The COMPLETE ILLUST
ENCYCLOPEDIA *of*
British & European
Birds

Publisher and Creative Director: Nick Wells
Project Editors: Cat Emslie and Sonya Newland
Copy Editor: Sonya Newland
Assistant Project Editor: Victoria Lyle
Picture Research: Victoria Lyle and Sonya Newland
Art Director: Mike Spender
Design Layout: Dave Jones and Mike Spender
Illustrator: Ann Biggs
Digital Design and Production: Chris Herbert
Proofreader: Dawn Laker
Indexer: Helen Snaith

Special thanks to: Claire Walker

08 10 12 11 09

1 3 5 7 9 10 8 6 4 2

This edition first published 2008 by
FLAME TREE PUBLISHING
Crabtree Hall, Crabtree Lane
Fulham, London SW6 6TY
United Kingdom

www.flametreepublishing.com

Flame Tree Publishing is part of the Foundry Creative Media Co. Ltd

ISBN 978-1-84786-225-9

A CIP record for this book is available from the British Library upon request.

Printed in China

The COMPLETE ILLUSTRATED ENCYCLOPEDIA *of*
British & European
Birds

David Chandler, Dominic Couzens,
Russ Malin, Stephen Moss

**FLAME TREE
PUBLISHING**

Contents

Anatomy, Behaviour & Habitat   10

Bird-watching & Identification   62

The Species   **90**

How to Use This Book

This book is divided into three main chapters, each designed to enhance an understanding of birds and bird-watching with the keen amateur in mind.

Anatomy, Behaviour & Habitat

This is an introduction to birds – their origins, their anatomy, breeding patterns and how and where they nest. It also includes sections on their different songs and calls, and an outline of the various habitats in which they can be found.

Bird-watching & Identification

This chapter offers a practical guide to bird-watching, including an outline of the best equipment to lay your hands on, what features to look out for when trying to identify birds – and what to beware of – and where to go both locally and abroad.

The Species

This chapter begins with an outline of bird names and how they are classified, which will help with understanding the family groups, with their similarities and characteristics.

It is followed by a series of sections organized by habitat. Across the spectrum of habitats there is an entry on all the key birds of Britain and Europe, organized within each section according to family groups. Every entry begins with a series of facts:

Size
Habitat
Population
Scientific Name
Similar Species
Identifying Features

GOSHAWK

SCIENTIFIC NAME: Accipiter gentilis

IDENTIFYING FEATURES: masked appearance; pale underparts with barring

SIMILAR SPECIES: Sparrowhawk, Buzzard

SIZE: 48–62cm (26–24 in?)
HABITAT: woodland
POPULATION: scarce

The juvenile bird has a streaked, buff-coloured breast. The Goshawk calls during display and often when approaching the nest site.

Feeding and Courtship Habits

Goshawks can be found in mature woodland, both coniferous and deciduous, as well as hunting in open country. Its range of prey is wide and it will eat almost any bird up to the size of a crow, although pigeons and jays are common prey. It has also been known to take mammals in the wild, particularly rabbits.

Courtship flights involve long periods soaring on the warm air currents known as thermals. This often gives the best chance of seeing this secretive bird and is best observed in March and April.

The Goshawk will build a loosely constructed nest of twigs high in a tree. It may also adopt old nests from other species. The average clutch size is three to four very pale blue eggs.

Goshawks are large, sometimes Buzzard-sized, birds of prey. They are rare breeders and nowhere near as common as the more diminutive Sparrowhawk. They became extinct in parts of Europe in the early 1900s but are now established again. It is believed that this new wave of birds originates from the accidental, or deliberate, release of falconers' stock but this has not been proved. Displaying birds in very early spring, at established sites, is probably the best chance to see these magnificent raptors.

The Goshawk is superficially similar to the Sparrowhawk. However, it is generally much larger, with a longer, more rounded tail. The male is grey above with a darker patch behind the eye, creating an almost masked appearance. At close range a distinct white eye stripe is noticeable. The underparts are pale and finely barred. The female is similar but brown rather than grey.

BELOW
Goshawk populations are widespread across Europe, but still little is known about their habits.

SPARROWHAWK

SCIENTIFIC NAME: Accipiter nissus

IDENTIFYING FEATURES: Rounded wings; speed in flight

SIMILAR SPECIES: Goshawk, Kestrel

SIZE: 28–38 cm (11–15 in)
HABITAT: woodland, parks and gardens
POPULATION: common

In the 1950s the Sparrowhawk was in trouble. Its numbers were seriously affected by the use of agricultural pest-control chemicals such as DDT. The more intensive the agriculture in a certain area the worse the problem became. With the tighter controls against these practices today, the Sparrowhawk is now quite common. As its name suggests, birds form largely the entire diet of this species. After killing its prey, the Sparrowhawk will often take it to a regular perch to be plucked.

Recovering Resident

Sparrowhawks are small and fast-flying birds of prey. The male has a slate-grey back with reddish barred underparts. The female is often considerably larger than the male and has browner upperparts and paler barred underparts. The female also has a characteristic white stripe above the eye. Both sexes have a series of four or five bars on the tail. Young birds have red-brown upperparts with some barring below. It is silent for most of the year but is known to make a shrill, four-syllable call when nesting.

Once heavily persecuted, the Sparrowhawk has made something of a recovery in recent years and is now a common resident. It can be seen in our gardens and parks as well as woodland and open country. It is another early nester and the display flight should be looked for in April.

The Sparrowhawk is a specialist of hunting smaller birds – not just sparrows, but also finches and tits. It has been known to take prey as large as a pigeon. A nest of twigs and sticks is made against the trunk of a tree, where the female lays four or five whitish eggs.

ABOVE
Although Sparrowhawks are mainly woodland birds, increasing numbers of them can be seen in urban areas.

Size

Gives the approximate size range of the adult species.

    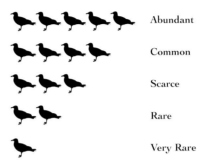

Small
(up to
15 cm/5⅞ in)

Medium
(16–30 cm/
6¼–11⅞ in)

Medium-large
(31–45 cm/
12¼–17¾ in)

Large
(46–70 cm/
18–27⅝ in)

Very large
(71 cm/28 in
and over)

Habitat

Summarizes the range of places where the birds can be found. Often this is in more than one particular type of habitat – birds may choose to breed somewhere different from their preferred environment the rest of the time, for example.

 Diverse

 Towns
Cities
Urban areas
Suburban areas

 Parkland
Gardens

 Coniferous woodland
Deciduous woodland
Mixed woodland
Ancient woodland

 Open country
Farmland/
agricultural land

 Moorland
Heathland
Grassland
Meadows

 Scrub
Hedgerows

 Reedbeds
Marshes

 Oceans
Seas
Coasts

 Ponds
Lakes
Rivers
Gravel pits
Open water

 Cliffs

 Islands
Beaches

 Upland and
tundra
Mountains

 Summer
visitor

Winter
visitor

Population

This gives a rough idea of how common – or scarce – the species is, and thus how likely you are to come across it. It is difficult to give specific figures for most species of bird, for obvious reasons, so instead standard terminology is used to describe the species populations, from rare, through common winter visitor, for example, to abundant.

Abundant

Common

Scarce

Rare

Very Rare

Scientific Name

This gives the bird's Latin or scientific name – the name by which it is classified by experts.

Identifying Features

These are suggested features to look out for when trying to distinguish one bird from another. Many birds – even those of a different group – may look similar from a distance or when camouflaged by a tree canopy, for example. Remember that a bird's plumage may change between seasons and between sexes, and these changes are noted where considered relevant.

Similar Species

This is intended partly as a guide to other species in a group but also to suggest pitfalls when bird-watching – similar species can often be mistaken for one another.

This information is followed by an introductory summary of the bird, and then a lengthier description of its preferred habitats and plumage, and its habits such as courting, mating, breeding, eating, nesting and the number of eggs that are typical.

Reference Section

At the end of the encyclopedia is a list of Useful Addresses, along with websites, with birding and wildlife organizations; there is also a list of Further Reading to expand on subjects and species covered here. A Glossary explains any terms that might be unfamiliar, and two Indexes (Scientific names and Common Names) will allow you to instantly locate a particular species.

Introduction

Bird-watching is one of the best ways of relaxing and enjoying nature, and it can be an extremely rewarding pastime if you know what to look for and where. The birds of Britain and Europe offer a feast of opportunity and quite an astounding diversity. From the ubiquitous pigeon to the rare Scottish Crossbill (the only species endemic to the British Isles), the familiar Mallard to the elusive Snowy Owl, there is something to be discovered wherever you are.

Essential Information

The encyclopedia begins with information about the history, behaviour and habitat of birds, from their origins and evolution to breeding patters, songs and displays. Birds have many fascinating behavioural habits and encountering these can be surprising and rewarding. The mating ritual known as lekking, in which males fight and perform displays to impress potential female mates – most notable with the Black Grouse – can be witnessed in particular known areas, for example.

This section also explains the main types of nest and colours and shapes of eggs. This can be key to successful bird-watching. Finding a nest of a particular shape and situation will give valuable information about its inhabitants and a little patience will almost certainly reward the watcher with a sighting.

Invaluable Advice

The second section offers a practical guide to bird-watching. The equipment you choose is important – what type of binoculars are best for you? What other items are essential in the field? Also important is where to go. What do you want to see? Are you willing and able to travel in search of specific species, or do you want to work within your local patch? Advice on attracting birds to your garden will enable you to be an armchair ornithologist!

The Species

The Species section of the encyclopedia is organized firstly by habitat. This should enable the reader to understand the types of birds they will find in a particular area. Of course, birds are not stationary creatures and few confine themselves permanently to a single habitat – some may be prolific in an area during the breeding season but rare outside it. It can also be difficult to categorize habitats neatly. Some water birds do indeed inhabit areas with freshwater, but many will also confine themselves to these areas within woodland regions, for example. The migratory habits of particular species should also be taken into account. There are thus many birds listed here that would comfortably fit into two or more habitat categories, so don't rule out a bird you think you have identified over farmland just because it appears in the Woodland section.

Sub-division
Within each habitat section, the birds are divided by family groupings. This is the order proscribed by the British Ornithologists Union and other organizations,

which allows birds to be seen with related species. Remember that just because a particular bird doesn't have the word 'duck' in its common name, does not mean it isn't a duck!

'Vital Stats'

Each entry in this section begins with a summary of key information – size, main habitats, population, scientific name, identifying features and similar species. The size of a bird will instantly enable the watcher to eliminate hundreds of species and focus on a particular size grouping, from small to very large. Habitats explains in more detail where the bird is likely to be seen. Population is intended as a guide to how likely you are to see a particular species. Actual bird populations are extremely difficult to measure and fluctuate wildly from year to year and indeed between seasons and

locations, so here you will find out whether the bird is abundant or just a winter visitor, a common sight in the named habitats or a passage migrant (a non-breeding visitor).

Identification

It is important to remember when looking for identifying features that plumage can change dramatically between seasons, between the sexes, and indeed between juvenile and adult birds. In the Identifying Features tag at the beginning of each species entry we have noted where plumage descriptions relate to specific seasons or sexes, but the main text of each entry will give more detailed information about plumage and other identifying features. To aid with identification, we have also named similar species with which the relevant bird might be confused. Colour photographs of all the birds give an immediate idea of what the species looks like, but also bear in mind that a bird may not look exactly like the picture! Often using features such as wing bars and other characteristics can be the best way to distinguish one species from another.

A Solid Foundation

This encyclopedia is intended as a guide to the interested amateur and should be used as a starting point for your bird-watching adventure. It is impossible to give every detail about every bird you are likely to encounter across this vast region, but those outlined in the Species section offer a good range of the types and families you might see. If your interest is piqued, investigate further by using one of the many excellent field guides available, which can be more specific. Today there is also a multitude of other media available to help you locate and identify birds – from CDs of birdsong to vast quantities of information on the Internet. At the back of this encyclopedia are listed some of the best websites to look at to find out more about birds and bird-watching.

Anatomy, Behaviour & Habitat

THE ORIGIN OF BIRDS

The origin of birds has been hotly debated by experts for many years. The current opinion, however, is that birds are the ancestors of a group of dinosaurs that evolved during the Mesozoic era (65 to 248 million years ago). The discovery of the primitive bird *Archaeopteryx* in 1861 suggested a close link between birds and dinosaurs, but the ongoing discoveries in China of feathered dinosaur fossils has shed new light on the subject, attracting the interest of both experts and amateurs alike.

Fossil Proof

Palaeontologists have usually classified birds as Archosaurs, a reptile group that includes dinosaurs and crocodiles. Questions about the origin of flight within this classification were historically seen as secondary concerns, since the anatomy of the group's members were similar. However, some ornithologists now argue that the origin of birds is closely linked with the origin of flight, and that the latter cannot be ignored when considering the former. This argument is based on the premise that birds evolved from small, lizard-like creatures that lived in trees and gradually adopted more aerial habits. Those who oppose the theory of the dinosaur origin of birds contend that because dinosaurs were ground-living creatures rather than small tree-living quadrupeds they could not have been related. They also point to the fact that the earliest known bird, *Archaeopteryx*, lived millions of years before the Theropods – the large carnivorous dinosaurs.

The Wishbone Debate

In the early 1900s, the Danish doctor Gerhard Heilmann wrote a book in which he pointed out that although there were many similarities between the skeletons of the carnivorous dinosaurs and those of birds, the Theropods lacked collarbones, or clavicles, which fuse together to become the wishbone in birds. He went on to argue that this feature could not be lost and then later re-evolved, so Theropods could not be the

ABOVE

The discovery of Archaeopteryx fossils suggested that birds evolved from dinosaurs.

BELOW

Crocodiles are classified as Archosaurs, the reptile group to which birds also belong.

ancestors of birds. However, later fossil findings have shown not only that Theropods had collarbones, but also that they were fused together to form a wishbone.

Fifty years later, a scholar from Yale University noted 22 common features in the skeletons of carnivorous dinosaurs and birds that were not found in any other creatures. Subsequent discoveries also indicated a tendency for certain bones in the legs to fuse and for those in the skull to be reformed in similar ways. Further similarities were found in the movement of the wrists – some dinosaurs folded their hands sideways in the same way that a bird furls and unfurls its wings.

Feathered Dinosaurs

In the late 1990s, Chinese researchers found a number of dinosaur fossils that suggested they may have had feathers. Although some ornithologists and scientists tried to discredit these findings by discovering fossils of non-dinosaurian reptiles with feathers, the evidence remained inconclusive. The development of feathers as a feature occurred before the origin of flight, and dinosaurs with feathers would not necessarily have been able to fly. Although feathered, many land-dwelling dinosaurs were flightless, like penguins.

Avian Dinosaurs

Many scientists now believe that birds evolved from a group of dinosaurs called Dromaeosaurs, which had many bird-like features. The wrist joints enabled them to fold their hands close to their arms, possibly to protect the feathers on their hands. Birds in flight perform

ABOVE

The furling and unfurling of birds' wings resembles the way dinosaurs folded their hands.

a similar folding action. Today, some experts believe that birds and dinosaurs have so many features in common that they call birds 'avian dinosaurs'.

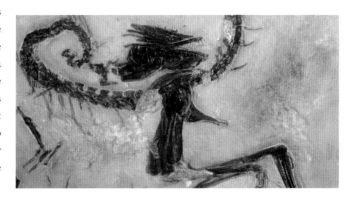

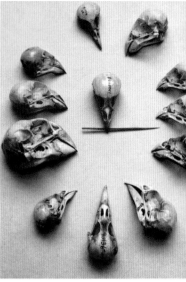

Regional Evolution

There are many bird species that are largely sedentary – they do not migrate or wander – but which are found in several different regions. Numerous species have evolved and adapted their habits or appearance but are still readily recognizable as their own species.

Regional Variations

In Europe, for example, the Wren, or Winter Wren, has its nominate form and then other forms on the Scottish islands of St Kilda, Shetland and Fair Isle, as well as Iceland. The wings, tails, bills and legs for this species get gradually longer the further away from the nominate race they get. This type of variation is referred to as a 'cline'. Where there is greater definition of separation, such as island groups, these are known as subspecies or races.

In America the Merlin offers a similar example. There are three documented races: the Taiga Merlin, Prairie Merlin and Black Merlin. The Taiga variety of Merlin appears darker in the east of the country and gets progressively paler as it is found further westwards. The variations with the Prairie Merlin relate to its size – it is noticeably larger than the other two races, although it is also generally a little paler. The Taiga Merlin is common along the coastal regions of the United States during migration, with some choosing to overwinter. Some Prairie race birds move south in the autumn, heading towards northern Mexico, while the Black Merlin will also winter in northern Mexico and California.

The skulls of the finches Darwin studied on the Galapagos Islands reveal their evolutionary process in the shape of their beaks.

Convergent and Divergent Evolution

When considering regional

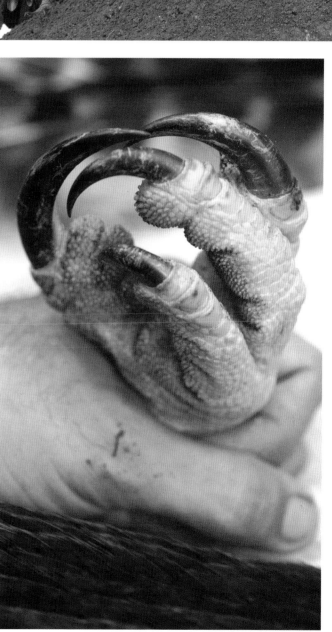

evolution in the same species it is important to also consider what is referred to as 'convergent evolution'. This can essentially be described as instances where species are not closely related (sometimes referred to as non-monophyletic), but which share similar behaviour and characteristics as a result of having to adapt to similar environments. The opposite end of the spectrum is 'divergent evolution', in which closely related species develop different characteristics to those of their near relatives.

Vultures are a good example of convergent evolution. The so-called New World Vultures, which include the Condor, were thought for many years to be of the same family as Old World Vultures, which include the African and Asian species such as the Griffon Vulture. They have many superficial similarities – both have similarly structured broad wings and have little or no feathering from the neck upwards. Both are also

prolific carrion feeders. However, research has shown that the New World Vultures are in fact more closely related to the stork family than Old World Vultures. These very different families have evolved similar – sometimes identical – adaptations despite their existence in different parts of the world.

Owls are another good example. Belonging to an order of birds known as Strigiformes, they range greatly in size but retain the same similar characteristics as a family. They are completely unrelated to the birds of prey, or raptors, such as hawks, buzzards and falcons. However, both groups have independently evolved several common features, such as sharp, hooked bills and talons.

RIGHT

Different species can evolve similar characteristics such as sharp talons.

Extinct Species and New Species

Over the last 500 years or so there have been recorded instances of the extinction of nearly 150 different species of birds, and this trend is continuing at a steady rate. There are many reasons for the extinction of bird species, but habitat loss tops the list. The loss of a species ecosystem, such as rainforests, can devastate wildlife populations, and most of these areas never recover.

Hunting and Predation

Hunting – both illegal and legal – is also causing bird species to die out. The Great Auk is one of the most famous examples. In 1844 the last two specimens of this majestic flightless bird where killed in Iceland by a group of three hunters commissioned by a collector. This barbaric practice still goes on in several parts of the world and has been responsible for the demise of many species.

Competition and predation by other species is also a factor. Many isolated populations can suffer when other animals are released there either accidentally or deliberately. In Guam, in the western Pacific, more than 60 per cent of the native species have been lost in just 30 years. The majority of this loss is attributed to the introduction of the Brown Tree Snake. There are in excess of 10,000 species of bird throughout the world, but more than 1,000 of these are at risk of extinction – and in nearly all instances the greatest threat comes from human activity.

New Discoveries

Despite the threat of extinction, there is good

news too: species are still being found that are new to science – albeit at a more modest rate. Somewhere in the region of five species a year are being discovered. And with the rapid advances in DNA technology there is also the possibility that extinction could one day become a thing of the past.

DNA Classification

DNA – deoxyribonucleic acid – is the material inside the nucleus of cells that carries genetic information. This genetic information tells us that birds are part of a monophyletic lineage. The word 'monophyletic' refers to any group of organisms that include the most recent common ancestor of all those organisms and all the descendants of that common ancestor. In essence, all birds are related through a common origin.

DNA Taxonomy

A taxonomy is a description of living things and the subject of bird taxonomy has been hotly debated. In the 1980s a new and somewhat radical bird taxonomy was proposed. This differed from the traditional list of birds, and was based on DNA and DNA hybridization. This new taxonomy created a classification of many levels; it began with Aves, the vertebrate class that includes birds, and branched out through numerous subclasses, families, subfamilies, right down to genera and species. This taxonomy, however, has its problems. Although ongoing genetic reconstructions lend themselves to DNA-based taxonomy, some studies reject many of the arrangements in the classification. Even DNA and DNA hybridization studies disagree with certain aspects of this structure. Despite these apparent flaws, though, this order of classification has been largely accepted and adopted by eminent ornithologists throughout the world.

ABOVE AND BELOW

The Saker Falcon (above) and the Ara Macaw (below) are both hybrid birds.

BELOW LEFT

A Lammergeier hatches in a breeding centre in Spain.

Ongoing research is taking a detailed look at the ancestry of our bird groups. This may well change the taxonomic order of our species yet again.

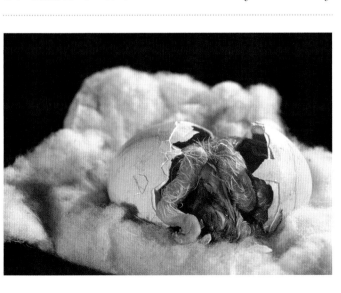

ANATOMY AND APPEARANCE

Birds differ from mammals in a number of ways. They walk on two legs and have two wings. They also have feathers instead of hair or fur. They have bills instead of jaws with teeth. Most birds have little or no sense of smell. Birds have also had to evolve a compact body shape in order to assist flying. There are, however, similarities with mammals – they are warm-blooded, with two eyes and ears (although the ears are not always visible).

Skeleton

The skeleton of a bird is, of course, designed for flight. Not only is it extremely lightweight but it will also withstand the rigours of flight such as alighting and landing. Because of the way that birds' bones are fused together, they generally have fewer individual bones than land-dwelling vertebrates such as mammals. Nor do birds possess a true jawbone or teeth. Instead they have evolved beaks, or bills, made up of a lower and upper mandible.

Bone Structure

To give structural strength and to aid flight, many of a bird's bones are hollow, with crossed or honey-combed struts for stability. The number of hollow bones within a skeleton differs between species. Birds that spend prolonged periods in the air, such as Swifts and birds of prey, will have more hollow bones. Flightless species have a predominately solid bone structure.

Birds also have more neck vertebrae than other animals – between 15 and 25 on

average. Another peculiar trait of a bird's skeleton is the collarbone, or wishbone, and the fused sternum or breastbone. This serves as an attachment for the muscles utilized in the process of flight.

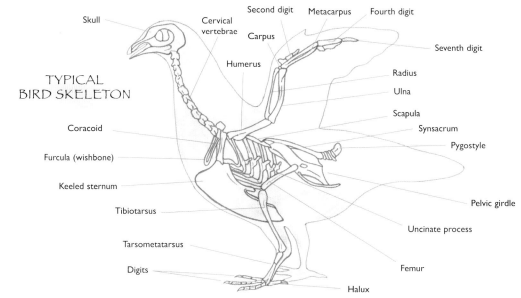

TYPICAL BIRD SKELETON

Skull, Cervical vertebrae, Second digit, Metacarpus, Fourth digit, Carpus, Humerus, Seventh digit, Radius, Ulna, Scapula, Synsacrum, Pygostyle, Coracoid, Furcula (wishbone), Keeled sternum, Tibiotarsus, Pelvic girdle, Uncinate process, Tarsometatarsus, Femur, Digits, Halux

TYPICAL BIRD BODY

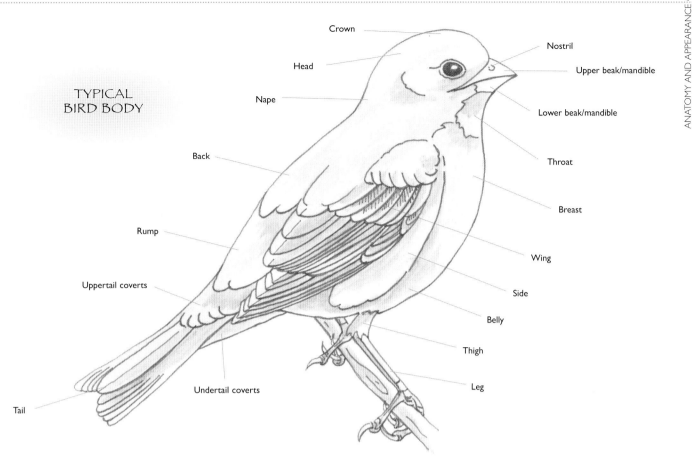

Crown

Head

Nape

Back

Rump

Uppertail coverts

Tail

Undertail coverts

Nostril

Upper beak/mandible

Lower beak/mandible

Throat

Breast

Wing

Side

Belly

Thigh

Leg

For flightless birds such as penguins these muscles are often adapted for swimming.

Skull

The skull of a bird is made up of five major bones: the frontal bone (the top of the skull); the paritel (the back of the skull); the premaxillary and nasal (which form the upper mandible); and the lower mandible. The skull makes up roughly one per cent of a bird's total body weight.

Pelvis

Another feature worthy of mention is that birds have a greatly elongated pelvis – a characteristic which is only really found in birds and reptiles. This could be a further link to their evolution from reptilian dinosaurs.

Skeleton Summary

The skeleton of a bird can be summarized as follows: the skull, the vertebral column, the pelvis and the pygostyle, or tail. The chest contains the wishbone, or furcula, and this and the scapula (shoulder and upper arm) make up the pectoral cage. The sides of the chest are made up of ribs that meet together at the sternum. Carpus and metacarpus bones form the 'wrists' and 'hands' of the bird. The upper leg is made up of the the femur, which connects to the tibiotarsus and fibula. The tarsometatarsus bones then form the main part of the foot. A bird's leg bones are generally heavier than the other bones in its skeleton.

Fascinating Facts

The skeleton of a bird weighs more than its feathers.

RIGHT

Heavier leg bones help maintain a low centre of gravity and aid flight.

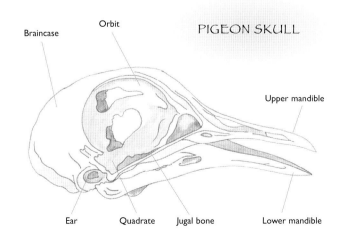

PIGEON SKULL

Braincase

Orbit

Upper mandible

Ear

Quadrate

Jugal bone

Lower mandible

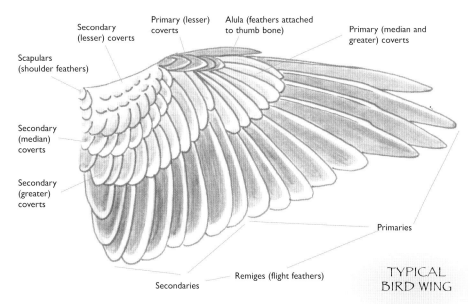

Wings

Wings are, of course, the key to flight. Each wing has a central section consisting of three bones – the humerus, ulna and radius. The 'hand' originally consisted of five individual digits but through evolution has reduced to three. These serve as an anchor point for the primaries – the two types of flight feather found on each wing. (The other flight feathers are called the secondaries). The primaries give the wing a streamlined shape.

Wing Shape

The shape of the wing is an essential factor in determining the style of flight for each species of bird. Different wing shapes relate to different characteristics such as speed. The shape of the wing as it is seen during flight is known as the planform. There are three main wing shapes: curved or elliptical, found in some hawks and non-migratory passerines; high-speed wings, found in falcons and swifts; and wings designed for soaring. These last usually have slotted primaries, or fingers, and this shape can be seen in eagles and other large birds of prey.

The Peregrine Falcon is the fastest bird in the world.

Secondary flight feathers are situated behind the carpal, or elbow joint. There is also a third group of wing feathers – the wing coverts.

Hovering, Take-off and Landing

Birds such as kingfishers and members of the kestrel family have wings that allow them to hover. In fact the old country name for the kestrel is the 'windhover'. Hovering uses up a lot of energy but is a very useful ability. It is basically generating lift through the flapping of the wings and nothing else – it does not require any thrust.

Apart from the time spent airborne, flight is essentially about two things: taking off and landing. For take-off a lot of energy is required to

Scapulars (shoulder feathers)

Secondary (lesser) coverts

Secondary (median) coverts

Secondary (greater) coverts

Primary (lesser) coverts

Alula (feathers attached to thumb bone)

Primary (median and greater) coverts

Primaries

Remiges (flight feathers)

Secondaries

TYPICAL BIRD WING

generate sufficient airflow to create lift. Landing is a little less demanding but there an amount of skill is needed to 'put the brakes on'. Species that aim for a target, for example a cliff-face nesting site, pull up reducing energy and lessening any airspeed at the point of impact. Birds that predominately land on water, such as geese or ducks, will twist and turn in flight to slow them down prior to landing.

Flight Mechanics
The physical role of the wing in relation to basic flight mechanics is not dissimilar to that used by commercial aircraft. The lift force created by a wing has two components – forward and vertical. The lift force is created by the action of airflow on the wing surface, like an aeroplane airfoil. This happens because of differing pressures between the top of the wing and the bottom.

When birds glide, they gain both a vertical and a forward force from their wings. This happens because the lift force is generated at a strict right angle to the airflow, which in level flight comes from slightly below the wing. The lift force therefore has a forward component. If the bird did not possess this forward component, a bird gliding would merely descend vertically. The downward stroke of the wing generates the majority of its thrust, and the upward stroke provides upward force.

Feathers

Feathers are incredibly lightweight, but they are strong and flexible. A bird has several different types of feathers, and each is adapted for a specific purpose – flight, insulation or for display. Bird feathers are made from a tough, fibrous material called keratin, a protein similar to the substance from which human hair and fingernails are made. A similar type of protein is also found in the scales of some reptiles.

Feather Construction

Flight feathers, found on the wings, are sometimes referred to as remiges. These feathers consist of a vane with a central shaft. The shaft is completely hollow and filled with air to make it lightweight. At the end of the shaft is the quill. The quill is directly attached to the bird via a follicle. When a bird raises its wing, the feathers open up and allow air to pass through. On the downward stroke, the feathers close up, presenting a solid surface to the air and generating the lift needed for the bird to remain in the air.

The vane of the feather is not solid but is made up of many thin filaments packed together tightly. Each of these

Feathers open up to allow air to pass through as the bird lifts its wings.

filaments are called barbs and on each barb there are hundreds of smaller barbs, or barbules, usually invisible to the human eye. The barbules

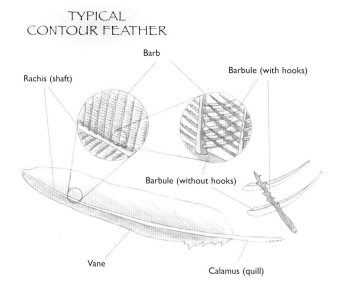

TYPICAL
CONTOUR FEATHER

Barb

Rachis (shaft)

Barbule (with hooks)

Barbule (without hooks)

Vane

Calamus (quill)

have tiny hooks that fasten over those adjacent to them. If feathers are displaced in any way a bird will preen itself to reconnect the separated barbs.

Other Types of Feathers

Bristle feathers are found around the eyes, nostrils and bills. They are very sensitive, and provide protection against dust and dirt, in a way similar to the whiskers of cats and dogs. These bristle feathers are particularly noticeable on insectivorous birds such as warblers, flycatchers and chats.

There are two basic types of down feather – those that are adapted for insulation, and powder down. Insulating down is a mess of tangled barbs that provides warmth.

This type of feather has remarkable insulating properties and is often collected, from the Eider Duck, for example, to be used as a filling for bedding. Powder down is a type of feathers with tiny barbs that turn to a dust. These feathers aid preening in species that do not possess preen glands, such as members of the dove family.

Plumage and Display

Feathers also provide incredible variations in plumage. There are several reasons for the vast array of feather colours. Camouflage is possibly the most important. For brown birds that need to blend in with their surroundings, their colour is created by a pigment called melanin.

Melanin also offers a large degree of UV protection.

For display purposes some species will possess brightly coloured feathers in reds, pinks and yellows. These colours are also created from pigments – carotenoids. These coloured pigments usually stem from diet of the bird. Blue colouration is not attributed to pigments, however. This is how the barbs of the feathers reflect light to create a sheen or iridescence. A good example of this is the blue-green

appearance on the head of a male Mallard. The various pigmentations also help with wear and tear – without pigmentation a feather is naturally white and would wear very quickly.

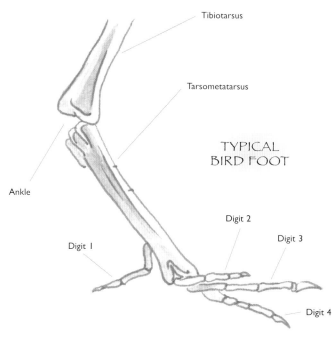

Tibiotarsus

Tarsometatarsus

TYPICAL
BIRD FOOT

Ankle

Digit 1

Digit 2

Digit 3

Digit 4

The form of birds' feet varies depending on habitat and use.

Passerines mainly use their feet for gripping while perching.

Legs and Feet

The two main purposes of feet are that of balance and walking. Some species are more reliant on their feet than others: birds of prey use theirs to catch and kill their food; other species use theirs for perching, climbing, swimming and even digging. Over the millennia, feet and legs have adapted to the habits and habitats of individual species. A perching bird, for example, has no need for webbed feet and likewise fierce, powerful talons would be of little or no practical use to a member of the goose family.

Most birds have four toes, usually with three toes pointing forwards and one backwards. There are exceptions to this, though. For example the swift, which spends nearly all its adult life airborne, has very short legs and all four toes point forwards. This helps it to perch on walls and rocks on the rare occasions that it comes to land. Another example of variation is the kingfisher, which has short legs with the third and fourth toes partially joined together; this helps when they are excavating their riverside nest tunnels. Even with all the individual variations across the species, there are essentially three types of feet.

Passerines

Perching birds, or passerines, which account for a large number of small birds, have a tendon that runs along the back of each of their legs. This tightens the feet and toes to ensure a firm grip while perching. This is also important for comfortable and safe roosting. Birds of prey share the same basic design, but with some variations. All birds of prey have long toes with extremely sharp claws. This increases their chance of a successful mid-air catch and helps to retain their grip on their prey until they can find a safe place to land and eat. An example of this is the Osprey. This bird is always found

breeding on, or near, lakes or reservoirs. The feet have specially formed gripping spines on them to ensure they keep a tight grasp on their prey – fish.

Walkers and Waders
Birds that spend their time walking and wading generally have longer legs and do not possess the same grip as the passerines because they do not need the same degree of dexterity. Many of these birds may also be missing the hind toe. Some species have basic webbing between the toes. This is particularly useful for species that feed on and in soft mud, for instance the very long legged Curlew, or birds such as herons and egrets, which often wade deep into open water looking for fish, frogs and toads. The basic webbing goes a long way to ensure adequate balance and to prevent sinking.

Similar to the wading birds, those that have feet adapted for swimming have webbing but generally this is attached to stronger, smaller legs. In birds such as ducks the webbed feet act as paddles to help in swimming. Grebes do not have webbed feet, but rather flaps of skin attached to each toe. These serve a similar purpose, as they push back against the water but then fold on their forward stroke like a miniature set of oars.

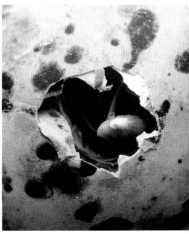

ABOVE

Nestlings use a special 'egg tooth' to help break out of the egg.

BELOW

Petrels belong to the family of tubenoses.

Bills

The bill, or beak, of a bird is quite simply an extension of its jaw. Not unlike humans, the top part is fixed while the bottom part is moveable (although there are a number of species that have some basic movement in the upper part). These parts are known as the upper and lower mandibles. Both are covered in a protective layer of hardened skin.

Nostrils

Nostrils are usually present on the upper mandible and although very visible on some species they can be hidden on others by feathering. One particular species worthy of mention is the Fulmar, which belongs to a family referred to as 'tubenoses'. These birds have a separate tube attached to the top of the upper mandible, which acts as a breathing aid. Birds of prey and pigeons have a softer, fleshy area around the nostrils known as the cere. Not all birds have nostrils. The Gannet dives head-first at great speed into the sea. To prevent water entering its lungs, it breathes through its mouth.

Bill Uses

Bills – like feet and legs – have adapted to serve a number of purposes: feeding, nest-building and preening. There are some species that also use the colour and shape of their bills to attract a mate through display.

A bird will first use its bill to break out of its egg. On the tip of the bill every chick has an 'egg tooth'. This is a small, bony growth that drops off once the nestling has hatched. The open mouth, or gape, of baby birds is often brightly coloured –

red or yellow – to attract the attention of the feeding parent. Another useful aid to feeding can be seen in the bills of adults of the larger species of gull, such as the Herring Gull or Lesser Black Backed Gull. The often yellow bill of the adult is marked with a prominent red spot. The chick will often use this as a target and repeatedly peck at the dot until the parent regurgitates its meal for the infant.

Bill Shapes

How a bird feeds and what it feeds on determines the bill shape and size in most birds. Birds of prey have razor-sharp, hooked bills, often with a notched tip. This enables the bird to not only kill the prey but also to tear its flesh.

Waders have longer, probing bills that come in a variety of lengths and shapes. Some waders have straight bills while others are curved

BELOW
Woodpeckers have very strong bills to allow them to make nest holes in trees.

SELECTION OF BEAK TYPES

Peregrine

Green Woodpecker

Shoveler

Bullfinch

Spoonbill

upwards or downwards. The tips of the bill are incredibly sensitive and can detect invertebrates and crustaceans in deep mud.

Insect-eating birds, such as flycatchers, have small bills. Often these will have small hairs around the base. This helps catch insects when the bill is open. Some birds, such as swallows, have tiny bills but unusually large gapes. This is important for catching flying insects while the birds themselves are airborne.

Woodpeckers have incredibly strong bills and have naturally occurring shock absorbers made up of spongy bone at the base. This reduces the potentially harmful impact when excavating nest holes in wood. Woodpeckers also use their bills to 'drum' against trees. This helps to establish territories and attract mates.

BREEDING

The majority of bird species are socially monogamous. This means that they will pair for the length of the breeding season or beyond – sometimes even for life. However, some demonstrate polygamous breeding patterns, where the females are able to raise broods without the help of a male, other than fertilizing the eggs.

Breeding Patterns

Breeding will usually involve a form of courtship display. These displays may be simple

or ornate depending upon the species. Many involve song, but might also include display flights, dancing or the passing of food to a potential mate. Birds will defend their territory during the breeding season. This is to protect both the family group and the chicks' potential food sources. Species that do not hold territories, including many sea birds, often nest in colonies.

Eggs are laid in a nest, the construction of which varies greatly from species to species (see page 34). Once the last egg has been laid incubation begins. This creates the optimum temperature for the chick to develop. Incubation periods range from 10 days to two

months, again depending on the species. Once hatched, the nestlings can be deemed either altricial, which are born blind, naked and

BELOW

Courtship rituals include the passing of food between the chosen mates.

immobile, or precocial, which means they are feathered and have a degree of mobility. The exact degree of parental care and its duration differs from bird to bird and in some species both parents care for nestlings and fledglings. Fledging can take from a few days up to a few weeks. Some migratory species stay with their parent, or parents, for their first migration flight.

Mating

Bonding and mating in birds ranges from long-term relationships, or pair bonds,

found in species such as swans, to occasional fleeting liaisons between males and females. There are several distinct types of paring.

Pair Bonds

A pair bond is generally formed between two birds as the result of an often complex and ornate display ritual. The longevity of a pair bond differs from species to species but generally lasts as long as both parents cooperate to feed and care for their offspring. Certain species have little in the way of pair bonds and only associate for the duration of mating. At the opposite end of the scale are birds such as the Canada Goose, which often mate for life. Canada Geese are extreme examples, however, and most birds fall somewhere in between. In most monogamous species the male and female remain together for the purpose of raising a family during one particular breeding season.

Other types of relationship include polygamy, in which a male mates with several females, and polyandry, in which a female mates with several males. There are a large number of species, including grouse and certain members of the sandpiper family, that are incredibly promiscuous and have numerous partners throughout the breeding season.

Lekking

One of the more unusual mating rituals is lekking. This is a variation on the promiscuous mating observed in some species. Generally species that participate are game birds and some waders.

During the breeding season, males gather in small clusters called leks. Each male then defends a territory, during which they perform intricate displays, which escalate as females enter the fray. As the female selects a mate, the act of mating takes place there and then. The female then retreats to a nest site and will probably never see the male again.

The Reproduction Process

In common with reptiles, male and female birds both possess cloacae. A cloaca is an opening in the body that allows eggs, sperm and waste matter to pass. During mating, the male and female birds push together both sets of cloacae, during which time the male transfers his sperm to the female. The female then lays an amniotic egg in which the young gestate. An amniotic egg is one that is covered by a shell and able to retain fluid. The fertilized egg is enclosed in a layer of albumen, which is the

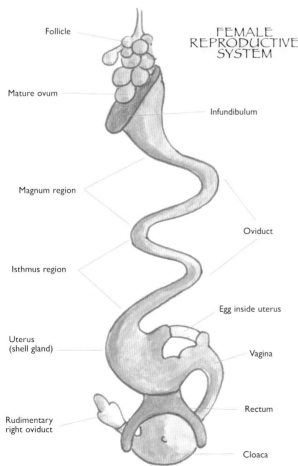

FEMALE
REPRODUCTIVE
SYSTEM

Follicle

Mature ovum

Infundibulum

Magnum region

Isthmus region

Oviduct

Egg inside uterus

Uterus
(shell gland)

Vagina

Rectum

Rudimentary
right oviduct

Cloaca

cytoplasm of the egg and accounts for 90 per cent of its total weight. It is then passed down the oviduct of the female and laid in the nest. With most species a single egg is laid each day and incubation starts once the final egg is laid.

Incubation

The female is usually responsible for incubation (although this is not always the case), while the male maintains the nest and finds food. The eggs are kept at a constant temperature by the bird covering the eggs, keeping them against the brood patch – an area that is largely devoid of any feathers. This allows direct contact between the warm skin of the bird and the outer layer of the eggshell.

A Black-necked Grebe lays an egg in her nest.

Incubation also helps to reduce evaporation of water from the shell. At

this constant temperature the eggs develop and hatch within a week or so.

Growth in the Egg

Inside the egg, the living cells are dividing to create the tissues and organs of the young bird. The yolk provides food and nutrition for the chick while the albumen is a source of sustenance. The eggshell and shell membranes are both permeable, so gases can pass through them. Oxygen thus diffuses into the air space and is absorbed by part of a large network of capillaries. In turn, these capillaries spread out over the yolk and then over a membranous sac called the allantois. The blood carries the oxygen to the embryo and a reverse process dispels the carbon dioxide through the eggshell.

Factors Affecting Reproduction

Birds often have a breeding season, and it is common in the Northern Hemisphere to find a multitude of chicks in the spring months. However, breeding is not exclusively confined to springtime. The breeding season is often affected by light stimulation, and the lengthening of daylight hours as spring approaches is the main reason for the flurry of breeding at this time. Breeding can also be affected by unseasonable cold or warm spells of weather. Some birds may breed twice a year, others only once.

Habitat can also affect reproduction – and this is one of the reasons many species are now endangered.

As habitats such as woodlands or forests are cleared, or even less wooded areas are cultivated for farmland, bird habitats are reduced and birds are unable to breed or are forced to move away from traditional areas to do so.

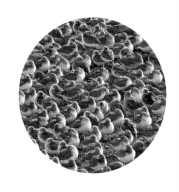

MIGRATION

Migration is the seasonal journey taken by certain species of birds. The distances and destinations involved differ from species to species, but the distance travelled can often be remarkable. The word 'migration' can also be used to describe instances where birds displace in response to changes in food availability, habitat or weather. Generally speaking these instances are irregular and often referred to as invasions or eruptions. Not all species migrate. Sedentary species are known as resident birds.

Reasons for Migration

The reasons for bird migration are not fully understood. A simple explanation might be a search for food or relocating to find a suitable and safe place to breed. Birds that breed in the summer in the extreme north, such as the Arctic Circle, benefit from an abundance of food, as plants and invertebrates flourish in the long daylight hours, and also because few large predators can survive the harsh winter conditions. With the ability to fly, birds can avoid the often punishing winter conditions by the act of migration.

Migratory Destinations

Birds that breed in the Northern Hemisphere, especially those in regions with definite seasonal differences, also tend to migrate, often travelling to the Southern Hemisphere. The Arctic Tern makes the longest journey of any species, migrating from the North Pole in the autumn months down to the South Pole, and then back again in the spring.

Birds that breed in the Southern Hemisphere also migrate. However, very few (except some sea birds) migrate from the Southern to the Northern Hemisphere. The warm temperatures close to the Equator are the wintering home of many birds, although many will choose a spot that is not as far but still warmer and has more food than their native country.

their breeding areas can overshoot and end up considerably further north than intended.

Reverse Migration

Another interesting variation is reverse migration. This is believed to occur because of genetic imbalances in juvenile birds and it can lead to extreme rarities landing as vagrants in areas possibly thousands of kilometres out of their normal migratory range. You may also hear reference to a drift migration. This occurs when strong winds blow often large numbers of birds off course during migration. This results in 'falls', where a large number of windblown migrants find land. This normally occurs at prominent coastal sites, such as headlands, promontories or offshore island groups. It can be a spectacular experience and the birds can often number hundreds of thousands.

Patterns of Migration

You might expect birds to fly in straight lines when migrating, to ensure the quickest journey time to their desired location. However, many migratory routes are far from direct, and there are a number of reasons for this. Water, such as open seas and oceans, can provide an obstacle to some species, while others cross them easily (the Arctic Tern, for example). Many birds are not fond of flying over deserts or mountain ranges, so they choose to fly around them. Another factor that might cause a different choice of route is prevailing winds.

Disorientation

There are various types of migratory patterns, including loops, doglegs and leap-

Fascinating Facts

Migrating birds fly in formation as a way of conserving energy, effectively flying in the slipstream of other birds.

FAR LEFT
Semipalmated Sandpipers amass in Novia Scotia during the autumn migration.

RIGHT
Ringing birds allows experts to trace patterns of migration.

frogging. Considering the complex patterns and incredible distances that some species undertake it is little surprise that some migratory birds can become disorientated, lose their way and be found outside their normal ranges. Often this can be due to flying past their intended destinations. For example, birds returning to

NESTS AND EGGS

Identifying nests and eggs belonging to different species can be one of the most rewarding experiences for a bird watcher, and it can often be easy to tell the species from the size, shape and materials used for the nest, as well as the size, shape and colour of the eggs.

Types of Nest

Nests are built to protect the eggs and baby birds from predation and other factors such as adverse weather. There are many different types of nest construction, the most common of which are described below.

Cup Nests

The cup nest is probably the most familiar, and is favoured by a large number of birds. Nesting materials can be varied but will usually be twigs, grasses, leaf litter, animal hair, feathers, lichen,

moss and very often man-made materials such as string or scraps of paper. The cup nest is typically lodged in the branches of trees and shrubs and supported from below.

Many common birds utilize the cup nest, including the Blackbird.

Suspended Cup Nest

Variations on the cup nest include the suspended cup nest, where rather than being supported from below the nest will be secured by the rim or sides of the nest. Examples of these types of nests can be found with the Goldcrest. Included within the cup nest group are those of species such as the Swallow or House Martin, which use a cup-like construction of mud and other materials, which will be literally stuck to the side of a building or in the eaves.

Platform Nests

A platform nest is a simple, flat construction made from a variety of natural debris. These nests are built by some larger tree-nesting birds, as well as some ground-nesting species, and also by a large variety of water birds, including grebes and swans, which will use aquatic vegetation to create their nest.

Scrape Nests

Other common types of nest include the scrape. Very often these scrape nests will be nothing more than simple depressions in the ground with little or no nesting material. These are typical

of some ground-dwelling woodland birds, such as the Nightjar, but are more often associated with waders and coastal nesting birds such as terns, gulls and plovers. In these instances, many species will be reliant upon well-camouflaged eggs to avoid predation.

Hole Nesting

Essentially there are two types of hole-nesting birds:

those that create their own holes, such as woodpeckers, and those that make use of existing cavities, either naturally occurring or vacant nests of other species. Old woodpecker nests will be used by a variety of other species including starlings, owls, flycatchers and members of the tit family. Some ducks, including the Goldeneye, nest in tree holes or in specially made wooden nest boxes.

Other hole-nesting birds worthy of mention are those that nest not in trees or man-made constructions, but in burrows or tunnels. The

Manx Shearwater cliff-top nest consists of a small burrow, but more familiar exponents include the Sand Martin and kingfishers. This brightly coloured resident of our riverbanks will excavate a hole in sand or soft earth. Generally the excavation hole will be sited one or two metres above the water level to prevent flooding of the nest chamber during prolonged wet weather. It normally slopes slightly upwards but may be horizontal, again to reduce the risk of flooding. This whole industrious process can take anything up to 12 days to complete.

Nesting Materials

The materials that a bird chooses for its nest can be as varied as the nest types themselves. Some ground-nesting birds that make a shallow scrape nest probably have little in the way of nesting materials, although a few may use feathers or plant matter. Sea birds that nest on cliff ledges will often have little more than a few centimetres of ledge, with nothing in the way of materials.

Plants, Fur and Feathers

Possibly the best example to consider when discussing materials is the cup nest. The outer layers of the nest are constructed of generally coarse materials such as twigs, branches and tree bark. These will often be bound together with mud. The nest lining itself is made using softer materials, such as feathers, leaves, mosses and lichens. This will give obvious comfort and warmth to the nestlings. Very often plants that produce down-like seed heads, such as thistles, are also found at nest sites. Animal hair and fur is also used. It is often possible to see birds collecting shed hair from fence posts and barbed-wire fences. The nest site is usually well maintained by the parent bird throughout the breeding season, with soiled nesting material removed and replaced with fresh. This is important particularly when animal matter is used, as the hair or fur may contain harmful ticks or mites.

Care of Nests

The cleanliness of a nest is very important to birds, particularly hole-nesting species such as woodpeckers and tits. There can often be a large number of young in very cramped conditions. However, these nests can usually be found immaculate and the nestlings clean. Each time the parent visits the nest to deliver food it leaves the site carrying a white sac containing excrement from the nestlings. With many passerines the excrement is held in a transparent sac of mucus. This enables the droppings to be removed without the parent bird soiling its bill. The sac can be deposited away from the nest site.

Other than issues of hygiene, the parent bird removes waste from the nest for safety. A heavily soiled nest site with characteristic white marks around the nest itself would advertise its presence to potential predators.

Birds of Prey

Birds of prey do not possess quite the same housekeeping skills as other species. The excrement of their young is expelled from the nest in a type of fluid that is not contained within a membrane. The young hawk or falcon will turn its tail towards the nest edge and expel the excrement with some speed, to a distance of a metre or so. This keeps the immediate nest area clean, but does advertise its presence.

Owls

One of the less hygienic bird families is that of the owl. Many owl species are hole nesters and where the nest site has been used for several breeding seasons the cavity can become very squalid. This is not because of nestling droppings – the parents do remove the excrement – but because of their diet. Owls dispose of indigestible parts of food, such as bone and fur, by regurgitating them in the form of a pellet. If the pellets are not regularly removed then they can accumulate in the nesting area.

the egg out through the oviduct. Strong muscles within the oviduct contract, pushing out the egg and forming the thinner pointed end as the egg is quite malleable at this stage.

Shape Variations

Variations on egg shape do exist, however. Species that make their homes on sheer cliff faces, such as auks and gulls, tend to have conical eggs. This helps them roll in a circular motion rather than rolling off the edge of the ledge – a shape believed to have developed due to natural selection. In a similar

Colour Variations

Essentially, the natural colour of all vertebrate species' eggs is white, because it is the natural colour of the material that makes the shell – calcium carbonate. Coloured eggs are created from naturally

Shapes and Colours of Eggs

Birds' eggs vary greatly in size and colour – they have almost as much variety as the species that lay them. However, most eggs are oval shaped. One end is rounded while the other is generally more pointed. This shape is formed as the female forces

way, many hole-nesting birds, including some owls, have almost spherical eggs as they are in little danger of rolling anywhere should they be knocked or nudged.

occurring pigments – biliverdin and chelate give a green or blue colour and the protoporphyrin produces brown or red colourations.

The cuckoo family is an excellent example of mimicry in egg colouration. The cuckoo chooses its host and, using these complex pigmentations, lays an egg that closely resembles that of its unwitting foster parent. Another interesting exponent of egg colouration is the guillemot. These birds nest in colonies in close proximity to other nests. The female lays eggs of a different colour to that of its immediate neighbours, so that it can identify its own eggs when landing on the crowded cliffs where it breeds.

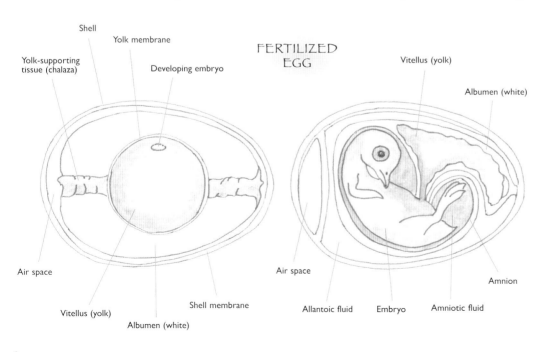

Shell
Yolk membrane
Yolk-supporting tissue (chalaza)
Developing embryo

FERTILIZED EGG

Vitellus (yolk)
Albumen (white)

Air space
Vitellus (yolk)
Albumen (white)
Shell membrane

Air space
Allantoic fluid
Embryo
Amniotic fluid
Amnion

LEFT

A cuckoo egg sits among unsuspecting neighbours in its host nest.

Protecting Eggs

Eggs are always at risk of predation, from other birds, mammals and reptiles. Sadly they are also at risk from humans. The once-fashionable pastime of collecting birds' eggs still exists today although thankfully it is not as prevalent as it once was. Many rare breeding species, particularly birds of prey, are at risk from egg hunters.

Camouflage

There are a number of ways that birds protect their eggs from natural predators. Quite often the eggs protect themselves by camouflage. While the adult birds are away from the nest it is important that the clutch remains safe. This is particularly true of ground-nesting birds such as the plover family. Often these eggs are laid on the ground in shallow scrapes in the earth, sand or shingle. Eggs of these species are covered with blotches and irregular markings that help to break up the distinctive outline and allows the clutch of eggs to sit unobtrusively.

Chicks are also often patterned in a way that they remain camouflaged once the eggs have hatched. Nightjars or Nighthawks, terns and many wading birds use this form of protection.

Decoy

Should the camouflage of the eggs not be sufficient then the adult bird has another method of protection. It will act as a decoy to any approaching predators. Usually this will take the form of the female feigning injury such as a broken wing or leg. The predator will then turn its attention to what appears to be fairly easy prey. Once they have been lured away from the nest site the bird will instantly take flight and often fly a considerable distance before returning, safe from the predator.

Fascinating Facts

The smallest eggs in the world are laid by the Vervain Hummingbird. They are about the size of a pea. The largest are Ostrich eggs.

ABOVE

An adult gull runs away with a stolen egg.

BELOW

Tern chicks are speckled like the eggs to offer camouflage protection against predators.

FAMILY LIFE

Other than searching for food, breeding and protecting eggs and young, there are a number of bird habits, including preening, displays to attract a mate and defining a territory. Many of these habits can easily be witnessed by a careful bird-watcher who knows where and when to look.

Preening and Displays

Preening is habit that can easily be witnessed in a lot of species. Its purpose is to keep the feathers clean and in optimum condition. Generally the bird moves its bill along the barbs of each feather in a nibbling motion. It will start at the quill end and work towards the tip of the feather. Many species have a small gland – the preen gland – situated underneath the tail that secretes a type of oil. The bird flicks or rubs its tail against the preen gland and spreads the oil over its feathers. This keeps the feathers lubricated and flexible, as well as assisting in waterproofing them and keeping bacteria and fungal infections at bay. The waterproofing is particularly useful in ducks, geese and sea birds as it prevents the bird from becoming waterlogged.

Display Habits

Display is an important step in the formation of a breeding pair. In certain species these displays are thought to have evolved as exaggerated routine behaviour such as feeding, preening and bathing.

Mating displays are not only essential steps in pair formation, they can also be fascinating to watch. Certain displays can be very elaborate and last a long time. Species such as grouse and some waders take part in communal displays called leks (*see* page 29). During the spring even the most common of urban birds will be displaying in some shape or form.

(*see* page 29)

BELOW LEFT

A Knot preens its feathers, stimulating the preen gland to release a protective oil.

BELOW

Ducks display by jumping, throwing back their heads or showing the white parts beneath their tails.

LEFT
*Thrushes have been known
to fiercely guard a berry-bearing
bush to prevent it being stripped
of its fruit.*

Protecting Territory

Many species of bird will attempt to stop other birds encroaching and occupying their home or its immediate area. They are defending their territory and laying claim on potential nest sites and the food sources therein. The act of territory protection is largely a vocal threat; however, if the vocal threat is ignored then the bird will adopt a threatening posture and sometimes even chase intruders. If all else fails, the bird will physically attack and sometimes kill.

Territory Size

The size of a bird's territory differs from species to species. Generally, the smaller the bird, then the smaller its territory. The territories for the sparrow family, for example, may only be a few square metres. Some birds of prey,

particularly buzzards and eagles can cover tens of square kilometres.

Breeding Season

Protection of territory is normally associated with the start of the breeding season and is largely targeted towards birds of the same

species that present a threat to potential mates. Threatening behaviour may also be directed towards birds with similar diets, which may threaten a food source.

Although the breeding season is the most common time for this activity, some birds will defend territory all year round. The European Robin, which can pair from as early as December, is one such example. Food may also motivate a bird into territorial protection during the winter months.

One trait that can be observed is, again during the breeding season, birds attacking their own reflection. This is purely a case of mistaken identity as they see the reflection of themselves as a rival male.

BIRDSONG

Bird songs and calls are a vital part of their daily lives. They are a means of communicating, of issuing warning, staying with a flock and attracting a mate. There is a huge variety of songs and calls, and some of them are very complex, although experts do not yet understand why this should be. Understanding the different songs and calls of birds – and even their meanings – is one of the best ways of identification for bird-watchers.

Purpose of Birdsong

A bird's vocal sound can be split loosely into calls and songs. The difference between the two is somewhat subjective, but a call is generally used to give alarm to warn of potential predators or to ensure contact is maintained with its flock, for example.

Song is used more to attract potential mates or to defend territory. Learning to differentiate between calls and songs can be useful in identifying different species. It is also useful to understand why and how birds learn to make these sounds.

Songs and Calls

Not all birds 'sing' – this is largely confined to perching birds, which make up only about half the species in the world. Calls, on the other hand, are made by all birds. Calls are usually (although not always) much simpler than songs. However, it is not always easy to distinguish a song from a call.

Songbirds

The male of the species sings for two reasons: to announce his territory to other males and to attract a mate. Very often the same song will be used to serve both purposes. How elaborate a song may be differs from species to species. Not all birds sing as much as warblers and thrushes, for example, but most perching birds possess a song, albeit a simple one.

Complex Songs

Though some birds sing relatively simple songs, others have more complicated ones involving many different phrases.

Fascinating Facts

Songbirds can be very good mimics, able to copy the sounds made by other bird species. Starlings and Mockingbirds are among the best avian mimics.

RIGHT

The Chaffinch has a range of songs which may serve different purposes.

Birds such as the Chaffinch may have several different songs. It is thought that in species with complicated songs, the females are more interested in the complexity of the song. Males with more complex songs therefore tend to find mates earlier in the season. Getting the pair bond formed early in the season is important because the sooner the pair can start raising a brood, the higher their chances of successfully rearing a second brood and thus increasing their reproductive success.

The Dawn Chorus

The dawn chorus is a well-known phenomenon but there are very good reasons for its existence. The time just around dawn in woodland is a good time to sing. The air is normally still and sound travels well in these conditions. It is also a time when many of the daytime predators are not yet on the move. There are several species, such as members of the tit family, that lay eggs in the morning, and the optimum time to mate is in the hour before the eggs are laid.

Identifying Birds from their Songs and Calls

Although getting to grips with birdsong can appear a little daunting, it is actually relatively easy. The best advice is to familiarize yourself with the inhabitants of your garden or local patch. Get to know these before venturing further afield. Do not expect to identify every species first time on the call alone. It is a good idea to invest in one of the many audio recordings available. Also, try to learn which groups of birds make which types of call. Narrowing it down to a particular family can save a lot of time when trying to identify to species level.

Water Birds

Swans, geese, ducks and similar species are not renowned for their vocal abilities, although most are able to vocalize in some form. Although you may not be able to use these sounds to identify them, the 'quack' of a Mallard, for example, is instantly recognizable, and the noise made by a large flock of geese as they alight can be nothing short of breathtaking.

Waders are a group that can easily be identified using calls and songs. Most of the species have a call, which ranges from a single 'peep' to multi-syllable trilling. These calls are often given in flight and although you may not be able to use this alone to identify the bird, it can be useful when used in conjunction with other features. As well as concentrating on the call or song, note other features such as colour of the rump, wing-bar etc.

Game Birds

Game birds are also not the most vocal of species, however the males of the grouse family in particular have very interesting songs and calls, especially during the breeding season. Gulls, terns and auks again make a variety of sounds but, perhaps with one or two exceptions, these generally will not be identified by that alone.

Passerines

Passerines are the real songsters and warblers probably steal the show

here. There is a bewildering array of these birds and an equally bewildering range of songs and calls. Again, do not be daunted, and do your homework with an audio guide if at all possible. Some native warblers have fluty, rich and melodic songs but are also quite capable of single-note calls as they move through the undergrowth. Beware of thrushes, however. Blackbirds and Robins have equally melodic songs and although their songs are more melancholy there is potential for confusion of these species.

Understanding the Dawn Chorus

Once you have reached a comfortable and competent level with birdsong you may wish to test your expertise with the dawn chorus, 40 minutes to an hour after daybreak. The thrushes are generally one

of the first species to be heard, including Robins and Blackbirds. Remember that this is not an exact science, however. Wrens and warblers may come next, followed by finches and other species. There is no guaranteed order, but there is a genuine tendency for some to start earlier than others. Individuals seeking territory are particularly active immediately after dawn, when it is light enough to move around but dark enough to forage for food safely.

There is also an evening equivalent to the dawn chorus – the dusk chorus. This does not quite have the magnitude or splendour of the dawn chorus, but is still an aural spectacle.

The Meaning of Bird Calls

Communication is vitally important to birds. Without a form of communication, many of them would starve, lose their way during migration or be unable to defend a territory or find a mate.

How Calls Are Made

Birds do not possess vocal cords. To produce sounds, vibrations are sent across the bird's voice box, the syrinx, located where the bronchial tubes meet the trachea. Generally, the more muscles a bird has attached to the syrinx the more vocalizations it can make. Warblers, for example, have many muscles and can produce a variety of sounds, while members of the pigeon and dove families have only one pair of muscles, which results in only a basic 'cooing' sound.

Mobbing

Each species has its own specific call or calls. Some birds have over a dozen calls in their repertoire, which serve different purposes. The alarm call is one of the clearest forms of communication a bird gives. This is particularly evident in mobbing. Mobbing is a very noisy and obvious way that birds protect themselves and their families from predators.

As soon as a predator is spotted the bird will emit their usual alarm call and on occasion fly at the predator, harassing it. Usually mobbing starts with one, possibly two birds. In a short space of time there can be a large number involved – very often of different species. The sound of this activity is often a tell-tale sign of a daylight roosting owl and is always worth following up. Crows, gulls and terns are also adept at mobbing although they tend to be more aerial. Birds of prey and herons can often be seen and heard mobbing. The loud alarm calls will attract every bird within earshot and lessen the chances of a successful catch. It is also thought that the calls are used to educate young birds. From such displays adults can impress on their offspring the appearance and behaviour of potential predators.

Mating and Location Calls

Calls are often made during the earlier parts of the breeding season when a bird is trying to attract a mate. However, birds tend to rely more on song than calls when breeding.

Group-feeding birds, such as members of the quail family, often call. When a feeding family disperses over an area, the young birds communicate with their parents through location calls. When split up they can pinpoint a location and then regroup through a series of gathering calls. Nestlings will also be quite vocal, especially when trying to attract a parent bringing food to the nest. The more vocal the young bird, the higher the chances of it getting first refusal with the food.

Understanding Calls

There is an ongoing investigation into the theory that birds hear calls differently to how humans hear them. It is thought that although many calls sound the same to the human ear, the pitch in which the call is delivered differs each time. By doing this the bird may be building a whole vocabulary of standard phrases that can easily be recognized by members of its own family and species. These calls are thought to be produced by both sexes throughout the year, and are thought to serve a variety of functions, including maintaining contact, raising an alarm and to coordinating flock activities.

ABOVE

Pigeons can only make a basic cooing sound because of the number of muscles in their throat.

BELOW LEFT

A flock of Avocets mob a Grey Heron.

BELOW

Quails call to indicate the discovery of food.

HABITAT

Birds can live almost anywhere – even in parts of the world with harsh environments and extreme temperatures. They can nest in the most unlikely places and have adapted to find food sources and withstand local predators. Birds with similar habits can of course be found in similar habitats, but some species will venture far from their natural environment in search of food, nesting places and warmer weather during colder months.

Ecology

Essentially ecology can be defined as the study of plants and animals, in this instance birds, in relation to their environment and habitat, the study of the distribution and abundance of bird species and the study of the structure and function of nature as a whole.

Each species of bird breeds and spends its non-breeding season in particular parts of the world. These are often the same regions for non-migratory species, which form the geographical range or distribution of that particular species of bird. Very often isolated species will develop in a different way to other members of the same family and create independent subspecies.

Behaviour Patterns

In these areas, birds occupy certain habitats and have certain characteristic behaviours. They also interact, directly or indirectly, with other species of birds, plants and animals that share the same habitat. The ecology of birds concerns the search for and study of patterns of behaviour and the principles that govern them. Birds are important for a large number of reasons, largely relating to their significance as predators at the top of many food chains. They are therefore important as ecological and environmental indicators – changes in their populations often reflect human impact on the environment.

Natural Selection

Natural selection states that the stronger species survive. When change occurs, for whatever reason, those birds best suited to the new circumstances will thrive and those that are not ideally suited will not be able to compete. The British naturalist Charles Darwin proposed this principle after observing some population variations in birds. He noticed that certain birds within a species often had slightly varied behavioural traits, and that those traits made some more suited to certain conditions. Darwin's theory was that, over a given length of time, the species that are better adapted would thrive and the others would die out completely. The resulting population would be entirely made up of those stronger, more adaptable species. Over time this could result in a species changing enough to eventually become a totally different creature.

Environmental Conditions

Questions have been raised about the validity of the theory of natural selection, but it cannot be denied that variations within a single species make some birds better suited to different circumstances. There is an important point to be made about the theory of natural selection, however. Should environmental conditions return to normal, the balance of that species would also revert to normal. For example, birds such as finches, with heavy, powerful bills may become dominant during periods of prolonged drought, since they can more easily break open nuts and other food sources. The species with regular bills will struggle in these conditions and their numbers diminish. However, once the drought is over, the population will revert to its former numbers.

Genetic Mutation

There are no known instances of a natural population experiencing a permanent, meaningful change. Observed genetic mutations are, in the natural world, usually fatal. While there is no doubt about the short-term function and effects of natural selection, its long-term effects are not fully understood.

TOP LEFT

A plover nest in a drought-stricken landscape – birds can survive in the most harsh environments.

Urban and Suburban Areas

Many people think that towns and cities must be rather dull in terms of wildlife, but in fact the opposite is true. Large numbers of bird species can be found in these built-up areas, including some that positively insist on being city dwellers.

One of the best-known species is the Feral Pigeon. These birds can be found in just about every large town and city. They are direct descendants of the rare and elusive Rock Dove, which makes its home on rocky coastal outcrops. Over the years the Feral Pigeon has developed to be the ultimate city slicker. They benefit from humans who directly feed them in town parks, and from those who feed

BELOW

A bird table in the garden can attract avian visitors even in the most urban settings.

them indirectly – food scraps from a late-night takeaway are eagerly devoured. Feral Pigeons nest on roofs, ledges and in buildings; they are often prolific breeders and can raise young almost all year round.

Garden Birds

Town gardens are vitally important for large numbers of bird species. The urban garden invites myriad visitors from the bird world. Should the garden benefit from a well-stocked bird table, so much the better. Members of the tit family will provide

endless entertainment as they tackle bird feeders primed with peanuts. Blackbirds and other members of the thrush family will search lawns and borders for slugs, earthworms and pretty much anything else they can find.

The Robin is often very tame in urban surroundings and can be tempted to feed from the hand.

Visitors

Listen out during the summer months for Swifts as they scream overhead. They also are big fans of towns and cities and choose to make their simple nests in roof spaces. Martins also visit urban areas during the summer. They construct fabulous cup-shaped nests under the eaves of houses to raise their young. During the winter months many members of the finch family

will move into urban areas to feed. Forced away from their normal habitats due to harsh weather and food shortages, they make a colourful addition to our gardens.

Gulls are often found in cities. Generally they will be more numerous during the colder months as they venture inland for food, but many now nest, particularly in coastal towns. The crow family is also often at home in urban settings. These natural scavengers collect scraps from city streets and rubbish dumps.

Birds of prey are also represented in urban habitats. Kestrels can be commonplace and the once rare Peregrine Falcon is now breeding in a large number of cities, using office blocks, churches, cathedrals and power-station cooling towers. The Feral Pigeon is its main quarry, so perhaps it is not surprising that it has chosen to settle in this particular habitat. The Tawny Owl is also often

encountered in the city and can be heard calling after nightfall.

Parks

Parks in towns and cities offer the bird-watcher a whole range of other birds that may be less frequent visitors to a garden. If the local park boasts a stretch of water, such as a pond or boating lake, this will increase the number and variety of species that could be

encountered. Here you will find ducks and geese, not to mention wagtails and kingfishers. Coots and Moorhens can also be found in good numbers. Again, during the harder weather a number of more unusual birds can find their way into our parks.

On first glance urban areas may appear uninteresting, but you are never far away from a range of interesting bird life.

Woodpeckers are one of the most fascinating sights in deciduous woodland areas.

Game birds such as pheasants usually make woodland their home.

Woodland

Woodland is an incredibly important habitat. It provides ample cover for nesting birds and holds an array of invertebrates that act as an all-important food source. Combine this with a wealth of seeds, nuts and fruit that are readily available and it is little wonder that our woodlands hold such a diversity of birds.

Broadleaved Woodland

Woodpeckers abound in broadleaved or deciduous woodland as do many species of warbler. Finches, sparrows and treecreepers are also at home here.

Most woodland has its fair share of larger birds as well. Species of buzzards, pheasants and woodpigeons are often numerous. If your local wood is within striking distance of a watercourse then you may be lucky enough to have a colony of herons. Their mass nesting sites are referred to, quite simply, as Heronries.

From July to September bird-watching in woodland environs can be quite demanding. Many birds are undergoing moult and birdsong is almost non-existent. Very often a solitary call from the undergrowth is the only available clue to the

woodlands' inhabitants. The arrival of winter causes the dropping of leaves and makes things a lot easier for bird-watchers. Sadly

warblers, redstarts and other summer visitors have long departed. However, there are still plenty of species to be seen on an

autumn or winter visit. During colder weather lots of different species amass in large mixed flocks. These are well worth close scrutiny and can often give up rare over-wintering warblers or normally elusive finches.

Coniferous Woodland

Coniferous woodland is also a habitat worthy of mention. In many parts of Europe, including Britain, there are not many indigenous conifers. There are several species of pine together with yews and junipers. However, a lot of coniferous plantations consist of introduced trees.

The bird life in coniferous woodland varies. Location is all important, as are the

often make for a dull place for birds. Younger coniferous plantations are often more attractive. If the plantations have open spaces, clearings and fire breaks this will often increase the number of

species, age and planting, or spacing, of trees. At an age of about 15 years, conifer trees form a thick canopy. Often modern forestry practices mean the lower branches are lopped and, combined with the light-reducing canopies, this can

different bird species. In certain areas shrikes, woodlarks and pipits will benefit from open areas and young growth.

There are many species that exist in coniferous woodlands which, quite simply, cannot

be encountered elsewhere. The crossbill family is a good example. These thickset, large-headed finches have adapted perfectly to life in the coniferous forests. Evolution has caused this bird to have elongated mandibles that cross at the tip (hence the name). This allows them to extract otherwise difficult seeds from fir cones. This evolutionary quirk makes them an extremely efficient feeder in areas that other species may find difficult.

Scour the woodland floor for dropped cones with the telltale sign of split scales – crossbills will not be far away.

Deciduous or coniferous, large or small, woodlands offer excellent bird-watching at any time of the year. Be patient during the summer months, brush up on bird calls and song and you will be rewarded with sightings of some very special birds.

Open Country

In recent years changes in farming practices have had a devastating effect on many native bird populations. Hedgerows have been removed and replaced by fencing, or simply removed to create larger fields. Any real diversity depends on hedges and, generally speaking, the older, wider and taller, the better. Hedgerows are the lifeblood of this type of habitat. Landowners are becoming more aware of the effects of this type of intensive farming and events may take a turn for the better.

Hedgerows
Hedgerows are obvious choices for nest sites. Finches, buntings and sparrows – to name but a few – all thrive in this

ABOVE

The Corn Bunting lives in open country and farmland.

environment. Game birds such as partridges are reliant on hedge bottoms to raise their young. Set-aside margins on field edges are

RIGHT

Despite its name, the Tree Sparrow prefers open country to woodland.

also very beneficial. Often these will be packed with wild flowers, which are an important food source for large numbers of insects, which in turn are an important food source for a number of bird species. Besides the bounties of the field edges there is also a lot

to be said for the fields themselves. If cereal crops are grown then this can provide valuable cover for numerous ground-nesting farmland birds. If the fields lie bare then lapwings and other species may nest.

Grasslands and Heaths

Other examples of open country include heaths and grasslands. Grasslands are found in both upland and lowland areas, and many of them overlap other broad habitat types. Although these places are normally rich in flowers and insects, they tend to have a limited, but nevertheless interesting, variety of birds. The spread of cultivation and use of chemical crop treatments have also damaged this important habitat, sometimes beyond recognition. However, there are several species that do very well in these conditions. Larks can often be abundant as they sing from high in the sky before plummeting to the ground as part of their spring display. Pipits and finches are also commonplace.

Heaths are generally flat expanses of land on sandy or rocky areas. Their soil type is generally quite acidic. These areas are broken up by deciduous and coniferous shrubs and trees that offer a good food supply as well as cover for nesting. Resident species in these habitats include members of the chat family, wheatears and some of the rarer warblers.

Fascinating Facts

Birds close their eyes when they sleep, but during the night they will open them at intervals to ensure there is no danger nearby.

RIGHT

Tree and Meadow Pipits can be found on open grasslands across Britain and Europe.

Freshwater and Marshland

Examples of freshwater habitats are varied. They can include lakes, rivers, reservoirs and streams. Land that has been previously mined for sand and gravel is often flooded and returned to a natural state. This can also be a rich habitat. Marshland is generally into three main groups. The dabbling ducks, such as the Mallard, feed on weeds and small insects on or just below the water's surface. Diving ducks, the Tufted Duck for example, search on the beds of rivers or lakes for weeds and insects. Sea ducks are primarily marine species that dive for animal prey such as fish – mergansers belong to this particular group.

defined as a wetland area, with grasses, rushes, reeds, sedges, and other herbaceous plants in or around shallow water. Both freshwater areas

During the winter months even sea ducks can be found wintering well inland.

Several species of geese can be encountered in freshwater, although apart from the ubiquitous Canada Goose these will tend to be winter visitors – unless you happen to be in the far northern areas, which are the breeding range of a number of goose species. There is also a small number of resident grebe species although, again in winter, you are likely to encounter other members of the family, together with divers or loons.

and marshland offer up an excellent array of birds and some fantastic opportunities for bird-watching.

Water Birds

Birds that can be found on open water include ducks, geese and grebes. Many of these species breed but their ranks are often swelled with large numbers of winter visitors. Ducks fall loosely

Open Water

Often wintering gulls will be found on open stretches of water, even many kilometres inland. Gulls choose large open bodies of water to roost on and with some patience bird-watchers can be rewarded by the occasional rare visitor during winter afternoons. The larger gulls can take up to five years to moult into adult plumage, the smaller gull species less so, and can provide a real identification challenge in their array of winter plumages.

During the summer large numbers of swallows and martins (Hirundines) can be seen over any expanse of open water, feeding on winged insects. They will also skim the surface and take up water to drink. Look out for kingfishers as they use branches and posts to perch on while they scan the water for prey. Wagtails will often be present around the muddy margins.

Marshland Birds

Marshland, and in part-icular the reedbeds that lie around the fringes, is an important habitat for birds.

Waders often dominate the marsh environment and can be found in good numbers, especially during the spring and autumn passage. Herons and egrets are also likely to be encountered. The reeds themselves can hold a selection of birds that make their homes there. Areas of reed, rush and sedge can often make for difficult viewing. The areas can be very dense and a great deal of patience may be needed. Bitterns can often be heard making their booming call during the spring but catching sight of one is rare, as they only come into open water to feed. Warblers and buntings breed in these conditions but, as with the bittern, their calls and songs may give them away but you are likely to get only a fleeting glimpse as they flit through the undergrowth.

BELOW

Gulls will winter inland over large expanses.

BELOW RIGHT

Bitterns are a common but elusive marshland resident.

Coasts

Coastlines provide an abundance of bird life. Sea birds have had to adapt to live and breed in these surroundings. Life can be arduous in this environment, especially during the winter months. Sea birds eat salty food such as fish, crustaceans and invertebrates, and ingest salty seawater, which would be impossible for most other species since their kidneys would not be able to dispel the excess salt in their blood. Sea birds have special glands situated behind their eyes, which remove the salt from the bloodstream. These glands then excrete a fluid, about five times saltier than their blood. Other species have adapted in different ways. Some, such as the Guillemot and other members of the auk family, are adapted for swimming with waterproof feathers, a dense plumage and a thick layer of body fat to increase buoyancy and encourage warmth. Their short legs make them look rather awkward on land, but at sea these enable them to maximize propulsion through the water and aid streamlining and steering. Their feet are webbed and their wings are used as flippers under the water.

Coastal birds such as auks have specially waterproofed feathers that help them swim.

Cliffs

Coastal cliffs can be teeming with breeding birds during the summer. Smaller gulls such as Kittiwakes nest on the ledges, while the larger gulls can be found on cliff tops. The seagull may be the first bird that comes to mind when considering this habitat, but in fact there is no such thing as a seagull; this is a colloquial term to describe the gull family. Terns will be attracted to breed on shingle beaches or, depending on the species, sand dunes. Also resident along coasts are members of the skua family. These dark, gull-like birds are voracious predators and feed on the chicks and adults of just about any species that nests in these environs.

Shorelines and Estuaries

Besides the seemingly inhospitable cliff faces, there are lots of other coastal attractions for birds. Beaches – whether sand or shingle – draw large numbers of wading

birds to feed along the tide and strandline on washed-up foodstuffs.

Bird life can be rich indeed at estuaries and saltings. Waders can often be prolific and during the winter large flocks gather on the estuary mudflats and creeks to feed on crustaceans and invertebrates. Egrets and herons, ducks and geese can also be found here. Wildfowl may have chosen to make this their winter home or may simply be stopping off to refuel on a bounty of food before recommencing their long migratory journey. Look carefully at the larger flocks of more common geese such as Brent Geese, as they can sometimes be joined by rare birds such as the stunning Red-breasted Goose.

Salt Marshes

A number of smaller birds can often be found on the foreshore and salt marshes.

Pay particular attention to large, mixed flocks as these can often contain buntings, Shore Larks and pipits. Wintering finches can also be found. Birds of prey such as the Peregrine Falcon often patrol the cliffs and beaches along the coast and can be looked for along with Ravens and other crow species.

During the summer the sight and sound of a thriving sea-bird colony can be quite breathtaking and, in sharp contrast, the desolation brought on with the onset of winter opens up a whole new world of avian visitors to this important habitat.

ABOVE LEFT

Razorbills can often be seen jostling with Puffins for position on a packed cliff ledge.

RIGHT

Although Ravens commonly make their homes in mountainous upland areas, they can also be seen patrolling cliffs along the coast.

Mountain and Upland

Mountains make up about one fifth of the earth's surface and can be found on every continent in the world. A mountain is generally considered to be land that rises well above its surroundings to a summit, usually greater than 610 m (2,000 ft). Areas below this level, and normally above any cultivated land, are generally referred to as uplands. Mountains, uplands and moorland may seem desolate and barren compared with other habitats. However, this unique landscape holds a larger number of resident bird species than it first appears.

The Merlin can be seen in the hills, and over the moorlands, of Scotland, Wales and northern England.

Food Sources

Generally speaking the high peaks hold the smallest amount of bird life but a single area of upland can hold an entire ecosystem all of its own. The bases of upland areas are often flower-rich, which encourages a large amount of invertebrate life, an important food source for many bird species. Open moorland has importance for a number of breeding waders and certain birds of prey. On higher ground the avifauna is restricted to smaller numbers of specialist species. Food sources are also less prevalent. The soil types higher up tend to be quite acidic. Although there are several specialized plants

that need this type of environment there is not anywhere near the variety, which has an obvious impact on the number of invertebrate species there.

Upland Residents

One resident that can be encountered this high up is the Ptarmigan, sometimes referred to as the Rock Ptarmigan. This member of the grouse family undergoes a moult during the year, which results in mottled brown summer plumage and an all-white plumage during the snow-filled winter months, camouflaging the bird and protecting it from predators. It feeds on a range of plant shoots, leaves, leaf buds, berries and insects. Other inhabitants of the high

upland areas include the Snow Bunting and several birds of prey, including the impressive Snowy Owl. The adult male is virtually pure white, but females and immature birds have some dark barring on their feathers. Its thick plumage, heavily feathered feet and colouration make the Snowy Owl well-adapted for life in upland areas.

Buntings and Eagles

Snow Buntings are large buntings, with striking plumages. Males in summer have all-white heads and underparts that contrast

The Dotterel is found mainly in upland areas of northern Scandinavia and Russia.

Fascinating Facts

The Pacific Golden Plover holds the record for the longest non-stop migratory flight, travelling from its native north, all the way to Hawaii. The journey takes them thousands of kilometres over open ocean.

TOP RIGHT

The Snowy Owl is one of the most impressive birds of the mountain habitat.

RIGHT

The Golden Eagle can be seen soaring over upland areas, particularly during the months of spring.

---

with a black mantle and wing tips. Females are a little more mottled above. In autumn and winter, birds develop a sandy/buff wash to their plumage and males have more mottled upperparts. Globally they breed around the Arctic from Scandinavia to Alaska, Canada and Greenland and migrate south in winter. They breed on the high ground but can be found on lower slopes during colder parts of the year.

One of the most majestic sights in upland and mountain landscapes is the Golden Eagle. This huge bird of prey likes to soar and glide on air currents, holding its wings in a shallow 'V'. Eagles have traditional territories and nesting places, which may be used for generations. They can be encountered all year round but in early spring they can often be found performing display flights. They feed on a range of birds and mammals, such as the Mountain Hare, and will also take carrion.

During the harsh winter months many mountain species will move further down the summits as the peaks become snowbound, making feeding difficult. This can often be a good time to observe some of these species without having to undergo arduous ascents.

Bird-watching & Identification

EQUIPMENT

Birds can be enjoyed without any equipment at all, but as your interest develops there are two items that you will want to acquire – a decent pair of binoculars and a good field guide. The first will help you see birds better and the second will help you put the right name to what you are seeing. There are other things that you might find useful too, but binoculars and a field guide are the basic kit.

Binoculars

Binoculars vary in price, quality and specification and not all of them are suitable for bird-watching.

Specifications

An 8 x 42 binocular magnifies eight times – that's what the first number means. The '42' tells you the size of the objective lenses – these are the large lenses at the front of the binoculars. An 8 x 42 binocular has objective lenses with a 42 mm diameter.

Most bird-watchers use binoculars with a magnification of between seven and ten times, with eight probably being the most popular choice. Do not be fooled into thinking that bigger is better! You can buy binoculars that magnify 20 times but most people would find them difficult to use for bird-watching. Higher magnifications make the bird appear closer, but you are unlikely to be able to hold them steady enough to enjoy the closer view – handheld binoculars are likely to wobble, and any movements are more obvious with a higher magnification. The field of view (the width of the viewing area) is likely to be narrower too, making it harder to find birds, and the image may not be as bright. Zoom binoculars are not a good choice for bird-watching.

Binoculars' objective lenses are their 'windows'. All things being equal, the bigger the windows, the brighter the view. But bigger lenses mean bigger and heavier binoculars and all things are not equal – the quality of glass and coatings used and the design of the binoculars also affect the brightness of the image. In practice, most bird-watchers use binoculars with objective lenses between 30 and 42 mm in diameter.

ABOVE

It is important to find a size and weight of binoculars that suit you.

Different Designs

The 'traditional' binocular design, where the eyepieces are not lined up with the objectives, is called a 'porro-prism'. Binoculars where the eyepieces and the objectives are on the same line are known as 'roof-prisms'. Either design can be used for bird-watching. A porro-prism will normally provide a higher-quality image than a similarly priced roof-prism. Many people find roof-prisms more comfortable to use, though, and roof-prisms tend to be more tolerant of rough treatment.

'Compact binoculars' have objectives with a diameter of around 25 mm or less and can be small enough to slip into a pocket. Some provide a very good image. They can be a good choice for children (whose hands may be too small for larger binoculars), as an 'always with me' binocular or for those who really do not want to carry something bigger.

To summarize, most bird-watchers use binoculars that magnify seven to ten times and have 30 to 42 mm objectives. If you need something smaller, try the better-quality compacts.

Focusing

Most binoculars have one central focusing wheel that focuses both sides of the binocular – this is the design you need for bird-watching. Some binoculars focus closer than others, perhaps to less than two metres. This is particularly useful if you want to look at insects such as butterflies and dragonflies.

Waterproofing

Some binoculars are waterproof, others are not. How important this is to you depends on how you use them. If you are a fair weather bird-watcher waterproofing will be less of an issue. You can also buy binoculars that are filled with nitrogen or argon. This stops them steaming up inside.

Rainguards

Rainguards are eyepiece covers that are threaded on to the binocular strap. They protect the eyepieces from the weather (and from crumbs!) and can be moved away from the eyepieces for viewing.

TOP LEFT

Carrying a small pair of binoculars with you while out walking will bring its own rewards.

TOP RIGHT

Compact binoculars are a good choice for children.

*It is important to ensure your
binoculars are correctly focused
before using them for spotting birds.*

LEFT
*Bird-watchers who wear glasses
should set the eyecups downwards.*

Making Your Choice

There is no one binocular that is the universal best bird-watching binocular.

Binoculars are a personal choice – buy a binocular that *you* are happy with. Try to buy from a specialist supplier who knows about the needs of bird-watchers. Work out a short list of models that suit your needs and budget (or ask the dealer for help) and, if at all possible, try before you buy. Do not compare more than a few binoculars at once or you will get confused. Here are some buying tips:

1. Adjust the distance between the eyepieces. When you look through a binocular you should see one circle. Some binoculars are not suitable for children because the eyepieces cannot be moved close enough together for their eyes.

2. Adjust the dioptre (*see* page 67). This will help you get the best out of a binocular.

3. Make sure the binoculars sit comfortably in your hands and that you can reach and move the focusing wheel easily. Is it easy to find the 'right' focus? Look for a bright, sharp image with no obvious 'colour fringing'.

4. Consider their weight. Can you hold them steady enough?

5. Ask for a strap to be fitted and see how they feel around your neck and how they sit against your chest. Imagine carrying them for several hours.

6. To get more for your money, think about buying a used pair of binoculars.

Setting Up Your Binoculars
Put the strap on and adjust it so that it is not too long. If necessary you can replace the supplied strap with one that is wider and more comfortable. Some straps have neoprene in them which makes the binoculars feel lighter than they are. To take the weight off your neck, try a binocular harness.

Adjust the distance between the eyepieces (the IPD or inter-pupillary distance) so that when you look through the binocular you see one circle.

Adjust the dioptre. One of the eyepieces, normally the right, will be adjustable – you can set this to compensate for any difference between your eyes. Here's how:

1. Cover the right-hand objective.

2. Choose something 50 to 100 m (160 to 300 ft) away with a crisp outline to focus on – a TV aerial for example.

3. Looking through the left side only, use the main focusing wheel to focus.

4. When it is sharp, cover the left-hand objective and focus the right-hand side using the adjustable eyepiece only.

5. Once the right-hand side is sharp, leave the adjustable eyepiece in that position. The binoculars are now set for your eyes – all you have to do from here on is use the main focusing wheel.

RIGHT
When bird-watching in wet or cold conditions, ensure that your binoculars and other equipment are kept dry.

Glasses
Most binoculars have eyecups that twist up and down. If you wear glasses when using binoculars twist the eyecups down – then you will see more of the field of view. If you do not wear glasses when using binoculars keep the eyecups up.

Binocular Skills
When you first use binoculars you may find it hard to 'get on to the bird'. Keep your eyes on the bird and bring the binoculars up to your eyes – do not take your eyes off the bird. It gets easier with practice!

Maintenance
Protect your binoculars from bumps and scrapes. If they are not waterproof and you are out in the rain, put them inside your jacket to keep the rain off. Use good-quality lens tissues or a lens cloth to clean the lenses and do not over-clean them – every time you clean them you risk scratching them. Make sure you blow off any dust or grit first.

Field Guides

Essentially, a field guide is a catalogue of the birds of a particular area, with illustrations and words to help the user correctly identify birds. There are many on the market, but some are better than others. But what may be regarded as 'the best' may not be the best when you first start out. In the UK, for example, what is widely regarded as 'the best' field guide covers the birds of Europe, North Africa and a good chunk of the Middle East. It includes over 700 species, most of which you are unlikely to see in the UK. When you are learning your birds, a reference with more limited geographical scope makes life much easier.

Choosing Your Field Guide

Look for a field guide that is portable enough for use in the field and that allows you to see all the words and pictures and the map for a species at the same time. If possible, listen to other bird-watchers' recommendations or read reviews, but try to find the book that works best for *you*.

Birds are variable beasts – males may look different to females, some wear different plumages at different times of year and young birds might not look like the

adults. It can be confusing, but a good field guide will include a range of illustrations to help you cope with the variety.

The text should be easy to find your way around and should quickly take you to the key things you need to look for to secure a confident identification. It will tell you how big the bird is, what it looks and sounds like (though the latter is not easy in a book!), how common it is

and where and when you are likely to see it.

Using Your Field Guide

Use it at home and when you are out bird-watching. In the UK, taking a field guide into the field used to be frowned on by some bird-watchers, but this is not the case in the US, and things may be changing in the UK. Do not be ashamed of using your field guide in the field and do not worry about getting it a bit dog-eared or dirty – it is a working tool.

RIGHT

Choose a field guide with clear pictures of the birds in your local area. Sometimes illustrations can be clearer than photographs.

Read the introductory pages at the beginning of the field guide. This will help you to understand how it has been put together, what any codes or symbols mean and what the colours on the maps mean.

Spend time on your field guide in the comfort of your home. Work out what you might see locally. Familiarize yourself with the names of the birds and what they look like. This can make quite a difference when you start seeing the birds for real. Try to get the hang of the order the birds are featured in, too – this may seem a bit peculiar when you first start. The logic is that the birds are arranged in scientific order, with the most primitive birds at the front of the book and the most advanced species at the back. Most books use a similar order. If it helps you, add your own notes to your field guide too.

Fascinating Facts

There are alternatives to a conventional, book-based field guide. Field guides can be installed on PDAs, iPods and iPhones for example. These are wonderfully portable and can include video clips and sound recordings. There are also some excellent DVD-ROMs which can be used at home.

RIGHT
Familiarize yourself with the birds in your garden before venturing further afield.

If you can afford it, get more than one field guide. No field guide is perfect and being able to check illustrations and descriptions in more than one book can be helpful.

Other Equipment

Notebook

A pocket-sized notebook can be very useful for recording what you see and for making notes on any birds that you cannot identify. The discipline of using a notebook can accelerate the learning process but, despite this, notebook use by bird-watchers has declined considerably.

Checklists that list the birds of an area offer a simple alternative for keeping a record of birds seen, and bird-recording software is available for PDAs too.

Telescope

A telescope provides the advantages of higher magnification and can be a very useful tool. Most telescopes come in two parts – the body and the eyepiece.

BELOW

This bird-watcher is videoing birds through his telescope.

You can choose between a fixed magnification eyepiece (a magnification of around 30x is typical), a zoom eyepiece (20 to 60x is typical), or both. Good zoom eyepieces can be expensive, though. To get enough light in, large objective lenses are required – most bird-watchers use telescopes with objective lenses that are around 60 to 80 mm in diameter, though there are some good-quality telescopes available with smaller objectives. You can also choose between those with a 'straight-through' eyepiece and those with an angled eyepiece (where you look down into the telescope at about 45 degrees). Shared viewing with people of different heights is easier with the latter and the viewing angle means that your tripod does not need to be as tall.

You will also need some kind of support for a telescope – handholding is not really an option. A tripod is the

commonest solution, with hide clamps offering an alternative for use in hides. Monopods and shoulder pods may be used, but these are not as stable as a tripod and are pretty useless for sharing the view with others.

Digiscoping

At its most basic, digiscoping is simply placing a compact digital camera over a telescope eyepiece and taking a picture. Positioning the camera correctly is very important and various adaptors are available to help with this, though some digiscopers make their own from plastic tubing at little expense. The ideal digiscoping setup uses a large objective telescope to let as much light in as possible and special digiscoping eyepieces are available. Surprisingly good results are possible – digiscoping has made bird photography accessible to a new audience.

Other Electronic Kit

Technology has changed bird-watching and, no doubt, will continue to do so. Bird songs and calls can be downloaded on to personal music players and listened to in the field. A 'pen' is available that plays a bird's songs or calls simply by pointing it at the right sticker in your field guide or the right part of a laminated list or special ring-bound field guide. A huge amount of information is available online, and the Internet provides a

RIGHT
Recordings of birdsong can be listened to in the field to help with identification.

medium for contacting bird-watchers from other areas and easy participation in ornithological surveys. Who knows what the future holds!

Other Reference Material

As your interest develops you will probably build a collection of bird books, and perhaps maps to help you explore new birding destinations. You might also want to acquire some good quality bird sound recordings, though may prefer some of the more portable electronic media for this.

News Services

For those that want to know the latest news on uncommon and rare bird sightings a range of services are available. There are websites that you can check and email and texting services that you can sign up to. Knowing what has been seen where has never been so easy.

Clothing

If your birding takes you to wild places or out in more extreme conditions you might need to purchase some specialist outdoor clothing, but there is plenty of bird-watching that can be done without investing huge amounts of money in what you wear!

IDENTIFYING BIRDS

To enjoy a bird you do not need to know its name, but for most bird watchers, putting a name to what they are looking at is very important. For some, identification is the end point. Arguably though, it is just the beginning – work out what the bird is and you can begin to find out more about it. Bird identification is about detective work. Collect as many clues as possible and come to a conclusion – an identification that is 'beyond reasonable doubt'.

Features to Look For

A bird watcher with even a modicum of experience may appear to have remarkable powers of identification to someone just starting out on their bird-watching journey. A confident identification of a glimpsed bird or of a brief blast of birdsong may feel like an unattainable level of expertise. The truth is, though, that a successful identification is simply the result of processing the available information to reach a conclusion. Sometimes, with experience, this can be done very quickly and when you know what you're looking for, some birds are very easy to

Habitat can narrow down the identify of a bird, as can distinctive bills (such as in this Large-billed Ground Finch from the Galapagos Islands).

identify. At other times it can be a lengthier process. Identification can be difficult, but with practice it gets easier. Below are some features to look out for.

Size

Estimating the size of a bird is a good starting point. Books express a bird's size in centimetres or inches – this is its length from the tip of its bill, over its head and along its back to the tip of its tail. Clearly it is of limited use when you are looking at a bird hopping about in a bush. The trick is to compare the bird with another that you know

reasonably well. Is it about the size of a sparrow, thrush or pigeon for example?

Take care when interpreting the sizes given in books. They are useful for comparisons, but remember that a bird with a long bill or tail will, according to the book, be 'bigger' than a bird with a short bill or tail but have the same sized body.

ABOVE

The distinctive shape of birds of prey can instantly help to narrow the options.

RIGHT

The Willow Tit (right) can be confused with the Marsh Tit.

Shape

Again, try to compare your mystery bird to one that you know. Even novice bird watchers will be surprised at how many bird shapes they already know: duck, heron, bird of prey, pheasant, owl,

Markings

Some birds have very obvious markings and these may be all that you need to see to identify the bird. In the UK, a pigeon with a white crescent across its wing has to be a Wood

pigeon, gull, kingfisher, sparrow and crow perhaps. Getting its shape right will help you get to the right pages in your field guide.

Pigeon. But sometimes subtler features need to be checked to confirm an identification. Marsh Tit and Willow Tit look very similar (and were not even recognized as different species until the late 1800s). One feature that helps to separate them is the Willow Tit's pale wing panel, though their voice can be even more helpful.

Make a note of any obvious markings, and if you have time, try to describe the whole bird, from bill tip to tail tip. If you have a field guide with you and have a rough idea of what you

might be looking at, you might want to have a quick look in the book before embarking on a lengthy description. Hopefully, the book will tell you what you need to check to sort out the identification and you can make that your priority, before the bird flies off. Traditional bird-watching 'wisdom' is that you should not work this way because the book may influence you to such a degree that you begin to see features on the bird that are not really there. This is a possibility, but a careful, intelligent approach should minimize this risk.

Sketching

Annotating a simple sketch can be a good way to quickly note down the details of a mystery bird. Your sketch does not need to be fine art – try using egg shapes to produce a basic bird shape. Learning some bird 'topography' can be useful

too. While some of the more technical language may be off-putting at first, much of the labelling is pretty straightforward. Knowing your way around a bird will help you to describe a bird accurately and to understand the descriptions used in some field guides.

What is It Doing?

A bird's behaviour can provide very useful clues to its identity. If you see a roughly pigeon-sized bird hovering over a roadside verge in the UK, it is a Kestrel. How birds fly or walk can give clues too. Some birds fly in a straight line (e.g.

Starling), others have an undulating flight (e.g. woodpeckers). Does it glide or flap its wings, or even alternate between the two?

Where is It?

While some birds are seen in many different habitats, others are more specific in their requirements. You would not expect to see a Puffin inland, for example. Not all the birds that occur in the UK are found in every part of the country – Ptarmigan and Capercaillie are only found in Scotland.

What Time of Year is It?

Some birds are residents – they spend the whole year in this country. Others are summer or winter visitors and spend the rest of the year somewhere else, and some birds just pass through when they are on migration (passage migrants). This information can help with identification.

Using Sounds

Bird songs and calls can provide excellent clues to help with identification. Do not leave learning songs and calls until you have got the hang of what birds look like – knowing some bird noises can make identification much easier and learning some songs and calls is not that difficult. Get to know some of the common birds first and take it from there. The descriptions of bird noises in books can be hard to interpret but using sound recordings can help, especially if you can take them out in the field with you. Alternatively, go bird-watching with a more experienced bird-watcher and learn from them or, when you hear a bird that you do not recognize, track it down and identify it visually too.

Some Tips

Get to know the local and common birds first and build your knowledge from there. Knowing the common birds well will help you to pick out the more unusual ones.

When faced with several species at once that you cannot identify, try to focus on just one of them. Some may 'get away' but you will gradually build your 'repertoire'. Try not to identify a bird on one feature alone. The 'safest' identifications are based on a range of different clues.

Expect to make some mistakes – it is part of the learning process. Stick at it and with time and application you will be the bird-watcher making those impressive split-second identifications!

Fascinating Facts

The best way to begin identifying a bird is by its 'bare parts' – its bill, legs and feet. Check their length, shape and colour, and this will almost always narrow it down considerably.

BELOW

If, on a winter's day, you see a wagtail with some yellow on it, it will be a Grey Wagtail and not a Yellow Wagtail – Yellow Wagtails are summer visitors to the UK.

BELOW RIGHT

The Willow Warbler and the Chiffchaff look very similar but are easily told apart by their song.

Fascinating Facts

Feathers do not go on for ever – they have to cope with a lot of wear and tear and are replaced by moulting. Worn feathers may look paler and tattier than new ones and may have lost their tips.

LEFT

Juvenile Robins do not have a 'red' breast.

BELOW

Male (below left) and female (below right) Tufted Ducks have quite dissimilar appearances. Be aware of such differences.

What to Beware of

Birds that look similar are not always the same species – look at some of the pipits for example. To add to the challenge, some birds that look dissimilar are not different species! Males and females may look different (e.g. ducks, Blackbird), some birds wear their breeding plumage for part of the year only (e.g. Grebes, Black-headed Gull) and young birds can look different to adults (some gulls take four years to acquire their adult plumage).

Juvenile Birds

A bird's juvenile plumage is its first set of 'proper' feathers. For a short period of time, until at least some of the juvenile feathers are moulted, the young bird can look quite unlike its parents. You may still be able to detect the character of the species though, and the juveniles of some species look like washed-out versions of the adults (e.g. Moorhen). One way to identify juveniles is to look for the adults who may be nearby.

Escapes

Not all birds seen in the wild are wild birds. Swans, ducks and geese escape from collections, and falconers and aviculturists lose birds sometimes. If you see a Black Swan it is unlikely to have made its way from the Antipodes!

Light Effects

The direction and intensity of the light can affect your perception of a bird's appearance. Colours may look different in different lights and a bird lit from behind may appear smaller than one lit from the front.

Abnormal Birds

Sooner or later you will see a bird that has some white feathers where it does not normally – a Blackbird with white wing feathers or white patches on the head for example. This is still a Blackbird, but for some reason, some of its feathers lack the normal black

ABOVE

If a bird has been feeding in mud, the true colour of its legs or beak may be obscured.

pigment. This is partial albinism – complete albinism is much more rare. Other birds may over-produce pigment. A melanistic bird is blacker or browner than normal. Abnormal pigmentation also produces other colour effects. Watch out for colour-dyed birds too – ornithologists may use a dye to mark a bird – to study the movements of swans or waders for example.

Not All 'Ducks' Are Ducks

To a beginner, Coots, Moorhens and Grebes may look like ducks. But when you search among the ducks in the field guide you won't find them. Most field guides are arranged in scientific order. All the ducks are together, but as these birds are not ducks you won't find them there. There is no easy solution to this apart from experience and leafing

through your field guide in advance and familiarizing yourself with the birds you are likely to see.

Your Field Guide is exactly that – a Guide

Good-quality field guides are a great identification tool. But they are only a guide – not all of the birds you see will look *exactly* like the illustrations of that species in the book. But normally they are pretty close.

Other Bird-Watchers

Many bird-watchers are friendly and more than happy to assist with a 'tricky' identification. Take care though – the 'experts' that you meet are not always right. Try to work out that mystery bird for yourself too, don't just take someone else's word for it. You will learn more that way too.

Recording Information

It is not compulsory to keep records of the birds you see but it can add a new dimension to your bird-watching. The process of recording your observations may improve your field skills – you will want to be confident of your identifications and may try harder to see or hear more species. Your records can help bird conservation – even observations of common species can add to the databank that helps ornithologists monitor bird populations. At a personal level, looking back over your notes can help you relive a great day's bird-watching.

The Practicalities

Do not rely on your memory – make notes while you are bird-watching. There are no rules about how you do this. You could try a simple notebook, a PDA, a portable Dictaphone or even make

notes on your mobile phone, or you might prefer a printed checklist. Experiment and find a method that works for you. When you get home you might want to transfer your records to something more permanent.

What to Record

Make a note of what you saw

or heard, where and when. You could add some brief notes on weather conditions too. Information on the numbers of birds present (even estimates) can be useful. One challenge you will face is trying to work out the number of birds in a big flock. The standard technique is to count a small portion of the flock and estimate the proportion that represents. Then it is simple multiplication. If you count 25 birds in what you think is about 1/20th of the flock, your estimate is 25 x 20 = 500 birds.

Any evidence of breeding or possible breeding is definitely worth noting. You may see the act itself, but subtler evidence includes birds singing or displaying to attract a mate or declare territorial ownership, birds nest-building or collecting

materials for nest-building and sightings of juvenile birds (though some species migrate in juvenile plumage). Make a note of any unusual things you see birds doing too.

BELOW

Count a small proportion of a flock and get a rough estimate of the total number by multiplication.

Rare Birds

Rare birds include rare breeding species that breed in small numbers, though may be more numerous at other times of the year, and birds that find themselves somewhere that they really are not meant to be (vagrants). The Fieldfare is an example of the former – a few pairs may breed, but in the winter, Fieldfares are not difficult to see. The Killdeer is an example of the latter. This plover is a bird of the Americas that, from time to time, turns up on the wrong side of the Atlantic.

Encountering Rare Birds

If you encounter a rare breeding bird, make sure that you do not disturb it and let the local bird recorder and the RSPB know as soon as possible. If you are fortunate enough to discover a vagrant, other bird-watchers will want to see it too, but this may not be in the best interests of the bird or of local people or landowners. News of rare birds can be disseminated very quickly with modern technology – but check with the landowner and local bird recorder if you have any doubts about the appropriateness of an invasion of bird-watchers.

To put things in perspective, if you are trying to identify a bird and have narrowed the options down to a common species or a rare one, it's very probably the common one. But not always!

ABOVE LEFT
The Killdeer is a vagrant.

ABOVE
The Flightless Cormorant, of the Galapagos Islands, is one of the world's rarest birds.

BELOW
The Fieldfare is a rare breeder.

WATCHING BIRDS

One of the joys of watching birds is that you can do it pretty much anywhere and everywhere. This section starts very close to home, with tips for attracting birds to your garden. It moves on to discovering and exploring your own 'local patch', a special place for any bird-watcher and, after some guidance on fieldcraft, gets more adventurous, introducing you to a range of different habitats and to the fun and frustration of overseas bird-watching.

LEFT

Bird feeders come in many shapes and sizes and can attract a variety of birds to your garden.

Attracting Birds to Your Garden

A garden can be your own private nature reserve. To attract birds to your garden think about the following things:

Providing Food

Feeding garden birds can be very simple – just put out some household scraps and wait. Birds will eat many different foods. You could try bread, biscuit or cake crumbs, windfall apples, boiled or jacket potatoes, cheese or raw pastry, for example. If you provide some feeders and perhaps a bird table, the number and diversity of birds that you attract should increase. A wide range of feeders and bird foods are available (seed mixes and sunflower seeds are probably the most popular), but some are better than others – if possible, buy products endorsed by a conservation organization. Squirrels can wreck bird feeders, so buy squirrel-proof feeders if this could be a problem. One specialist food worth experimenting with is nyjer seed. This very small seed is put out in special feeders with small feeding holes. It attracts Goldfinches, though other birds sometimes feed at nyjer feeders.

Position your feeders or bird table where you can see them, but out of the reach of

marauding cats. To reduce the risk of disease (in visiting birds) clean your feeders and bird table periodically with diluted disinfectant and move them around the garden. Clean up food waste and uneaten food to reduce the risk of attracting rats.

Birds can be fed throughout the year, but do not put out any foods during the breeding season that are large enough to choke a nestling (such as whole peanuts or chunks of bread). Foods that contain salt should always be avoided, as should mesh bags that might trap birds.

ABOVE

A wildlife pond provides another reason for birds to visit your garden!

BELOW

It can be fascinating to watch the comings and goings of your bird residents.

Think about how you manage your garden too. Limit or eliminate the use of artificial pesticides and include insect-friendly plants and plants whose seeds or fruit provide 'natural' food. If you do not have a garden you can buy feeders that stick on to the outside of a window and these can provide some very close encounters.

Providing Water

A shallow dish is all that is needed to provide birds with something to drink and bathe in, though a wildlife pond is much better. A floating ball will help to stop ice forming – do not add antifreeze or salt.

Providing Nest Sites

Nest boxes can be built or bought, and may provide nest sites for a range of different species. There are different sizes and designs, including small open-fronted boxes for species such as Robins, boxes with a hole entrance for Blue and Great Tits and large

'chimney' boxes for birds such as Tawny Owls. Nest boxes should be sited out of the reach of predators and in a position that provides some protection from the weather, including summer heat. Get them up before mid-February if you want them to be used that year. They can be cleaned out after the breeding season but make sure the box is not in use and do not do this before August.

Think about how you garden, too. With the right plants and some good cover, birds will nest in your garden without using nest boxes.

LEFT

Even urban areas, such as parks, can possess bird-spotting potential.

BELOW

Churchyards can be popular haunts for owls and other birds.

A Local Patch

Discovering and exploring your own local patch is a very rewarding but often neglected form of bird-watching. It is easy to spend all or most of your bird-watching hours at well-known sites, and chasing rarities is easier than ever in this information-rich age. But there is a very different satisfaction that comes from working your own patch – somewhere local, and possibly somewhere that attracts no other bird-watchers.

A local patch is somewhere that you can get to easily and frequently, ideally on foot or by bike. Because you can go there often you can get to know it and its bird sights and sounds really well. It is a great place to cut your birding teeth, and with time you may well become the expert on the area's birds.

Finding a Local Patch

You may already know your local area well but even if you do it is worth looking at a good-quality map to help you find a local patch. Ordnance Survey 1:25,000 scale maps are very good and you can look at OS maps online free of charge. For a variety of birds, try to choose somewhere with a variety of habitats. A patch that includes an area of water could be very good. Check the rights of way and make sure that you can access the site safely and legally. You may even be able to persuade a local landowner to allow you access to private property if you explain what you want to do. Do not choose an area that is too large – you need to be able to cover it in a couple of hours or less or you are unlikely to visit it enough. Even urban areas

can provide good local patches – a park, reservoir or churchyard perhaps.

For a more demanding local patch, you could decide to explore your parish or other similar area. This is likely to mean that you will be covering a number of local sites – it is much more ambitious and means that you will get to each site less often, but it will encourage you to explore parts of your local area that you might otherwise never visit. You may be surprised at what you find tucked away on your own doorstep.

Working Your Local Patch

Visit it frequently and keep notes on what you see and hear. With time, you will discover that some birds are often seen in the same part of your patch. Spring and summer visits will give you some idea of which species are breeding where, and perhaps how many pairs there are. You will see changes in the bird population, as summer and winter visitors come and go, and may see migrants passing through in spring and autumn. Birds that are common elsewhere but rare on your patch will give you a special thrill if they show up, and you might even find a species that is notable on a wider scale, a bird that may never have been found if you had not found it.

Make sure that your records are sent to the local bird recorder and/or the BTO

(British Trust for Ornithology). Local patch records really do count – other people may be submitting records from the well-known sites, but you could be the only one watching your patch. Your data may even help to protect the site from damaging development. Without data it is very difficult to put the conservation case forward, and you won't know the significance of your local patch unless you get out there.

RIGHT
Keep a count of the birds you see when you are out and about.

Fieldcraft

Fieldcraft is what you do and what you know that helps you see more birds and see birds better. There are a number of guidelines to follow.

1. Dress to be warm enough, or cool enough, and comfortable. Camouflage gear is not *de rigueur*, though bright colours are not a good idea. Avoid clothes that rustle – they make it harder to hear birds.

2. Move gently, look and listen and stop frequently. Some birds are easy to see, others give their presence away by a movement or sound. Get into your bird-watching mindset – concentrate on finding and watching birds – leave life's problems behind.

3. Take your time. Look and look again – you will not see every bird on just one scan of a lake, for example. Birds may move out from behind islands or vegetation, surface from a dive or fly into view.

4. Keep an eye on the sky – birds can fly!

5. Use binoculars to look for birds, not just at birds. Look in likely places – where there is food, water, shelter or somewhere to nest. Check 'edges' – watch the trees along a woodland edge or ride, look carefully along the edge of a reedbed or scan around the edges of a lake or reservoir, for example.

6. As an alternative to 'strolling and stopping', find a comfortable viewing place and sit and watch. This can be a good strategy in woodland and is how most sea bird-watching is done (unless you go out in a boat – special 'pelagics' are organized to take bird-watchers out to sea to get closer to sea birds).

7. Try to plan your bird-watching so that you are not looking into the sun, especially when the sun is low in the sky. This makes for much easier viewing.

8. Do not walk on the skyline – it makes your presence very obvious and could scare off birds. To get closer to birds, use whatever cover is available – if they show signs of unrest, wait a while and

sometimes very close by. When you are in a hide keep your voice down and resist the temptation to put your arm out of the viewing slot to point at something. Scan to the left and right, near and far. Eavesdrop on others' conversations to find out what they are seeing and ask for a bit of help if you need it. But don't just take their word for it – try to identify the birds for yourself.

back off if necessary. Few bird-watchers do it, but getting down on your belly and gradually moving closer can give you some great views. Alternatively, sometimes just sitting and waiting will reap rewards when the birds make their way towards you.

9. The man-made cover provided by hides and viewing screens can provide some comfortable and wonderful views of birds,

10. Get up very early! Daybreak and the next couple of hours may provide the best birding of the day. The tail end of the day can be good too.

11. Know what birds you are likely to see at what time of the year and where. If you are looking for particular species, plan your visit accordingly.

12. Always follow the Birdwatchers' Code (as outlined by the RSPB):

• Avoid disturbing birds and their habitats – the birds' interests should always come first
• Be an ambassador for bird-watching
• Know the law and the rules for visiting the countryside, and follow them
• Send your sightings to the County Bird Recorder and the Birdtrack website
• Think about the interests of wildlife and local people before passing on news of a

rare bird, especially during the breeding season.

13. Finally, and very importantly, enjoy your bird-watching. That is why you are doing it.

ABOVE

Hides are for everyone to use, not just the 'experts'.

BELOW

Find somewhere to sit and watch – grassy banks can be good vantage points – patience will be its own reward.

Sparrowhawks are a good find in woodland areas.

You will find a greater variety of birds in deciduous woods than in coniferous woods, though conifers can be good for Coal Tits, Goldcrests, Siskins and Crossbills. Strolling and stopping works in woods, but find somewhere with some bird activity and try just waiting too. Early morning visits are good – a spring dawn chorus visit is recommended. Use your ears to help you find birds and check sunny patches carefully – where there are insects, there may be birds.

Exploring Different Habitats

To broaden your repertoire and experience a wider range of bird species you need to spend time bird-watching in different habitats. Below are some of the main habitats and the types of birds to look for.

Farmland

Look for: Buzzard, Kestrel, partridges, Pheasant, Golden Plover, Lapwing, Redshank, Snipe, gulls, Wood Pigeon, Stock Dove, Turtle Dove, Barn and Little Owls, Swallow, Yellow Wagtail, thrushes, warblers including Whitethroat and Lesser Whitethroat, tits, Starling, Magpie, Jackdaw, Rook, Carrion Crow, finches, buntings.

Scan fields carefully and pay special attention to the hedgerows, especially older and more diverse ones. Damp grassland may hold breeding waders. If there are grazing cattle look for Yellow Wagtails. Rough grassland, including field edges, can be good for Barn Owls.

Woodland

Look for: Sparrowhawk, Buzzard, Stock Dove, Wood Pigeon, Tawny Owl, woodpeckers, Wren, Dunnock, Robin, Redstart, thrushes, Garden Warbler, Blackcap, Wood Warbler, Chiffchaff, Willow Warbler, Goldcrest, Flycatchers, tits, Nuthatch, Treecreeper, Jay, finches.

Lakes and Reedbeds

Look for: grebes, Cormorant, Bittern, Grey Heron, Mute Swan, Greylag and Canada Goose, ducks, Marsh Harrier, Hobby, Water Rail, Moorhen, Coot, migrating waders, gulls, Common Tern, Swift, Kingfisher, Swallow, House Martin, Sand Martin,

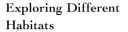

Grey Wagtail, Sedge and Reed Warblers, Bearded Tit, Reed Bunting.

Look once, look twice then look again – there are probably more birds there than you realize. Do not assume that all the birds in a flock are the same species – have a good look. Watch the airspace; Swallows, martins and dragonflies are food for hunting Hobbys. Check reedbed edges and scan the reed-tops too. Use your ears to help you find warblers.

Estuaries
Look for: grebes, Cormorant, Little Egret, Grey Heron, swans, geese, Shelduck, Wigeon, Red-breasted Merganser and other ducks, Peregrine, Oystercatcher, Ringed and Grey Plovers, Lapwing, Knot, Turnstone, Dunlin, Redshank, Curlew and other waders, gulls, terns, Rock Pipit, Linnet, Twite.

For winter waders visit around high tide when birds will be concentrated in smaller areas. Research your waders before you visit. Get to know the common species – Dunlin is a 'reference point' in small-wader identification. A telescope is useful but you can enjoy estuaries without one. If a flock takes to the air there could be a Peregrine about.

Uplands
Look for: Hen Harrier, Buzzard, Golden Eagle, Merlin, Peregrine, grouse, Dotterel and other breeding waders, Short-eared Owl, Meadow Pipit, Skylark, Whinchat, Stonechat, Wheatear, Ring Ouzel, Raven, Twite.

ABOVE
Knots are common visitors to estuaries.

BELOW RIGHT
A visit to a rocky coastline can be rewarded by sightings of colonies of birds such as the ledge-nesting Fulmar.

Upland birds can be few and far between but some are very special. Some have very limited distributions – what you see depends on where and when you go. Dress appropriately and allow plenty of time.

Heathland
Look for: Hobby, Nightjar, Wood Lark, Stonechat, Dartford Warbler, Yellow-hammer. Visit around dusk during May or June to hear, and hopefully see, Nightjar.

Rocky Cliffs
Look for: Fulmar, Gannet, Cormorant, Shag, Herring Gull, Kittiwake, Guillemot, Razorbill, Black Guillemot (Scotland and Ireland), Puffin.

Bird-watching at a sea bird colony is very memorable – full of sights, sounds and smells! June is a great time to visit. Scan the cliffs to work out where the birds are then check the ledges carefully – there may be more birds than you realized.

ABOVE AND LEFT

When travelling abroad, be aware of differences in similar species, such as Pied and White Wagtails.

BELOW

Take the opportunity to do some bird-watching while on holiday.

In Foreign Places

Bird-watching abroad can be exciting and frustrating. Exciting because of the wonderful birds you will see, and frustrating because you might not be able to work out what all of them are and you will not see everything that you want to.

A trip within Europe can be a good first step. You will be seeing some birds that you are already familiar with and others that may be new to you. However, even the familiar species may not be quite the same – the 'Pied' Wagtails might look a bit odd, for example. This is because Pied Wagtails are the British subspecies of White Wagtail, and it is White Wagtails that you will be seeing on the continent. Visit South America or some other far-flung destination and the learning curve could be much steeper, with new *families* of birds to get to grips with.

Wherever you go, do your homework in advance. Get hold of a good field guide and familiarize yourself as much as possible with the species that you are likely to see.

Opportunistic Overseas Bird-Watching

A business trip or family holiday abroad may offer limited opportunities for bird-watching, especially if you're the only one interested. Finding time for birds can be a challenge, though early mornings or evenings (depending on the light) could be a solution and don't forget that there may well be birds at 'non bird-watching' tourist destinations. Birds are everywhere so look for local opportunities to see them – the hotel grounds or a park could be good. Try to leave the crowds behind; a short walk out of a resort could get you into much more interesting countryside, and sea-watching may reap dividends.

Do some advance planning and find out if there are any bird-watching hotspots within reach of your destination. Then, if you are able to devote a day or half a day to bird-watching you will be able to use it well. Think about your personal safety when bird-watching abroad. Binoculars and other bird-watching

paraphernalia may attract unwanted attention and can be viewed suspiciously in some countries. Take particular care near military establishments.

Dedicated Bird-Watching Holidays

You can organize your own bird-watching holiday or buy a bird-watching package from a specialist provider.

Organizing your own takes much more planning and without expert guidance and local knowledge you may see many fewer birds. Finding birds may be harder too, but on the up side, the thrill of finding your own

may be manageable, but others may get away, though you can still enjoy them. Organizing your holiday will take time but there are books and online resources that will help.

Many companies offer specialist bird-watching holidays – you will see their adverts in bird-watching magazines. Think carefully about the type of holiday that you want. How big a group do you want to be in and what ratio of leaders to participants do you want? How much of your time do you want to spend bird-watching? What level of expertise are you looking for

and identifying them for yourself may more than compensate. If you do go it alone, accept that you will not be able to identify every bird you see or you could have a very frustrating holiday. Birds that are in good plumage and seen well

in the leaders and in the other holidaymakers? Do you want to look at wildlife other than birds or are you totally bird-focused? Get personal recommendations if you can and speak to the company before you book to get some idea of their style and ethos.

The Species

CLASSIFICATION

Birds belong to the class Aves. Aves are, in turn, part of the Phylum Chordata and the Subphylum Vertebrata. The class of Aves is then divided into 23 orders, 142 families, somewhere over 2,000 genera and finally over 9,700 species. Over half of the world's species of birds fall into one order, the Passeriformes, also known as the passerines. The rest of the population belongs to the remaining 22 orders. Generally speaking, birds of the same order share similar characteristics.

Names

Bird names are more complicated than they first appear. Take, for example, the bird *Carduelis tristis*. In America this bird can be known as American Goldfinch, Flying Canary, Outdoor Canary, Wild Canary, Yellow Bird or simply Goldfinch. Yet all these names refer to the same species. In Britain and Europe the Goldfinch known to bird-watchers is a completely different bird altogether.

Scientific Names

To avoid confusion, every species of bird is given a scientific name. Many of these names are Latin, as used by the Romans, but many are derived from Greek. There are also scientific names that include Norwegian, Russian, Old English and some of the various native South American languages. The scientific names are often used as generic titles, such as *Columba*, meaning pigeon and *Passer* which means sparrow. Scientific names (a better term than Latin names, given the varied origins of many) ensure that the correct species is being described, wherever in the world it may be. It is rare for bird-watchers to refer to scientific names in everyday terms, however, and the common names are usually a point of reference.

TOP

The Long-eared Owl may get its common name from its characteristic feature.

Common Names

Common names are normal, non-scientific names. Very often this name can give an indication about the bird. There are numerous different sources for common names but essentially they can be categorized into a number of groups. The first is where they are named for their appearance. Examples of this are Blue Jay, Purple Sandpiper or perhaps Long-eared Owl. However, these can sometimes be misleading. The Red-bellied Woodpecker does not have a red belly, nor are all members of the blackbird family actually black.

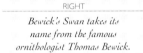

Behaviour and call may also lead to a common name – Kittiwake, Curlew and Whimbrel are all named after their vocal sounds. However, although some of these are quite straightforward, certain others might require a degree of imagination to make the connection. Turnstone is an apt name as this bird literally turns stones on beaches as it feeds. The word Nuthatch comes from the bird's habit of wedging a nut into a crevice and hammering the kernel until it hatches.

Geographical names also abound but bear in mind that a bird's range can increase or decrease greatly over a short period of time, so they may not be entirely accurate. Common examples of geographical naming are American Bittern and Arctic Tern. However, beware of birds such as the Eurasian Starling, which is as abundant in North America as it is in Europe.

Often birds will be named after the people who discovered them. Pallas, Wilson, Audobon and Bewick are all familiar prefaces to birds' names and all are well-known scientists and ornithologists.

The final example comes from common names that illustrate a bird's relationship. Cattle Egrets are often found feeding around livestock. Cliff Swallow and House Sparrow both have indications in their names that give a clue as to their preferred habitats. Other good examples of this include Water Pipit and Tree Swallow.

Differences in Names

One big problem can be the difference in names between two countries. North America and the United Kingdom illustrate this point. In the UK, 'buzzards' refers to large hawks, while in North America the term 'buzzard' is usually used to describe members of the vulture family. On the face of it we share several common species – Robin and Goldfinch together with Blackbirds, for example, but in every case they are very different species. Other peculiarities between the two regions are many. The sea duck referred to in America as the Oldsquaw is the Long-tailed Duck in Europe and the Goosander in Europe is the Common Merganser on the other side of the Atlantic.

Regional Names

As well as the common and scientific names of birds there are also colloquial, regional or country names. The Nightjar or Nighthawk was given the name of Goatsucker, referring to the species' habit of flying close to the ground around livestock. They do this to feed on the insects that are attracted to the cattle, but it was believed that they were draining milk from goats' udders. In Europe, the Mistle Thrush is still referred to in certain areas as the Storm Cock. This is because of its habit of singing from the tallest possible exposed perch in the foulest weather.

Whatever the bird, there is usually an explanation as to how its name came about. Plover derives from the Middle English and

Old French *plouvier*, from the Latin *pluvial* ('rain'), so it is the rain bird – also a regional name for the Green Woodpecker in parts of Europe. Bittern seems to come from the Old French *butor*, itself derived from Latin *butio* and *taurus*, 'bittern' and 'bull'. Oriole is fairly clearly linked to Latin *aureus*, 'golden'.

Middle English is the source of other names as well. The Dotterel's name, for example, is related to 'dote' and 'dotage'; the bird's trusting nature apparently made it easy to catch, so they thought it slow-witted.

Classical Names
Many birds owe their common names to the classical languages. Phalarope means 'coot-foot': in classical Greek *phalaris* means coot and

The word 'osprey' is said to derive originally from the Latin ossifragus, *literally 'bone-breaker'.*

pous/podos means foot – as in 'chiropodist'. The very natural-seeming name of the Ring-necked Pheasant was originally introduced from the Far East. Its name goes back to the Greek *phasianos*, 'bird of the river Phasis', in present-day Armenia.

Many more bird names recall Anglo-Saxon, Germanic and Scandinavian languages. Auk is from Old Norse *alka*, Skua comes via Faroese from Old Norse *skufr*. Snipe and tit are also probably of Scandinavian origin. The Germanic bird names include Redstarts – *staart* is Dutch for 'tail'.

Orders

Understanding the orders of birds can assist greatly in bird-watching, as it can help you understand which birds are related to which, and share common features. However, it is important to remember that birds which may seem similar (or that share similar common names) are not necessarily of the same order.

Podicipediformes

The first order of birds in Britain and Europe are Podicipediformes, which are the grebes. Grebes are a widely distributed order of freshwater diving birds, some of which visit the sea when migrating and in winter. This order contains only a single family, the Podicipedidae.

Procellariiformes and Pelecaniformes

Procellariiformes, sometimes referred to as tubenoses, include those giants of the sea Albatrosses, together with Shearwaters and Petrels. Sea birds also make up the order Pelecaniformes. As the name implies, this order contains the pelican family, as well as tropicbirds, gannets, cormorants, shags and boobies.

Anseriformes

Geese, ducks and swans belong to the order Anseriformes. There are only two families in the order, but it consists of over 150 species. Species in the order are highly adapted for an aquatic existence at or on the water's surface. All are web-footed for efficient swimming, even though several species have subsequently become largely terrestrial.

Ciconiiformes

Ciconiiformes are members of another wide-ranging order, which includes herons, bitterns, egrets, ibises and storks. Traditionally, the order Ciconiiformes has included a variety of large, long-legged wading birds with large bills.

Falconiformes

Birds of prey, or raptors, belong to the order Falconiformes. This order is a group of about 290 species that includes the diurnal birds of prey. Raptor classification is complicated and there is some confusion regarding this order. Historically all raptors are grouped into four families within this order. In Europe, though, it has become common to split the order into two:

Falconiformes, which contains about 60 species of falcons and caracaras; and Accipitridae, which contains the balance of the order including hawks and eagles. Whichever lineage you follow, this order is the most diverse on the planet by way of size. The smallest falcons can measure little more than 15 cm (5⅞ in) and the largest members of the order – eagles and vultures – have wingspans in the region of 3 m (9⅞ ft).

Galliformes

Game birds belong to the order Galliformes. Included in this order are turkeys, grouse, quails and pheasants. There are somewhere in the region of 250 individual species within this order. One common characteristic is the presence of a sharp spur-like projection on the backs of males' legs, which is used in fighting rival males.

Gruiformes

Gruiformes are an interesting and diverse order. *Gruiform* means 'crane-like'. The order contains a large number of species, both living and extinct, that appear to have little in common with each other. Historically waders and some land birds did not seem to belong in any of the other orders and as such were placed together in Gruiformes. Included here are cranes, crakes and rails, together with a number of very small families with very few species.

Charadriiformes

The Charadriiformes include small to medium-large birds. There are approximately 350 species and the order has families in all parts of the world. Most Charadriiformes live near water and eat invertebrates or other small animals. However, some are pelagic (sea-going) while others occupy deserts or thick forest. Traditionally this order was split into three suborders: waders, or

Charadrii, typical shorebirds that generally feed by either probing in the mud or collecting food items off the surface in both freshwater and coastal environs; gulls, or Lari, and their close relatives generally take fish or other foods from the sea; and auks or Alcae, strictly coastal species that nest on sea cliffs.

Gaviiformes

Loons, or divers, belong to the order Gaviiformes. There is only one family, Gaviidae within this order, which contains all living species of loon or diver. The European name 'diver' comes from the habit of plunging into the water to catch fish and the North American name 'loon' comes from the bird's haunting cry.

Columbiformes

Columbiformes include pigeons and doves. This order is widespread and successful. As well as pigeons and doves this order also had the extinct Dodo in it. Like many other species, all Columbiformes are monogamous, meaning that they have only one single mate at any one time. Unlike most other birds, however, members of this order are capable of drinking by sucking up water, without needing to tilt the head back.

Cuculiformes

The order Cuculiformes traditionally included three families, of which only one is present in our region. Essentially this order comprises the near-passerine species known as cuckoos.

Also within this order are Anis, although they are sometimes considered as subfamilies.

Strigiformes

Owls are in a separate order to the day-flying raptors, that of Strigiformes. There

BELOW

Cuckoos belong to the order Cuculiformes.

are in the region of 200 species within this order and they are split loosely into Tytonidae, which are Barn Owls and their close relatives, and Strigidae – all other species.

Caprimulgiformes

Caprimulgiformes includes Nightjars and Nighthawks and Poor-Wills. Traditionally, they were regarded as being midway between owls and the swifts. Like owls, they are nocturnal hunters with a highly developed

sense of sight, and like the swifts they are excellent flyers with small, weak legs.

Apodiformes

The order Apodiformes contains three living families of which there are two in our region, the swifts and the hummingbirds. In some circles the hummingbird has been removed from this order and given a new grouping of its own. Apodiformes translates as 'footless'. They have small legs with limited functions other than that of perching.

Coraciiformes

Coraciiformes are classed as near passerines and are generally a colourful group of birds. They include kingfishers, bee-eaters and rollers. As an order they generally have three forward-pointing toes (although this is missing in many kingfishers).

Piciformes

Piciformes are the penultimate group. There are six families within the group, but the best-known is the Picidae, or woodpeckers. Of the 400 or so species within the order, around half of these are woodpeckers. In general this order is insectivorous.

Passeriformes

Passeriformes make up a gigantic order – more than half of the world's species belong here. Passeriformes are sometimes referred to as perching birds. Both the names 'passerine' and 'passeriformes' are derived from the scientific name of the House Sparrow, *Passer domesticus*. *Passer* is Latin for 'true sparrows' and other similar small birds. Over 5,000 species of bird are included in this order, which covers warblers, chats, flycatchers, orioles, finches and buntings.

RIGHT

Passeriformes is the largest order, and includes birds such as the Sparrow.

Urban & Suburban Areas

Even the most densely populated urban areas can provide excellent opportunities for bird-watching. City centres may appear devoid of wildlife but they very seldom are. Pigeons, House Sparrows, starlings, swifts and martins are a familiar sight and are all birds that have adapted to live side by side with humans. Certain birds of prey are also utilizing our cities. The Peregrine Falcon is one such species. It is now a regular breeding bird in even the largest cities, using cathedrals and tower blocks to nest in place of its typical cliff- and quarry-face nest sites.

Green spaces within cities – parks, gardens and sports fields – open up other opportunities. Here can be found species such as tits, finches and thrushes. Gardens with well-stocked bird tables will usually have a plentiful array of birds. Winter can bring birds that would normally avoid urban areas into towns and cities in search of food. Ponds or boating lakes in parks should be checked during periods of harsh weather – as temperatures in urban areas are higher than in more rural areas, unusual species of duck and grebe may venture to these places if their normal haunts are frozen over.

Grass verges on main roads or railway embankments can also offer a green oasis in industrial environments. Such areas are often rich in flowers and consequently have a good selection of insects. This makes for some rich pickings for insectivorous birds such as warblers and chats.

Wasteland, although not particularly attractive, can also provide bountiful food sources for birds such as finches and buntings, particularly during winter when they can be found feeding on thistle heads and teasels.

FERAL PIGEON

SCIENTIFIC NAME: Columba livia

IDENTIFYING FEATURES: Very variable plumage

SIMILAR SPECIES: Rock Dove

SIZE: 31–34 cm (12¼–13⅛ in)

HABITAT: Towns and cities

POPULATION: Abundant

The Feral Pigeon is a truly urban bird. It is descended from the Rock Dove, a rare species restricted to coastal cliffs. It is a familiar resident of towns and cities, providing bird life in even the most built-up areas.

The Feral Pigeon has an incredibly varied plumage. Cross-breeding with domestic stock has led to an array of appearances. Essentially, however, the true Feral Pigeon has a blue-grey body with a greyer back. It normally has two black wing bars and a paler rump.

It can be found literally anywhere where humans live – it is probably the most urban of all our resident bird species. The Feral Pigeon has adapted to breed in the most unlikely surroundings and can often rear young throughout the year. It will feed on a variety of seeds, but will also scavenge food waste. The nest site is not grand and is usually sited on a ledge. A normal clutch consists of two white eggs.

LEFT

The Feral Pigeon is a common sight, and sadly not always a welcome one – especially when in their most abundant numbers.

WOOD PIGEON

SCIENTIFIC NAME: Columba palumbus

IDENTIFYING FEATURES: White wing bar and neck patch

SIMILAR SPECIES: Stock Dove

SIZE: 40–42 cm (15¼–16½ in)

HABITAT: Gardens, parkland

POPULATION: Common

The Wood Pigeon – a large, heavy pigeon and a gregarious feeder – is generally a bird of open country, where it is shot for food, but it has adapted well to life in the city. It is now a regular sight in town parks and gardens.

The Wood Pigeon is grey-brown above with a pale pink breast. It has distinctive white crescents or wing bars and a

white and iridescent green patch on the neck. Sexes are alike but juveniles lack the neck patch, although the wing bar is present. Its call is a five-syllable 'coo'.

Originally a farmland bird, the Wood Pigeon has now colonized most towns and cities where it can be found with relative ease. It breeds very early in the year – often as early as February – but this is dependent upon the availability of food. Grain and seeds are its natural diet but the Wood Pigeon has adapted to eat all manner of food. Its nest is a thin, fragile-looking platform of twigs, where it lays one or two white eggs.

COLLARED DOVE

SIZE: 31–33 cm (12¼–13 in)

HABITAT: Gardens and parkland

POPULATION: Common

SCIENTIFIC NAME: Streptopelia decacto

IDENTIFYING FEATURES:
Pinkish-buff plumage with thin, dark neck bar

SIMILAR SPECIES: Turtle Dove

Habits

Collared Doves can be found in parks and gardens, although they are equally at home in more open country. They are quite adaptable and will frequent bird tables; many are very approachable.

The species has a prolonged and prolific breeding season. It can often raise multiple broods in a single year, and may keep the same partner for many seasons. It feeds on a range of grain, seeds and fruit. It will also take bread and scraps when natural food sources are scarce.

The Collared Dove's nest is a shallow and untidy platform made of twigs, usually situated near the trunk of a tree. The bird typically lays two white eggs.

Fascinating Facts

Since the 1950s, the Collared Dove has expanded its range from India at a phenomenal rate, to colonize the whole of Europe as far north as Scandinavia.

BELOW LEFT

Collared Doves have an impressive courtship flight where they splay their feathers on the glide down.

The history of the Collared Dove is a rather short one. This bird originated from India, and spread across Europe. It arrived in Britain in the 1950s when a single pair bred. This rise continued for the next 20 years but has now eased off. Its rise has been nothing short of meteoric and can now be encountered in numerous habitats. The success of the Collared Dove can perhaps be attributed to its breeding season. Often three but sometimes as many as five or six broods can be raised each year by a single pair. It has a distinctive three-syllable call.

The Collared Dove is a pale, fawn-coloured bird with a pinkish breast tinge. The thin black collar on the neck is also a key feature. Its long tail has a prominent black bar with a white tip. The juvenile birds have a duller, paler plumage with no black collar. The Collared Dove has a distinctive display flight, which consists of a steep rise into the air before gliding down.

SWIFT

SCIENTIFIC NAME: Apus apus

IDENTIFYING FEATURES:
All dark with scythe-shaped wings

SIMILAR SPECIES: Swallow, House Martin

SIZE: 16–17 cm (6¼–6¾ in)

HABITAT: Towns and Cities

POPULATION: Common summer visitor

Often called 'The Devil Bird' because of its screaming call, the Swift is a common summer visitor. What is remarkable about this bird is its ability to spend large amounts of time in the air. Only when it is nesting does it come to land and roost normally. It is thought that a young Swift can spend the first two years of its life on the wing without ever landing.

Swifts have a dark, sooty plumage and although they appear black they are actually dark brown, often with a distinctive whitish throat and chin. Their profile in flight is also distinctive, with scythe-shaped and exceptionally long wings that arch backwards. They also have a shallow notched or forked tail, which gives greater control in flight. The loud screaming call is a common sound in towns during the summer months.

Breeding and Feeding Habits

Swifts are found in all urban habitats, choosing to nest in roof spaces and eaves. Churches, cathedrals and towers are also favoured locations. They demonstrate an interesting breeding pattern for an insectivorous bird, in that the young hatch at carefully staggered intervals. This is to ensure that in poor summers at least the first-hatched chick will survive, even if the subsequent nestlings do not.

Swifts eat an array of flying insects, including gnats and midges. They are thought to catch in excess of 10,000 insects each day, from around 300 different species.

The Swift's nest is a shallow cup of its own feathers and detritus, bound together by its saliva. Two or three eggs are typical per brood and these are creamy white.

Fascinating Facts

Not only does the Swift feed and sleep on the wing, it also often mates in mid-air. It only ever lands to roost or lay eggs.

BELOW
Swifts are often summer visitors to our towns and cities.

HOUSE MARTIN

SIZE: 12 cm (4¾ in)

HABITAT: Towns and cities

POPULATION: Common

SCIENTIFIC NAME: Delichon urbica

IDENTIFYING FEATURES: Distinctive white rump

SIMILAR SPECIES: Swallow, Sand Martin

Another summer visitor to towns and villages across Britain and Europe, the House Martin is smaller and daintier than the Swift, but just as agile in the air. It builds distinctive mud cup nests under the eaves of houses. During prolonged summer droughts its numbers may be fewer, as it is heavily reliant upon mud for the construction of its nest. Once the summer is over the House Martin returns to Africa, but exactly where it spends the winter months remains something of a mystery.

Adult House Martins have iridescent blue upperparts with darker wings. The underparts are white and they also have a distinctive white rump. The tail is quite short but with a small but noticeable fork at the tip.

Homes and Food

Originally, before the onset of human dwellings, the House Martin nested on cliffs. These days the majority of these birds reside in towns, cities and villages. They are summer visitors and should be looked for from May onwards. Towards the end of summer large numbers will gather on wires as they prepare for the migration back to Africa.

They are not social nesters particularly, but often when there is more than one brood the earlier young will take on some of the parental care, feeding chicks from subsequent broods. House Martins feed on winged insects, taken in flight.

The nest of the House Martin is largely constructed of mud and small amounts of plant material. This is generally positioned under the eaves of a roof with an opening at the top. The eggs are white and a typical clutch size is between four and five.

BELOW LEFT

House Martins will return to the same nest site year on year.

WAXWING

SCIENTIFIC NAME: Bombycilla garrulous

IDENTIFYING FEATURES:
Starling-sized with a prominent crest and black bib

SIMILAR SPECIES: Starling

SIZE: 18 cm (7 in)

HABITAT: Gardens and parkland

POPULATION: Winter visitor

This rather exotic-looking, Starling-sized bird is a prize winter target for a lot of bird-watchers. The success or failure of its food crop determines the numbers that visit in winter. It is seldom seen in some years while in others many thousands may arrive. These sporadic invasions are referred to as 'eruptions'. The Waxwing gets its name from the pink waxy tipped secondary flight feathers on each wing.

The Waxwing is, quite simply, a beautiful bird. The head, distinctive crest and underparts are a pink colour. They have a sweeping black eye stripe and a black bib on the throat. The wings are darker with white and yellow lines with the telltale pink tips to the secondary flight feathers. These wing markings, including the waxy pink tips, are thought to be related to the age and sex of the bird. However, it is very difficult to ascertain either of these features – perhaps only by looking for the duller markings of juvenile birds. The tail is rather short but with a bright yellow tip.

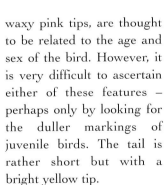

Where to Look

In a good winter Waxwings can be found in parks and gardens. Some years will bring large numbers of these visitors, while others may bring none at all. Although it does not breed in our region, it nests very late in the year – often late June – and both parents share the duties of bringing up the young.

They are incredibly gregarious feeders. Their winter diet consists almost entirely of berries such as rowan, hawthorn and ornamental shrubs such as cotoneaster. In the summer months it develops a taste for insects, particularly mosquitoes.

They have cup-shaped nests containing usually four or five eggs, which are incubated for two weeks. The young fledge after a further two weeks.

WREN

SIZE: 9–10 cm (3½–3⅞ in)

HABITAT: Gardens, parkland and woodland

POPULATION: Common

SCIENTIFIC NAME: Troglodytes troglodytes

IDENTIFYING FEATURES:
Tiny with tail often cocked

SIMILAR SPECIES: Dunnock, Goldcrest

The Wren is an active, tiny bird common throughout our region. In harsh winters this species is very susceptible to the cold and to help combat this they have communal roosts. These can sometimes number more than 50 birds in a single nest box or similar. The male Wren often creates more than one nest during the spring and whichever one the female chooses, and lines with feathers, is where the young will be raised that year.

This minute bird is a reddish-brown colour above with slightly paler barred underparts. It also has a noticeable cream-coloured eye stripe. Its short tail is often cocked and is a good feature to look for. The combination of the short tail and small head give the Wren a very rounded appearance. Its flight is generally fast, direct and very low to the ground. Its song is surprisingly loud for such a small bird and consists of a metallic rattle.

Habits and Habitat

The Wren can be found in a variety of habitats although parks, mature gardens and woodland are particular favourites. The male is often polygamous, having two or more mates. It can construct up to a dozen nests for the female, or females, to choose. If the male is monogamous then it will help to rear the young with the female. This is less common in polygamous birds. It is an insectivorous bird and feeds on spiders, ants, caterpillars, beetles and mites.

The nest site is usually low down in a tree crevice or situated in ivy or creepers. It is made of plant material and is domed. The female lays around five eggs, which are white with faint red mottling.

Fascinating Facts

The scientific name of the Wren, *Troglodytes troglodytes*, comes from the Latin for 'cave dweller'. This is a reference to its domed nest, with cave-like opening.

DUNNOCK

SCIENTIFIC NAME: *Prunella modularis*

IDENTIFYING FEATURES:
Brown upperparts with blue-grey underparts

SIMILAR SPECIES: Wren, warblers

SIZE: 14 cm (5½ in)

HABITAT: Gardens, parkland and woodland

POPULATION: Common

The Dunnock is an unremarkable bird to look at, its name derived from 'dun-coloured bird'. It is also occasionally referred to as the Hedge Sparrow, although it is not a member of the sparrow family at all but belongs to the Accentors. During the spring, look for males, often several in number, as they perform their wing-waving display. Despite its drab appearance and habits a male Dunnock can often attract multiple females, and three females in attendance is not uncommon.

Adult Dunnocks are a tawny-brown colour streaked with black. The head, with its darker face mask, and breast are a slate-grey colouring. There is also a paler wing bar, which is sometimes noticeable in flight. Juvenile birds are more heavily streaked with some mottling.

BELOW
Dunnocks have a single-note call but a surprisingly rich and pleasant warbling song.

Mating and Nesting

Dunnocks will be found in most gardens, often visiting bird tables, but they also favour woodland settings. This is a bird that will often have multiple partners during a single breeding season. In these instances an unusual feature of the Dunnock is that of stimulating a female using his bill. This is thought to encourage the female to eject sperm from any previous mating encounter, thus ensuring that he is the male to fertilize the eggs.

The Dunnock has the slim bill associated with insect-eaters and will hunt for food under hedges and on lawns. However, it is quite capable of eating and digesting small seeds during the winter months when live food may be less plentiful.

It creates a cup-shaped nest of leaves, grasses and roots, lined with softer material. It is usually found low down in a hedge or bush. It has four to five eggs, which are a vivid turquoise colour.

ROBIN

SIZE: 14 cm (5½ in)

HABITAT: Gardens, parks and woodland

POPULATION: Common

SCIENTIFIC NAME: Erithacus rubecula

IDENTIFYING FEATURES: Distinctive red breast

SIMILAR SPECIES: None

The Robin is a familiar bird, which always seems to be associated with Christmas, although it can be seen year-round. Its striking red breast is incredibly distinctive but avoid confusion with the juvenile birds, which do not possess this colouring. The Robin will pair from early December and are one of the few birds that hold territory all year. They are fiercely territorial and males have been known to attack and, on occasion, kill other Robins that pose a threat.

A distinctive species that is apparently much loved amongst bird-watchers, both sexes share the red breast, bordered by pale blue-grey feathering. The upperparts are a dull olive brown. Younger birds tend to have a mottled breast turning to red after moult. During late summer adult birds undergo a post-breeding moult, during which time they can become extremely secretive and difficult to observe. Their song is a pleasant but mournful thrush-like warble and is often delivered in the dead of night.

Courtship

When protecting their territories, Robins will display their red breasts with vigour to any potential intruders. The female will chase the male during the breeding season until she is accepted. Once this has happened, the male Robin can be seen feeding the female as part of the courtship process.

The Robin is largely an insect-feeder but will also take earthworms. It will, however, take fruit and seeds and is fond of berry-bearing plants.

The nest is made of leaves, moss and grass, and often a Robin will build a nest in sheds or outhouses. A typical clutch size is four or five eggs although six or seven is not uncommon. The eggs are creamy white spotted with red.

Fascinating Facts

British Robins are joined during the winter months by migrants from the continent. These are noticeably more wary than the resident birds, possibly due to the massacre of migrant birds that are still hunted in southern Europe.

BELOW

The Robin is a common bird in our gardens and can become very tame and tolerant of man.

BLACK REDSTART

SCIENTIFIC NAME: Phoenicurus ochruros

IDENTIFYING FEATURES: Dark with red sides to the tail; male has white wing flashes

SIMILAR SPECIES: Redstart

SIZE: 14–15 cm (5½–5⅞ in)

HABITAT: Cities

POPULATION: Scarce

The Black Redstarts notably made their homes in former Second World War bomb sites across Britain and Europe, colonizing these seemingly desolate areas in large numbers. Although it is much more scarce today, the Black Redstart can still be found in some large towns and cities. It seems particularly partial to power stations, canal-side buildings and railway stations. Sometimes hard to spot in this type of environment, listen for its metallic song, said to resemble the rattling of a bunch of keys.

The adult male Black Redstart has a sooty black plumage that contrasts with a paler white wing panel and orange-red tail with a darker central streak. The female bird shares the characteristic tail colouring but is a uniform brown. Juveniles are similar in appearance to the adult female, but even in this immature stage can sing and hold territory. The distinctive song is usually delivered from a prominent high perch. When on the ground it moves with a distinctive hopping motion, its red tail constantly flicking and quivering. It can also dart off perches to catch insects in a flycatcher-type motion.

Urban Dweller

The Black Redstart is essentially an inner city bird, although there are isolated pairs breeding on cliffs around our coastlines. Nowhere is the Black Redstart common and you are possibly more likely to encounter it as a passage migrant. Given its preferred habitats very little is known about its breeding patterns or courtship rituals.

It is mainly dependent on insects for its diet but will also adapt to seeds, berries and similar. The nest is built in a hole or crevice from grasses and leaves, then lined with feathers, fur or wool. The Black Redstart lays between four and six eggs normally, which are white.

LEFT

A male Black Redstart, with its distinctive red tail, perches with food or nest materials.

BLACKBIRD

SIZE: 24–25 cm (9½–9⅞ in)

HABITAT: Gardens, parkland and woodland

POPULATION: Abundant

SCIENTIFIC NAME: Turdus merula

IDENTIFYING FEATURES:
Male black with distinctive yellow bill

SIMILAR SPECIES: Ring Ouzel

Where to Look

Blackbirds can be found pretty much anywhere, and they are regular visitors to gardens. Although they will visit bird tables they are more likely to be found feeding on the ground, on lawns and in borders. Blackbirds are quite territorial. Actual physical attacks on other males are rare but have been documented.

During the summer months they will eat a range of insects and worms. In winter they will eat seeds and berries. They build a tidy cup nest of mud and mosses, lining it with grass. The eggs are an attractive blue-green colour with brown speckles. There are often two broods, each consisting of four to six eggs.

The Blackbird is one of the best-known and best-loved city-dwelling birds and can be found with ease in most habitats. Only the male Blackbird is actually black, with a distinctive yellow bill and eye ring. Females are a mixture of browns. Watch for Blackbirds as they run along lawns, stopping with their head cocked to one side, as they search for earthworms. Although this creates the impression that they are listening for movement, they are in fact looking.

The unmistakeable adult male has jet-black plumage, although in flight the wings can appear somewhat paler. The female is much duller and has a mottled throat and breast. Young male Blackbirds are superficially similar to adult females. They have a dull bill that turns to the familiar yellow after the spring moult. They often retain the brownish wing feathers grown as nestlings until after the first full moult. Their song, which is usually delivered from a prominent position, consists of notes that are formed together into phrases.

RIGHT
Blackbirds are often one of the first species to start singing and one of the last to stop, singing well into the evening.

SONG THRUSH

SCIENTIFIC NAME: Turdus philomelos

IDENTIFYING FEATURES:
Distinctive spotted breast and orange underwings

SIMILAR SPECIES: Mistle Thrush, Redwing

SIZE: 23 cm (9 in)

HABITAT: Gardens, parkland and woodland

POPULATION: Common

The Song Thrush is an attractive speckled bird and a familiar sight, although in recent years it has undergone something of a decline. Snails form a large part of its diet and it will regularly use a rock or stone to break open the shells. These are referred to as 'anvils'.

The Song Thrush has warm brown upperparts but is paler underneath. The buff-coloured breast is covered in familiar black spots. It also has a distinctive orange underwing. Its song is melodic and consists of a phrase of two or three notes repeated.

Once common in gardens, the Song Thrush has undergone a decline in numbers. However, they can be found with relative ease in gardens and woodlands. As well as snails, they will feed on earthworms, a variety of insects, fallen fruit and berries.

The nest is made of leaves and twigs and the Song Thrush lays four or five eggs, pale blue and spotted with black.

MISTLE THRUSH

SCIENTIFIC NAME: Turdus viscivorus

IDENTIFYING FEATURES:
Boldly spotted underparts and white underwing

SIMILAR SPECIES: Song Thrush, Fieldfare

SIZE: 27 cm (10.5 l)

HABITAT: Gardens, parkland and woodland

POPULATION: Common

The Mistle Thrush has the old country name of 'Storm Cock'. This is largely due to its habit of singing from the tops of tall trees in the most inclement of weather. This bird is larger and noisier than the Song Thrush and has a noticeable white underwing.

The Mistle Thrush is the largest of the resident thrushes. They are superficially similar to the Song Thrush but larger. The spotting on the breast is much heavier and they have a white underwing. Although they will be seen in large, mature gardens they are more likely to be encountered in parks and woodland.

It is a very early breeder, starting to attract a mate as early as December and often eggs can be laid in February. It will eat some insects but is particularly fond of fruit and berries. The nest is rather untidy and is laid in the fork of a tree. Clutch size will be between three and five eggs and although the egg colour can be variable they are generally brown and speckled.

Fascinating Facts

As well as Storm Cock another ancient country name for the Mistle Thrush is the Throstle.

BLUE TIT

SIZE: 11–12 cm (4¼–4¾ in)

HABITAT: Gardens, parkland and woodland

POPULATION: Common

SCIENTIFIC NAME: Parus caeruleus

IDENTIFYING FEATURES: Yellow underparts; white cheek with black line through the eye

SIMILAR SPECIES: Great Tit

A charming, inquisitive member of the tit family, the Blue Tit is a welcome addition to any garden bird table. They are single-brooded and usually time their breeding to coincide with an abundance of their foodstuff – caterpillars. They can lay up to 15 eggs in this brood but if the food is not plentiful enough then there is no second brood. Installing a nest box will help attract Blue Tits to your garden all year round.

History and Habitat

The Blue Tit began life as a woodland species but has adapted to more urban habitats. It is now a familiar sight in gardens as it visits bird tables in the winter and uses nest boxes. Blue Tits are prolific breeders and a brood in double figures is not unusual, as is the presence of a second brood during the season, should an adequate provision of food allow.

Caterpillars are the mainstay of a Blue Tit's diet. They are very active feeders and as they are so light they can seek food at the tips of the thinnest twigs, giving them quite an advantage. The Blue Tit is a hole-nester and as well as using nest boxes it will utilize holes in trees and buildings. Clutch size can be anything from seven to 15 eggs; these are white with reddish-brown spots.

Fascinating Facts

Blue Tits are renowned for pecking the foil tops from doorstep milk bottles, but they also remove putty from windows. It is thought that they do this while searching window frames for spiders.

The Blue Tit is an attractively marked bird with a vivid blue cap, wings and tail. Its underparts are a bright, clean yellow in colour. The face is white with a noticeable darker eye stripe. Younger birds have greener caps with a yellow, rather than white, face. Its vocabulary is a mixture of thin, high-pitched churring calls.

GREAT TIT

SCIENTIFIC NAME: Parus major

IDENTIFYING FEATURES: Black cap, collar and throat with a black line running down the breast; white cheeks

SIMILAR SPECIES: Blue Tit, Coal Tit

SIZE: 14 cm (5½ in)

HABITAT: Gardens, parkland and woodland

POPULATION: Common

The Great Tit is a larger, more boisterous relative of the Blue Tit, essentially another woodland bird that has adapted to be at home in parks and gardens. It is a very adaptable bird and is renowned for utilizing a large variety of unusual nest sites. It has one of the most varied vocabularies of all our birds and if you hear an unfamiliar call in your garden, there is a higher than average chance that it will be a Great Tit.

The adult Great Tit has a striking combination of white cheeks with a black crown and bib, and a bright yellow breast. It has a thick black band running vertically down the centre of its breast. The wings and tail are blue-grey in colour with the tail having prominent white outer feathers. Although both sexes possess the breast band it is noticeably broader on the male and unbroken, whereas it is much thinner on the female. It has an extremely varied voice with myriad calls, phrases and notes, although the song is a repetitive 'teacher, teacher, teacher'.

Feeding and Breeding

The Great Tit is a species that feeds largely on caterpillars but will also take seeds, fruit and peanuts. During the winter they regularly drop to the ground tossing aside leaf litter and moss as they search for food.

Nest boxes are a favourite but they will often take advantage of man-made sites such as holes in pipework. Clutch sizes can be large but on average number five to seven. The eggs are white with red spotting. The male is another territorial species and the female is known to hiss at predators should they approach the nest site.

BELOW
Gardens and woodland are home to the Great Tit and they are a common resident in both.

STARLING

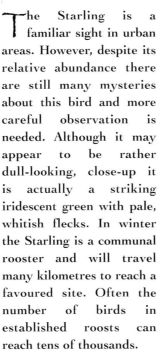

SIZE: 21 cm (8¼ in)

HABITAT: Gardens, parkland and woodland

POPULATION: Abundant

SCIENTIFIC NAME: Sturnus vulgaris

IDENTIFYING FEATURES: Blackish bird with green-blue sheen; heavy speckling

SIMILAR SPECIES: Blackbird

The Starling is a familiar sight in urban areas. However, despite its relative abundance there are still many mysteries about this bird and more careful observation is needed. Although it may appear to be rather dull-looking, close-up it is actually a striking iridescent green with pale, whitish flecks. In winter the Starling is a communal rooster and will travel many kilometres to reach a favoured site. Often the number of birds in established roosts can reach tens of thousands.

Fascinating Facts

Female Starlings will often remove eggs from another bird's nest and place them gently on the ground, intact, and then use the empty nest space to lay her own eggs.

RIGHT

The Starling is found in any urban location, often gathering in large numbers.

At close quarters the Starling is really quite an attractive bird. During spring the male is a glossy mix of green and black with a distinctive yellow bill. At the base of the bill is a blue patch. This is pinkish on the female. After its autumnal moult the tips of the feathers are pale, giving a speckled appearance. Juvenile Starlings are a dull

grey-brown with a dark bill. The song is not particularly grand – more a long mixture of rattles. However, the Starling is an exceptional mimic and can impersonate many other species as well as other sounds such as car alarms and telephones.

Eating and Nesting

This is another species that is often polygamous. Another interesting, but inexplicable, fact about this bird is that where a group of Starlings are nesting the egg-laying between the pairs will be synchronized so that they are all laid at the same time.

Insects and their larvae are the preferred food of the Starling but it will eat largely anything, particularly in an urban setting.

They nest in holes and crevices in buildings and trees using a variety of materials. Research has shown that certain plants are chosen to line the nest. These possess some types of natural toxins to eliminate parasites. The eggs are pale blue and number between four and six per clutch.

HOUSE SPARROW

SCIENTIFIC NAME: Passer domesticus

IDENTIFYING FEATURES:
Slate-grey crown; distinctive black bib

SIMILAR SPECIES: Tree Sparrow

SIZE: 14 cm (5½ in)

HABITAT: Gardens, parkland and woodland

POPULATION: Abundant

Humans and Sparrows

Most urban areas will have groups of House Sparrows. They are also present on farmland – in fact, wherever humans are, House Sparrows will follow. They are real opportunists and have managed to colonize the majority of the globe.

Essentially the breeding season is from May to July; however, there is an increasing tendency amongst this species to nest all year round, and three or four broods are not unusual.

The House Sparrow has seen a decline in numbers in the last few years, although it is still quite abundant. It is an excellent example of humans living side by side with birds. It can be found in the most urban of areas and although largely sedentary, ringing recoveries have shown some individuals can travel in excess of 300 km (200 miles) away from their normal areas. The House Sparrow is easily recognized by its slate-grey cap and prominent black bib.

The male House Sparrow is quite distinctive, with a black bib, grey crown and grey rump. The wings are a mix of warm browns with a whitish wing bar. The female is drab by comparison – a rather nondescript greyish brown. The House Sparrow is quite a vocal bird but with a limited vocabulary of cheeps and twitters. They often congregate in large groups and the combined chattering can be quite a sound.

House Sparrows have a varied diet but strictly speaking they are seed-eaters. They will also readily eat berries and buds. In towns and cities, though, they will feed on scraps and discarded food waste.

The nest is a rather untidy affair largely constructed of grass and straw. They will nest in holes or make loose nests in bushes. Three or four eggs are typical but a female can lay as many as seven. The eggs are greyish with fine darker speckles.

CHAFFINCH

SIZE: 14–15 cm (5½–5⅞ in)

HABITAT: Gardens, parkland and woodland

POPULATION: Common

SCIENTIFIC NAME: Fringilla coelebs

IDENTIFYING FEATURES: White shoulder stripe and wing patch; male has pinkish breast and cheeks

SIMILAR SPECIES: Brambling, Bullfinch

The Chaffinch is probably the most common resident finch, and the male is a very attractive bird indeed. Although the resident population in Britain does not really wander, the winter sees the arrival of large numbers of Chaffinches from the continent moving in search of food. The Chaffinch builds an elaborate nest of grasses which it then decorates. For such a small bird they are long-lived and research has found individuals that have survived for 13 years.

Habitat and Habits

Largely resident, this bird can be found in parks, gardens and open country as well. It is normally absent from very urban areas.

The short, stubby bill tells us that the Chaffinch, in common with other finches, is a seed-eater but will take a range of other foods, including insects.

The Chaffinch pairs in late winter and is usually single-brooded. However, two broods are not uncommon. The nest of a Chaffinch is built low in a bush or tree, often in the fork of a branch. It is a cup nest that is lined with feathers and grasses. The exterior of the nest is usually decorated with lichens stripped from surrounding trees. The eggs are dark spotted and greenish. Four or five eggs is typical.

BELOW
Chaffinches will spend more than a week building their nests.

There can be no mistaking the Chaffinch. The handsome male has a pink breast with a blue-grey head that shows a noticeable peak. A double white wing bar is also evident, particularly in flight. Look also for the white outer tail feathers. The female is a much toned-down version of the male but can still show a faint pink wash to the breast. The female also has the distinctive white wing bars. In early spring the Chaffinch song can be heard – a short descending series of trills ending with a flourish. At other times it can be heard making a two-note chipping call, 'pink, pink'.

GREENFINCH

SCIENTIFIC NAME: Carduelis chloris

IDENTIFYING FEATURES:
Olive-green with prominent yellow wing flashes

SIMILAR SPECIES:
Siskin, Goldfinch, female Crossbill

SIZE: 15 cm (5⅞ in)

HABITAT: Gardens, parkland and woodland

POPULATION: Common

The Greenfinch is another easily found urban dweller. It is a fairly thickset finch with a characteristic undulating flight. These are increasingly familiar garden birds and are particularly partial to sunflower and niger seeds. They are solitary during the summer months but can form sizeable flocks during winter.

As its name suggests, the Greenfinch is green in colour, although this is offset by yellow flashes in the wing and tail. The female is a little duller, streaked brown and with less vivid yellow colouration. The song is a mix of pleasant twittering notes.

Found in parks and gardens, especially during the winter months, it can also be encountered in a variety of other habitats such as woodland. Its diet is a wide range of seeds, berries and cereals.

Greenfinches are aggressive birds during the breeding season, and they build nests of twigs and moss in bushes and hedges, laying four to six whitish speckled eggs.

GOLDFINCH

SCIENTIFIC NAME: Carduelis carduelis

IDENTIFYING FEATURES: Distinctive red, white and black face; yellow wing flashes

SIMILAR SPECIES: Greenfinch, Siskin

SIZE: 12 cm (4¾ in)

HABITAT: Gardens, parkland and woodland

POPULATION: Common

Fascinating Facts

At one time the Goldfinch was a popular cage bird. It was trapped using a primitive cage called a Chardonneret. Chardonneret is also the French name for the Goldfinch.

RIGHT
The Goldfinch can be identified by its striking facial markings.

Possibly the most colourful of all resident finches, the Goldfinch is a beautiful bird. It is less frequent in gardens than some species, but look for it on waste ground in winter. Here it will feed on its favourites of thistle heads and teasels.

The Goldfinch is slim built with a striking facial pattern of red, black and white. Prominent yellow wing flashes on black wings are another key feature. During the spring it can be seen with two brownish patches on each side of the otherwise pale breast. Goldfinch song is a very liquid mix of twittering. The Goldfinch is another seed-eater, with a preference for members of the thistle family.

They can be found occasionally in gardens but are more likely to frequent waste ground. They build tidy cup nests, constructed of wool and mosses, usually at the end of a branch. Eggs are bluish with some streaking and spotting, usually numbering five or six.

117

SIKIN

SIZE: 12 cm (4¾ in)

HABITAT: Gardens, parkland and coniferous woodland

POPULATION: Common

SCIENTIFIC NAME: Carduelis spinus

IDENTIFYING FEATURES:
Yellow-green plumage with yellow wing bars

SIMILAR SPECIES: Greenfinch

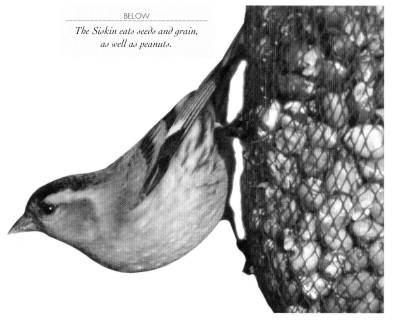

BELOW
The Siskin eats seeds and grain, as well as peanuts.

This species has undergone something of a population increase in recent years, thought to be linked to the spread of coniferous forestation. It is another predominately yellow and green finch, but is smaller and slighter than the Greenfinch. Combine its appearance with a charming, twittering song and it is not surprising that the Siskin was prized in Victorian times as a cage bird.

The Siskin is a small, lively finch, largely green and yellow. The male has a black cap, chin and throat. Yellow wing flashes and a yellowish rump are also noticeable. Another good feature is the notched tail, which can be seen clearly in flight. The female is much greyer and shows far less yellow in its overall plumage, with paler, streaked underparts. The Siskin has a varied twittering song and a shrill single-note call.

Garden Attractions

Today the Siskin can be seen regularly in urban and suburban gardens during winter months, when bird table nuts are a big draw. Siskins will often form large flocks. Outside the winter months it is closely associated with coniferous woodland, where it breeds. It can also be seen with some regularity in damp woodland, particularly where alder trees are present. The bill shape of the Siskin makes it an ideal tool for extracting the seeds of birch and alder – two of its preferred foods.

During the spring the display flight of the male is quite elaborate and his song is delivered in flight, while circling the tops of trees. It has a delicate cup nest made of twigs and moss. This is usually built high in a conifer. The eggs are a deep blue colour and a normal clutch will have four or five eggs.

BULLFINCH

SCIENTIFIC NAME: Pyrrhula pyrrhula

IDENTIFYING FEATURES: Black cap and white rump; male has vivid pinkish underparts

SIMILAR SPECIES: Chaffinch

SIZE: 14 cm (5½ in)

HABITAT: Woodland; also visits gardens

POPULATION: Common

The Bullfinch is a stout, dumpy finch with a reputation for doing vast damage in orchards, where it feeds on the buds of fruit trees. For a bird with such a vivid plumage the Bullfinch can often be secretive. The female is a toned-down version of the male in terms of plumage and they can often be encountered feeding in pairs. The noticeable white rump in flight is a good identification feature.

There can be few resident finches as striking as the Bullfinch. It is a plump, large-headed finch with a very short stubby bill. Its wings, tail and cap are all a glossy black in colour. The breast, underparts and cheeks of the male are a glorious rich pink. The female is nowhere near as colourful, with a pinkish-brown wash. The noticeable white rump is present in both sexes, as is a silvery white wing bar. Its song is a quiet warble, but is rarely heard.

A Secretive Species

The Bullfinch is an urban visitor during the winter months, but in the spring and summer it retreats to woodland or mature parkland to breed. During the winter its population is swollen by migrants from the continent.

In terms of breeding patterns the Bullfinch is unremarkable. Its secretive nature has made it difficult to study. One interesting fact, however, is that during the breeding season the adults develop a pouch within their mouths to carry food.

The staple foods of the Bullfinch are buds from a variety of trees. Oak and hawthorn are favoured, as are the buds of fruit trees. These preferences make the Bullfinch a pest species for commercial growers.

It nests between May and July in flimsy-looking nests of twigs and mosses. Here the female will lay four to five bluish-green eggs.

Fascinating Facts

The Bullfinch can enjoy a long life – the oldest bird of this species recorded was over 17 years old.

Woodland

Woodlands are fabulous places for birds. There are three main types of woodland areas: deciduous woodland, where the leaves fall during the winter; coniferous woodland made up predominately of firs and pines; and mixed woodland, which has a combination of the two.

Mature deciduous woods offer possibly the largest selection of birds, particularly during the spring and summer. Warblers often dominate but other species that make this their habitat include flycatchers, woodpeckers and finches. Early mornings are one of the best times for this particular habitat, as the birds are generally very active and vocal. The dawn chorus is a fabulous experience and will often test your knowledge of birdsong. One factor to be wary of, however, is that during the spring and summer the dense foliage and natural cover can make some species very difficult to see. During the autumn and winter months this becomes less of a problem, but there may be fewer species at this time of year.

Coniferous woodlands generally hold fewer species than deciduous woodlands. The newer coniferous plantations are worth visiting, though, particularly if there are clearings and rides. These areas are often home to pipits, flycatchers and chats. Several species of the tit family prefer a coniferous environment, as do Siskins and the crossbill family. Members of this last have adapted in a remarkable way to live in coniferous woodland. Their upper and lower mandibles have become crossed or twisted. Although this may look a little comical, it makes them more adept at removing seeds from fir cones than any other bird.

CAPERCAILLIE

SCIENTIFIC NAME: Tetrao urogallus

IDENTIFYING FEATURES:
Large bird with glossy black plumage

SIMILAR SPECIES: Black Grouse

SIZE: 60–88 cm (23⅝–34¾ in)

HABITAT: Mature coniferous woodland

POPULATION: Scarce and very localized

Lekking

Like other game birds, the Capercaillie forms groups called leks during the early spring. These leks will contain a number of females and often several males. The courtship ritual is prolonged and can be quite aggressive at times.

Despite its large size this bird can be found in the tops of trees, where it feeds on pine buds and needles. It will also eat berries and various seeds. The nest is a large but shallow scrape on the woodland floor, often at the base of a pine tree. There can be as many as eight eggs, and these are buff-coloured and speckled with brown.

The ancient Caledonian forests are home to this enormous game bird. The turkey-sized males are fiercely territorial and have been known to attack humans in defence of these areas. A combination of habitat loss and hunting led to its extinction in the 1800s in Britain, but birds from Scandinavia were introduced to replace the original stock and the descendants of these survive today. The best way to see this bird is early morning in spring, as groups of birds assemble at established areas for the displays known as leks.

The male Capercaillie is a huge black bird with dark brown wings. It has a distinctive red wattle above the eye and a characteristic small white shoulder patch.

The female is a mixture of tawny and rufous colouring with a strongly barred orange breast. The fanned tail of the female helps distinguish it from other female grouse species. Its call is a throaty crescendo of notes said to sound like a cork popping from a bottle. The population is established and steady but can suffer greatly from disturbance.

BELOW
The populations of Capercaillie fluctuate across Europe depending on changing disturbances in their traditional habitats.

GOLDEN PHEASANT

SCIENTIFIC NAME: Chrysolophus pictus

IDENTIFYING FEATURES: Smaller than Common Pheasant; male has exotic plumage

SIMILAR SPECIES: Common Pheasant, Lady Amherst's Pheasant

SIZE: 60–115 cm (23⅝–45¼ in)

HABITAT: Woodland

POPULATION: Rare

In common with a lot of game birds, the Golden Pheasant was introduced to Europe from Asia. The male is an incredibly exotic-looking bird with a rich plumage of reds and golds. The female is much drabber by comparison and is similar to the female Common Pheasant. Despite the striking plumage, Golden Pheasants can be very hard to find. It is a secretive bird and nowhere is it particularly common.

The male Golden Pheasant is unmistakeable. It has orange red underparts with a distinctive golden yellow head. The upperparts are a dark green and it has black and yellow barred feathers on the side of the neck that are used in display. The tail is long and brown. The female is a yellowish-brown with finely barred underparts. Juveniles resemble the female bird but with less obvious barring of the underparts. Both sexes are smaller than the Common Pheasant. This is not a particularly vocal bird and is seldom heard, although it is said to emit a crowing noise in the breeding season.

A Rare Sight

Since being introduced from China over 100 years ago, the Golden Pheasant has spread to many parts of Europe, although it is now quite rare and numbers appear to be declining further. It favours dark and dense woodland, and consequently can be very hard to see.

During the breeding season the male Golden Pheasant is very territorial and fierce fights between males can ensue.

Little is known about the exact diet of this species although it has been reported feeding on grain, buds and some insects.

The nest is a shallow depression on the ground. A typical clutch size would be in the region of five to eight eggs but often up to 12 can be laid. The eggs are a pale olive-green colour.

BELOW

The Golden Pheasant is something of a mystery to experts – little is known of its habits in the wild.

LADY AMHERST'S PHEASANT

SCIENTIFIC NAME: Chrysolophus amherstiae

IDENTIFYING FEATURES:
Larger than Golden Pheasant; exotic-looking male

SIMILAR SPECIES:
Common Pheasant, Golden Pheasant

SIZE: 70–120 cm (27⅛–47⅛ in)

HABITAT: Woodland

POPULATION: Rare

Lady Amherst's Pheasant is also a species introduced from Asia. This is another exotic male pheasant and the female adopts the drab brown plumage in common with members of this family. Its numbers are much reduced and unless you are fortunate to be aware of established groups of these birds it is unlikely you will encounter them.

The male is quite splendid, with a dark green face, neck and back, with red feathering that hangs behind the head. Its back is red and yellow and males have an extraordinary long black and white tail. The female is reddish-brown with a pale belly. Their call is similar to that of the Golden Pheasant but said to be more metallic. They tend to be found in young conifer plantations or mixed woodland.

They seem to be less territorial than the Golden and Common Pheasants, but little is actually known about their breeding patterns in the wild or their diet, although these pheasants have been observed eating berries, seeds and insects.

The nest is a shallow scrape on the floor which will typically contain between six and nine pale green eggs.

Fascinating Facts

The Lady Amherst's Pheasant was named after the wife of the Governor-General of India when it was first introduced in 1828.

HONEY BUZZARD

SCIENTIFIC NAME: Pernis apivorus

IDENTIFYING FEATURES: More slender than Common Buzzard; variable marked underparts

SIMILAR SPECIES: Common Buzzard, Rough Legged Buzzard

SIZE: 52–60 cm (20½–23⅝ in)

HABITAT: Deciduous and coniferous woodland

POPULATION: Scarce summer breeder

The Honey Buzzard is an uncommon summer visitor that breeds in dense, mature woodland, often at established locations. In flight it can be difficult to distinguish from other raptors, particularly the Common Buzzard. However, the strongly barred underparts can be obvious in certain individuals.

The Honey Buzzard varies greatly in its plumage, although essentially the male has a grey head, greyish-brown upperparts and barred underparts. In flight the barred underparts can be noticeable, as can a dark patch near the bend of the wing. The Honey Buzzard is generally silent. As the name suggests, the Honey Buzzard feeds largely on the larvae of bees, wasps and other grubs.

Breeding takes place in generally established locations and their soaring display flight can be seen from May onwards. Honey Buzzards often adopt the nests of other birds such as Common Buzzards or Crows. They normally lay two eggs, which are creamy white with reddish-brown markings.

GOSHAWK

SIZE: 48–62 cm (19–24⅛ in)

HABITAT: Woodland

POPULATION: Scarce

SCIENTIFIC NAME: Accipter gentilis

IDENTIFYING FEATURES: masked appearance; pale underparts with barring

SIMILAR SPECIES: Sparrowhawk, Buzzard

Goshawks are large, sometimes Buzzard-sized, birds of prey. They are rare breeders and nowhere near as common as the more diminutive Sparrowhawk. They became extinct in parts of Europe in the early 1900s but are now established again. It is believed that this new wave of birds originates from the accidental, or deliberate, release of falconers' stock but this has not been proved. Displaying birds in very early spring, at established sites, is probably the best chance to see these magnificent raptors.

The Goshawk is superficially similar to the Sparrowhawk. However, it is generally much larger, with a longer, more rounded tail. The male is grey above with a darker patch behind the eye, creating an almost masked appearance. At close range a distinct white eye stripe is noticeable. The underparts are pale and finely barred. The female is similar but brown rather than grey.

The juvenile bird has a streaked, buff-coloured breast. The Goshawk calls during display and often when approaching the nest site.

Feeding and Courtship Habits

Goshawks can be found in mature woodland, both coniferous and deciduous, as well as hunting in open country. Its range of prey is wide and it will eat almost any bird up to the size of a crow, although pigeons and jays are common prey. It has also been known to take mammals in the wild, particularly rabbits.

Courtship flights involve long periods soaring on the warm air currents known as thermals. This often gives the best chance of seeing this secretive bird and is best observed in March and April.

The Goshawk will build a loosely constructed nest of twigs high in a tree. It may also adopt old nests from other species. The average clutch size is three to four very pale blue eggs.

BELOW

Goshawk populations are widespread across Europe, but still little is known about their habits.

SPARROWHAWK

SCIENTIFIC NAME: Accipter nissus

IDENTIFYING FEATURES:
Rounded wings; speed in flight

SIMILAR SPECIES: Goshawk, Kestrel

SIZE: 28–38 cm (11–15 in)

HABITAT: Woodland, parks and gardens

POPULATION: Common

In the 1950s the Sparrow-hawk was in trouble. Its numbers were seriously affected by the use of agricultural pest-control chemicals such as DDT. The more intensive the agriculture in a certain area the worse the problem became. With the tighter controls against these practices today, the Sparrowhawk is now quite common. As its name suggests, birds form largely the entire diet of this species. After killing its prey, the Sparrowhawk will often take it to a regular perch to be plucked.

Sparrowhawks are small and fast-flying birds of prey. The male has a slate-grey back with reddish barred underparts. The female is often considerably larger than the male and has browner upperparts and paler barred underparts. The female also has a characteristic white stripe above the eye. Both sexes have a series of four or five bars on the tail. Young birds have red-brown upperparts with some barring below. It is silent for most of the year but is known to make a shrill, four-syllable call when nesting.

Recovering Resident

Once heavily persecuted, the Sparrowhawk has made something of a recovery in recent years and is now a common resident. It can be seen in our gardens and parks as well as woodland and open country. It is another early nester and the display flight should be looked for in April.

The Sparrowhawk is a specialist of hunting smaller birds – not just sparrows, but also finches and tits. It has been known to take prey as large as a pigeon. A nest of twigs and sticks is made against the trunk of a tree, where the female lays four or five whitish eggs.

ABOVE

Although Sparrowhawks are mainly woodland birds, increasing numbers of them can be seen in urban areas.

WOODCOCK

SCIENTIFIC NAME: Scolopax rusticola

IDENTIFYING FEATURES: short legs; long, tapering bill

SIMILAR SPECIES: Snipe

SIZE: 33–35 cm (13–13¼ in)

HABITAT: Woodland

POPULATION: Common

Fascinating Facts

The Woodcock has the extraordinary habit of flying with its nestlings, one by one, between its legs to relocate them in the event of any danger. Several trips must often be made to ensure the whole family is moved to safety.

The Woodcock is unusual in that it is a wader that makes its home in deciduous and coniferous woodland. Its subtle brown plumage makes excellent camouflage for this ground-nester. This can be a

difficult bird to see but warm spring evenings are a good chance when they are displaying or – as it is sometimes called – roding.

The Woodcock is a large bulky wader with a very long bill and short legs. Its overall colouring is reddish-brown above with obvious black barring on the crown. Underparts are a warm buff with barring.

The Woodcock makes its home in deciduous and mixed woodlands. In severe weather it can be encountered almost anywhere. It eats a wide range of insects, grubs and worms.

During the breeding season, when roding, the male flies bat-like with slow, deliberate wing beats in the hope of attracting a female. It nests on the ground in a shallow scrape and lays between three and five blotchy brown eggs.

TURTLE DOVE

SCIENTIFIC NAME: Streptopelia turtur

IDENTIFYING FEATURES: Small and delicate; distinctive diamond-shaped tail

SIMILAR SPECIES: Collared Dove

SIZE: 26–28 cm (10¼–11 in)

HABITAT: Woodland and copses

POPULATION: Scarce summer visitor

The Turtle Dove is a summer visitor here and is also the smallest species of dove. It is a delicate, long-tailed bird that is attractively marked. Its numbers have declined in recent years. Its

RIGHT

The cooing of the Turtle Dove is a familiar sound in the summer months.

favoured nest sites include mature, tall hedgerows. These are often removed in farming nowadays and this has had a negative effect on the Turtle Dove. Listen for its purring call between May and August.

Turtle Doves can be recognized by their brown and black upperparts, giving a

tortoiseshell effect. They have a subtle pink tinge to the breast with a black and white striped neck patch. Their song is a long, cat-like purring call.

Despite a recent decline in numbers this species can still be found with some regularity in open woodland, copses and occasionally farmland. It feeds mainly on

the seeds of wild plants as well as cereals and grain and nests on a flimsy platform of twigs, laying one or two white eggs.

CUCKOO

SCIENTIFIC NAME: Cuculus canorus

IDENTIFYING FEATURES: Slim body; long tail;
resembles a bird of prey in flight

SIMILAR SPECIES: Sparrowhawk

SIZE: 26–28 cm (10¼–11 in)

HABITAT: Woodland and copses

POPULATION: Scarce

The Cuckoo is probably one of the first birds that comes to mind in the summer months. The Cuckoo is a brood parasite, which means that it lays its eggs in the nests of other species which then raise the young Cuckoo as their own. More often heard than seen, in flight the Cuckoo can be confused with the Sparrowhawk. As it has no parental responsibilities during the summer, it is one of the first birds to migrate back to Africa.

The upperparts and breast of the Cuckoo are blue-grey in colour with paler, heavily barred underparts. The tail is long and rounded with a pale tip, although this can be difficult to see. When at rest the Cuckoo droops its wings in a characteristic pose. The sexes are similar, although the female is browner. There is a rare form of the adult female where the colouration is a reddish-brown. In flight the long tail and angled wings give the impression of a bird of prey. The call is the very familiar two-syllable phrase that gives the bird its name.

Foster Parents

The Cuckoo favours woodland, parkland and open country. It is rarely encountered in urban areas. This species is largely insectivorous but will also eat eggs and nestling birds. Some Cuckoos do maintain territory while others simply gather near numbers of potential host species. The female makes no nest, choosing instead to lay her egg in the nest of a suitable foster parent. Typical host species include Dunnocks, warblers and pipits. The female removes an egg from the nest of the host species and eats it. She then lays hers in its place. The colours of the eggs are incredibly varied and normally resemble that of the host.

Fascinating Facts

Although the Cuckoo only lays one egg per nest it is not unusual for a female to lay up to 25 eggs, in different nests, during the course of a season.

TAWNY OWL

SCIENTIFIC NAME: Strix aluco

IDENTIFYING FEATURES: Largish owl;
reddish-brown; well-rounded wings

SIMILAR SPECIES: Long-eared Owl,
Short-eared Owl

SIZE: 37–39 cm (14⅝–15⅜ in)

HABITAT: Woodland,
parks and gardens

POPULATION: Common

The Tawny Owl is the most common breeding owl. Originally a woodland species, it has adapted to life in parks and gardens. Given its strictly nocturnal nature, the Tawny Owl can be a difficult species to see. During the day its presence can be made known by the anxious chattering of other birds as they come across a roosting owl. These verbal attacks can be quite prolonged.

The Tawny Owl is a thickset owl with a large rounded head. It is reddish-brown in colour with noticeable white markings on the wings as well as on the crown. Around its face is a ring of darker feathers, creating what is called a facial disc. There is also a grey form of the Tawny Owl but these are not commonly recorded. Its call is a well-known hoot but it also has a sharp 'ke-wick' that can often be heard.

Nesting and Feeding

Deciduous woodland is where the Tawny Owl makes its home, although they are also found in large, mature gardens and parkland. The male is particularly territorial during the breeding season and they have been known to attack people should they feel a threat to the nest site.

The nest is made in the hole of a tree or in a nest box, although there have been instances of this species nesting on the ground. Eggs in a normal clutch number between two and five and are white.

Small mammals make up the main part of this species' diet, such as mice and voles. They also take small birds, beetles, frogs and earthworms. The Tawny Owl has even been recorded snatching fish from the surface of water.

Fascinating Facts

Tawny Owls dispel the indigestible parts of their food in the form of a pellet which they regurgitate. Pellets on the ground can be an obvious clue to a roosting or nesting owl above. These pellets can be dissolved in warm water, where you will find animal bones, teeth and fur.

RIGHT
Tawny Owls are the most widespread of any bird species in the world.

LONG-EARED OWL

SCIENTIFIC NAME: Asio otus

IDENTIFYING FEATURES: Slim-looking with noticeable ear tufts

SIMILAR SPECIES: Short-eared Owl, Tawny Owl

SIZE: 25–39 cm (9⅞–15⅛ in)

HABITAT: Woodland, often coniferous

POPULATION: Scarce

The Long-eared Owl is a scarce breeding resident. Its preference is for mature coniferous woodland, rather than deciduous woods. The ear tufts, which give the owl its name, are only raised when it is curious or alarmed. In a relaxed state the tufts are flat. In winter this species often roosts socially and can be encountered during daylight hours as they roost in hedgerows and woodland. These roosts can occasionally number 10 or 12 birds.

The Long-eared Owl is a small, slim owl with characteristic ear tufts, which are not always visible. The plumage is a warm buff brown with darker streaking. The paler underparts are boldly streaked. When seen up close note the orange eyes. In flight the Long-eared Owl is difficult to distinguish from the related Short-eared Owl, although the Long-eared Owl has more uniform wings without the pale buff edge. The seldom-heard call is a drawn-out cooing, although younger birds make a noise said to sound like a creaking gate.

Breeding Season

The Long-eared Owl breeds in coniferous or mixed woodland. Outside breeding season it can be found in a wider variety of habitats. The success of a breeding season is largely dependant upon the success of its main prey, voles. In a good vole year Long-eared Owls should prosper, but in poorer years they will be less common.

They normally adopt the nest of another species, such as a crow or Magpie, or on occasion a squirrel nest. In poorly wooded areas they will nest in a shallow scrape on the ground. They lay between three and five white eggs.

LEFT

Long-eared Owls can adapt their preference for nesting sites depending on the materials and places available.

WRYNECK

SCIENTIFIC NAME: Jynx torquilla

IDENTIFYING FEATURES: Finely barred tawny plumage

SIMILAR SPECIES: None

SIZE: 16–17 cm (6¼–6¾ in)

HABITAT: Woodland and large, mature parkland

POPULATION: Passage migrant

The Wryneck is a very close relative of the woodpecker. Not unlike the Green Woodpecker, the Wryneck's diet is composed almost entirely of ants. One big difference, however, is that unlike woodpeckers the Wryneck is migratory. It was once a breeding species but Wrynecks are now more likely to be seen on spring and autumn passage at coastal locations. The bird's curious name comes from the way it twists its neck right around to look behind it.

Wrynecks are small, slim birds, with short legs and bills. They are predominately grey-brown in colour, with a distinctive brown diamond marking that runs from the crown to the base of its back. The underparts are buff but gently barred. It also has a dark brown eye stripe. Sexes are similar. They are generally silent birds but will occasionally emit a falcon-like call during the breeding season.

Population Decline

The Wryneck no longer breeds in this area and is generally found to be a displaced passage migrant, particularly along the coast. Where it does breed it utilizes a wide range of habitats including woodland, orchards, parks and large gardens. The breeding season will fail unless its nest site is in close proximity to their staple food, ants. As well as ants they will also eat beetles, moths, grasshoppers, spiders and flies.

The Wryneck is a hole-nester, normally in trees but it will also make its home in walls, sandbanks or nest boxes. They use no nest material at all and will lay up to 10 white eggs.

The European population has fallen by more than 50 per cent in recent years and the loss of old pasture with a plentiful supply of ants' nests is thought to be one of the main factors.

Fascinating **F**acts

Wrynecks have the longest tongue in relation to their bodies – largely because this helps them scoop up their main prey – ants. The tongue is two-thirds the length of the bird's body.

ABOVE LEFT

Wrynecks do not make their nests, but rather use holes in trees or walls.

GREEN WOODPECKER

SCIENTIFIC NAME: Picus viridis

IDENTIFYING FEATURES:
Predominately green plumage; red crown

SIMILAR SPECIES: Golden Oriole

SIZE: 31–33 cm (12¼–13 in)

HABITAT: Woodland

POPULATION: Common

Green Woodpeckers are the largest species of woodpeckers. Both sexes share the bright green plumage and red crown, but the red moustache stripe is only seen on the male. Once spotted it is largely unmistakable, with its vivid plumage and deep, undulating flight – a common characteristic of the woodpecker family. Ants and their larvae are the Green Woodpecker's main diet and the birds can often be seen plundering an ant hill.

This is a large and distinctive woodpecker. The upperparts are a dark green while the underparts are paler and greyer. The red crown is present in both sexes but the male also possesses a red moustachial streak, which is entirely black in the female. Juveniles are similar in plumage but tend to have heavy barring on the breast and flanks. The call is an easily recognized laughter-like call. They do not normally drum, like some woodpeckers, but when they do it is weak.

Where to Look

Green Woodpeckers can be found in deciduous woodland, parkland and open country, occasionally visiting gardens. Despite being a woodpecker, they will often feed away from trees in open grassy areas such as lawns, playing fields and open pasture.

When breeding the Green Woodpecker is particular about its nest site and quite precise on location. The nest is usually about 4 m (13 ft) above ground with an entrance hole no wider than 6 cm (2⅜ in). The nest chamber is then excavated to a depth of around 30 cm (11⅞ in). Ants, together with their eggs and larvae, are a large part of the Green Woodpecker's diet, as are beetles, flies and caterpillars.

Mature trees, particularly oak and ash, are favoured. The nest chamber is lined

Fascinating Facts

When feeding the Green Woodpecker can extend its tongue to 10 cm (3⅞ in). The sticky tip of the tongue is then used to collect the prey.

with wood chippings and a typical clutch size is five to seven glossy white eggs.

GREAT SPOTTED WOODPECKER

SIZE: 22–23 cm (8⅝–9 in)

HABITAT: Woodland

POPULATION: Common

SCIENTIFIC NAME: Dendrocopus major

IDENTIFYING FEATURES: Black and white with red under-tail feathers

SIMILAR SPECIES: Lesser Spotted Woodpecker

Great Spotted Woodpeckers are usually found in deciduous and mixed woodland, but they are also a visitor to gardens. They have a distinctive pied plumage with flashes of red on the nape of the neck and base of the tail.

The large and obvious white wing patches are a useful aid to identification in flight. Its drumming sound is a familiar noise in woodlands. It can be seen with regularity away from woodland haunts, where it travels to feed at garden bird tables. Most of its natural food – a large variety of insects and their larvae, particularly beetle larvae – is obtained by repeated pecking of dead and decaying wood and bark.

Both sexes excavate a nest chamber and incubate between four and six white eggs in an unlined nest chamber.

LESSER SPOTTED WOODPECKER

SIZE: 14–15 cm (5½–5⅞ in)

HABITAT: Woodland

POPULATION: Scarce

SCIENTIFIC NAME: Dendrocopus minor

IDENTIFYING FEATURES: Small with a black and white plumage

SIMILAR SPECIES: Great Spotted Woodpecker

This small, sparrow-sized woodpecker shares the black and white plumage of the Great Spotted Woodpecker. The male has a crimson crown which is absent in the female. The drumming sound is weak and said to sound like it is drumming on split wood or cane.

Despite its attractive markings, the Lesser Spotted Woodpecker can be notoriously difficult to see. Numbers of this species have declined rapidly in recent years and it can be difficult to find. Look for it in deciduous woodland, orchards as well as riverside alders and willows. The nest site is also usually very inconspicuous and hard to find.

An insect-feeder, it will eat a wide range of larvae together with aphids. In common with other members of the family it excavates a nest chamber, often in birch or alder. It will lay up to eight white eggs.

NIGHTINGALE

SCIENTIFIC NAME: Luscinia megarhynchos

IDENTIFYING FEATURES: Warm brown colour;
reddish-tinged tail; distinctive song

SIMILAR SPECIES: Redstart, Robin

SIZE: 16 cm (6¼ in)

HABITAT: Woodland and scrub

POPULATION: Scarce

Eating and Nesting

The Nightingale is slowly recovering from a decline in its numbers but this has some way to go and it is common nowhere. It breeds in a variety of habitats from woodland and coppices to low scrub. It eats most invertebrates, including beetles and flies together with berries and other plant material.

It makes a bulky nest of grass and leaves lined with softer material, on or just above ground height. The eggs are bluish-green but heavily speckled and number four or five.

The rich, fluty song of the Nightingale is a well-known sound. In fact, one of the earliest recordings included the song of this bird. Its musical warbling tones are best listened for at dawn and dusk during the summer months. Contrary to its fabulous vocals, the Nightingale is a rather unremarkable-looking bird. A plumage of warm browns can make it very hard to spot; look for a flick of its distinctive chestnut red tail.

The Nightingale is most easily located by its song. It is extremely elusive, so a great deal of patience may be needed to actually see this bird. It is slightly larger than a Robin and has warm brown upperparts. Its rump and tail are reddish-brown. The underparts are paler with a brown tinge to the flanks and a whitish throat. It has a noticeable black eye. Sexes are similar but the juvenile birds are heavily speckled and very similar to juvenile Robins. The voice is a tremendous rich series of notes delivered from thick undergrowth. The song is often delivered at night but can be heard during the day.

Fascinating Facts

One of the reasons for the recent demise of the Nightingale is persecution by hunters in Europe who trap, on lime sticks, and kill large numbers of this species. They are a delicacy in some parts and are often pickled and eaten.

RIGHT
The Nightingale is perhaps the most famous song bird heard in Britain and Europe.

REDSTART

SIZE: 14 cm (5½ in)

HABITAT: Deciduous and mixed woodland

POPULATION: Scarce

SCIENTIFIC NAME: Phoenicurus phoenicurus

IDENTIFYING FEATURES: Black face and throat; orange-red underparts

SIMILAR SPECIES: Black Redstart

The Redstart is a bird of oak and mature mixed woodland, and is a summer migrant – one of the earliest returning summer visitors. The Robin-sized male is striking, with a mixture of red, black, grey and white plumage. The female is much duller but retains the reddish colouration of the tail. Redstarts sing from often exposed perches in woodland and choose to nest in holes in trees or occasionally nest boxes.

The male Redstart is unmistakeable. Its tail and rump are bright orange-red, as are the breast and flanks. It has a black face and throat and the upperparts are blue-grey. The female's upperparts are a grey-brown and she has a pale throat. The red tail is present but toned down slightly. Juveniles are heavily spotted but also have a reddish tail. Their song in spring is a loud, melodic warble ending with a mechanical sounding flourish. They also have a warbler-like two-syllable call. Redstarts are very active birds and spend a lot of time flitting and hovering between the branches.

Declining Species

The Redstart is another declining species. It favours oak and mixed woodland as well as mature parkland and upland areas with a scattering of trees. Its diet is largely insect-based, such as flies, beetles and ants. It also eats fruit from a variety of wild plants.

The Redstart nests in a tree hole or crevice. It will also take up residence in open-fronted nest boxes. The female constructs the nest using grass and moss. The incubation of the eggs is undertaken solely by the female birds. Generally there are between five and seven eggs of an unmarked pale blue.

BLACKCAP

SCIENTIFIC NAME: *Sylvia atricapilla*

IDENTIFYING FEATURES:
Noticeable black cap, brown in the female

SIMILAR SPECIES:
Garden Warbler, Marsh and Willow Tits

SIZE: 13 cm (5 in)

HABITAT: Woodland, parks and larger gardens

POPULATION: Common

The Blackcap is also a summer visitor; however, increasing numbers of this species have adapted to overwinter here. The black cap that gives it its name can only be seen in the male. The female has a reddish-brown cap. For such a small warbler, the Blackcap can be surprisingly dominant and aggressive. Often when feeding the male will puff out its breast feathers to make it appear larger, although this is also an added protection against colder temperatures.

Slightly smaller than a House Sparrow, the Blackcap is a common sight in our woodlands. The male is grey-brown above with paler underparts. The distinctive black cap is only to be found on the male, in the female it is chestnut brown. Besides the cap colouring it is a rather ordinary-looking warbler.

The juvenile is a duller version of the female. The song of the Blackcap is a pleasant melodic tune made up of rich, clear notes and generally ending with a flourish.

Food and Nests

It is common in our woodlands during the summer and many birds choose to overwinter here. During the winter they will often enter gardens in search of food. Summer food is made up of caterpillars, flies and beetles. During the winter, however, it will feed on fallen fruit, bread and other scraps from the bird table.

When breeding it is a very aggressive bird and will challenge rival males that enter its territory by puffing out its breast feathers and raising its cap. The male builds several nests. The female will choose a nest and then adapt it into a tidy, delicate cup-shaped nest. These can be found in dense vegetation such as brambles. It generally lays five eggs and they are creamy white with brown speckling.

GARDEN WARBLER

SCIENTIFIC NAME: Sylvia borin

IDENTIFYING FEATURES: Dull with no obvious features

SIMILAR SPECIES: Blackcap, Chiffchaff

SIZE: 14 cm (5½ in)

HABITAT: Woodland

POPULATION: Common

This warbler is rather nondescript and has no obvious outstanding features. It is vaguely reminiscent of the Blackcap but without the coloured crown. However, it does possess a glorious song and rates as one of the most musical song birds. The song is quite quiet and mellow with long phrases punctuated with short silent intervals. It often stays on late in the season, adapting its largely insectivorous diet to take in the autumn crop of berries and small fruits.

The Garden Warbler is a dumpy, plain brown warbler with a short and stout bill. The upperparts are largely brown with paler underparts. As the breeding season progresses the adults tend to become greyer. Sexes are alike and the juveniles are similar to the adult birds, appearing more olive when the plumage is fresh. The song can be heard from April and is a mixture of

RIGHT
Garden Warblers have a long, melodic song.

musical phrases that is remarkably similar to the Blackcap, although the deliverance of the Garden Warbler's song is more sustained, often lasting in excess of a minute.

Warbling Insectivore

Despite its name, the Garden Warbler is rarely found in gardens, unless these are large and mature. It breeds in deciduous and mixed woodland where there is thick undergrowth to give cover. It can occasionally be found in open country where there are copses or hedgerows. The Garden Warbler is insectivorous and will eat most invertebrates. They are also known to eat berries and other fruits.

The male, like many in this family, builds a number of rudimentary, unfinished nests. They allow a female to choose and then she completes the finishing touches. The cup-shaped nest is built low down in a bush or hedge and constructed using grass, leaves and small twigs. Clutch size is usually five eggs and these are off-white with darker blotches.

WOOD WARBLER

SCIENTIFIC NAME: Phylloscopus sibilatrix

IDENTIFYING FEATURES: Attractive leaf warbler with rich yellow colouring

SIMILAR SPECIES: Willow Warbler, Chiffchaff

SIZE: 12 cm (4¾ in)

HABITAT: Mature woodland

POPULATION: Scarce

In terms of breeding warblers in this region, the Wood Warbler is probably the most scarce. It is an attractive leaf warbler with vivid green upperparts and paler underparts, although this plumage weakens as the breeding season progresses. An unusual feature of this bird is that it possesses two entirely different songs. It is found feeding in tree canopies but unlike its close relatives it prefers to nest on the ground where it rears its single brood.

Wood Warblers are large, green leaf warblers that have a broad-shouldered appearance. They have short tails but are long winged. In fresh plumage they appear bright and clean. They have pale green upperparts with a distinctive yellowish eye stripe. The throat and breast are a bright yellow and the underparts are white. Sexes are alike. Their song is a rich warble that accelerates towards the end. They rarely sing twice from the same perch, preferring to move to another spot to begin their song again.

Oak Habitats

Wood Warblers have a preference for mature upland oak woods, but they can be found with regularity in beech and mixed woodland where they spend their days high in the canopies. Wood Warblers feed on caterpillars, crane flies and beetles. They also eat spiders but rarely take berries or fruit.

When breeding, males may defend territories but often nest in small clusters. The male will often attempt to attract a second mate. They nest on the ground, sometimes under fallen branches or trees. They lay between five and seven eggs and usually have one brood. The eggs are white with reddish speckles.

BELOW

Wood Warblers favour upland oak woods and spend much of their time in the treetops.

CHIFFCHAFF

SIZE: 11–12 cm (4¼–4¾ in)

HABITAT: Woodland, gardens and parks

POPULATION: Common summer visitor

SCIENTIFIC NAME: Phylloscopus collybita

IDENTIFYING FEATURES: Dull green upperparts; paler breast; dark legs

SIMILAR SPECIES: Willow Warbler, Wood Warbler

Like the Blackcap, the Chiffchaff often overwinters in our region, although it is essentially a summer migrant. It is very similar to the Willow Warbler in appearance, but is generally not as brightly coloured and has darker legs. It arrives early and its familiar two-syllable call, from where it gets its name, can often be heard from March onwards. It can often be found feeding on the ground, particularly during spring and autumn passage and will repeatedly flick both its tail and wings.

The Chiffchaff is a familiar bird of our woodlands. Its upperparts are generally dull green or brownish with a contrasting pale rump. It also has a pale eye stripe. The underparts are a dull yellow. It is similar to the Willow Warbler, although it is a duller bird with dark legs, whereas the Willow Warbler's legs are pale. The species are, however, best separated by their songs. The song of the Chiffchaff is like its name, and this phrase is usually repeated three times.

An Early Nester

Chiffchaffs can be found in deciduous and mixed woodland, parks and some gardens. They are largely absent from coniferous woods. They feed mainly on insects, including midges and flies, but will occasionally take berries and seeds (although this is unusual).

The Chiffchaff is an early nester, from late April. The female builds a dome-shaped nest, low down in the undergrowth. Four to six eggs are typical – white with faint darker markings.

WILLOW WARBLER

SCIENTIFIC NAME: Phylloscopus trochilus

IDENTIFYING FEATURES: Greenish-brown upperparts; yellowish underparts

SIMILAR SPECIES: Chiffchaff, Wood Warbler

SIZE: 11–12 cm (4¼–4¾ in)

HABITAT: Woodland and parks

POPULATION: Common summer visitor

The Willow Warbler is a close relative of the Chiffchaff and is a common summer visitor. They have a pleasant, tuneful descending song. They are very similar to Chiffchaffs but generally much cleaner in appearance and with flesh-coloured legs. However, there are many variations in both species and often the voice can be the only determinable feature. It feeds actively on insects and can often hover or dart out from a favourite perch, not unlike a flycatcher.

The Willow Warbler is a small, slim leaf warbler. It has green-brown upperparts but is noticeably pale yellow underneath. As the summer progresses this yellow will fade. It has pale legs and a dark line through the eye with a pale yellow stripe above. These are features to

ABOVE
Willow Warblers have adapted to a range of habitats, including woodland and even urban areas.

help distinguish the Willow Warbler from the Chiffchaff. Willow Warblers are also noticeably longer winged.

Their song is a liquid series of notes ending with a pronounced flourish.

Variety of Habitats

Willow Warblers can be found in a variety of habitats, including deciduous and mixed woodland. They are also found in open country, especially where there are hedgerows. They are becoming increasingly urban and can be found in large gardens. Their diet is a range of insects including flies, caterpillars and beetles. They

will also eat berries and similar fruits, particularly in the autumn.

Some male Willow Warblers are polygamous. They normally have one brood per year but the polygamous males will often raise a second brood with a different female. The Willow Warbler usually nests on the ground in a delicate domed nest, with an entrance at the side. The nest is constructed from grasses and moss. There are between four and eight eggs and these are white with reddish-brown speckles.

GOLDCREST

SIZE: 9 cm (3½ in)

HABITAT: Coniferous woodland, large gardens

POPULATION: Common

SCIENTIFIC NAME: Regulus regulus

IDENTIFYING FEATURES: Active bird with yellow or orange crown stripe

SIMILAR SPECIES: Firecrest

The Goldcrest, along with the Firecrest, is our smallest bird, measuring in the region of 9 cm (3½ in). It is a tiny but very active bird with a striking orange or yellow crest which it raises when agitated. In can be found in all types of woodland, although it prefers to nest in conifers. It creates a cup nest usually suspended from a branch. Goldcrests can often be seen during the winter months in the company of other birds, such as tits, in large mixed flocks.

This minute bird is rather round-looking with short wings. The upperparts are a dull green in colour while the underparts are pale off-white. The male has a distinctive orange crown patch, which is more yellow in the female (from where it gets it name). The crown patch, or crest, is used in display to attract a potential mate and ward off any intruders. There are also two faint white wing bars. The juvenile is similar to the adult birds but without the crown patch. Both song and call are a high-pitched series of notes.

Diverse Habitats

The Goldcrest can be found in a range of different habitats. Woodland, scrub, gardens, parks and churchyards all attract this species. It feeds almost exclusively on insects, such as flies and caterpillars, and spiders. Occasionally it will also take small seeds.

When it comes to the breeding season the Goldcrest will favour coniferous woodland and plantations. The nest is an ornate cup of mosses, lichens and spiders' webs. The nest is suspended from each end and it is built towards the end of a branch. The Goldcrest will lay up to eight eggs, which are white with faint spotting.

BELOW

Goldcrests rarely descend from their camouflage of conifer trees and can thus be hard to see.

FIRECREST

SCIENTIFIC NAME: Regulus ignicapillus

IDENTIFYING FEATURES:
Orange and red crown stripe; dark eye stripe

SIMILAR SPECIES: Goldcrest

SIZE: 9 cm (3½ in)

HABITAT: Deciduous and
coniferous woodland

POPULATION: Rare

The Firecrest is quite similar to the Goldcrest. Although it breeds in Britain and Europe, it does not do so in great numbers. However, it is quite likely – especially given its diminutive size – to be overlooked, and may be more common than we think. The crown of the male Firecrest has a deep orange central stripe, from where it gets its name. Probably the best chance of seeing this species is on the coast during passage migration in the autumn months.

The Firecrest is fractionally larger than the Goldcrest at a little over 9 cm (3½ in), but the two can easily be confused. Generally it is a brighter bird with greener upperparts. The underparts are cleaner and whiter than that of the Goldcrest. There is an obvious dark stripe through the eye with a white eye stripe above it. The crown is a striking orange red in the male while the female has a yellow crest. The juvenile is very similar to a young Goldcrest but the white eye stripe is noticeable, which is lacking in juvenile Goldcrests. Their song is lower-pitched than the Goldcrest and slightly louder and faster.

LEFT
The Firecrest can be distinguished from the Goldcrest by the dark stripe through the eye.

Habitat Preference

Firecrests are insectivorous birds that feed on a range of invertebrates including aphids and caterpillars. It will also take small snails. This species is less dependant upon conifer trees than the Goldcrest, although these are still a preference, particularly Norway Spruce. Mixed woodland will also attract Firecrests, although they are a rare breeder. You are more likely to see Firecrests during migration, when they can be found in a range of habitats, predominately coastal.

Outside the breeding season Firecrests can be found in mixed flocks of other species including tits. These flocks should always scrutinized be for this little gem of a bird. The nest is a suspended dome made from mosses, lichens and spiders' webs. The female lays between seven and 10 eggs, which are a pinkish-white with faint blotched markings.

SPOTTED FLYCATCHER

SIZE: 14–15 cm (5½–5⅞ in)

HABITAT: Woodland, parks and gardens

POPULATION: Common

SCIENTIFIC NAME: Muscicapa striata

IDENTIFYING FEATURES: Grey-brown with streaking on a paler breast

SIMILAR SPECIES: Dunnock, Tree Pipit

The Spotted Flycatcher is the most common member of this family. It has creamy pale underparts with darker brown upperparts. It is heavily reliant on insect prey and often arrives late when there is an abundance of its food. It usually adopts a favourite perch and darts out repeatedly to catch prey. Spotted Flycatchers do not feed entirely on insects and the female will often take woodlice and snails. It is thought that this is to ingest calcium to strengthen eggs.

This is a plain, but rather nicely patterned flycatcher. The upperparts are grey-brown in colour while the underparts are off-white with noticeable streaking. The wings have pale edges to the feathers. Both the wings and tail are quite long and the bill is dark and broad at the base.

LEFT

An adult Spotted Flycatcher perched on a branch with nest material.

Sexes are alike and the juvenile is a mottled, blotched version of the adult. The call is said to resemble a squeaky handcart, while the song is a quite melodic but high-pitched scratchy warble.

Feeding and Migratory Habits

Spotted Flycatchers have declined in recent years but can still be found in deciduous and mixed woodland. They are also found in mature gardens, parkland and particularly churchyards. As its name implies, this species hunts flying insects, usually from a prominent post or perch. It will dart out, catch its prey and often return to the same perch to start again. During less clement weather it will search among leaves to find aphids and caterpillars. Cold, damp weather in May and June will curtail its feeding activities and it may well abandon breeding for that season.

Most Spotted Flycatchers arrive in May to breed, which makes it one of the last migrants to arrive. It is a long-distance migrant and starts its return journey as early as July, unless it is double brooded in a particular season. It is also a nocturnal migrant, choosing to fly only at night.

It nests on ledges or open-fronted nest boxes. Very often it will nest using ivy as a cover. The nest is a cup nest, loosely assembled using twigs and grasses. The eggs are white with pale red blotches and usually number between four and five.

PIED FLYCATCHER

SCIENTIFIC NAME: Ficedula hypoleuca

IDENTIFYING FEATURES: Adult male is a distinctive black and white; female is brown

SIMILAR SPECIES: Pied Wagtails

SIZE: 13 cm (5 in)

HABITAT: Woodland

POPULATION: Scarce summer visitor

The Pied Flycatcher, as the name suggests, is a black and white bird. It is also a summer visitor and flying insects form a large part of its diet. The male is often bigamous and may have a second female. This second nest may be a considerable distance from that of its original partner. They do not have the same aerial predation techniques as the Spotted Flycatcher and often collect their food from leaves, branches and tree bark.

The Pied Flycatcher is slightly smaller and dumpier than the Spotted Flycatcher. The upperparts are a dullish black with a distinctive white wing patch. The underparts are white and it has a small white mark above the bill. In the female the black is replaced with brown and the underparts are pale washed with brown. After breeding the male quickly moults and takes on a similar appearance to the female but the white in the wing is usually more obvious. Juveniles resemble the female but have a scaly, mottled appearance.

Woodland Specialist

Pied Flycatchers are scarce, although in certain parts of the country they can be fairly numerous. They are an oak and birch wood specialist. They are particularly fond of upland areas but can also be found in mature parkland. Not quite as aerial as the Spotted Flycatcher, they still feed on airborne insects. They will also readily eat spiders, woodlice and other invertebrates.

Males often have two, or occasionally more, females and will often have nests several kilometres apart simultaneously. Migrating males always arrive back before the female and start to seek out suitable territories.

The Pied Flycatcher is a hole-nester, often utilizing a vacant woodpecker nest. It makes a loose nest in the chamber using grass and moss. Here they will lay up to nine eggs of an unmarked pale blue.

Fascinating Facts

The Fork-tailed Flycatcher holds the world record for having the longest tail feathers in relation to its body size – 27 cm (10⅝ in).

LONG-TAILED TIT

SCIENTIFIC NAME: Aegithalos caudatus

IDENTIFYING FEATURES: Extremely long tail; attractive black, white and pink plumage

SIMILAR SPECIES: Pied Wagtail

SIZE: 14 cm (5½ in)

HABITAT: Woodland

POPULATION: Common

Over two-thirds of this bird's body length is its tail. Despite its name and similar appearance the Long-tailed Tit is not actually a member of the tit family. It belongs to the babblers, a group not often encountered in our region. It is quite unmistakeable, with its extremely long tail and distinctive plumage. Often during the winter large flocks of Long-tailed Tits can be seen, sometimes 20 or 30 in number.

The Long-tailed Tit is a small and dumpy bird with a remarkably long tail. It is a pinkish brown above and paler below, with a pinkish tinge. The head is largely white but with distinct black lines above the eyes. There are pink and white patched on an otherwise dark wing. Sexes are similar. Their song is rarely heard but is an extension of its high-pitched calls. The birds can be found along deciduous woodland edges and also in parkland and gardens.

It feeds on flies, beetles, caterpillars and a range of other invertebrates. Its nest is an elaborate oval construction made with moss and leaves, then bound with spiders' webs. Eggs will number between eight and 12 and are white, spotted red.

CRESTED TIT

SCIENTIFIC NAME: Parus cristatus

IDENTIFYING FEATURES: Brindled face pattern; distinctive black and white crest

SIMILAR SPECIES: Blue Tit

SIZE: 11–12 cm (4¼–4¾ in)

HABITAT: Ancient coniferous woodland

POPULATION: Rare

Crested Tits are restricted to established Caledonian pine woods; resident in reasonable numbers but not common and often difficult to locate. The black and white crest, which gives the Crested Tit its name, is an obvious identification feature. Aside from the crest and its attractive face pattern, it is a rather dull little bird. It is sedentary, meaning that it does not migrate or wander, and can be looked for at any time of the year.

This Highland specialist is brown above with paler buff underparts. It has a pale head with black streaking on the face and crown, which extends to a long crest. The Crested Tit feeds on caterpillars, aphids and other insects. The nest is in a hole that is self-excavated, often in a rotting stump. They lay five to seven eggs, which are white with pale red blotches.

COAL TIT

SCIENTIFIC NAME: Parus ater

IDENTIFYING FEATURES: Black head with white cheek patches and nape

SIMILAR SPECIES: Great Tit, Crested Tit

SIZE: 11–12 cm (4¼–4¾ in)

HABITAT: Woodland, often coniferous

POPULATION: Common

ABOVE
Coal Tits can be separated from others of the family by the distinctive white nape.

Although the Coal Tit can be seen in deciduous woodland, its home is really coniferous woodlands and pine plantations. It is a rather dumpy and short-tailed tit but extremely agile and acrobatic when feeding. The males and females of the species are identical but juvenile birds can usually be identified by their more yellow plumage. Coal Tits have a distinctive single-syllable call that often gives its presence away in thick, dark pine woodland.

The Coal Tit is smaller than the Great Tit, with similar black head markings and white cheeks. It lacks any yellow plumage and is a dull bluish-grey above with paler buff underparts. The characteristic white nape is distinctive. They can be found breeding in coniferous woodland but at other times of the year can be encountered elsewhere, including gardens. They feed mainly on insect larvae but during the winter will eat seeds and peanuts from bird-table feeders.

Another hole-nester, Coal Tits tend to nest low to the ground. They lay between seven and 10 red-spotted white eggs.

WILLOW TIT

SCIENTIFIC NAME: Parus montanus

IDENTIFYING FEATURES: Dull black cap with large black bib

SIMILAR SPECIES: Marsh Tit

SIZE: 11–12 cm (4¼–4¾ in)

HABITAT: Woodland and gardens

POPULATION: Scarce

The Willow Tit can be difficult to distinguish from the Marsh Tit, although it is more tolerant of different habitats and can be found in coniferous woodland, parkland and gardens. It is thought to be more common than the Marsh Tit and perhaps this is down to its habitat adaptability. It is slightly thicker set than the Marsh Tit, with a duller crown and larger bib.

The overall appearance of the Willow Tit is almost identical to a Marsh Tit. A couple of identifying features are a duller cap with a pale patch in the wing. The call is a distinctive, nasal 'eez, eez, eez', which is nothing like the call of the Marsh Tit. It is a little less conservative in its choice of habitats and can be found in most woodland, coniferous or deciduous, as well as gardens and parkland. It is another insect-eater and has a bill less strong than the Marsh Tit, so is unable to enjoy the same varied diet. It nests close to the ground in a cavity, often in a rotten tree stump. Eggs number six to ten and are white with reddish spots.

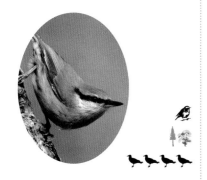

NUTHATCH

SIZE: 14 cm (5½ in)

HABITAT: Woodland

POPULATION: Common

SCIENTIFIC NAME: Sitta europa

IDENTIFYING FEATURES: Blue-grey above with pinkish underparts

SIMILAR SPECIES: Blue Tit, Great Tit

Upperparts are blue-grey while it has paler underparts. The lower flanks are a rich chestnut colour. Sexes are similar and the juveniles resemble the adult birds but with less chestnut colouration on the flanks. Their call is a loud 'tewit, tewit, tewit, tewit', which increases in intensity when alarmed.

Habitat, Nests and Eggs

Nuthatches can be found in deciduous woodland, parkland and large, mature gardens. They are rarely seen in coniferous woodland but will venture into mixed woodland to feed on fir cones during the second half of the year.

Despite its name, during the spring, the Nuthatch feeds on a range of invertebrates including beetles and spiders. During the autumn and winter months it will feed on the nuts and fruits of acorns, hazel, beech mast and similar. It is a hole-nester, but adopts old nests rather than excavating its own. Occasionally it will use a nest box. The females lay on average six to 10 eggs which are white with pale red markings.

Nuthatches are dumpy, rather solid-looking little woodland birds. They possess long thick bills to enable them to break open acorns and beech mast. They are hole-nesters but do not excavate their own; they use a ready-made site and then proceed to plaster the rim of the entrance hole with mud. This is done to prevent larger predators entering the nest cavity. Its black eye stripe is a distinctive feature when seen at close quarters.

The Nuthatch is a fairly common woodland bird, roughly the size of a Great Tit but resembling a diminutive woodpecker. The bill is dark and dagger-like, and there is a distinctive black stripe through the eye.

MARSH TIT

SCIENTIFIC NAME: Parus palustris

IDENTIFYING FEATURES:
Black cap and small black bib

SIMILAR SPECIES: Willow Tit

SIZE: 11–12 cm (4¼–4¾ in)

HABITAT: Deciduous woodland

POPULATION: Scarce

The Marsh Tit is not a rare bird but neither is it a common one. It can be incredibly difficult to separate from the closely related Willow Tit. In fact they were, until 100 years ago or so, thought to be the same species. It is unusual to find the Marsh Tit away from its woodland habitat, although in severe winters it may be encountered in gardens. The Marsh Tit has a strong bill and will often hammer seeds to obtain the fruit within.

The Marsh Tit, like the Willow Tit, has been sadly declining in numbers over the last two or three decades. Marsh Tits are a similar size to the Blue Tit, but have a distinctive black cap and bib with pale cheeks, plain brown wings and buff underparts. There are several clues to distinguish it from the very similar Willow Tit. Generally the Marsh Tit has a glossier cap, which does not extend as down the back of the neck as it does with the Willow Tit. However, it is best separated from this species by its call. Its main call is a two-syllable 'pit-u', which is quite unlike that of the Willow Tit.

Winter Gardener

Its habitat is generally open deciduous woodland but will also visit gardens, particularly during the winter months. It is largely insectivorous but will also eat seeds and some berries. Although the bill is quite small it is also capable of breaking open nuts. The nest is a hole, low down, which it usually lines with moss and other materials. It rarely uses nest boxes. The female lays anywhere between six and 10 eggs, which are white with red markings.

TREECREEPER

SIZE: 12–13 cm (4¾–5 in)

HABITAT: Woodland

POPULATION: Common

SCIENTIFIC NAME: Certhia familiaris

IDENTIFYING FEATURES:
Mouse-like with obvious curved bill

SIMILAR SPECIES: None

Treecreeper are so high-pitched it can be difficult for humans to hear.

Broods

The Treecreeper makes its home in deciduous and coniferous woodland. It can also be found in copses, parks and gardens. In the winter it may also be seen in open country where there are mature hedgerows. It will eat insects of most kinds and during the autumn and winter will also eat small seeds, particularly those from pines and spruce.

The Treecreeper is generally single-brooded, however, research has shown that pairs nesting in coniferous woodland often raise a second brood. They nest in a cavity, usually behind ivy; the nest is lined with small twigs and plant material before being finished with moss and spiders' webs. They lay between four and eight red-spotted eggs.

The Treecreeper is a small and delicate mouse-like bird with a thin down-curved bill. It uses this bill to probe tree bark for insects and aphids. It can often be watched as it spirals and winds up the length of a tree. It very rarely climbs downwards, preferring to leave the tree and start at the base of another nearby. It nests in cracks in trees or behind pieces of loose bark.

The Treecreeper's upperparts are barred brown with paler streaks. It has a noticeable pale stripe above the eye. Underparts are white and it has a brown rump. The tail feathers are long and pointed. In flight the pale wing bar is often noticeable. Sexes are similar and the juvenile is difficult to distinguish from the adult birds. Its voice is a high-pitched two-syllable call, and its song is a high-pitched warble. In fact, the songs and call of the

RIGHT

Note the pale stripe above the eye in the Treecreeper.

JAY

SCIENTIFIC NAME: Garrulus glandarius

IDENTIFYING FEATURES:
Pinkish brown with blue, black and white wings

SIMILAR SPECIES: None

SIZE: 34 cm (13⅓ in)

HABITAT: Woodland

POPULATION: Common

The Jay is an attractive member of the crow family, or corvids. It is well marked with salmon-pink colouration, iridescent blue feathering in the wing and a distinctive crest. Despite its handsome appearance the Jay can be incredibly wary and secretive. Listen for its unusual cat-like call. Jays can be encountered with more regularity in autumn as they forage for acorns, one of their staple foods. They will often collect these in large numbers and stash them away by burying them, retrieving them during the winter.

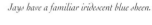

LEFT
Jays have a familiar iridescent blue sheen.

Habitat

They favour deciduous woodland, particularly oak. They can be incredibly secretive during the breeding season and are often heard rather than seen. During the autumn months they become more obvious as they forage for acorns. The Jay adores these nuts, although they will also take beech mast and other fruits. Like other members of the crow family they will also take eggs and nestlings of other birds.

Jays are very colourful members of the crow family, roughly the size of a Jackdaw. They are largely pinkish-brown with the underparts being slightly paler. The head has a black and white marked crown or crest. They have a black moustachial streak and a whitish throat. The white rump contrasts starkly with the black tail. The iris of the eye is a pale blue while the bill is black and the legs are pale pink-brown. The wings are mostly dark with white patches but also have striking iridescent blue patches.

The nest of twigs is built by both birds in a tree or shrub. Jay eggs are a pale blue-green or olive with darker blotches. A typical clutch size is between four and five.

JACKDAW

SIZE: 33 cm (13 in)

HABITAT: Woodland; occasionally urban areas

POPULATION: Common

SCIENTIFIC NAME: Corvus monedula

IDENTIFYING FEATURES:
Black but with silvery sheen to the nape

SIMILAR SPECIES: Carrion Crow, Rook

LEFT

Once a Jackdaw finds a mate, they will often stay together for a number of seasons.

Jackdaws are members of the crow family and have the uniform black plumage associated with these birds. When seen at close quarters the beady pale eye is one of their most distinguishing features. They are quite long legged and walk with a peculiar gait. They are noisy birds and can often be quite aggressive. They nest, often in large groups, in old trees. However, they are becoming increasingly urban and can be found in towns and villages where they nest on buildings, often using old chimney pots.

The Jackdaw is a small crow that appears all black from a distance; up close, however, they have a grey neck and pale eyes. Most of the plumage is black or a silvery greyish black except for the cheeks, nape and neck. These are light grey to silver. The iris of adults is greyish white and is quite noticeable at close range. The sexes are similar but juvenile birds show a pale blue iris rather than grey. The call is a harsh 'tchak, tchak'.

Sociable Breeders

They are found in both coniferous and decidous woodland, as well as open country, towns, villages and more urban areas. The bird is a sociable breeder, nesting in often large colonies. Pairs of Jackdaws will often stay together for several years. They usually nest in colonies in cavities of trees, cliffs or ruined and sometimes inhabited buildings, usually in chimneys, and sometimes in dense conifers. The eggs usually number four to five and are a pale blue-green in colour.

Jackdaws are largely ground-feeders, where they eat insects and other invertebrates. They will also eat seeds and grain and when in an urban environment, will eat scraps.

BRAMBLING

SCIENTIFIC NAME: Fringilla montifringilla

IDENTIFYING FEATURES: Distinctive orange and black plumage, more subtle in winter

SIMILAR SPECIES: Chaffinch

SIZE: 14–15 cm (5½–5⅞ in)

HABITAT: Woodland, particularly beech

POPULATION: Common winter visitor

The Brambling is a winter visiting finch. It is regular in number and in certain years Bramblings can be prolific. Very occasionally odd pairs will linger after the winter and breed, although this is unusual. Males in breeding plumage are a striking sight, but in winter the plumage is a little drabber. Beech mast is a particular favourite food of this bird and you will often find the Brambling in the company of other finches. Any large finch flock that you encounter during winter will be worth scrutinizing for this handsome bird.

The Brambling is similar in size and shape to a Chaffinch, but has a paler rump and lacks the white outer tail feathers. It has a dark back, orange breast and whitish belly. The large double wing bars are orange or white.

The breeding male is unmistakeable, with his orange underparts and black head and back, although in winter, when it is most likely to be encountered, it is a lot paler.

Winter Visitor

The Brambling is predominately a winter visitor, very often in large groups, although several pairs do breed in the far north most years, but never in any great numbers. Coniferous or mixed birch woodland is favoured for breeding. It usually builds its nest in a tree fork, and decorates the exterior with moss and lichens to give it a degree of camouflage. The nest is similar to that of a Chaffinch but more untidy. Bramblings will lay between four and eight eggs.

The Brambling is a seed-eater and has a particular preference for beech mast. In good years beech woodlands can hold hundreds of this species. They will also eat other seeds and fruits, although young birds are fed exclusively on insects.

COMMON CROSSBILL

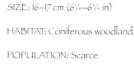

SIZE: 16–17 cm (6¼–6¾ in)

HABITAT: Coniferous woodland

POPULATION: Scarce

SCIENTIFIC NAME: Loxia curvirostra

IDENTIFYING FEATURES: Brick-red plumage in males; subtle green in females

SIMILAR SPECIES: Scottish Crossbill

periods high in the canopy. They come to drink at woodland puddles frequently and can often be encountered there. They are incredibly similar to other members of the family and are often best separated by their call, which is a metallic 'chip, chip, chip'.

Pine Habitat

Crossbills are very early breeders, often as early as January. This ensures that the young are raised at an optimum time for availability of the pine-cone crop. They feed on a variety of pine seeds. As a result, Crossbills can be found in areas containing large stands of pine. They can be fairly numerous in these areas and have their numbers increased during the winter with large numbers of migrants. Some years are so-called irruption years, when many thousands of birds will be present. They nest in conifer woods and plantations, laying four eggs of an off-white colour with bold spots.

The Common Crossbill has evolved in a quite remarkable way. Over time the upper and lower mandibles of the bill have twisted and crossed at the tip. This crossing can be either right to left or left to right. Although it may appear a little odd-looking this bill is an effective tool for extracting seeds from cones produced by various species of pine tree. The males are red in colour but the females have green colouration. In winter the numbers of Crossbills are swelled by migrants.

Male Crossbills tend to be brick-red or orange in colour, and females greenish-brown or yellow, but there is much variation. The bizarre crossed mandibles of the bill are enough to tell this species from other members of the finch family. They are pine-feeders and often spend long

FAR LEFT
The Common Crossbill is unmistakeable because of its curious bill shape.

SCOTTISH CROSSBILL

SCIENTIFIC NAME: Loxia scotia

IDENTIFYING FEATURES:
Virtually identical to Common Crossbill

SIMILAR SPECIES: Common Crossbill

SIZE: 16–17 cm (6¼–6¾ in)

HABITAT: Coniferous woodland

POPULATION: Rare

The Scottish Crossbill is restricted solely to the Caledonian pine forests of northern Scotland. It is pretty much identical to the Common Crossbill and thus incredibly difficult to distinguish. Scottish Crossbills were only established as a species in their own right a few years ago, and there is an ongoing debate regarding their status, with some ornithologists claiming that the Scottish Crossbill is a subspecies of the rarer Parrot Crossbill.

This bird is very closely related to both the Common Crossbill and the Parrot Crossbill. Its size is roughly intermediate between these two species. It is Britain's only endemic species and is restricted solely to the ancient Caledonian pine forests in northern Scotland. As with the Common Crossbill, males are orange-red while the females are a brown-green colour. It is also a pine-feeder although it is thought to have adapted its bill slightly from the Common Crossbill as it feeds largely on Scots Pine. It nests in pines and lays two to five eggs, which are off-white and blotched.

Fascinating Facts

The Scottish Crossbill is the only bird endemic to the British Isles – that is, all other birds found there can also be found in other countries.

HAWFINCH

SCIENTIFIC NAME: Coccothraustes coccothraustes

IDENTIFYING FEATURES:
Short tail; black eye stripe and bib

SIMILAR SPECIES: None

SIZE: 18 cm (7 in)

HABITAT: Deciduous and mixed woodland

POPULATION: Rare

The Hawfinch is a large bulky bird and our largest finch. The large thick bill and bull neck of the Hawfinch, combined with a short tail, makes for a distinctive silhouette in flight. It is not a common finch and despite its huge size this bird can be incredibly elusive.

Its head is an orange-brown colour and it has a noticeable black eye stripe and bib. Its bill is very large and is black in summer but paler in the winter months. The upperparts are a dark brown and the underparts are an orange colour. The white wing bars and tail tip are striking in flight. The call is a hard 'chikk'. The song is quiet and rarely heard.

Deciduous or mixed woodland with large trees, especially hornbeam, is favoured for breeding although they can be found in a variety of woodland habitats during the winter months. The fruit from the Hornbeam is the Hawfinch's staple food but it will eat a variety of other seeds and fruit, splitting the kernel with its powerful bill.

LEFT
Hawfinches are rarely heard or seen.

Open Country

'Open country' is a blanket term for a number of British habitats, each with its own set of birds. It includes the broad spectrum of different farming habitats, plus rough grassland, heath, moorland and scrub. In such places are some of our most familiar birds, such as the Skylark, the Pheasant, the Carrion Crow and the Swallow.

On the whole, open country, by definition, suggests a lack of trees, and this has several implications for the bird community. Many species live primarily on the ground, or among deep cover, and this means that, when the time comes to attract a mate, they have to be very obvious or very noisy – or both. Thus the Skylark leaves the ground to make itself heard and seen on its marvellous song-flight, while the Common Whitethroat leaves the brambles to do the same, although on a more modest scale. Other spectacular visible courtship displays are made by the Montagu's Harrier, the Lapwing and both the

Meadow and the Tree Pipit, while such birds as Quail, Red-legged Partridge, Corncrake and Nightjar make astonishing and far-carrying sounds, often at night.

Interestingly, birds of open areas usually have higher-pitched songs than woodland birds. High-pitched sound quickly dissipates in leaves, so the birds sing lower pitches to compensate. Thus the Skylark or the Meadow Pipit might have difficulty making themselves heard in more enclosed habitats.

Most of the birds of this section will be found on farmland, but some are more specialized. The Dartford Warbler, Woodlark, Great Grey Shrike and Nightjar, for example, are typical birds of lowland heath, while the Corncrake requires damp meadows and the Grasshopper Warbler low scrub. Naturally, there are plenty of birds that also intrude into other habitats, such as crows and Magpies into towns, but they are at heart open country birds, and are treated as such here.

Red-legged Partridge

Scientific name: Alectoris rufa

Identifying features: Short tail; red legs; white throat, black necklace; black on flank stripes

Similar species: Grey Partridge, female Common Pheasant

SIZE: 32–34 cm (12⅝–13⅜ in)

HABITAT: Open country and farmland

POPULATION: Common

Introduced into Britain in the eighteenth century from the Continent, the Red-legged Partridge has found this country thoroughly to its liking ever since, recently leaving the native Grey Partridge far behind in terms of population. It is less slavishly a ground bird than the Grey Partridge, and sometimes surprises observers by sitting on roofs, gateposts and haystacks. It is even possible to imagine that it once perched in the branches of a pear tree, giving rise to the famous Christmas song.

If you should ever hear what seems to be the puffing sound of a steam-engine in the middle of a field at sunset, the chances are you will actually be listening to the territorial call of a Red-legged Partridge. This extraordinary performance is delivered by the male to proclaim rights to a patch of land. If an intruder threatens, the territory-holder will stand upright, puff out its white throat, raise its colourful flank feathers and, in a state of high dudgeon, make frenetic half-circles around its visitor. Look harder, and you can almost imagine steam coming out of its head.

Flocks and Breeding

This non-native Partridge is a common bird of slightly more open, less grassy habitats than the Grey Partridge, but is still a regular sight flying off on rapid wing-beats across open fields. In common with most game birds, it is sociable outside the breeding season, sometimes gathering into flocks of 50 or more. These flocks forage mainly on seeds, roots and leaves, which they unearth from bare ground using the bill, rather than the feet as in most of their relatives.

The Red-legged Partridge shows an unusual breeding quirk. Although many pairs bring up young together, a female will sometimes lay two clutches of eggs, one for herself to incubate, and the other for her mate. Each adult is then responsible for the welfare of their resulting chicks, although the two halves of the family may meet up again in midsummer.

LEFT

The Red-legged Partridge originated in mainland Europe and was introduced to Britain.

Grey Partridge

Scientific name: Perdix perdix

SIZE: 29–31 cm (11½–12¼ in)

HABITAT: Farmland, grassland, hedgerows

POPULATION: Scarce and declining

Identifying features: Ground-dwelling bird with short tail; heart-shaped mark on breast

Similar species: Red-legged Partridge, female Common Pheasant

---

Few birds leave the ground as seldom as the Grey Partridge. Apart from the occasional escape flight to avoid predators, and despite being able to fly powerfully when necessary, Grey Partridges much prefer to walk or run everywhere, and their whole lives may be lived within the confines of a few fields. At night they roost out in the open, small groups of birds gathering into a circle, each individual facing outwards so that communal vigilance is maintained in all directions.

Although Grey Partridges are usually seen well away from cover, hedgerows and other thick vegetation play an important part in their lives. The nest is hidden among long grass or under a hedge. The clutch is relatively enormous, frequently containing 10 to 20 eggs, with a record of 29. This is one of the highest clutch numbers of any bird in the world. Not surprisingly, Grey Partridge nests make a bounteous meal for a predator such as a Red Fox *Vulpes vulpes*, so the female sits tight and the youngsters do not hang around for long once hatched. In contrast to their parents, the chicks have a diet of 90 per cent insects, while adults are almost wholly vegetarian.

LEFT

The population of Grey Partridges is declining due to their focus for hunters.

Family Unit

The social unit of the Grey Partridge is the 'covey'. This tends to consist of a single pair and their surviving youngsters, but non-breeding birds sometimes attach themselves, and sometimes two families get together. Whatever the makeup, it is a temporary winter measure, and by the end of February the covey splits up and everyone goes their own way. Pairs form when wandering males visit a female's home range and display at her. The male stands up straight, showing off its impressive heart-shaped mark on the breast. Meanwhile, the female seems most interested in her potential mate's brown flank-stripes, sometimes passing her bill over them, but not quite touching.

Quail

Scientific name: Coturnix coturnix

Identifying features: Explosive wing-beats;
stubby tail; if seen well, face markings distinctive

Similar species: Young Partridge or Pheasant;
Skylark, Corn Bunting

SIZE: 16–18 cm (6¼–7 in)

HABITAT: Grassland, downland
and agricultural fields

POPULATION: Scarce
summer visitor

There is something mysterious about the Quail. When encountered, it is usually nothing but a disembodied voice calling softly from the depths of a barley or pea field, usually after dark on a night in high summer. The 'wet-me-lips' phrase carries some distance, but the direction is easily lost in the slightest breeze, and the call has ventriloquist qualities. Equally mysterious are the Quail's migratory habits, which are still being worked out, and the complicated breeding arrangements, which have only come to light in recent years.

The Quail is a summer visitor, usually arriving in April or May, but for many years unexplained mass arrivals have also occurred in late summer (July). It is now known that these are birds that have already bred once in the year, probably in North Africa, and have arrived in the north to breed again, along with their first-generation youngsters. This is a situation almost unknown in birds, but frequent in butterflies. The birds themselves migrate at night, usually low to the ground or sea, and they always travel together, often in large numbers. Huge arrivals often appear from nowhere, as recorded long ago in Biblical times.

Breeding Centres

The birds settle in agricultural fields, where they feed on small seeds and, in quantities unusual for a game bird, insects. As soon as they arrive, birds in the same locality form 'breeding centres', to which both males and females are attracted but nobody holds territory. Suitable partners pair up, and then the female lays up to 13 eggs in a small scrape in the ground. These hatch extremely quickly, in some cases after only 11 days, one of the shortest periods of any European bird. More remarkably, however, the young become sexually mature after only 12–15 weeks, potentially allowing them to breed in the very year in which they hatched.

Pheasant

SIZE: 53–89 cm (21–35 in) of which tail up to 47 cm (18½ in)

HABITAT: Mainly farmland and woodland edge; edges of marshes

POPULATION: Common

Scientific name: Phasianus colchicus

Identifying features: Male unmistakeable; sometimes has white ring round neck; female has longer tail than other game birds

Similar species: Partridge, Red and Black Grouse

The true home of the Pheasant is East Asia, but it has managed to settle with great ease into the foreign fields of both Europe and North America. True, its populations are maintained by annual releases for hunting purposes, but it is likely that, even without this somewhat dubious help, it would still be a common, albeit incongruous, feature of the landscape. It is really so familiar, indeed, that it is easy to overlook the male's quite astonishingly colourful, spangled plumage, topped by its superb, elegant long tail.

Not that the female is particularly interested in the complexities of the plumage. What marks the best males out for her is the extent of the red wattles on the male's face, which inflate slightly when the bird is excited. The male will show its intent, too, with some delightful, courteous displays, one of which involves circling the female and spreading its slightly open wings on the ground in front of her.

A Territorial Bird

Male Pheasants are highly territorial, and seldom aim to attract just one female to their patch of ground; instead, they work hard to acquire a small harem which, very occasionally, may number 10 or more females, but usually two or three.

These females lay eight or more eggs each, in what can be a very productive season for a successful male. On the down side, however, some males cannot acquire a territory at all, and spend a frustrating season harassing paired females.

After breeding, male and female Pheasants often gather into single-sex flocks and spend their time scratching with their feet for grain, seeds, roots and snails, or using their bills to dig and pick. At night they roost up in the trees, often giving loud calls prior to settling down, which are slightly strangled versions of the familiar coughing crow.

BELOW

Pheasants can run surprisingly fast, carrying their tails slightly above the horizontal.

Red Kite

Scientific name: Milvus milvus

Identifying features:

Similar species: Buzzard,
Marsh Harrier (at a distance)

SIZE: 60–66 cm (23½–26 in)

HABITAT: Farmland, sheep country;
breeds in woodland

POPULATION: Once very rare,
can now be locally common

It is the Red Kite, not the kite with a string, that came first. The toy was named after one of Britain and Europe's masters of the air – a bird that can change direction with the mere twitch of its unusual forked tail, or dive down with a flick of the wings. The Red Kite's history is as up and down as any aerial manoeuvre it might perform: once common as a scavenger in London and other big cities, it was persecuted to near extinction by the beginning of the twentieth century, before a strong, conservation-driven recovery in recent years, aided by the introduction of birds brought from the Continent.

Despite its reputation as a scavenger, a bird that once frequented the gallows in medieval times and now frequents rubbish dumps and even bird tables, the Red Kite is also a well-adapted predator. In the spring, especially, it is perfectly capable of snatching living food such as voles and other small mammals, and even the occasional bird. It uses a quick pounce, striking feet first, and thus tends to surprise its victims.

Red Kites build a nest of sticks at a modest height in a tree, often in a traditional site used down the generations. They sometimes betray their status as scavengers by adding such adornments as rags, plastic bags, dung and sheep's wool to the structure; even underwear has been recorded! The young, of which there are between one and three, hatch after 31 days into these moderately insalubrious surroundings and, in contrast to the situation in some birds of prey, grow up without murderous sibling aggression.

One bird that does excite the Kite's ire however, is the Carrion Crow. Crows sometimes attack Kite nests and the Kites respond in kind, while at a good feeding site the two species constantly bicker over corpses, with much thieving and counter-thieving.

Fascinating Facts

Red Kites were once thought to be vermin in much the same way pigeons are now, and by the end of the eighteenth century they had been largely exterminated. A conservation programme established by landowners brought them back from the brink of extinction.

LEFT

Red Kites were once a rare sight in Britain and Europe, but conservation efforts have seen their population rise once more.

Montagu's Harrier

Scientific name: Circus pygargus

SIZE: 43–47 cm (17–18½ in)

HABITAT: Mainly agricultural fields

POPULATION: Rare summer visitor

Identifying features: Long tail and narrow wings held in a V; narrower than other harriers

Similar species: Marsh Harrier, Hen Harrier

LEFT
Like other birds of prey, Montagu's Harrier feeds on small mammals and sometimes other birds.

This can be a difficult bird to see. It is rare, scattered, irregular and often occurs in agricultural fields – habitats that tend to be neglected by bird-watchers. It is also, in contrast to the other harriers, exclusively a summer visitor, present only between April and September, in which months some continental migrants also pass through. Identification is not straightforward either, because the Montagu's Harrier has similar plumage to the Hen Harrier, but with experience, the far more elegant and buoyant flight of the Monty's, together with a slimmer body and slender wings, soon pick it out.

The Montagu's Harrier hunts in typical harrier fashion, flying slow – up to 30 km/h (9 mph) – and low to the ground, often following natural lines, such as the edges of fields, or ruts. By approaching low it can easily surprise prey, which is then grabbed by the talons, which have a wide grasp. In the breeding season the Montagu's Harrier seems mainly to feed on small birds, many of which are from their nests, but will dabble in small mammal catching where necessary, and takes the occasional lizard and snake. On the whole this raptor finds its food in open areas with only low vegetation, and it tends to be drawn to the drier, warmer parts of the country.

Sky Dancer

Breeding is prefaced by a 'sky-dancing' display, in which the male will often repeatedly dive from a great height before sweeping back upwards at the last moment, and it will also twist and turn playfully, as if out of control. It puts those same flying skills to good use later in the breeding cycle, when it alone will be responsible for catching food for itself, the female and the early-stage young. The Montagu's Harrier's nest is usually placed within a tall crop, or in the long grass, where it is well concealed.

Buzzard

Scientific name: Buteo buteo

Identifying features: Short tail; often pale 'necklace'; soars with wings in shallow V

Similar species: Honey Buzzard

SIZE: 51–57 cm (20–22⅛ in)

HABITAT: Upland and lowland farmland or moorland with nearby woodland or crags

POPULATION: Common and widespread

Much the commonest large bird of prey in Britain, the Buzzard is also the most confusing. It shows a bewildering variety in its plumage, with some birds all-dark and others pale and creamy, depending on the individual. Little is consistent, except the broad wings, with 'fingers' at the tip, and the Buzzard's short tail. Thus it is a species that often leaves even experienced bird-watchers with red faces.

It is almost as unpredictable in its feeding habits. Although a large bird, with a presumably healthy appetite, it is as likely to be seen wandering over ploughed fields in search of worms as it is to be pouncing from a height on to a young rabbit, or some other favourite delicacy. A catholic diet is the norm, with voles nevertheless a consistent feature, together with carrion from roadkills and a few larger, more cumbersome birds such as Wood Pigeons or crows. The Buzzard can sometimes be seen hovering, or at least 'hanging in the air', while homing in on prey below. Typically, it will also perch upon fences and roadside poles, looking more like a surveyor of traffic than a voracious predator.

Nesting Habits

Buzzards are more territorial than other birds of prey and are reluctant to allow others within their borders, so it is a common sight to see quite a number of these birds in the air at once, circling at their invisible boundaries. They are also more vocal than other raptors, uttering a marvellous wild mewing call.

Pairs are relatively sedentary, remaining in the territory throughout the course of the year. In the breeding season they build a substantial nest out of sticks and twigs, which is typically lined with fresh green material, possibly as a sort of chemical disinfectant to keep away parasites. Up to four young may fledge from successful nests.

Kestrel

SIZE: 32–35 cm (12½–13¾ in)

HABITAT: Open country

POPULATION: Common but declining

Scientific name: Falco tinnunculus

Identifying features: Easiest to identify by its hovering habit; long tail; narrow, pointed wings

Similar species: Hobby, Peregrine, Merlin

You cannot separate the Kestrel from its distinctive mode of hunting. This is the bird so often seen hovering over the verges of motorways and other major roads, or over agricultural fields, moorland or wasteland. Although it does hunt in others ways, for example sitting on a high perch (such as a telegraph pole or wire) and dropping down on to prey, it is never so easy to see as when it is hanging in the air, flying into the wind with wings steadily beating and its head absolutely still.

The main food of the Kestrel is small mammals, especially voles. Voles are diurnal, but the Kestrel will also hunt at dusk and dawn for mice, and has also been recorded hovering by moonlight. Interestingly, recent research has shown that this small raptor is able to see in the ultraviolet spectrum, which is bad news for voles, because their urine has an ultraviolet component. Since the voles use urine for scent marking and rarely go for long without relieving themselves, this enables the Kestrel to use urine-trail density to assess the abundance of voles in a particular area.

Early Courtship

For Kestrels, living in open areas, it is often a problem to find a suitable nest site, and this certainly limits its abundance. Nests are usually located in holes in trees, buildings or cliffs, while the birds also take readily to open-fronted nest boxes. Another major nest site is in the abandoned nests of birds such as crows, and this reflects the fact that Kestrels do not make any significant structure of their own. The most DIY they attempt is to make a shallow scrape for the four to six eggs.

The breeding cycle, however, begins long before eggs are laid. Males may start displaying to females as early as February, two to three months in advance; they plunge from a height towards the female and veer away at the last moment, and otherwise show off their aerobatic skills.

Fascinating Facts

Kestrels are able to spot prey from amazing distances. They can locate a beetle from some 50 m (165 ft) away.

ABOVE

The Kestrel is one of the most distinctive open country birds, hovering in the air before swooping on its prey.

Hobby

Scientific name: Falco subbuteo

Identifying features: Slim build; sharply
pointed wings; dark above, with black face-mask;
streaks down breast

Similar species: Kestrel, Merlin, Peregrine

SIZE: 30–36 cm (11⅞–14⅛ in)

HABITAT: Heathland and farmland
with scattered trees

POPULATION: Uncommon
summer visitor

Hobby and Kestrel are of similar size and shape, and
should really be tricky to tell apart, but they are not.
For a start, the Hobby virtually never hovers at all, which
the Kestrel does, and it is a far more aerial hunter than its
close relative, flying much higher and sweeping the skies
with more style and panache. At a distance, with its long,
swept-back wings and fairly short tail, it is frequently
compared to the Swift. But if so, it is a Swift in slow
motion, without the frenetic wheeling of the smaller bird,
and with more menace.

The prey items of the Hobby
can be divided into two
categories – insects and
birds. As far as the former
are concerned, the Hobby
tends to take the larger
forms, such as beetles, moths
and dragonflies which, apart
from being good meals, are
also speedy and difficult to

catch. Dragonflies, which
often fly high into the
Hobby's airspace, are a mid-
to late-summer speciality,
and Hobbies often commute
several kilometres to a bog
or other wetland where these
insects are common. When
hunting dragonflies, the
birds can be seen to snatch

them in the talons and
then transfer the bodies
seamlessly to the bill, where
they are eaten in mid-air.

Bird Food

Birds eaten include many
open country species, such as
larks and pipits, and those
that share the Hobby's aerial
habitat: House Martins,
Swallows and even Swifts.
Swifts are exceedingly quick
and manoeuvrable in the air,
and the only chance a Hobby
has is to take one unawares.
When a Hobby catches a
bird, it has to return to a
perch to consume it.

Hobbies do not build their
own nests, but use an old
crow's nest or raptor nest in
a tree on the edge of open
country. These birds are
among the latest to breed,
rarely producing eggs before
mid-June. They do this in
order to take advantage of
the midsummer glut of
young fledgling birds, which
make good meals for their
clutch of two to four young.

LEFT

*Hobbies inhabit areas where large
populations of dragonflies can be
found – one of their favourite foods.*

Spotted Crake

SIZE: 22–24 cm (8⅝–9½ in)

HABITAT: Large freshwater marshes

POPULATION: Very rare summer visitor and scarce passage migrant

Scientific name: Porzana porzana

Identifying features: Short bill, spots on plumage

Similar species: Water Rail, Moorhen

The Spotted Crake is a challenging bird to see in Britain, owing to its small size, almost paranoid secretive habits and general rarity in the country. The best chance is in the autumn, when juvenile birds pass through in quite high numbers and can occasionally be quite confiding. If you are fortunate enough to see one, it will probably be a bird scuttling along on the mud at the base of a reedbed, its body held close to the ground, the tail flicking nervously, and the head bobbing in chicken-like fashion. It is the short bill, rather than the peppering of spots on the plumage, that best distinguishes this bird from the larger Water Rail.

It would be near-impossible to know that Spotted Crakes were breeding in an area were it not for the male's distinctive advertising call, which can be heard in still conditions from 2 km (1.2 miles) away. It is an endlessly repeated 'whit', heard once every second, sometimes for many minutes on end, and usually in the depths of the night between dusk and dawn. The sound is often compared to a whiplash, but, at the same time, it has been likened to the squeak made by a pair of waterproof trousers as someone walks along, or to the dripping of a tap into a water container.

Foodstuff

This small bird eats a wide variety of items gathered at its feet, mainly animal matter including worms, snails, insect larvae and small fish, but also plant fragments such as algae, seeds and shoots. It forages mainly on the mud, but is also found over water up to about 7 cm (2¾ in) deep. The nest is a thick-walled cup of vegetation built very close to the water's surface; it can be as much as 10 cm (3⅞ in) tall, constituting a lot of hard work for the builders. In a good season Spotted Crakes can produce two broods of 10 chicks each, although early mortality is very high.

ABOVE

It is a rare treat to see a Spotted Crake; the best way to find them is to follow the distinctive call of the male in breeding season.

Corncrake

Scientific name: Crex crex

Identifying features: Pale brown, streaked, grey about head; wing rusty-brown

Similar species: Partridge, Quail

SIZE: 27–30 cm (10⅝–11⅞ in)

HABITAT: Grassland and meadows

POPULATION: Rare summer visitor

Mainly encountered as a strange, disembodied voice, the Corncrake is now a rare bird. Once found in hayfields, meadows and pasture throughout the country in summer, it is now confined to the Western Isles, Ireland and a few other scattered locations. Modern farming has been the problem; the cutting of grass for silage in spring and summer, coupled with the removal of damp, grassy corners from fields, is not compatible with this bird's need for a little long-grass privacy for the chicks. Recent conservation efforts using traditional hay-making methods have, however, begun to halt the decline.

The Corncrake is a very skulking bird, hard to see, and its presence would probably go unrecorded most of the time were it not for the male's loud advertising call. This is well rendered by its scientific name *Crex crex*, and it can also be likened to the sound made by running a comb along the edge of an empty matchbox twice. The advertising is far-carrying and is usually made in the middle of the night; it is very much redolent of warm nights on rich summer meadows.

Breeding Habits

Recent work has shown that the ever-elusive Corncrake can be polygamous, the male bird acquiring more than one mate. It seems that the male, having attracted one female, simply goes on calling in the hope that another will appear. If this happens, the original male will expand its territory to encompass another site for a shallow-cupped nest, much to the irritation of its male neighbours.

Corncrakes lay between eight and 12 eggs and, after the breeding season, they migrate in August or September away from Britain and Europe and all the way to South East Africa, to return again in mid-April. Despite their weak-looking appearance in flight, they can cross the Sahara Desert in a single flight.

RIGHT

Like the Spotted Crake, the Corncrake can be difficult to find in its grassland habitat.

Lapwing

Scientific name: Vanellus vanellus

Identifying features: Iridescent green above with purple tints, white below; toffee-coloured undertail; wispy crest

Similar species: None

SIZE: 28–31 cm (11–12¼ in)

HABITAT: Agricultural fields, marshes, coastal mudflats

POPULATION: Common

The Lapwing is no ordinary wader. For one thing, it does not like wading or getting its feet wet. It is not even particularly fond of water, often being found well inland on agricultural fields and pasture, where it feeds in large flocks on earthworms, leatherjackets, caterpillars and ants. And for another, it looks unlike any other related bird. Not only does it have glistening iridescence on its upperparts, which glints spectacularly in the sun, but it also has peculiarly broad, rounded wings, which are beaten in a slow, lazy manner, quite unlike the usual powerful, fast wing-beats of other waders.

In spring and early summer, those unusual wings are put to good use during the Lapwing's sensational courtship routine. The male takes to the air and immediately flaps its wings with unusually deep beats, gaining height in what is known as the 'butterfly flight'; it will then make a series of ascents and steep plunges, often lurching from side to side, apparently out of control, and even flipping briefly over on to its back. This wild flying is accompanied by equally excited yelps, like a child on a rollercoaster, together with strange tearing and whooping sounds, and the wings, for their part, add in a loud throbbing.

Mating Displays

Further, more subtle displays take place on the ground. A bird of either sex settles down and scrapes away dirt with its feet. This is a prelude to nest building. The four eggs are laid in a small depression made in the same way, and the female sits tight for a month before they hatch. During this time, both parents often become highly agitated as one after another, various intruders going about their business are harassed by the noisy birds. Harmless cows and sheep, as well as crows and birds of prey, are subjected to mock attacks and overwrought squeals.

Fascinating Facts

Lapwing eggs used to be a popular food. During the rationing of the Second World War they were collected and used to make dried egg powder.

LEFT

The Lapwing is unlike any other species of wader – eschewing water in favour of farmland.

Stock Dove

Scientific name: Columba oenas

Identifying features: Dark eyes, short tail;
plum-pink breast; iridescent neck mark

Similar species: Woodpigeon, Feral Pigeon

SIZE: 32–34 cm (12⅝–13⅜ in)

HABITAT: Open woodland,
farmland, cliffs

POPULATION: Common

Few birds are so overlooked or under-appreciated as the Stock Dove, a very classy and attractive bird of woodland and farmland. It is smaller and less cumbersome than the similar Woodpigeon, with a more intense ash-grey colour to the body, and a vivid iridescent neck-ring lacking the adjacent white patch. It flies with faster wing-beats than the Woodpigeon and looks more compact. It is rarely seen in large numbers, and is thus much less of an agricultural pest than its irrepressible relative. Furthermore, Stock Doves feed on a wider range of vegetation than their relatives, taking seeds, shoots and leaves from many different types of plants, not just crops.

Another distinction from other pigeons and doves is that the Stock Dove usually makes its nest – such as it is, which is not more than a few twigs at most – inside a hole in a tree. Sometimes it will use a hole in a cliff or wall instead, but essentially the Stock Dove is limited to places where suitable holes are found adjacent to short-grass turf and pasture land, where the birds forage. In common with other pigeons, the Stock Dove lays two white eggs, and the young are fed for their first few days on 'pigeon milk', a rich, paste-like substance formed in the crop.

Stock Dove Call

These birds can breed almost throughout the year, but they can be very unobtrusive. In contrast to the Woodpigeon's loud, insistent song, for example, Stock Doves merely utter a soft, repeated, somewhat questioning coo, which is easily drowned out by the chorus of birds and other woodland sounds. In addition, their flight display is also distinctly understated; pairs of birds simply fly around in a wide circle, sometimes daringly raising their wings in a shallow V as they do so. The whole performance, as so much about the Stock Dove, is easily missed.

Barn Owl

Scientific name: Tyto alba

Identifying features: Pale plumage; heart-shaped face

Similar species: Other owls will look similar in silhouette, especially in flight

SIZE: 33–35 cm (13–13¼ in)

HABITAT: Farmland, marshes and grassland

POPULATION: Fairly common

ears are not symmetrical; the left is higher on the skull than the right. This means that sound travelling from below or above will arrive at one ear before the other, and this difference helps to compute the direction from which the sound is coming. In short, the Barn Owl has three-dimensional hearing. It is able to catch food in complete darkness.

Fascinating Facts

Barn Owls have the keenest sense of hearing of any bird in the world.

BELOW LEFT

In the dark it can be difficult to distinguish Barn Owls from other owls, but in fact its appearance is quite different.

The pale, ghostly shape of the Barn Owl, most often seen as it hunts silently over fields at dusk, has excited much fear and suspicion among country-dwellers in the past, especially when the bird has uttered its typical rasping shriek – a sound to make the blood run cold in the semi-darkness. But in truth this bird poses no threat to humankind. Instead it is a ruthless and efficient hunter of small mammals, such as rats, mice and shrews, often doing a farmer a considerable service by nesting in an outbuilding or barn and keeping mammal numbers down.

Selecting a Mate

Barn Owls breed not just in barns, but also in churches and other buildings, as well as natural sites such as caves and tree holes. There is no real nest, the female just lays the four to seven eggs on the floor, often among old discarded owl pellets. The young hatch out after about 30 days, and then it will be another three months at least before they are independent. Interestingly, recent research has shown that males prefer to breed with females with plenty of spots on their thighs, an individual feature that appears to reflect a bird's state of health.

The Barn Owl looks quite unlike other owls, with its peculiar heart-shaped face and small, black eyes. The arrangement reflects how it uses its senses. The eyes are only of secondary importance in hunting; it is the ears that hold sway. The facial discs help to amplify sounds, while the silent flight, typical of all owls, keeps background noise to a minimum. Internally, the

Little Owl

Scientific name: Athene noctua

Identifying features: Fierce yellow eyes; white 'frown'; white spots on brow

Similar species: None (all other owls much larger)

SIZE: 21–23 cm (8¼–9 in)

HABITAT: Farmland, parkland and rocky country

POPULATION: Fairly common

Although it occurs on the near-continent, the Little Owl is not a native species to Britain. It was introduced several times in the nineteenth century, started slowly and only became common in the second half of the twentieth. These days it does well enough, inhabiting mainly open areas with scattered mature trees. The trees provide the roosting and nesting sites, while the open ground allows it to hunt for terrestrial prey, including worms, insects and smaller mammals and birds.

Somewhat oddly for an owl, this bird can be seen quite easily during the day, usually sitting on the low branches of a tree, on a rock or even a fence post, often bobbing its head in characteristic fashion. This tendency towards being awake during daytime is rather unusual, especially considering that it usually hunts for food between dusk and midnight, and then again at dawn. It is often perfectly possible to hear it calling by day, too, giving a loud, rather intense mewing call. The male's slightly questioning hoot can be heard in the early spring.

Permanent Homes

Little Owls live in the same territory throughout their lives, giving plenty of time to get used to the area and to discover the best places for foraging. Pair bonds are also stable, with male and female staying together all year round. Within the territory are several nest sites which, although usually in holes in trees, do not always have to be in such conventional sites. Some Little Owls have been known to raise a family in a rabbit hole, or in a hole among the roots of a tree. Up to four young may be raised in a year, wherever that might be.

Among the Little Owl's enemies are large birds of prey such as Goshawks or Peregrines and, bizarrely, other larger owls, including the Tawny Owl.

BELOW

The Little Owl is, as its name suggests, far smaller than other members of the owl family.

Nightjar

SIZE: 26–28 cm (10¼–11 in)

HABITAT: Heathland, moors and open woodland

POPULATION: Widespread but uncommon summer visitor

Scientific name: Caprimulgus europaeus

Identifying features: Large head, minute bill and long body; sits along, not across, perch

Similar species: Kestrel, Hobby or Cuckoo in flight.

The Nightjar is quite unlike any other European bird. It is about the size of a Kestrel, but it has an enormous gape and a minute bill, together with short legs and weak feet. The wings and tail are long, giving it great manoeuvrability in the air, while the plumage is all over highly cryptically coloured, making the Nightjar almost impossible to see when perched or on the ground. All these are adaptations to something very unusual: a nocturnal aerial lifestyle.

The main food of the Nightjar is made up from flying insects, such as moths and large beetles, and it is the only bird to tap into this rich resource in darkness.

Prey is snatched on the wing and, contrary to what you might expect, the Nightjar does not trawl randomly through the skies with its mouth open, but actually targets its prey using sight. Nightjars have special adaptations in the eyes allowing them to see contrast very brightly, and they often use the sky as a backdrop to snatch a meal from below. Moonlit nights are also good times for hunting.

Left

The Nightjar has an unusual and very distinctive call, known as 'churring'.

Unusual Call

Apart from its feeding technique, the other remarkable aspect of the Nightjar's life is the male's extraordinary advertising call. Known to bird-watchers as 'churring', it consists of a long trill alternating between two pitches, with an odd, hollow quality, a little bit like a muffled pneumatic drill, or the engine of a two-stroke motorcycle. It is a superbly atmospheric sound, of heaths and moors on summer nights.

Nightjars lay two well-concealed eggs straight on to the ground, in a small scraped patch created by the birds themselves. The female does most of the incubation, but the male takes over at dawn and dusk, to allow its mate time to feed. After about 18 days, the eggs hatch and the young can take wing about 16 days after this, although they will be dependent on their parents for a while until they can feed themselves.

Hoopoe

Scientific name: Upupa epops

Identifying features: Pink with black and white wings and tail; long, curved bill; fan-like crest

Similar species: None

SIZE: 26–28 cm (10¼–11 in)

HABITAT: Areas with short turf for probing

POPULATION: Rare migrant; very rare breeder

The Hoopoe looks too exotic to adorn the lawns of Britain and Europe and yet it is a regular visitor and has actually bred on occasion. Not a single year goes by without some records, and in most years there are about 100 sightings, especially in March and April when birds are returning from Africa and overshoot their destinations. Global warming might make it more common. In contrast to many rarities, there cannot ever be much doubt about its identification. **With its strange pink plumage, fan-like crest, odd shape and butterfly-like flight, no other bird looks remotely like it.**

In Europe, where it is common, the Hoopoe feeds on the larger kinds of insects, such as beetles and mole-crickets, which it obtains by probing into short turf. The bill is long and strong, enabling the bird to probe it into the soil and then open it slightly, increasing the circumference of the hole made and making prey easier to find. Hoopoes will often feed in a small patch of ground for quite some time, working thoroughly and surprisingly unobtrusively. You often fail to notice them until they suddenly take wing, flopping away unsteadily. When Hoopoes are alarmed or excited, they open their crests to reveal the full extent of the fan-like shape.

Poor Housekeepers

The Hoopoe gets its name from the male's advertising call, a three-note 'hoo-poo-poo' delivered at even pace. Once the pair has been formed, the birds select a hole in a tree or wall in which to place their nest and lay the seven to eight eggs. Abroad, Hoopoes have a reputation for being poor housekeepers and, indeed, most nests smell quite disgusting. Both adults and young secrete a foul-smelling substance that presumably keeps the nest free from sensitive-nosed predators. But if it does not, the young are able to fire faeces hard at any intruder foolish enough to make too close an approach.

Woodlark

Scientific name: Lullula arborea

Identifying features: Short tail and long buff supercilium to the nape; black, pale-tipped primary coverts

SIZE: 15 cm (5⅞ in)

HABITAT: Heathland, open woodland

POPULATION: Scarce

Similar species: Skylark

The Skylark might be the more renowned singer in the lark family, but many would say that the Woodlark actually has the better voice. It sounds less shrill than the Skylark, and never dominates the atmosphere like the commoner bird, but for sheer mellifluous subtlety it is unrivalled. Progressing down the scale in semitones, it is a short, lilting phrase, and it gives rise to the bird's imaginative scientific name, *Lullula*. It is usually uttered when the bird is aloft, circling and looping in the sky. Paired males usually sing from about 50 m (165 ft) up, but unpaired birds, with a need to broadcast, may perform from twice the height.

The Woodlark is a scarce bird, mostly confined to southern regions, a fact that betrays this bird's preference for warm, sunny places. As its name suggests, it also has a most unlark-like affinity for trees, which are essential in the territory, used by males as song-posts when aerial singing seems like hard work. A territory also needs some low vegetation, plus some suitable short turf over which the birds forage preferentially for mid-sized

insects and spiders. Thus Woodlarks are quite fussy in their requirements, being confined to heathland and some open woodland.

Nesting

These birds nest very early in the year, often having eggs by mid-March. Pairs form a bond for the season only, but males usually retain their territory from one year to the next. The nest is placed on the ground, usually under some bracken or other low vegetation, and the first building task requires excavating a surprisingly deep hollow (up to 55 mm/2⅛ in) in which the nest will be placed. Most nests face north-west or south-east to avoid direct sunlight. The female lays between three and five eggs and, once the young have hatched, they may be flying after only 10-13 days. This is extremely quick, and at first they do not fly with much expertise – but to avoid danger it makes sense to leave the nest as quickly as possible.

Skylark

Scientific name: Alauda arvensis

Identifying features: Distinctive hover; white trailing edge to the wings and white outer tail feathers

Similar species: Other small brown birds

SIZE: 18–19 cm (7–7½ in)

HABITAT: Farmland, grassland, coastal areas

POPULATION: Common

There can be few more famous songsters than the Skylark, a bird commemorated in great music and literature for its sweet-sounding outpourings. And indeed, there are fewer more vivid experiences than walking in the countryside and being drenched in lark song for hour after hour. To deliver its song the male rises from the ground in a slow, hovering flight, and once it has reached its preferred height, often 30 m (100 ft) or more in the air, it will seemingly hang there, fluttering, as the song reaches its zenith.

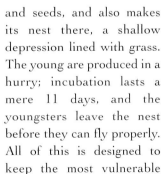

In common with many great songsters, the Skylark is not very impressive to look at. It is surprisingly large, approaching the Starling in bulk, and, apart from its pert crest, has little to distinguish it. Of course, being bold and colourful is something of a liability for a bird that, like the Skylark, is mainly terrestrial and needs to be unobtrusive. It feeds on the ground, on insects and seeds, and also makes its nest there, a shallow depression lined with grass. The young are produced in a hurry; incubation lasts a mere 11 days, and the youngsters leave the nest before they can fly properly. All of this is designed to keep the most vulnerable stages to a minimum.

Winter Visitor

Many people think that Skylarks are only found in Britain in the summer, but this is not the case. The birds are resident, and large numbers of visitors actually come from the Continent to spend the winter season on our damp, relatively frost-free island. Most of the time they keep a low profile, feeding and roosting on the ground, often in flocks. But occasionally, on a mild winter's day, the odd bird is encouraged to sing, in readiness for the warmer season ahead.

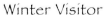

ABOVE

The Skylark is known for its familiar and melodic song.

Swallow

SIZE: 17–19 cm (6¾–7½ in)

HABITAT: Open country, including farmland and villages, usually near livestock and water

POPULATION: Abundant summer visitor

Scientific name: Hirundo rustica

Identifying features: Long tail-streamers; royal blue upperparts and breast-band, with red-brown throat; creamy belly

Similar species: Swift, House Martin, Sand Martin

There can be few more famous and popular birds than the Swallow. With an empire encompassing much of the world, it is welcomed as an incoming migrant wherever it goes, be it to the Northern Hemisphere (Eurasia and North America) in summer, or the Southern Hemisphere for the rest of the year. Everywhere it goes it lives in close association with people, feeding over fields grazed by livestock, and nesting on man-made structures, often on the eaves of barns.

With its long tail and swept-back wings, the Swallow is a master of the skies. However, in contrast to Swifts and most other members of its family, it usually hunts low down, zooming just above ground and having to dodge large animals by side-flips; this enables it to catch larger prey than other similar aerial birds, notably blowflies and horseflies, those pests of summer. With the Swallow's wide gape, it might seem as though it could simply fly along with its mouth open and snatch what it needs, but in fact every catch is made by sight, and carefully targeted.

Social Interaction

Swallows either breed as single pairs or in colonies, although the latter are small by the standards of their family. Within either system their social relationships are particularly fascinating. Experiments have shown that, within the population, some males have longer tails than others, and some pairs of streamers at the ends of the tail are of equal length, and others not. Females, it seems, prefer both length and symmetry in tails, and males so blessed acquire a mate rapidly. They are also favourites for copulation outside the pair bond.

The Swallow nest is a cup, lined with feathers or hay but made primarily out of pellets of mud, sometimes a thousand or more. This need for fresh mud ensures that these birds are usually found near a ready source of water.

Fascinating Facts

There are about 100 species of swallow found around the globe, including members of the martin family.

BELOW
Swallows are usually seen in open countryside, often in farmland where livestock is raised.

Tree Pipit

Scientific name: Anthus trivialis

Identifying features: Pumps tail up and down; streaks on breast peter out towards flanks

Similar species: Meadow Pipit

SIZE: 15 cm (5⅞ in)

HABITAT: Open woodland, young plantations and heathland

POPULATION: Fairly common summer visitor

The Tree Pipit is something of a bird-watcher's bird, too brown and streaky to be appreciated by anyone else. It does, however, perform an eye-catching display flight, and is also a migrant, delighting enthusiasts by dropping down almost anywhere, unexpectedly, in the spring and autumn. It can readily be distinguished from most other small brown birds by its habit of walking on the ground, instead of hopping like the rest, yet conversely, for a pipit, it is decidedly arboreal.

Every Tree Pipit requires tall trees in its territory, and the male may spend most of the day simply perching in the crown. Nevertheless, every so often it will, perhaps a little grudgingly, take to the air, rising at a steep angle, and begin to sing. Uttering a fast, trilling phrase, it will reach some 10 m (30 ft) and then, having reached the top of its flight-path, will suddenly stop flapping and descends instead with wings and tail rigid and splayed, legs dangling. The descent follows a circular course and eventually ends at an elevated perch, usually another treetop. This helps to distinguish it from other pipits, whose similar 'parachute flights' end up on the ground.

Double Brooders

When not singing the Tree Pipit is an unobtrusive bird. It feeds primarily on the ground, just walking around, picking items from low grass or other plants, minding its own business. Its main food is invertebrates, such as beetles and weevils, but it will also take some plant material in late summer and autumn. The nest is well concealed, a cup placed in a shallow depression on the ground, but it can sometimes have quite an open aspect. Tree Pipits lay between two and six eggs and, if all goes well, are capable of fitting two broods into their busy summer schedule.

Meadow Pipit

SIZE: 14.5 cm (5⅝ in)

HABITAT: Open country

POPULATION: Very common

Scientific name: Anthus pratensis

Identifying features: Pink legs; small, thin bill; heavily streaked down belly to flanks

Similar species: Tree Pipit, Rock Pipit

It might look small and feeble, but the Meadow Pipit is a tough bird. It is one of the few species that occurs on bleak uplands, moorlands, chilly fields and coasts throughout the year, eking out a living by eating small seeds and insects. It often rises from the feet with an air of complete panic, flying this way and that, shouting out 'tsip, tsip!', seemingly unable to decide what to do. On the ground it can look equally gormless, just wandering around aimlessly.

In the spring, however, the male Meadow Pipit performs a flight-song similar to that of the Tree Pipit, with the same parachuting finish. The display does, however, go on for longer, and the song is more monotonous than the Tree Pipit's, repeating a single note incessantly in the manner of a modern-style alarm clock. Its purpose is to defend a territory from other Pipits, as well as to attract a mate; both of these essential tasks are difficult to do while on the ground, and Meadow Pipits tend to occur in places without many elevated perches.

BELOW
Meadow Pipits often fall prey to animal predators and nest-stealers such as Cuckoos.

Dangers of Ground-nesting

Breeding can be perilous. The ground nest is vulnerable to predators such as weasels, crows and snakes, but this bird also has the added worry of attracting the attention of a Cuckoo. It is one of the Cuckoo's favourite hosts in Britain, and the larger bird will often home in on the Pipit's nest by monitoring the alarm reaction of the parents, which tend to become more and more agitated the closer the parasite gets.

The Meadow Pipit should lay three to five eggs, which hatch after about two weeks, the young fledging after another 10–14 days. Some may raise three broods in a season.

Whinchat

Scientific name: Saxicola rubetra

Identifying features: Broad white/buff supercilium, white-edged tail

Similar species: Stonechat

SIZE: 12.5 cm (4⅞ in)

HABITAT: rough grassy areas, usually with bracken, including moorland

POPULATION: Fairly common summer visitor, common passage migrant

In contrast to Stonechats, Whinchats are exclusively summer visitors, arriving in April and departing from August onwards. They are long-distance migrants, travelling all the way to tropical Africa for the winter, while Stonechats move within the country, or stay put close to their breeding grounds. Interestingly, the Whinchat has longer wings than the Stonechat, since these are more energy-efficient for extended flights.

Breeding Territory

Once it has arrived the male Whinchat sings a somewhat scratchy, fitful song full of imitations of nearby birds, and it sometimes embellishes its performance with a brief up-and-down song-flight. Males are extremely territorial, and quarrels between them are common. Their patches of ground, where they feed on insects gathered on brief excursions from an elevated perch, are very important to them. The bonds between male and female are not very strong, and last for a single brood at best, rather than a whole season.

The nest is placed on the ground, usually among long grass or bracken, plants that typify Whinchat country, and while Stonechats almost always seem to have gorse in their breeding territory, despite their name ('whin' is an alternative name for gorse) Whinchats often do not. The female lays four to seven eggs and when these hatch, unattached birds sometimes help the pair in feeding the youngsters.

To most British bird-watchers the Whinchat is far less familiar than its relative the Stonechat, especially with its tendency to occur in wilder habitats, such as bracken-covered moorland, and to be present for less of the year. So it is exciting when this bird's prominent pale eyebrow gives away its identity, especially on migration when Whinchats can turn up almost anywhere, well away from their favourite haunts.

RIGHT

The bond between male and female Whinchats lasts less than a season.

Stonechat

Scientific name: Saxicola torquata

Identifying features: Small, dumpy bird
with a habit of standing upright and staying
still on low perches

Similar species: Whinchat

Size: 12.5 cm (4⅞ in)

Habitat: Open country, typically
with gorse, especially heathland

POPULATION: Common resident

This is the sort to delight bird-watchers, with its habit of perching in full view of observers for minutes on end, making itself easy to see and admire. The habit comes from its foraging technique. It feeds on invertebrates that move across patches of open ground, or fly through the air nearby; by sitting still it can watch for movement, and then fly suddenly to snap up whatever morsel it has spotted. The technique is similar to that of the Robin, although the Stonechat rarely perches on spades.

The Stonechat is a bird of various kinds of open country, anywhere where suitable perches are readily available. While the closely-related Whinchat can sit comfortably on the thinnest stems, including rushes and bracken, the Stonechat prefers more secure watch points, such as treetops, posts and gorse bushes. Although it is probably commonest of heathland, it is also drawn to coastal sites, including the rough ground above cliffs.

Call and Meaning

Even if the Stonechat were not conspicuous, it would still be an easy bird to find, simply because it cannot keep its mouth shut. It has a distinctive call, 'sweet-sack!', the latter half of which sounds vaguely like two small stones being tapped together. Recent studies have shown that the

BELOW LEFT

The Stonechat gives itself away with its characteristic song and call.

'sweet!' part of the call is a code to any nearby young to keep their heads down. Meanwhile, the male has a pleasing if slightly strained song which, if the bird is in a flamboyant mood, is given in a brief display flight.

The Stonechat nest is an untidy cup of grass and leaves placed on the ground, usually under a gorse bush. The young are turned out at almost factory speed, with broods overlapping so that, while the previous youngsters are still not independent, the male feeds these while the female is already incubating the next batch of eggs.

Fieldfare

Scientific name: Turdus pilaris

Identifying features: Smoky-grey on rump, lower back and head; black tail; chestnut back; yellow bill

Similar species: Mistle Thrush, Song Thrush, Redwing

SIZE: 25.5 cm (10 in)

HABITAT: Scrubby country, hedgerows, fields

POPULATION: Abundant winter visitor

LEFT

Fieldfares feed on invertebrates and berries – a favourite in the autumn months.

M uch as the first Swallow is a sign of spring, so the arrival of Fieldfares, usually in October, heralds the impending winter. These large thrushes arrive in Britain every autumn in enormous numbers from Scandinavia and north-central Europe, where they are abundant breeding birds, and they remain here until March or April. As they move about nomadically, they fly in characteristically loose flocks, intermittently giving distinctive 'shack-shack' calls, the sound of the season.

Fieldfares are closely related to our other thrushes, such as the Mistle Thrush, but they are highly distinctive to look at, with a tasteful combination of grey on the back and head, velvet back and black tail. The 'spots' you see on the breast are actually chevrons and arrowheads. These birds are almost always seen in loose flocks, usually moving over open ground on the lookout for soil invertebrates such as worms and leatherjackets, hopping a little and then standing still, watching around them, before pecking and digging into the soil. When they first arrive most Fieldfares are actually on the lookout for the autumnal crop of berries, which they gobble down with alacrity. Their favourite types are the larger ones such as sloes and rowan, although they also take haws.

Territorial Defence

Although Fieldfares are peripheral breeding birds in Britain, with minute numbers, they do have a very interesting and surprising aspect to their breeding biology. Nesting in large groups, the adults in a neighbourhood often club together when their colony is under threat from some predator such as a Hooded Crow. They all take to the air and, one after the other, bombard the intruder, pelting it with well-aimed excreta. A few minutes of such rough treatment soon moves the chastened predator on, sometimes with seriously soiled plumage. A few attacks can be fatal and, not surprisingly, the vicinity of Fieldfare colonies is an unusually safe place for other unrelated birds to place their own nests.

Redwing

SIZE: 21 cm (8¼ in)

HABITAT: Scrubby country, hedgerows, fields, woodland edge

POPULATION: Common winter visitor

Scientific name: Turdus iliacus

Identifying features: Broad pale supercilium and pale stripe below ear-coverts; rusty-red flanks and underwing

Similar species: Song Thrush

Often referred to collectively with Fieldfares as 'winter thrushes', Redwings move in the autumn from Scandinavia to spend the cold season in Britain, where frosts are brief, snow is rare and the berry crop is excellent. In common with Fieldfares they live a nomadic lifestyle, moving across the countryside in informal flocks, checking out the hedgerows and damp field corners for food. In contrast to Fieldfares, Redwings also commonly enter woodlands to feed, where they search the leaf-litter for invertebrates.

The Redwing resembles a Song Thrush but is easily distinguished by its striking head pattern and, given a decent view, also by the eponymous leak of brownish-red under the wing. It also gives a distinctive piercing 'tsee' call when flushed, a sound that can also be heard when the birds are travelling about. They usually do this on still nights and, in the darkness, intermittent calls can give their presence away up in the sky above rooftop height, unseen. These birds are great travellers, and individual birds that spend one season here may well go elsewhere the next, to Spain or Greece, for example.

Taiga Bird

Although a very small number of Redwings breed in Scotland, this thrush generally has a more northerly range than its co-traveller the Fieldfare, essentially inhabiting the taiga forest belt of Northern Eurasia. Here it eschews forming large colonies itself, but will often nest next to Fieldfare colonies for safety. It builds a cup-nest in typical neat thrush style, and will often bring up two broods in a season.

Male Redwings have a curious singing quirk. Each individual sings just one phrase, repeated again and again; males in the same area share the same song. For a thrush, a family renowned for singing excellence and variety, this is rather surprising.

Grasshopper Warbler

Scientific name: Locustella naevia

Identifying features: Olive-brown with heavily streaked back; heavy-looking tail; short wings

Similar species: Reed, Sedge and Cetti's Warblers

SIZE: 12.5 cm (4⅞ in)

HABITAT: Scrubs and marshland

POPULATION: Locally fairly common summer migrant

LEFT

The Grasshopper Warbler has an unusual, 'reeling' song that is instantly identifiable.

Mouse-like on the ground, insect-like to listen to – the Grasshopper Warbler seems to live in denial of being a bird. Spending most of its time amidst thick, low undergrowth about 1 m (3 ft) tall, it tends to feed on or close to the ground, walking or running rather than hopping, in search of small invertebrates.

It gives away its presence, however, with an extraordinary song, an extended reeling sound rather like a freewheeling bicycle. The male sings from a low perch, and this is one time when it can make itself visible. As it sings it turns its head, making the volume of the song rise and fall from the perspective of the listener. The song often carries on during the night.

The nest is placed on or close to the ground, often in a tussock. It is a thick cup of grass and other material placed on a base of dead leaves.

Lesser Whitethroat

Scientific name: Sylvia curruca

Identifying features: White underparts; grey head; dark brown, uniform upperparts

Similar species: Common Whitethroat, Blackcap

SIZE: 12.5–13.5 cm (4⅞–5¼ in)

HABITAT: Tall scrubby areas

POPULATION: Locally fairly common summer migrant

An altogether cleaner and more smartly turned-out bird than its close relative the Common Whitethroat, the Lesser Whitethroat is nonetheless much more difficult to see. It is shyer and more skulking, rarely showing itself in the tall scrub and low trees in which it lives.

In common with most warblers, it is much easier to hear than to see. Oddly, however, it has a habit of delivering its trilling song phrase just once or twice before moving on to another bush, thus never settling long at a single song-post.

Lesser Whitethroats travel to Britain by way of an extraordinary route. Although they winter in Western Africa, they always travel by way of the Eastern Mediterranean, following an enormous curve. In transit, Lesser Whitethroats are quite sociable, gathering in small flocks, although they are territorial when they arrive.

The male builds several nests for the female to inspect before breeding begins. Four to six eggs are laid in a cup-nest, well hidden in thick vegetation.

Common Whitethroat

Scientific name: Sylvia communis

Identifying features: Chestnut-brown panel on wing; dull pinkish underparts except for brilliant white throat

SIZE: 14 cm (5½ in)

HABITAT: Low scrub, hedgerows

POPULATION: Common summer visitor

Similar species: Lesser Whitethroat, Garden Warbler, Blackcap

The Common Whitethroat is a perky, effervescent species of low, thorny scrub and copious undergrowth. Here it lives a fairly skulking life from April to September, picking insects and spiders off leaves and occasionally indulging in the odd berry, especially in late summer.

It would be hard to see were it not for its curiosity, and its need to perform its short, scratchy song. The latter is delivered either from a perch, sometimes a high perch such as an overhead wire, or during a brief display flight, in which the bird hovers in the air, rising and falling slightly. In the spring this song is performed almost all day long.

Common Whitethroats nest low down in dense vegetation, sometimes among nettles. The male builds

several nest structures, from which the female selects one to refurbish for breeding, and then she lays four or five eggs. These hatch after nine to twelve days and, once they leave the nest, the brood may be split so that each bird is responsible for feeding its allotted young.

Dartford Warbler

Scientific name: Sylvia undata

Identifying features: Very long tail; dark grey-brown above, reddish below

SIZE: 12.5 cm (4⅞ in)

HABITAT: Heathland

POPULATION: Scarce

Similar species: None

Once famous for being a great rarity, the Dartford Warbler has benefited in recent years from a long run of mild winters, and is now commoner than it has probably ever been in Britain, with a couple of thousand pairs scattered across southern England.

It is very much a bird of heathland, requiring a combination of heather and gorse to be present if it is to thrive. It feeds exclusively on small insects and spiders, picked off from low vegetation. While feeding, these birds are almost impossible to see, keeping well hidden and only making short flights on whirring wings just above the heather. However, if it is spotted, the dark plumage and long tail, often held cocked, ensure that the Dartford Warbler is always easy to identify.

This bird is highly unusual among warblers in being resident, not migrating away in the autumn, and thus having to survive the damp and the cold. If things go badly one season, Dartford Warblers can raise three broods the next season and build up the population again.

ABOVE

The Dartford Warbler winters in Britain and Europe, rather than migrating to sunnier climes.

Red-backed Shrike

Scientific name: Lanius collurio

Identifying features: Long, white-edged tail; hooked bill; male has black face-mask, grey head, warm-brown back

Similar species: Great Grey Shrike

SIZE: 17 cm (6¾ in)

HABITAT: Scrub, hedgerows

POPULATION: Scarce passage migrant

The Red-backed Shrike was once a familiar summer visitor to hedgerows and scrubby areas in southern England. Sadly, however, after a long decline, it is now all but extinct as a breeding bird, just appearing in the autumn as a scarce passage migrant. Nobody is sure why it suffered such a catastrophic decline, but it is likely to be related to losses elsewhere in Europe, where its habitat has been much reduced by land clearance and the intensification of farming.

Its disappearance is not lamented by the small animal community, however, because for a diminutive bird the Red-backed Shrike is a fierce predator, subsisting mainly on meat. Its main prey consists of large insects, especially beetles, but it will also catch

Fascinating Facts

Shrikes will often impale their prey on sharp posts or barbed-wire fences as they catch them.

and kill small vertebrates such as mice, voles and small birds. These are spotted as the Shrike sits up on an elevated perch, watching the comings and goings around it. Once it sees something edible, it flies down to the ground and pursues the animal on foot or, sometimes, in a pursuit-flight, finally holding its capture down with the feet and despatching it with bites of the bill, aimed at the back of the head. Interestingly, the Red-backed Shrike sometimes catches more

than its immediate needs dictate. When this happens it caches the items, impaling their limp bodies from thorns or barbed wire: this unusual habit has earned it the colloquial name 'Butcher-bird'.

Habitat

In order to be successful, Red-backed Shrikes can only thrive in habitats with a combination of plenty of lookout posts, such as bushes and small trees, plus

a certain amount of open ground where insects can be spotted as they walk around. Thus hedgerows and scrubby areas are the best in which to look for them. These birds also require shelter and, in truth, warm climates suit them best.

Great Grey Shrike

SIZE: 24–25 cm (9½–9⅞ in)

HABITAT: Open country, especially heathland

POPULATION: Rare winter visitor

Scientific name: Lanius excubitor

Identifying features: Long tail; hooked bill; mainly grey, with black on face-mask, wings and tail

Similar species: Red-backed Shrike

Fewer than 100 Great Grey Shrikes winter in Britain each year, and sometimes only half that, depending on the year. But they are popular with bird-watchers, bringing a dash of excitement and drama to the winter landscape. These birds often inhabit quite impoverished off-season habitats, such as heaths and moors, and occupy enormous territories, making them difficult to track down. Once seen, however, they are unmistakable, with their three-colour pattern, and habit of perching high up on wires or trees, tails twitching.

These are highly predatory birds, and rely on the presence of small animals to keep them going. In common with other shrikes this prey mainly consists of large insects, but mammals, such as voles, are also important; birds are usually too difficult to catch, but that does not stop the Shrikes trying. The various items recorded for Great Grey Shrikes include some impressively large animals; this includes birds up to the size of a Fieldfare (odd, because the two species often nest close by each other in the summer), and mammals, incredibly, up to the size of a stoat. The latter is a fierce predator itself – quite a coup for a Shrike.

Habitat and Habits

Most Shrikes are birds of warm, sunny climates, but the Great Grey Shrike operates in cold, windy and wet conditions. If times are really hard it will sometimes abandon its usual high-perching and simply hop over the ground instead, like the Blackbird from hell, hoping to locate some beetle or other ponderous insect. It will also sometimes pursue both insects and birds in flight, the former in Sparrowhawk-style, after approaching them stealthily, for instance from behind a bush.

In its customary harsh habitats food is usually at a premium, so if things go well, the Shrike will keep on hunting, even on a full stomach. The excess is stored, impaled on thorns, and the larders of Great Grey Shrikes are usually busier than those of its near-relatives.

LEFT

The Great Grey Shrike can prey on quite large birds and animals.

Magpie

Scientific name: Pica pica

Identifying features: Black and white with long tail; black on wing; iridescent sheen

Similar species: None

SIZE: 44–46 cm (17⅓–18 in)

HABITAT: Suburbs, farmland, woodland edge

POPULATION: Very common

Everyone knows the Magpie, one of Europe's most familiar birds. But not everybody likes it. It has a reputation for thieving, which is based on myth. It has a reputation as a merciless killer of young birds and eggs in the garden, which is wildly overstated to the point of prejudice. It also has a mischievous chattering call and a pushy, wide-boy personality which undoubtedly grates with Middle England. But really, it is just a successful, opportunistic omnivore and deserves a bit of admiration.

Fascinating Facts

Magpies are known for destroying the nests of other birds, but they are fearless and can attack larger creatures too. They have been known to attack weak newborn or sickly sheep and cows by pecking at them.

RIGHT

Magpies' nests are complicated structures of twigs and mud.

Magpie society is quite complicated. It consists of two classes, one consisting of territory-holding pairs, the other of non-breeding birds that live in loose flocks. Every Magpie aspires to be a territory holder, because it is only these birds that can breed; the rest must wait for a vacancy, or try to sneak in by force. If you see a large, noisy gathering of Magpies assembled during the day, a fight over territory could be taking place, with one or more flock members challenging established birds. At night-time, Magpies also may gather in groups to roost in thick scrub, sometimes with the two classes mixing.

Spotting Magpie Nests

You can assess the abundance of Magpies in the area by waiting until winter and counting the distinctive domed stick-nests, usually placed quite high in a small tree. These nests are complicated structures, carefully interwoven and with a mud cup in the middle. The pair often begin building, or refurbishment, in the dead of winter. The birds only attempt to bring up one brood a year, and the clutch varies a lot in size, from only three to a challenging nine, the latter only attempted by experienced birds.

It is primarily when their young hatch that Magpies may predate the eggs or nestlings of smaller birds. It is a highly seasonal and peripheral activity, and they do not kill adult birds; but their reputation, it seems, is fixed in stone.

Rook

SIZE: 44–46 cm (17½–18 in)

HABITAT: Farmland, towns

POPULATION: Common

Scientific name: Corvus frugilegus

Identifying features: Bare, dirty white bill and face; steep forehead

Similar species: Carrion Crow, Jackdaw, Raven, Chough

LEFT
Rooks and Crows are often mistaken for one another but can be distinguished by their more sociable tendencies.

Brooding

Rooks attempt just one brood a year, the eggs hatching at a time when the chicks' main diet, worms, is abundant in the damp spring soil. Each female lays between two and five eggs and, although Rook partners pair for life, these eggs may carry the genetic matter of more than one male. Rape is a common fact of life in Rookeries, and the birds seem to be predisposed to some promiscuity anyway.

from the feeding areas, and they are extremely noisy, making a wide range of caws and higher pitched sounds, the latter resembling the breaking of an adolescent voice. The commuting of Rooks between their nests and feeding areas in the spring, undertaken by direct flights, is almost certain to be the origin of the term 'as the crow flies'.

It is often said that if you see a flock of crows they are Rooks and, while this is not quite accurate, there is little doubt that the Rook is by far the more sociable of these large black birds. For one thing, it nests in colonies, known as Rookeries, while crows nest singly. It also tends to feed in large flocks, which may cover whole fields as each bird digs around in the soil for invertebrates such as worms and beetle larvae.

The Rook is one of the earliest of our birds to nest in the spring, fitting in some nest-building before the turn of the year, and reaching the stage of incubating eggs by the middle of March. This is helped by the fact that immature birds tend to pair up in the autumn, while the adult pairs stay together for life. The stick-nests, placed high in trees, are a familiar part of the rural landscape, especially in winter when the leaves are absent and the stick platforms are most obvious. Once the residents have settled in, however, they are equally impossible to overlook, since the birds are forever coming and going

Carrion Crow

Scientific name: Corvus corone

Identifying features: Feathered face; dark bill; flat crown

Similar species: Rook, Raven, Jackdaw

SIZE: 45–47 cm (17¾–18½ in)

HABITAT: Diverse

POPULATION: Abundant

Being clad in black all over and having the word 'carrion' in your name is not ideal for a positive image. And indeed, this crow is one of our least popular birds: farmers allege that it harms livestock, and gardeners shoo it from the bird table, claiming that it scares more attractive birds away.

There is little substance in either claim, but the crow is immune to all this anyway, and is a hugely successful bird, occurring in almost any habitat. It has a catholic diet which can include some live animals, plenty of dead meat and everything from scraps to fruit and berries.

In contrast to Rooks, Carrion Crows nest as single pairs, usually high in a tree, but also atop a cliff or building. The nest is a surprisingly complex structure, with at least four layers of different sticks and mud. Crows raise up to seven young, and as the nestlings grow the nest can be a noisy place indeed: high-pitched croaks are quickly added to the adults' irritable cawing.

Hooded Crow

Scientific name: Corvus cornix

Identifying features: Smoky-grey nape, mantle and underparts below the chest

Similar species: Carrion Crow, Jackdaw

SIZE: 45–47 cm (17¾–18½ in)

HABITAT: Diverse

POPULATION: Common

Recent genetic studies have shown that this form, long regarded as a race of the Carrion Crow, should be considered a species in its own right. There do not seem to be many differences in behaviour between the two, but the habitats are slightly different: the Hooded Crow takes over at higher altitudes and in wilder landscapes.

Although crows often live as single pairs, this does not apply to the whole population. If birds are unable to acquire a territory, they live with others of their kind in loose associations, forming flocks that roam around – so they are quite sociable. These birds also often join together in communal roosts at night, sometimes coming from miles around.

Hooded Crows are a regular sight at roadsides, tucking in to the latest traffic victim, such as a rabbit or fox. They often have competition from other scavengers in this regard, including Magpies. On the whole these two species do not get along with each other, and will sometimes interfere with each other's nesting attempt.

Tree Sparrow

SIZE: 14 cm (5½ in)

HABITAT: Farmland, woodland edge

POPULATION: Increasingly scarce

Scientific name: Passer montanus

Identifying features: Brown cap and white cheek with black spot; small black bib

Similar species: House Sparrow

Environmental Issues

In common with House Sparrows, Tree Sparrows live in small colonies with a fixed membership. The colonies remain true to their patch all year round except just after the breeding season, when all the birds of an area meet up in rich feeding areas for something of a knees-up. After a few weeks, the well-

---
LEFT

Contrary to its name, the Tree Sparrow is not a true woodland bird.

The Tree Sparrow was once a common bird across Britain and Europe, but it is now becoming so rare that bird-watchers travel kilometres to see it. It seems that the decline is related to the agricultural landscape becoming less and less suitable. Intensification reduces waste and spillage, there is less spring tilling, less stubble, fewer hedges and more use of chemicals – all of which reduce the amount of food available to these birds, especially in winter.

Within its hole the nest is made from the simple technique of stuffing material in – leaves, stems and roots, hair and feathers. The clutch of, typically, five eggs is incubated for 11–14 days, and the young leave after another two or three weeks.

The Tree Sparrow does not quite live up to its name because, although it often selects a hole in a tree for breeding, it can also use buildings and is by no means a true woodland bird. Thus it does overlap with the House Sparrow in some areas. The two species look very similar, but the Tree Sparrow is much less grimy and scruffy than its urban counterpart, with clean underparts and a neat white cheek centred with a black spot.

fed adults, plus a few recruits from the young of the year, return to the colony site to re-establish territories and, in some cases, to form new pairs.

Interestingly, male and female Tree Sparrows look similar whereas, in House Sparrows, they are quite different. This quirk can be explained in that having radically different female plumages prevents these two closely related species interbreeding.

Linnet

Scientific name: Carduelis cannabina

Identifying features: Longish, forked tail with white edges; white wing-panel; pale patches on face

Similar species: Redpoll, Twite, Greenfinch

SIZE: 13.5 cm (5¼ in)

HABITAT: Open country with bushes

POPULATION: Common

Linnets in books always look spectacular, tending to show off the male's brilliant crimson breast and forehead, contrasting pleasingly with its grey head and warm-brown mantle. The reality, though, is that this bright colour scheme is only worn for a comparatively short part of the spring and summer, and for the rest of the year Linnets look like rather dowdy, small brown birds. They are, however, highly effervescent, sociable and talkative, so what they lack in colour they make up for in character.

Most bird-watchers come across Linnets in flocks, usually feeding in a corner of a weedy field. They do

RIGHT
Linnets eat virtually no insects at all, and even the young are fed on a vegetarian diet.

not feed in trees, nor even in bushes, but instead cling to stems or seed-heads, or stay on the ground. This bird's exceptionally short, stubby bill is adapted for taking very small seeds, especially those of weeds such as charlock, dock, mustard and buttercups, as well as oil-seed rape.

Nesting

The Linnet was once commonly kept as a cage-bird, on account of its

pleasant, cheery demeanour and, especially, its song. The latter is a rambling affair, often delivered somewhat fitfully; but when it really gets going it is a wild, pacey, very varied and musical set of trills, a real delight.

Linnets often nest earlier in the year than other finches, from April, mainly because their favoured seeds are available before those favoured by other species – thistles for Goldfinches, for example. The structure is often placed in a thick bush, such as gorse, and tends to be lower down than most finch nests, sometimes even on the ground. Although many pairs nest alone, it is quite usual for three or four to use the same clump of bushes. Such birds often go on joint seed-hunting expeditions.

Lesser Redpoll

SIZE: 11.5 cm (4½ in)

HABITAT: Edges of woodland, along rivers, heaths, commons

POPULATION: Fairly common

Scientific name: Carduelis cabaret

Identifying features: Brown, streaky plumage; buff wing-bars; black bib; red forehead

Similar species: Linnet, Twite, Siskin

This delightful bird is an easily overlooked species of woodland edge, scrub and commons. At first sight it is just a small brown bird, but closer inspection will reveal a characteristic black bib, raspberry-red forehead and buff-coloured wing-bars. In spring the male is more colourful, with a strong stain of red on the breast; interestingly, though, this makeover does not arise from a moult, but from the wearing away of the fresh, dull coloured feather tips, leaving the colourful sub-terminal band exposed.

Redpolls rely year-round on very small tree seeds, such as those of birch and alder. In contrast to Linnets or Twites they customarily take these from up in the branches, often in company with Siskins and Goldfinches. However, in the late spring, when the seeds begin to fall, Redpolls will descend to the ground, and once there they often take the opportunity to drink.

Pairing and Clutch Size

Pairs of Redpolls often meet up in winter flocks. They do not hold much of a territory and, indeed, small groups often nest close by each other. The nest is a rather messy cup made up from twigs, grass, moss and, as a special furnishing, flower-heads. Meanwhile, it is lined with feathers and plant down, making the structure look white at a distance. There are four to six eggs in the clutch and, in common with other finches but unusually for small birds, the young are fed mainly on seeds.

In the winter, the resident population of Redpolls in Britain may be joined by

immigrants from Europe's northern birch forests. These Redpolls are larger and paler than indigenous birds, and they have white wing-bars.

ABOVE

The Common Redpoll is very similar to the Lesser Redpoll, but is larger and paler.

In recent years they have been upgraded to separate species status, and are called Common Redpolls, *Carduelis flammea*. They do not come every year and they are never very common, but if you see a large flock of Redpolls, it would be worth checking if this species was involved.

Yellowhammer

Scientific name: Emberiza citrinella

Identifying features: Male very distinctive and yellow, especially around head; female not as bright, but yellow wash usually obvious. Both have chestnut rump

Similar species: Cirl Bunting

SIZE: 16–16.5 cm (6¼–6½ in)

HABITAT: Farmland with hedgerows, grassland, scrub

POPULATION: Widespread and common

A few years ago almost everyone would have known the song of the Yellowhammer, encapsulated in the phrase 'A little bit of bread and no cheese'. Nowadays, however, the bird is no longer found at the corner of every field, and its favourite hedgerow habitat has been so drastically reduced that the declining Yellowhammer has faded from cultural consciousness, along with its dry, repetitive phrase. Its brilliant plumage, adorning bush-tops throughout the year, is also now an increasingly unusual sight.

The marvellous yellow plumage of the male in spring would, you might think, be wholly adequate to attract a mate; but in fact it is not the yellow, but the small red patches on the face that make the difference. The amount of red reflects the health and strength of the male, a measure of its ability to manufacture pigments from the seeds in its diet. Meanwhile, the song is a territorial tool to keep other males at a distance. It is sung quite incessantly, sometimes as often as 7,000 times a day, and for a long part of the year, right into midsummer and beyond.

Well-defended Territories

Yellowhammer nests are almost always built on the ground, the most typical site being at the base of a hedge, often on a slight bank. It is a well-hidden cup of grass and hay sprinkled with moss, into which the female lays between three and five eggs.

Yellowhammers, in common with many ground-nesting birds, do not allow their chicks much time in the nest, and the latter leave after just 10 days or so, before they can adequately fly.

After breeding, the well-defended territories break down, and the birds become much more sociable. They often form flocks, although the membership is not fixed and individuals wander freely in search of grain and weed seeds. In the autumn the plumage is not so bright as in spring, and many people mistakenly think that Yellowhammers are summer visitors.

Cirl Bunting

Scientific name: Emberiza cirlus

Identifying features: Olive-green rump; male head-pattern distinctive; female has pencil-thin streaks on breast and belly

Similar species: Yellowhammer

SIZE: 15.5 cm (6 in)

HABITAT: Farmland with hedges

POPULATION: Rare

Breeding Attempts

Cirl Buntings, in common with other buntings, feed mainly on seeds in the winter, mainly those of typical farmland weeds, including grasses. In the breeding season, however, they will add in a few insects, such as grasshoppers, bugs and aphids, and these form the main food for the young. Cirl Buntings are not specialized for insect catching, so most of these are simply picked up from the ground.

The nest is an untidy structure placed low down in dense herbage, although not usually on the ground, as the Yellowhammer's can be. The female lays three or four eggs, which she incubates for 12–13 days and, if all goes well at the start of the breeding season, the pair may fit in two, or even three, breeding attempts. Cirl Buntings are quite sedentary birds and, if both survive, the same male and female will pair up year after year.

At heart the Cirl Bunting is really a bird of warm Mediterranean-type climates, so it is perhaps not surprising that it is rare in Britain, with a maximum of about 700 breeding pairs, although it was once much commoner. It is a famously awkward species, with a host of habitat requirements. For example, it will only search for food within 30 m (100 ft) of cover, so it eschews the large, open fields that can be used by Yellowhammers. It also prefers south-facing fields, preferably on a slight slope.

Even in areas with many Cirl Buntings, this can still be a very difficult bird to see. It is a real skulker that can 'disappear' as it feeds unobtrusively on the ground, and it spends much time hidden in more substantial cover. The male's song is not as persistent as that of the Yellowhammer, and it is easy to miss amidst the bird chorus. The song itself lacks the 'cheese' element at the end of the phrase, so it is little more than a dry-sounding rattle.

RIGHT
The Cirl Bunting prefers Mediterranean climes to the more extreme northern parts of Europe.

Corn Bunting

Scientific name: Emberiza calandra

Identifying features: Plump with fairly short tail and heavy bill; streaks on breast often coalesce into central breast spot

Similar species: Yellowhammer, Reed Bunting

SIZE: 18 cm (7 in)

HABITAT: Grassland and arable fields

POPULATION: Localized fairly common

It might not look much, but the Corn Bunting is actually a highly individual bird, with an instantly recognizable song and a distinctly intriguing breeding system. In appearance it usually just looks like a featureless lump on an overhead wire or the top of a herb, but the dry, jangling song, sounding very much like somebody shaking a bunch of keys, makes the lump come alive and is very much a part of the atmosphere of arable fields on warm summer days.

Unusually for a small bird, there is a considerable difference in weight between sexes, with the males up to 20 per cent heavier than the females. The breeding system is also unusual, with a high proportion (up to a third) of males being polygamous. Most such males can aspire to attracting two or three females, but one is on record for somehow acquiring the attentions of 18 females in a single season. At the other end of the scale, some males attract no females at all. The difference appears to be related to the quality of a given male's territory.

Nest Style

The nest is a large, loosely constructed cup made up from grass and other plant stems and roots, and it is usually placed on the ground. This can be among crops and, if so, it is usually at the edge of a field. Being on the ground makes the structure vulnerable, so production schedules are hasty: the eggs are incubated for a mere 12–14 days, and the young are turfed out sometimes after only nine days, before they can actually fly.

The young are fed on insect food but, once they can fend for themselves, their diet switches principally to vegetable matter. Corn Buntings eat a wide variety of seeds, including cereals such as barley, and plenty of farmland weeds, often feeding in flocks in the winter months.

RIGHT

The song of the Corn Bunting is one of the most recognizable of all those heard in open country.

Freshwater & Marshland

Wetland habitats – freshwater marshes, rivers, streams and lakes, and the range of associated bogs, swamps and reedbeds – are amongst the most productive of all places for birds, holding the greatest variety of species of any habitat. This is because water really is the stuff of life, supporting a wide range of insects and other invertebrates, fish, crustaceans and other items suitable as prey for birds of all shapes and sizes.

The most obvious birds of freshwater and marshland habitats are water birds, of which the majority of species are from the order Anseriformes – the ducks, geese and swans. These have evolved to exploit a wide range of different water levels and types of watercourse: from shallow water (dabbling ducks, swans) to deep water (diving ducks). But not every water bird you see is from this group: other groups, including divers, grebes, and two members of the rail family – Moorhen and Coot – are also represented.

Long-legged wading birds also love marshy areas: from the herons, egrets and bitterns, to members of the various wader families such as plovers and sandpipers.

Amongst such a range of water birds, it is easy to overlook members of other bird groups, not normally associated with water, that find their home here. Some songbirds have adapted to a more watery existence: notably the Dipper, which has become truly aquatic. Other songbirds, from warblers to buntings and the Bearded Tit to the Sand Martin, are also associated closely with water. And who could forget the monarch of all the water birds: the dazzling, orange and electric-blue Kingfisher?

So if you want to enjoy close-up views of some fascinating and varied species, and watch their behaviour at close hand, head for your nearest wetland – whatever the time of year, and whatever the location, you will not be disappointed.

MUTE SWAN

SCIENTIFIC NAME: Cygnus olor

IDENTIFYING FEATURES:
Large, white; orange and black bill

SIMILAR SPECIES: Whooper and Bewick's Swans

SIZE: 140–160 cm (55–63 in)

HABITAT: Rivers, lakes and ponds

POPULATION: Common

Britain's largest bird is also one of its best-known and best-loved. Long associated with the royal family, Mute Swans are often supposed to be owned by the Queen, though in fact this only applies to some birds. They are also legendary for their aggressive nature, with many urban myths suggesting that they are able to break a man's arm! In fact, although male swans will vigorously defend their territory they are unlikely to do much more than hiss at you.

Our only resident swan, the Mute Swan can be easily told apart from its two relatives, Whooper and Bewick's Swans, by virtue of the orange, rather than yellow, colour of its bill. Mute Swans also have a prominent black knob on the front of their bill – slightly larger in the male than the female.

Ugly Ducklings

Youngsters – the proverbial ugly ducklings – are grey when they first fledge, gradually acquiring their snow-white adult plumage during their first year of life.

Mute Swans are found over most of lowland Britain and Europe, including many offshore islands. They will colonize a wide range of freshwater habitats, including rivers, large streams, lakes, ponds and lochs.

Well known for their habit of pairing for life, swans build a large nest out of sticks, and lay up to eight eggs, which often become stained by vegetation during incubation, which lasts up to six weeks. The young swim immediately, and stay with their parents for several months afterwards.

Mute Swans feed by dabbling or ducking their head underneath the water, to pick up aquatic vegetation – they also occasionally take animals such as frogs and worms. They were once under threat from lead weights used by anglers, but following a ban populations are now well on the way to recovery.

LEFT

Mute Swans have a reputation for aggressiveness, but in fact they will only hiss when defending territory.

BEWICK'S SWAN

SIZE: 115–127 cm (45¼–50 in)

HABITAT: Tundra in breeding season; freshwater lakes and marshes in winter

POPULATION: Winter visitor

SCIENTIFIC NAME: Cygnus columbianus

IDENTIFYING FEATURES: Black bill with yellow base; smaller size than other swans

SIMILAR SPECIES: Mute and Whooper Swans

Fascinating Facts

Swans are able to float so well partly because of the oil they excrete, which they coat their feathers with when preening.

LEFT
Bewick's Swans move from their Siberian breeding-grounds to north-western Europe in the winter.

Named after the eighteenth-century engraver and publisher Thomas Bewick, this is the smallest of Europe's three species of swan. Found across the whole of the Holarctic region from Alaska and Canada to Siberia, there are two distinct populations of this species; of which the race *bewickii* is confined as a breeding bird to northern Russia. In autumn these head westwards to flee the coming harsh winter weather, and many winter in Britain and Western Europe, attracted by the mild climate.

Noticeably smaller than its two larger relatives (Mute and Whooper Swans), Bewick's Swan shares the Whooper's black and yellow bill; though whereas the larger species has less black than yellow, Bewick's generally sports more black. The black and yellow bill pattern is not just attractive, but unique for each individual bird, allowing scientists to follow named individuals from year to year. This extraordinary fact was discovered by the great conservationist Sir Peter Scott.

Winter Home

Bewick's Swans start to arrive in their winter quarters in October, though the bulk come westwards in November and early December, forming large flocks at well-known wintering sites. Like all swans, they prefer lowland fresh-water areas such as lakes and marshes, generally near grassy areas where the birds can graze for food.

On the Siberian tundra, Bewick's Swans nest on open areas of swampy tundra; often associating with birds of prey such as Peregrines and Gyr Falcons that help warn them of approaching predators like Arctic Foxes. They build a nest from a mound of vegetation on a raised area, safe from flooding, and lay between three and five rounded eggs. The young fledge quickly, so they can accompany their parents on the long journey to the wintering grounds.

WHOOPER SWAN

SCIENTIFIC NAME: Cygnus cygnus

IDENTIFYING FEATURES:
Large size; yellow and black bill

SIMILAR SPECIES: Bewick's and Mute Swans

SIZE: 145–160 cm (57–63 in)

HABITAT: Freshwater marshes

POPULATION: Winter visitor

As large as a Mute Swan, the Whooper Swan is a winter visitor to the British Isles from its breeding grounds far to the north, in Iceland and Scandinavia. Named after its haunting call, it is one of the most elegant of all wintering wildfowl; especially when seen in flight. Like other swans, it migrates in family parties, with adults guiding their young on their first migration south each autumn.

Like Mute Swans, Whooper Swans are huge, white birds, with a long neck and dazzling plumage. Unless seen at a great distance, they can be told apart from Mutes by their yellow and black bill, a feature they share with their smaller relative the Bewick's Swan. Identifying them from Bewick's is not always easy, especially if you encounter a lone bird; but the Whooper Swan's larger size, longer neck and longer bill (with more yellow than black) is usually distinctive.

Creatures of Habit

Like Bewick's Swans, Whoopers are creatures of habit, with individuals and families returning to the same communal wintering sites year after year; though they are also sometimes found in smaller flocks and family parties, especially on migration.

On their northern breeding grounds, Whooper Swans start nesting even before the snow has thawed, enabling them to raise their brood of up to seven cygnets before the autumn cold sets in. Like other swans, they feed mainly on aquatic vegetation, upending themselves to reach down into the water.

One migrating party of Whooper Swans was recorded flying at a height of over eight thousand metres off the Scottish coast; but most travel at much lower altitudes – perhaps a few hundred metres above the sea.

GREYLAG GOOSE

SIZE: 75–90 cm (29½–35¼ in)

HABITAT: Lakes and marshes

POPULATION: Common

SCIENTIFIC NAME: Anser anser

IDENTIFYING FEATURES: Large size; pink bill, pale forewing in flight

SIMILAR SPECIES: All other 'grey' geese

The classic 'grey goose', the Greylag is the ancestor of most domestic breeds of goose, and has bequeathed to them its large size, ungainly gait and loud, honking call. Once mostly seen in the north of Britain, Greylag Geese are now much more widespread, due to escaped birds forming feral populations. Though yet to rival the much commoner Canada Goose in numbers, the Greylag population threatens to dominate many wetlands if they continue to increase.

Greylag is the largest goose found in the region, with a thick neck, bulky body and large bill. Like many of its relatives, its feet and legs are pink, as is the bill – a distinguishing feature from Pink-footed, White-fronted and Bean Geese which all have a partially dark bill. In flight Greylags look large and heavy, and usually utter their distinctive honking call.

Social Interaction

Truly wild Greylag Geese inhabit fairly remote areas, often on islands or remote wetlands. Feral birds can be found in a wide range of lowland freshwater sites, usually with areas of open water as well as grassy places for grazing. Like other geese, Greylags graze on grass, and also eat a wide range of aquatic plants, obtained from beneath the water's surface.

Greylags are sociable, gregarious birds, breeding in loose groups, and building their nests in a variety of places including in hollows on land and on floating vegetation in the water. They usually have a brood of around half a dozen goslings, though can have as many as a dozen.

The name 'greylag' has been explained in several ways: it may refer to the bird's habit of 'lagging behind' on migration, but it is equally likely that 'lag' is an ancient name meaning goose.

BELOW
The Greylag is the largest member of the goose family found in this region.

CANADA GOOSE

SCIENTIFIC NAME: Branta canadensis

IDENTIFYING FEATURES: Large size; pale belly; dark neck and head with white face-patch

SIMILAR SPECIES: None

SIZE: 90–100 cm (35⅓–39⅓ in)

HABITAT: Lakes, rivers and marshes

POPULATION: Common

Celebrated as a long-distance migrant in its native North America, the Canada Goose has a much less romantic reputation on this side of the Atlantic, having grown to pest proportions since it was originally introduced here more than two centuries ago. Brought to Britain and Europe by aristocratic landowners to decorate the lakes of their stately homes, its large size and aggressive habits have enabled it to spread throughout our cities, towns and countryside.

One of the easiest geese to identify thanks to its large size, and distinctive dark neck and head with contrasting white patch running from the base of the neck across each cheek. Birds occasionally hybridize with other geese, but their

facial pattern is usually dominant enough for the observer to tell the parentage.

Wild Geese

Canada Geese are found on most kinds of waterway, from rivers and lakes to large park ponds and freshwater marshes, throughout lowland England and Wales and in parts of southern Scotland.

They are resident, although each autumn a handful of truly wild Canada Geese – often of one of the smaller, more compact races – cross the Atlantic and can be seen at locations in the north and west. These genuinely wild birds are much more wary of humans than their feral cousins, and usually associate with other wild geese such as Greenland White-fronts.

Canada Geese build a large nest out of leaves, grass and reeds, usually on the ground within easy reach of water – often on small islands where they can be safe from ground predators such as foxes. The young are, like many goslings,

ABOVE

The cute Canada Goose goslings resemble many goslings, with their yellowish-brown down. They are perfectly at home in the grass on the banks of a lake.

covered in yellowish-brown down, and fledge after about six or seven weeks. Like most geese, they feed mainly on plants.

EGYPTIAN GOOSE

SIZE: 63–73 cm (24⅞–28¾ in)

HABITAT: Wide range of freshwater habitats including park ponds

POPULATION: Scarce but on the increase

SCIENTIFIC NAME: Alopochen aegyptiacus

IDENTIFYING FEATURES: Dark mask; white wing-bar; buffish plumage

SIMILAR SPECIES: None

African Native

In its native Africa this species has a fairly catholic choice of watery habitats, enabling it to adapt well to life in more temperate climes, where it has colonized city parks, wild reed-fringed broads and swampy woodlands. It is an early breeder, laying eggs from March or April – and even earlier in urban locations during mild winters. Egyptian Geese will nest in a range of sites, from the ground to rocky cliff ledges, where it lays its clutch of up to a dozen creamy white eggs.

It is also a fairly adaptable feeder, eating a range of leaves, seeds, grass and crops such as sweet potatoes, and may also take small creatures such as insects.

BELOW
The Egyptian goose actually falls into a category somewhere between a goose and a duck.

This bizarre looking 'goose' is in fact a member of the Shelduck tribe, considered by ornithologists as a sort of 'halfway house' between true geese and ducks. Originally confined to (mainly sub-Saharan) Africa, the Egyptian Goose was brought to Britain by a Norfolk aristocrat, and for many years was confined to the area in the immediate vicinity of his stately home. However, in recent decades it has begun to spread throughout southern and eastern England, and may yet prove itself almost as adaptable and able to spread as its Canadian cousin.

Unlike any other European species of wildfowl, the Egyptian Goose sports a unique combination of buffish–brown plumage, chestnut wing tips, a white and green wing pattern, and a dark mask around the eye. In flight the broad and prominent white wing-bars are very obvious, although these are almost hidden when the bird is on the ground.

MANDARIN DUCK

SCIENTIFIC NAME: *Aix galericulata*

IDENTIFYING FEATURES: Bright colours and orange 'sails' on male; greyish plumage speckled with white on female.

SIMILAR SPECIES: Feral Wood Duck (North American)

SIZE: 41–49 cm (16–19 in)

HABITAT: Lakes fringed with dense trees and shrubs.

POPULATION: Scarce

One of the world's most striking and beautiful birds, the Mandarin Duck was, like several other exotic species of wildfowl, brought to Britain from its native China to provide ornament for stately homes. This tree-nesting duck has found the temperate woodlands of parts of southern Britain to its liking, and a small but well-established population continues to thrive in various parts of the country, including the London suburbs.

The male Mandarin Duck is, quite simply, unmistakeable. No other bird boasts the same combination of features: the colourful head pattern and bright orange-red bill; the delicate feathering on the sides of the neck and, most striking of all, the two orange 'sails' poking up from the bird's back. Females are much less conspicuous – as befits their status as main parent at the nest. Nevertheless, their combination of contrasting greyish-brown speckled with white creates a very pleasing appearance.

Habitat and Breeding

Mandarin Ducks prefer large, tree-lined lakes – often favourite destinations for recreation – yet are often quite wary of humans. They frequently seek out the cover of waterside vegetation,

only flying when flushed unexpectedly from their hiding place.

They nest in holes in trees, sometimes as much as 10 or even 15 m (33–50 ft) above the ground, from which the young must jump soon after hatching. Like so many hole-nesting species, the eggs are white, and are incubated for four weeks. The young remain with the parents until fledging about six weeks later.

Fascinating Facts

It used to be thought that the small British population of Mandarin Ducks was a significant proportion of the total world population, but discoveries of larger numbers in China and Japan mean that this is not the case; nevertheless, it is a welcome addition to our avifauna.

WIGEON

SIZE: 45–51 cm (17¼–20 in)

HABITAT: Freshwater marshes, often near the coast

POPULATION: Scarce breeder; common winter visitor

SCIENTIFIC NAME: Anas penelope

IDENTIFYING FEATURES: Male has chestnut head, pinkish breast, grey plumage

SIMILAR SPECIES: Female Gadwall, Mallard

One of the most attractive of all the dabbling ducks, due to its attractive plumage and haunting, whistling call, the Wigeon is a classic bird of coastal freshwater marshes. The sound of a flock of whistling Wigeon on a wild and windswept wetland is one of the classic sounds of winter birding – though many observers fail to realize that only the males make that distinctive whistle, while the females utter a low-pitched, purring growl.

Distinctive Shape

The female Wigeon is far less distinctive, being mainly rufous brown in colour, and can easily be confused with other female dabbling ducks such as the Mallard and Gadwall (both larger) and the Teal (much smaller). But even in silhouette, both males and females have a very distinctive shape, with the rounded head and steep forehead creating a quite different 'feel' from other ducks.

A few hundred pairs of Wigeon breed in Britain, but the vast majority of birds seen in the British Isles arrive outside the breeding season from the north and east. From autumn onwards, they gather in large flocks on coastal marshes and other wetland areas where they can search for food. Unlike most ducks, Wigeon prefer grazing to dabbling or diving, and characteristically move across a short grassy area in large flocks, picking up morsels of vegetation with their delicate bills.

BELOW
The white patch at the base of the tail is a good way of identifying a Wigeon.

The male Wigeon is one of our most distinctive ducks: sporting a handsome combination of chestnut head (with a paler orange stripe running from the bill to the crown); pinkish breast; and grey back and flanks. In flight the males also show prominent white bars on the upper surface of their wings, a very useful feature for identifying the species at a distance.

GADWALL

SCIENTIFIC NAME: Anas strepera

IDENTIFYING FEATURES: Male is greyish overall, black under tail; female has orange bill, grey face

SIMILAR SPECIES: Female Mallard, Wigeon, Shoveler

SIZE: 46–56 cm (18–22 in)

HABITAT: Freshwater lakes and gravel pits

POPULATION: Common in winter; scarce breeder

Both the scientific and English names of this charming but often overlooked dabbling duck refer to the sound it makes. 'Gadwall' derives from 'gaddel', suggestive of the species' chattering call, while *Anas strepera* literally means 'noisy duck'! Like other members of its genus, the male sports a more distinctive plumage than the female, although both sexes can be distinguished at a distance from even close relatives by their distinctive compact body shape.

The Gadwall is one of the most subtle in plumage of all ducks. The basically brown female can easily be confused with other female dabbling ducks such as the Mallard, Shoveler and Wigeon, although her greyish head and face, yellowish tinged bill and white speculum

(the area showing of the folded wing) are all good identification features.

Plumage

At a distance, the male Gadwall appears basically grey, apart from a clear white speculum and jet black under the tail. However, on close examination, a subtle and variegated plumage becomes apparent: tiny vermiculations of black, white and grey,

varying in width from broader on the breast to very fine on the flanks.

Gadwall can be found on a wide range of fresh water courses, including lakes, reservoirs and gravel pits,

though they prefer shallow water surrounded by vegetation. They nest on the ground, usually close to water and with the nest hidden by vegetation.

Gadwall are often in mixed flocks with other dabbling ducks, and associate especially with Coots, which by diving regularly for food appear to bring morsels of vegetation to the water's surface, where the Gadwall pick it up by dipping their heads underwater.

BELOW
Gadwall frequent shallow, lowland waters, feeding on vegetation.

TEAL

SIZE: 34–38 cm (13⅜–15 in)

HABITAT: Small ponds and marshes

POPULATION: Common winter visitor; scarce breeder

SCIENTIFIC NAME: Anas crecca

IDENTIFYING FEATURES: Male has chestnut and blue-green head pattern; female has green speculum

SIMILAR SPECIES: Garganey

Our smallest dabbling duck, the Teal is a favourite among birders for its diminutive size, beautifully marked plumage and secretive habits. It is often found in habitats where other ducks do not venture, such as tiny marshy pools and the edges of reedbeds, where small flocks can feed without being disturbed. Uniquely for a common bird, the Teal has never been known by any other name. The word itself has been adopted by interior decorators and fashion designers to refer to the rich, bluish-green colour of the patch running behind the male's eyes.

No other dabbling duck, apart from the Garganey, even approaches the Teal in smallness of size, which is often the easiest way to identify the species even at a distance, especially when it is associating with other ducks. Seen at closer range, the male's deep orange-brown head, contrasting with the bluish-green patch running from the eye to the back of the nape, are distinctive. Males also show a pale, yellowish stripe along their sides, and a noticeable yellow patch beneath the tail. Females are typically much less distinctive: basically speckled browns and buffs, with a darker cap and green speculum.

Habitat and Feeding

Outside the breeding season, Teal can be seen on a wide range of water courses,

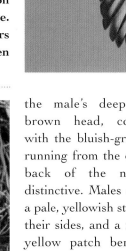

BELOW
The Teal can easily be identified by its diminutive size.

including large reservoirs as well as the smallest pool. When breeding they prefer to seek out thick cover to conceal their nest and eggs.

Teal feed by using several methods: on water they skim the surface or pick up tiny items of plant and animal matter; they also paddle slowly through shallow water or mud, filtering items as they do so.

MALLARD

SCIENTIFIC NAME: Anas platyrhynchos

IDENTIFYING FEATURES: Male has bottle-green head; female has large size, orange-yellow bill

SIMILAR SPECIES: Female Gadwall, Shoveler, Pintail

SIZE: 50–65 cm (19¼–25⅝ in)

HABITAT: Any freshwater

POPULATION: Abundant

The classic, ubiquitous dabbling duck, from which most domestic breeds of duck are descended. The Mallard is often overlooked because it is so common and widespread, being found on most waterways from village ponds, through rivers and lakes, to man-made gravel pits and reservoirs – the Mallard has adapted to them all. Mallards also have a dark side, noticeable in the breeding season, where gangs of males will pursue and harass a lone female until she gives in through exhaustion and mates with them – or occasionally dies trying to fight them off.

The male Mallard is quite simply unmistakeable, with his bottle-green head, yellow bill, white collar and magenta breast. Mallards are the largest of our dabbling ducks, a useful way

to identify females if they are in a mixed flock with other female dabbling ducks such as Shoveler and Pintail. Females can also be identified by their prominent speculum: a purplish-blue bordered with white and black at the sides.

Eclipse Plumage

During the summer months, all dabbling ducks undergo a period of moult known as the 'eclipse plumage', when they are often flightless for a period of time as their new feathers grow. At this time, male Mallards may resemble a darker version of the female.

The key to the Mallard's success is its adaptability both in its breeding and feeding habits, and its sociable, gregarious nature. Although most breed in the spring, during mild winters eggs may be laid even before Christmas, with broods of

ducklings out and about by December or January. Mallards are also highly opportunistic and catholic feeders, taking a wide range of plant and animal food – ducklings are even known to snatch tiny insects from mid-air.

PINTAIL

SIZE: 51–66 cm (20–26 in)

HABITAT: Freshwater marshes, often near the coast

POPULATION: Common winter visitor; very scarce breeder

SCIENTIFIC NAME: Anas acuta

IDENTIFYING FEATURES: Male has long tail, brown head, white breast; female has slender shape

SIMILAR SPECIES: Female Mallard; Shoveler

Surely our most handsome and elegant dabbling duck, the male Pintail sports the long, central tail-feathers that give the species its English and scientific names. The pioneering seventeenth-century ornithologist John Ray also noted two folk-names: 'cracker', after its call; and 'sea pheasant' from its distinctive appearance. Because of its extensive global range, the Pintail was once thought to be the world's commonest duck, but after declines that title probably now goes to the Mallard.

The male Pintail is, like so many members of the dabbling duck genus *Anas*, unmistakable, even in silhouette, with his long tail and long, slender neck obvious even at a great distance. Closer to, we can appreciate the greyish vermiculations along the back, the pale buffish yellow undertail, and the chocolate brown head contrasting with the snow-white breast. In flight the slender shape and long tail feathers are very distinctive.

Dabbling Ducks

Females are also very distinctive, not least because they share their mates' long, slender neck and body shape. They have the typical speckled appearance of all female dabbling ducks, along with a plainer brown head.

When breeding, Pintails prefer open areas of wet grassland or tundra, with nearby water. Outside the breeding season, they tend to congregate on freshwater areas near the coast such as estuaries, where they often gather in quite large flocks with other dabbling ducks such as Shoveler, Wigeon and Gadwall.

When feeding, Pintails usually up-end in quite shallow water in order to pick up morsels of food (both plants and small invertebrates) from the muddy bottom. They are also known to graze in fields.

LEFT

Pintails are essentially birds of northern Europe, preferring tundra habitat to most others.

GARGANEY

SCIENTIFIC NAME: Anas querquedula

IDENTIFYING FEATURES: Brown head with white eye-patch (male)

SIMILAR SPECIES: Teal

SIZE: 37–41 cm (14⅝–16⅛ in)

HABITAT: Freshwater pools, often fringed with reeds

POPULATION: Scarce summer visitor

The only summer visitor to Britain of all wildfowl (ducks, geese and swans), the Garganey is a scarce and secretive bird, rarely seen except on passage in spring and autumn. It may once have been commoner, as shown by the fact that it has gained several folk-names, including 'summer teal' and 'cricket teal' – the latter a reference to one of its distinctive calls, which sounds rather like a buzzing insect, and may be a useful clue to the bird's presence.

The male Garganey is one of the smallest and most exquisite ducks, rivalling the Teal for compactness and beauty. In full breeding plumage, males have a very distinctive brown, grey and white plumage, the most obvious distinguishing feature being the broad creamy-white stripe running from just in front of the eye to the back of the nape, and contrasting with the dark, chocolate-brown head, face and breast.

RIGHT

Garganeys are totally migratory, spending their winters in sub-Saharan Africa.

Distinguishing Male from Female

The female Garganey is typically rather drab, and can be hard to tell apart from the female Teal. The differences are that the Garganey has a bluish forewing (usually only viewable in flight) and a more distinctively striped head pattern, with a prominent dark crown and eye-stripe contrasting with a paler buff supercilium.

The Garganey is one of our earliest spring migrants to arrive, usually returning from its African winter quarters in March or April. At this time they can be quite easy to see, but soon move on, with only a few pairs staying to breed in Britain. In August or September they can also be seen on their return journey south.

Despite its rarity in Britain, in world terms, the Garganey is one of the most abundant ducks throughout Europe and Asia, and at least two million overwinter in West Africa.

SHOVELER

SIZE: 44–52 cm (17½–20½ in)

HABITAT: Freshwater habitats, especially shallow ones

POPULATION: Common winter visitor; scarce breeder

SCIENTIFIC NAME: Anas clypeata

IDENTIFYING FEATURES: Huge bill; male has white breast, green head, brown flanks

SIMILAR SPECIES: Mallard

The unique, spoon-shaped bill that gives the Shoveler its popular English name is one of the most extraordinary of all British birds, and allows the Shoveler to feed in its distinctive style. Groups of Shovelers will often feed huddled closely together, driving forward across the surface of the water and hoovering up morsels of food as they go. Oddly, in past times, the name 'shoveler' was also attached to the Spoonbill, and vice versa.

The male Shoveler is the only duck, apart from the much larger and goose-like Shelduck, to show a combination of green, chestnut-brown and white in its plumage, with a bottle-green head, snow-white breast and chestnut flanks. The female also sports the huge, spatula-shaped bill, but otherwise is very similar to other female dabbling ducks, with a speckled brown and buff plumage. In flight the female shows pale greyish-blue on the forewing.

Feeding and Nesting

Like most dabbling ducks, which feed on the surface of the water rather than by diving down beneath it, the Shoveler prefers shallow areas of fresh water, often with reeds or other vegetation where they can take cover should a predator reveal itself.

They usually nest close to water, on the ground amongst low vegetation, without necessarily taking the trouble to conceal themselves, but instead relying on the female's camouflaged plumage. The male is more territorial than other ducks, frequently driving away rivals if they come too close to the nest.

When feeding, the broad bill really comes into its own: the Shoveler sucks in water through the sides, where fine hairs act as a filter to trap tiny morsels of animal and plant food.

BELOW
Shovelers like to breed on shallow lakes bordered by rushes.

RED-CRESTED POCHARD

SCIENTIFIC NAME: Netta rufina

IDENTIFYING FEATURES: Male has orange head,
[re]d bill, black breast; female has dark head with pale
cheeks, reddish bill

SIMILAR SPECIES: Pochard

SIZE: 53–57 cm (21–22⅛ in)

HABITAT: Large lakes and gravel pits

POPULATION: Scarce

This handsome and striking diving duck is a rare visitor to Britain, though in recent years escaped birds from wildfowl collections and city parks have established feral breeding populations **in several parts of the country, making it difficult to distinguish them from truly wild birds.**

Originally from central Asia, where it breeds in large numbers on reed-fringed lakes, the Red-crested Pochard is also found in pockets of wetland in eastern and southern Europe, where it is expanding its range westwards.

One of our most striking ducks, the male has what looks like a bouffant 'hair-do' of fluffy orange, which he puts to good use during courtship displays.

Red-crested Pochards are partial migrants, heading southwards to avoid the snow and ice, though only going as far as the Mediterranean and the Indian subcontinent.

POCHARD

SCIENTIFIC NAME: Aythya farina

IDENTIFYING FEATURES: Male has chestnut
head, pale grey body, black breast

SIMILAR SPECIES: Female Tufted Duck

SIZE: 42–49 cm (16½–19¼ in)

HABITAT: Larger areas of fresh water

POPULATION: Common winter
visitor; scarce breeder

A large, stocky diving duck, the Pochard's unusual name comes from its feeding actions, which are supposed to resemble that of a poacher. Like its relatives, it gathers in large flocks outside the breeding season, often on exposed reservoirs and gravel pits, with deep enough water to obtain its food.

The male Pochard is easily identified by the combination of a chestnut head, black breast and pale grey back and flanks. Females are much less distinctive: pale greyish-brown on the body with a brown head and breast.

Pochards often associate with other diving ducks, especially Tufted Ducks, outside the breeding season – sometimes in huge flocks of more than a thousand birds. They nest mainly on larger lakes across the steppes of Asia.

TUFTED DUCK

SCIENTIFIC NAME: Aythya fuligula

SIZE: 40–47 cm (15¾–18½ in)

HABITAT: Large, open water

POPULATION: Common, especially in winter

IDENTIFYING FEATURES: Male has black and white plumage; female has slight tuft on back of head

SIMILAR SPECIES: Scaup

The commonest and most widespread diving duck in Britain, this smart black and white bird with its distinctive tuft of feathers on the back of the male's head is found in a wide range of freshwater habitats, from huge, concrete-banked reservoirs to park ponds in the heart of our cities. It feeds with a highly effective diving action: using its powerful feet to propel itself down to the bottom of the water to find food.

Like almost all ducks, the male and female Tufted Duck are very different in appearance: so much so that beginners often mistake them for two completely different species. The male is basically black and white: with black head, breast, back and under the tail, and contrasting white flanks.

Identifying Ducks

Look closer and you will see that the 'black' also gives off a purplish sheen, more noticeable in bright sunlight. The eye is bright yellow, and the male also has a prominent black tuft of feathers on his head that

gives the species its name. The female, by contrast, is mainly brown, though paler on the flanks in a vague echo of the male's plumage. She too sports a short tuft of feathers, though nothing like as prominent as that of the male. The female may also have a pale patch around her bill, similar to that of the larger and bulkier female Scaup.

Tufted Ducks nest on the ground, often on islands, or in the open but in colonies of gulls or terns which give them protection.

The ducklings dive almost as soon as they are hatched, though stay with their parents until they fledge after about seven weeks.

ABOVE
Tufted Ducks get their name from the crest on the back of their heads.

SMEW

SCIENTIFIC NAME: Mergus albellus

IDENTIFYING FEATURES: Male has white plumage striped with black, black mask; female has chestnut cap, white cheeks

SIMILAR SPECIES: None

SIZE: 38–44 cm (15–17⅜ in)

HABITAT: Gravel pits and reservoirs

POPULATION: Scarce winter visitor

Habitat Choices

When breeding, Smew prefer dense forests, where they readily take to nest boxes where provided. On migration and in winter they favour a range of freshwater habitats, generally with fairly deep water enabling them to obtain their food by diving. They often gather in small, tight flocks, associating with other wintering ducks such as Goldeneye and Goosander. Shy and retiring, they fly easily when disturbed.

Smew are prone to hard weather movements, and will often spend the early part of the winter in the Netherlands or Baltic, and only move westwards in search of milder climes if harsh weather sets in.

LEFT
Female Smews compete in the looks department with their chestnut crown.

Sometimes the most simple colours and patterns can be the most beautiful, and nowhere is this better illustrated than in a male Smew, whose delicate black and white markings create a truly stunning image. A bird of the northern boreal forests, where it nests in holes in trees, the Smew migrates south to more temperate latitudes in winter. In Britain, it often appears, rather incongruously, on suburban gravel pits and reservoirs, where it brings a touch of the exotic to a winter day's birding.

impression of a precious vase that has been dropped and put back together! The female – also known along with immature males as a 'redhead' – has a grey body, chestnut crown and prominent white cheeks. In flight both males and females show white on the upper wing.

The male Smew is impossible to confuse with any other duck: small and compact, with a snow-white plumage overlaid with broad and narrow black stripes and grey vermiculations on the flanks, as well as a black mask – giving the overall

GOOSANDER

SIZE: 58–68 cm (22⅞–26⅞ in)

HABITAT: Upland rivers when breeding; reservoirs and gravel pits in winter

POPULATION: Scarce but increasing

SCIENTIFIC NAME: Mergus merganser

IDENTIFYING FEATURES: Male has dark green head, pale body; female has chestnut head, grey body

SIMILAR SPECIES: Red-breasted Merganser

The largest of the three European duck species known as 'sawbills' (the others being Red-breasted Merganser and Smew), the Goosander is one of the handsomest of our ducks – especially the smart male. Despite coming into conflict with anglers over fish stocks (and even having a bounty placed on their heads as recently as the 1970s), the Goosander is thriving as a British breeding bird, having more than doubled in numbers and spread south from its Scottish strongholds to colonize England and Wales.

The male Goosander is a truly stunning creature: his dark, bottle-green head and crimson bill are offset by the pale breasts, flanks and underparts – which glow with a salmon-pink tinge when in full breeding plumage. In flight the dark wingtips and head contrast

RIGHT

Female Goosanders (such as here) may sometimes nest together.

with the paleness of the rest of the body. The female is very similar to the Red-breasted Merganser, though larger and stockier, and with a noticeable border between the chestnut head and pale neck. It has a slightly less shaggy crest than the Red-breasted Merganser, though this can be variable.

River Breeders

When breeding, Goosanders are often found on fast-flowing rivers, usually in upland areas. They nest in holes in trees, and in Scandinavia and Russia have been known to nest in the walls of buildings and houses. Up to 22 eggs have

been found in the same nest, almost certainly as a result of two females laying together.

Outside the breeding season, during the autumn and winter months, Goosanders gather in flocks on large, open areas of water such as reservoirs and gravel pits; more generally inland than the Red-breasted Merganser. They may be seen displaying on bright winter days.

RUDDY DUCK

SCIENTIFIC NAME: Oxyura jamaicensis

IDENTIFYING FEATURES:
Sticking-up tail; rufous plumage

SIMILAR SPECIES: None

SIZE: 35–43 cm (13¾–17 in)

HABITAT: Variety of
freshwater habitats

POPULATION: Common

This rather odd-looking species, originally from North America, is the only member of the 'stifftail' tribe to be found in Britain. Its presence here is down to the misguided release of captive birds more than fifty years ago; like other introduced wildfowl, the lack of competition has enabled the Ruddy Duck to thrive. However, it is now under threat because of its habit of interbreeding with a rare relative in southern Europe, and may fall victim to an official cull.

The male Ruddy Duck is one of our most distinctive species of wildfowl: tiny (barely larger than our smallest duck, the Teal), and with a rich rufous plumage, white cheeks, a dark crown and impossibly bright blue bill. He also sports a prominent, sticking-up tail which he puts to good use in wooing the female. Females and juveniles are basically the same shape as the male, but with a less prominent tail and much duller, brownish plumage; though immature males also show the white cheeks.

Courting

When courting, the male Ruddy Duck sticks his tail vertically in the air, puffs up his chest and struts around the water banging his bill on his chest in a Tarzan-like manner.

Unfortunately the Ruddy Duck's aggressive courtship behaviour has now got him into trouble: male Ruddies are thought to have interbred with Spanish populations of the endangered White-headed Duck, thus threatening their genetic heritage. The good news for lovers of the Ruddy Duck is that culls of birds tend to fail because new birds simply move into the area vacated by the culled ones. So the future of the Ruddy Duck – at least on this side of the Atlantic – now hangs in the balance.

RED-THROATED DIVER

SCIENTIFIC NAME: Gavia stellata

IDENTIFYING FEATURES: Slender bill;
red throat (in breeding season)

SIMILAR SPECIES: Black-throated and Great
Northern Divers

SIZE: 55–67 cm (21¼–26⅛ in)

HABITAT: Freshwater lochs;
coast and open sea

POPULATION: Scarce

Divers are amongst the most primitive of all birds, with a vaguely prehistoric feel about them. They are also some of the most aquatic, spending the vast majority of their lives on water, and only coming ashore during the breeding season to nest. Like all divers, the Red-throated has a haunting and mysterious call, which has given rise to a wide range of superstitions and folklore.

The Red-throated is the smallest of the divers – about the size of a large duck, but much more slender and elongated in shape, with a pointed bill. In the breeding season both adults sport the red throat patch that gives the species its name, and an elegant pale grey head. But for most of the year they are in their non-breeding garb, with a grey cap, mottled greyish back and clean white face, throat and neck.

The Rain Goose

When breeding, Red-throated Divers prefer small lochs on remote Scottish islands or coastal areas, usually fairly near the sea. Outside the breeding season they are usually found on the sea itself, and may be driven inshore by bad weather, especially in autumn and winter.

They lay their two eggs in an untidy nest made from aquatic vegetation, either floating on the water or right beside it on the shallow bank. The eggs are incubated for about four weeks, and the young swim almost as soon as they are hatched, but remain with the parents until fledging about five to seven weeks later.

The Red-throated Diver's habit of living in some of the wettest regions means that its call is often associated with rain; and the bird has been named the 'rain goose'.

BELOW
Red-throated Divers are the smallest of this family, although still about the size of a duck.

BLACK-THROATED DIVER

SCIENTIFIC NAME: Gavia arctica

IDENTIFYING FEATURES:
Contrasting plumage; straight bill

SIMILAR SPECIES: Red-throated and
Great Northern Divers

SIZE: 58–73 cm (22⅞–28¾ in)

HABITAT: Lochs (when breeding);
reservoirs and coast in winter

POPULATION: Scarce breeder
and winter visitor

The Black-throated Diver breeds in some of the most far-flung and inaccessible parts of Britain, on tiny lochs in the northern and western reaches of the Scottish Highlands and Islands. It can only survive there because the fish it eats are too small to attract any competition from other species of water bird, allowing this beautiful creature to indulge in elaborate courtship dances in which rival pairs work out the borders of their territories.

In breeding plumage, the Black-throated Diver is a very handsome bird, with highly contrasting black and white plumage, a pearl grey head, and the black throat patch which distinguishes it from its close relative the Red-throated Diver. Both sexes are alike, and the same applies outside the breeding season, when the diver loses its black throat and adopts contrasting dark upperparts and white underparts. At this time of year it can be hard to distinguish from the other two divers, but a pale patch on the flanks and straighter bill than Red-throated, and smaller size compared with Great Northern, make it possible to identify given decent views.

Fascinating Facts

Increased breeding figures for the Black-Throated Diver in the UK may be thanks to man-made rafts anchored in Lochs.

LEFT

Black-throated Divers spend most of their lives on the water, and only come on to land to breed.

Diving Bird

Like all divers, the Black-throated is a highly aquatic bird, diving frequently for its food – sometimes for up to two minutes at a time – and only coming on to land to breed. The nest is built either close to the shoreline, or on a floating platform on the water itself. Black-throated Divers normally lay two eggs, and the young remain with the parents through a long fledging period of about two months, after which they leave the breeding area. They do not breed until they are two or three years old.

LITTLE GREBE

SCIENTIFIC NAME: Tachybaptus ruficollis

IDENTIFYING FEATURES: Small size, fluffy rear end

SIMILAR SPECIES:
Black-necked and Slavonian Grebes

SIZE: 25–29 cm (9⅞–11½ in)

HABITAT: Freshwater marshes, lakes and ponds

POPULATION: Common

This tiny grebe (the world's second smallest after the Least Grebe of the Americas) is sometimes mistaken for a baby duck, due to its small size, fluffy plumage and endearing features – hence the widespread folk name still in use, 'dabchick'. It is a widespread and fairly common bird, often overlooked because of its unobtrusive habits.

All year round the Little Grebe can usually be told apart from any other water bird by its diminutive size and fluffy rear end – though beware non-breeding plumage Black-necked Grebes which can also look very small. In spring and summer, Little Grebes adopt a smart breeding dress, with a pale greenish patch at the base of the bill, and a rufous patch on the sides of the face and throat. The rest of the head and body, apart from the paler rear end, is dark brown.

Adaptable Grebes

Little Grebes can be found on some of our smallest waterways, including canals, ponds and marshes – often suitable for no other birds apart from the equally unassuming and ubiquitous Moorhen. They rarely appear on larger areas of water such as reservoirs, though well-vegetated gravel pits are also suitable for breeding and wintering.

Little Grebes are mainly carnivorous, devouring a wide range of aquatic invertebrates, especially insect larvae, molluscs and crustaceans. Like other grebes, they build a floating nest from vegetation, and lay four to six (occasionally as many as 10) eggs. The tiny young are able to swim virtually as soon as they are hatched, but enjoy hitching a ride on the adults' backs for some time afterwards!

LEFT

Like all the members of its family the Little Grebe is an accomplished swimmer and diver.

GREAT CRESTED GREBE

SCIENTIFIC NAME: Podiceps cristatus

IDENTIFYING FEATURES:
Prominent orange crest (in breeding season only)

SIMILAR SPECIES: Red-necked Grebe

SIZE: 46–51 cm (18–20 in)

HABITAT: Gravel pits, rivers and lakes

POPULATION: Common

The largest European member of its family, the Great Crested Grebe is celebrated for two things: one behavioural, the other historical. It has one of the most elaborate courtship displays of any bird, culminating in the famous 'penguin dance'. The species also played a crucial part in the history of bird protection, being one of the prime reasons for the founding of the Royal Society for the Protection of Birds – formed in the late nineteenth century to prevent the use of grebe skins in women's fashion.

In breeding plumage, both male and female Great Crested Grebes sport an elaborate headdress of orange feathers tipped with brown. In winter, these are discarded, and the bird can best be identified by its large size relative to other grebes, pinkish bill and all-white neck.

Courtship Display

The courtship display often begins very early in the New Year, with male and female facing each other in the water and engaging in a very formal series of head turns and beak twitches. Sometimes this comes to nothing, but once paired up, they need to cement the bond. This is when they wave weed in each other's faces, while frantically paddling to stay vertically upright in the water – hence the comparison with penguins.

Great Crested Grebes build a floating nest out of water weed, and lay anything between one and six pale, elongated eggs. These are soon stained greenish-brown because of being covered up by water weed to deter predators when the adults are away from the nest. The young are striped like old-fashioned humbugs, and hitch rides on the adults' backs for as long as they are able to.

RED-NECKED GREBE

SCIENTIFIC NAME: Podiceps grisegena

IDENTIFYING FEATURES: Chestnut-red neck, yellow base to bill

SIMILAR SPECIES: Great Crested and Slavonian Grebes

SIZE: 40–50 cm (15¾–19¾ in)

HABITAT: Freshwater marshes, lakes and reservoirs

POPULATION: Scarce winter visitor

Like other members of its family, the Red-necked Grebe has a very distinctive change of plumage between the breeding season and at other times of year. During the autumn and winter, it can be confused with both the larger Great Crested and the smaller Slavonian Grebe, especially in distant views on choppy reservoirs. However, its dagger-shaped, yellow bill, dark cap contrasting with white cheeks, and most importantly the dusky neck, should make identity certain.

Territories

In the spring and summer the Red-necked Grebe is a much easier bird to identify, sporting the brick-red neck that gives the species its name. It is also more vocal than other grebes at this time of year, with territorial birds 'singing' to each other to mark their boundaries.

In its eastern European strongholds, the Red-necked Grebe is found mainly on small, well-vegetated waters, with plenty of emergent vegetation such as reedbeds, where the bird will conceal its nest. Like other water birds, it often chooses to nest amongst large colonies of gulls, which will often drive away potential predators, thus safeguarding the Red-necked Grebes and their families.

After breeding the birds disperse: firstly to larger inland waters, and then, after a westward and southward migration, to the coast.

The second largest of Europe's grebes, the Red-necked has always been a fairly scarce visitor to Britain, although influxes occur periodically when harsh winter weather on the Continent drives the birds westwards in search of milder conditions. Red-necked Grebes occasionally summer in Britain too, and have attempted to breed, though so far without great success. As climate change takes hold, the species is likely to become even scarcer in winter, but may perhaps eventually breed here.

BELOW
The Red-necked Grebe changes its plumage in the breeding season.

SLAVONIAN GREBE

SCIENTIFIC NAME: Podiceps auritus

IDENTIFYING FEATURES:
Straight bill; pale neck

SIMILAR SPECIES: Black-necked and
Red-necked Grebes

SIZE: 31–38 cm (12¼–15 in)

HABITAT: Freshwater marshes,
reservoirs, coastal waters

POPULATION: Scarce

Also known as the Horned Grebe, because of the prominent golden-yellow head feathers sported by both the male and female during the breeding season. The original English name of the Slavonian Grebe derives from a region in eastern Croatia, from where the bird is supposed to have originated, although it is actually only a winter visitor to the Balkans. The breeding range of Slavonian Grebes extends right across the northern temperate zone, from Europe, through Asia, to North America.

Slavonian is a medium-sized grebe, often confused with its slightly smaller relative the Black-necked (or Eared) Grebe. In breeding plumage, look out for the chestnut (not black) neck, and much more prominent head feathers extending from the bill and above and behind the eye. Outside the breeding season, Slavonian has a more 'capped' appearance, with a white neck and cheeks. At all times of year, the Slavonian's straighter, dagger-shaped bill is a good identification aid.

Protection of Chicks

Slavonian Grebes breed on sheltered lakes and lochs, usually with vegetation where they can gain some protection for their floating nests. Like other grebes, they will carry their four or five young on their backs, with the striped chicks often concealing themselves completely in the parents' feathers to avoid danger.

The chicks soon learn to dive for their own food: mainly aquatic beetles and their larvae, although they will also take small fish and other aquatic creatures.

After breeding, Slavonian Grebes are more likely to head to coastal waters than their relatives, and are often seen in harbours and offshore bays – where their black and white plumage may cause confusion with winter plumaged auks such as the Guillemot or Razorbill.

LEFT

The dagger-shaped bill of the Slavonian Grebe is a useful feature for identifying this water bird.

BLACK-NECKED GREBE

SIZE: 28–34 cm (11–13⅜ in)

HABITAT: Freshwater marshes, reservoirs

POPULATION: Scarce

SCIENTIFIC NAME: Podiceps nigricollis

IDENTIFYING FEATURES:
Upturned bill, dark neck

SIMILAR SPECIES: Slavonian and Little Grebes

The Black-necked Grebe is an enigmatic little bird, particularly in its breeding habits. Although widespread as a breeding bird across Europe, Asia and North America, and even found in eastern and southern Africa, its distribution is often very patchy – with colonies appearing in a particular location, breeding successfully for a few years, and then disappearing for no apparent reason. Outside the breeding season it may gather in vast numbers, such as the million or more birds that winter on Mono Lake in northern California.

The other name for the Black-necked Grebe – and the one used in North America – is 'Eared Grebe', which applies solely to the bird in its handsome and striking breeding garb. The golden-yellow feathers behind the eye are similar to those of the Slavonian Grebe, but do not extend in front of the eye and are confined to the side of the face rather than sticking out behind the head as in those of the Slavonian.

How to Spot

Other key identification features during the breeding season are the coal-black neck, and the rather fluffy rear-end, reminiscent of the Little Grebe. In autumn and winter the resemblance to the Little Grebe is even more striking, and care must be taken not to confuse the two species. Black-necked appear larger, and have more obvious pale cheeks contrasting with the dark cap (though far less obvious than in the Slavonian).

Black-necked Grebes breed on marshy pools, usually fringed with reeds, and often alongside large, noisy colonies of gulls or marsh terns, which provide protection against intruders and predators. After breeding they disperse to a range of habitats, including coastal ones as well as lakes, gravel pits and reservoirs.

BELOW

It can be easy to confuse the Black-necked Grebe with other members of the grebe family.

BITTERN

SCIENTIFIC NAME: Botaurus stellaris

IDENTIFYING FEATURES:
Streaked brown plumage, large bill

SIMILAR SPECIES: None

SIZE: 69–81 cm (27⅛–32 in)

HABITAT: Reedbeds

POPULATION: Scarce

The Bittern is an extraordinary bird: rarely seen, yet often heard as it emits its low-pitched, booming call. This is one of the furthest-carrying of any bird sound, being audible at a distance of up to several kilometres away, and often heard at dawn or dusk.

When seen, the Bittern is unmistakable: more like a shaggy owl than a heron,

with its unkempt brown feathers seemingly too big for its body. Against reeds, the Bittern is perfectly camouflaged, with the blacks and browns of its plumage perfectly mimicking its habitat, especially when it points its bill upwards in its alert posture.

Outside the breeding season, Bitterns venture to new areas, and may be seen in

some surprising locations; though they will always seek

out the safety of a dense reedbed where they can.

LITTLE BITTERN

SCIENTIFIC NAME: Ixobrychus minutus

IDENTIFYING FEATURES: Small size;
pink wing-patches

SIMILAR SPECIES: Night Heron (very rare)

SIZE: 33–38 cm (13–15 in)

HABITAT: Freshwater marshes and reedbeds

POPULATION: Very rare

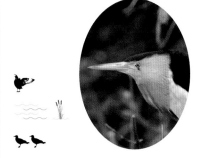

This tiny heron (second in size only to the Least Bittern of North America)

is incredibly elusive, often hiding in dense reedbeds, where it uses its powerful

legs to clamber about the vegetation and hunt for its favourite prey of frogs and fish.

Like some other herons the Little Bittern is essentially crepuscular in habits – emerging mainly at dawn and dusk. It is most likely to be seen in flight, when its small size, and long broad wings

with their pinkish wing-patches, are the best means of identification. Females are more like a miniature Bittern in appearance, with streaked black and brown plumage ideal for camouflage in their reedy home. Apart from during the breeding season, Little Bitterns are essentially solitary birds: secretive, lone hunters.

LITTLE EGRET

SIZE: 55–65 cm (21³/₄–25⁵/₈ in)

HABITAT: Freshwater marshes, lakes and ponds

POPULATION: Scarce but increasing

SCIENTIFIC NAME: Egretta garzetta

IDENTIFYING FEATURES: Pure white plumage

SIMILAR SPECIES: Cattle Egret (very rare)

LEFT

The Little Egret is distinguishable by its snow-white plumage.

This elegant, snow-white heron is a familiar sight in wetland areas across much of the warm temperate and tropical zones of the Old World, from western Europe and Asia to Japan and Australia, and throughout sub-Saharan Africa. In recent years the species has shown the ability to colonize new areas, including Britain; while increasing numbers of Little Egrets are now appearing on the other side of the Atlantic Ocean, in places such as Trinidad and Tobago in the Caribbean.

Like several other species of egret, the Little Egret has a primarily snow-white plumage, offset by a dark bill, yellow patch around the base of the bill and the eye, dark legs and bright yellow feet. It can be told apart from its larger relative the Great White Egret purely on size, but is much harder to distinguish from its sibling species, the North American Snowy Egret.

A Fashionable Bird

Like many other species of heron and egret, Little Egrets are colonial breeders, nesting together in noisy colonies, usually in trees. In the breeding season the adults adopt delicate, feathery plumes extending from the back of the head and down the back – plumes that were once nearly the Little Egret's downfall. In the nineteenth century, these plumes were much in demand to use in ladies' fashions; protests against which eventually led to the founding of the Royal Society for the Protection of Birds (RSPB) in Britain.

When feeding, Little Egrets use both the 'stand and wait' and 'stalk and hunt' methods, jabbing at their intended prey with that dagger-shaped bill. They have a catholic diet, including frogs, fish, snakes, lizards, snails, worms and a wide range of aquatic invertebrates.

GREY HERON

SCIENTIFIC NAME: Ardea cinerea

IDENTIFYING FEATURES: Large size; grey plumage

SIMILAR SPECIES: Purple Heron (very rare)

SIZE: 84–102 cm (33–40 in)

HABITAT: Freshwater marshes, lakes, rivers and ponds

POPULATION: Common

Europe's largest species of heron, the Grey Heron stands up to a metre tall, dwarfing other water birds in the region. In flight, it can resemble a large bird of prey, though its broad, bowed wings, trailing legs and hunched neck make it fairly easy to identify even at a distance or in silhouette. Herons can be unpopular, especially for people who own a garden pond, as they are able to remove exotic fish very effectively.

Grey Herons are tall, elegant birds, most often seen standing by the side of a waterway such as a river, lake or marsh, where they may pose stock-still for several minutes before a rapid movement sees them grab an unwary fish or frog from the water around their feet. They are quite shy, however, and close approach tends to flush them; often uttering a deep, croaky 'fraaank' call as they fly away on sturdy, down-curved wings.

Plumage and Nesting

The plumage is mainly grey, with a paler front (with fine black streaking) and a striking black stripe through the eye, contrasting with the yellow bill. Juveniles lack the black on the head.

Herons are one of the earliest nesting birds, gathering in their colonial heronries soon after the New Year, and adding a few sticks to their huge, untidy nests before settling down to breed. They lay between three and five eggs, which hatch into rather comical-looking youngsters, which remain in the nest being fed by the parents for about seven weeks after hatching.

ABOVE

The Grey Heron is the largest of its family to be found in Europe.

Although rather thin and scraggy in appearance, the heron was considered a delicacy for medieval English kings, though later writers who tried it considered it to have a rather foul taste!

PURPLE HERON

SIZE: 78–90 cm (30¾–35⅛ in)

HABITAT: Freshwater marshes, reedbeds

POPULATION: Very rare

SCIENTIFIC NAME: Ardea purpurea

IDENTIFYING FEATURES: Purplish plumage

SIMILAR SPECIES: Grey Heron

Unlike its larger relative the Grey Heron, the Purple Heron is a very shy and elusive bird, rarely seen except occasionally when flushed. When seen, it often poses very still by the edge of a reedbed, its purplish-brown plumage blending in surprisingly well with the vegetation. When frightened, it will freeze with its bill pointing upright rather like its reedbed-dwelling relative the Bittern. Either on the ground or in flight, its long, sinuous neck gives it a faintly reptilian appearance.

If you are fortunate enough to get close views of this rare and elusive creature, the subtleties of its plumage become apparent: the purples, browns and buffs contrasting with the creamy, streaked breast – with hues of cinnamon, grey and burgundy also present. Juveniles are much browner and paler, and may be mistaken for a Bittern – though are far more elegant in shape than that species.

Colonial Birds

The Purple Heron prefers warmer climatic zones than its larger relative and is found in a wide range of wetland habitats across southern and eastern Europe, Asia and parts of East Africa (including Madagascar).

Purple Herons are semi-colonial when breeding, building an untidy nest out of dead reed stems on a pile of reeds; or occasionally also in trees (when sticks and twigs are used instead of reeds). They lay four to five eggs, incubated for about four weeks; with the young staying in the nest until they fledge about six or seven weeks after hatching.

In recent years the Purple Heron has decreased both in numbers and breeding range

ABOVE

Purple Herons are widespread across southern and eastern Europe, as well as Asia and Africa.

– probably due to increased disturbance and pollution on existing wetlands, and the draining and destruction of others. It may, however, be able to extend its range north following the effects of global climate change in Europe.

WHITE STORK

SCIENTIFIC NAME: Ciconia ciconia

IDENTIFYING FEATURES:
Large size; black and white plumage

SIMILAR SPECIES: None

SIZE: 110–115 cm (43¼–45¼ in)

HABITAT: Freshwater marshes

POPULATION: Very rare

This legendary bird is supposed to bring babies – and to this day many people in southern and eastern Europe put up a platform on their homes especially for the White Stork to nest – bringing good luck to the family and the wider community.

This huge black and white bird, with its dagger-like scarlet bill, is hard to confuse with any other European species. In flight the large size, long neck, and black feathers along the wings are obvious. When breeding, the adults will often clatter bills in a form of greeting, which also helps to strengthen the pair bond between them.

Storks are long-distance migrants, though being so heavy they need thermal air-currents to travel; so can be seen in vast numbers at key places such as the Bosphorus, Gibraltar and the Red Sea during spring and autumn.

SPOONBILL

SCIENTIFIC NAME: Platalea leucorodia

IDENTIFYING FEATURES: Large, white; spoon-shaped bill

SIMILAR SPECIES: None

SIZE: 80–90 cm (31½–35⅜ in)

HABITAT: Freshwater marshes

POPULATION: Rare

This extraordinary bird has one of the most incredible bills of any bird: a spatula-shaped appendage which it sweeps from side to side through the water to obtain small aquatic organisms, such as insects, small fish and frogs, to eat.

Seen well, the spoon-shaped bill is the key identification feature; but the bird's distinctive shape, white plumage tinged with yellow, and in the breeding season short, drooping crest, are also helpful ways to identify the species.

Spoonbills nest in large colonies, often with other species of ibis and heron. When pairing up, the male and female display to each other, pointing their bills up in the air and raising their head feathers. Spoonbills are sociable and gregarious outside the breeding season as well, usually being seen in small flocks, especially on migration.

MARSH HARRIER

SIZE: 48–56 cm (19–22 in)

HABITAT: Marshes, reedbeds, farmland

POPULATION: Scarce but increasing

SCIENTIFIC NAME: Circus aeruginosus

IDENTIFYING FEATURES: Male has variegated plumage; female has brown plumage, pale cap

SIMILAR SPECIES: Hen and Montagu's Harriers

Harriers are amongst the most elegant fliers of all birds of prey, using their long, narrow wings to glide low over the ground while hunting. As its name suggests, the Marsh Harrier is more suited to freshwater habitats than its other European relatives, but it will also hunt freely over coastal marshes and farmland. Now that they are better protected, Marsh Harriers are doing rather well, despite the loss of many wetland habitats throughout their range.

Male and female Marsh Harriers are very different in appearance. The smaller male shows a variegated pattern in flight: with brown, black and grey on the upper wings, giving it a distinctive appearance quite unlike any other European bird of prey.

The female is much larger and bulkier – sometimes resembling a Buzzard in shape, though with much longer wings. Her plumage is mainly deep chocolate brown in colour, set off by the distinctive creamy yellow cap.

Breeding and Migration

They breed in a range of habitats: often in reedbeds, but also on the ground in farmland habitats, where they may clash with their smaller relative Montagu's Harrier. Like other harriers, the males indulge in a spectacular 'sky-dancing' display to impress the female, and also offer her morsels of food, exchanged in mid-air, to cement the pair bond. Once she is incubating, the male will bring prey back to the nest at regular intervals to sustain his mate.

Marsh Harriers usually migrate south in autumn, though with milder winters more are staying out in western Europe for the whole of the year. Others either head south to the Mediterranean and North Africa, or cross the Sahara Desert to spend the winter in equatorial Africa.

BELOW

Most Marsh Harriers nest in protected reserves. They are rare, but the population is increasing.

OSPREY

SCIENTIFIC NAME: Pandion haliaetus

IDENTIFYING FEATURES:
Pale underparts; head-pattern

SIMILAR SPECIES: None

SIZE: 55–58 cm (21¾–22⅞ in)

HABITAT: Freshwater lakes and lochs

POPULATION: Scarce but increasing

The Osprey is one of the world's commonest and most adaptable birds of prey, being found in wetland habitats in a wide range of climatic zones from Scotland to Japan, the Himalayas to Australia, and Canada to the West Indies. It is also known as the 'fish-hawk' for its supreme ability to catch fish by plunge-diving into the water – helped by its ability to reverse one of its toes to keep a grip on its slippery prey.

Africa. Recent developments in radio-tracking technology have revealed the challenges these birds face: especially the youngsters, making their first journey alone. On migration Ospreys may turn up in unexpected places such as suburban gravel pits and reservoirs, before continuing on their travels.

BELOW
The Osprey displays its amazing 'fishing' skills.

Seen well, it is hard to mistake the Osprey for any other bird of prey: the dark upperparts contrasting with the white underparts, and the distinctive dark face mask, are diagnostic. In flight, the long-winged Osprey looks more like a gull or heron than a raptor, often flying on bowed wings, which it tends to flap more than other birds of prey.

Osprey Nests

When breeding, Ospreys build a large nest out of twigs in a tall tree or on a man-made platform, where they lay two or three eggs. Before this, the male displays to the female by circling above the nest site carrying a fish, and uttering a high-pitched yelping call.

After breeding, the adults and young migrate south, spending the winter in

Fascinating Facts

The name Osprey translates as 'bone-breaker', and may originally have been applied to other raptors such as the Lammergeier, which do drop bones from a great height in order to break them and get at the contents.

WATER RAIL

SIZE: 23–28 cm (9–11 in)

HABITAT: Reedbeds, freshwater marshes

POPULATION: Common

SCIENTIFIC NAME: Rallus aquaticus

IDENTIFYING FEATURES:
Dagger-shaped bill; streaked flanks

SIMILAR SPECIES: Moorhen, Spotted Crake

Identifying Water Rails

The Water Rail's plumage is subtle but striking: upperparts chestnut streaked with black, underparts purplish-grey, and the flanks barred black and white. The long, red bill and bright white undertail are also useful ways of telling the species from a juvenile Moorhen, with which it may be confused. The chicks are little black balls of fluff, and are rarely seen, as like their parents they prefer to seek out cover in dense reedbed vegetation.

Water Rails are very vulnerable to harsh winters, and will sometimes seek out alternative habitats when their reedbed homes are iced over. As a result, they are benefiting from the recent run of mild winters, which has reduced their mortality rate at this tough time of year.

The name 'rail' comes from the ability of these secretive birds to squeeze their bodies laterally, and so to pass through the tight and narrow gaps between clumps of reeds – hence the popular expression 'as thin as a rail'. The Water Rail uses this ability to hunt down a wide range of aquatic creatures, including frogs, beetles and small fish, which it grabs with its dagger-shaped bill.

Often the first indication of the Water Rail's presence is the extraordinary squealing call: variously compared to a klaxon horn, grunting hedgehog and a stuck pig – and often sounding as if the bird is in considerable distress. Having established by sound that Water Rails are actually present, the best way to see them is to sit patiently by an area of soft mud next to a reedbed, and simply wait for a bird to emerge. Dawn and dusk are the best times of day to see Water Rails, and you may be rewarded by close views.

RIGHT
You are likely to hear a Water Rail rather than see one – they can be elusive birds.

COOT

SCIENTIFIC NAME: Fulica atra

IDENTIFYING FEATURES: Black plumage; white bill

SIMILAR SPECIES: Moorhen

SIZE: 36–38 cm (14½–15 in)

HABITAT: Freshwater marshes, rivers and lakes

POPULATION: Abundant

Taken for granted by many people because it is so common and ubiquitous, the Coot repays closer attention than it usually gets. During the breeding season, Coots become highly territorial, and will engage in prolonged and vicious fights between individuals, each using their powerful feet to try to force their rival under the water. Outside the breeding season, however, they are gregarious and sociable birds, gathering in flocks numbering in the thousands in some locations.

Seen well, the Coot is hard to confuse with any other species. No other British water bird has the combination of all-black plumage (at closer range actually a very dark grey as well as black) offset by a white bill and face-shield – a feature which gave rise to the saying 'as bald as a Coot'. Juvenile birds are smaller and greyer than the adults, with pale beneath; while downy chicks may be confused with their close relative the Moorhen on account of the fact that they have red on their heads.

Ground-based Birds

Coots are rarely seen in flight, as like all members of the rail family they are clumsy in the air; while on land they reveal their extraordinary feet: not webbed like ducks, but with small lobes on the edge of each toe, rather like grebes.

Coots nest early in the spring, laying between six and 10 eggs in a bulky nest made from plant material, often floating on the water (but secured in the base of a tree or by attaching to some other vegetation).

Outside the breeding season they gather in large flocks, often on much more open water such as reservoirs and gravel pits, where they often accompany dabbling duck flocks.

MOORHEN

SIZE: 32–35 cm (12⅛–13¾ in)

HABITAT: Freshwater marshes, lakes, ponds, rivers

POPULATION: Abundant

SCIENTIFIC NAME: Gallinula chloropus

IDENTIFYING FEATURES:
Red and yellow bill; whiteundertail

SIMILAR SPECIES: Coot

streaks along the sides that distinguish them from their close relative the Coot.

Floating Nests

Like Coots, Moorhens often build a floating nest out of plant material; but as befits a surprisingly adept climber they will also occasionally nest high up in a bush or tree. They lay between five and nine eggs, and after hatching the young stay with their parents until fledging – any time between six and 10 weeks later.

This unassuming and attractive member of the rail family is found on most small areas of water, often managing to thrive where no other waterbird can. As a result of this ability to live in almost any damp habitat it is one of the commonest and most widespread of all wetland species. The name 'moorhen' derives from the old sense of 'moor' meaning marsh or lake (as in the word 'mere') – so simply means 'bird of the lake'.

Moorhens are members of the rail family, but like the world's other species known as 'gallinules' they have adapted to swim on open water rather than creep about in enclosed vegetation. Seen well, the adult is hard to confuse with any other bird: its combination of purple and brown plumage, offset by a jagged pale line along the flanks, pale under the tail and that gaudy red and yellow bill are unmistakable. Youngsters are duller: mainly brown, with a yellowish bill; but they usually also show the pale undertail and the

After breeding, Moorhens tend to stay close to where they nested, and are virtually never seen on large areas of open water like other water birds. Yet they are also able to colonize new habitats, suggesting that they do take to the wing – though at night, to avoid being caught by aerial predators.

LEFT

Moorhens are a common sight on freshwater lakes and rivers all over Britain and Europe.

COMMON CRANE

SCIENTIFIC NAME: Grus grus

IDENTIFYING FEATURES:
Tall; grey plumage; long tail plumes

SIMILAR SPECIES: None

SIZE: 110–120 cm (43¼–47⅛ in)

HABITAT: Freshwater marshes and wet grasslands

POPULATION: Rare

This stately bird is one of the best-known and best-loved of all European species, due to its statuesque appearance, notable migrations and extraordinary courtship behaviour. In many northern European cultures, the annual return of the Cranes is celebrated as a sign that winter is finally over and spring has come – a celebration made even more special by the Cranes' elegant courtship dance. Like so many water birds, however, the Crane is under constant threat because of the loss of its wetland habitats.

Cranes are hard to confuse with any other European bird – apart, perhaps, from the Grey Heron. But their much larger size (about one third taller), elegant (almost human-like) posture and key plumage features usually make identification straightforward. On the ground, the impression is of a tall, stately bird: with a long, straight neck, predominately grey plumage, and elaborate plumes sticking out from the bird's rear end – giving the impression of a Victorian lady in a formal dress! The head pattern – black neck offset by white cheeks and scarlet crown – is also highly distinctive, and distinguishes the Common Crane from its other relatives around the world.

Wetland Habitats

Cranes depend entirely on unspoilt wetland habitats in both their breeding and wintering quarters, as well as on migration. They breed in the freshwater bogs and marshes of the north, often building their nests on a low mound to keep the eggs dry. In winter and on migration they frequent a wider range of habitats, including traditional farmland; but usually near water.

Fascinating Facts

Some long-legged birds will often stand on one leg to conserve heat. Drawing one leg up close to the stomach feathers stops heat escaping through both long legs.

BELOW LEFT
The Crane is one of the most distinctive water birds in the region.

Cranes are seen as key indicator species of the health of our wetland habitats, and as such have suffered a major decline over the past three centuries or so. However, signs are that careful conservation measures may now have turned the corner for this wonderful bird.

LITTLE RINGED PLOVER

SCIENTIFIC NAME: Charadrius dubius

IDENTIFYING FEATURES:
Yellow eye-ring; lack of pale wing-bar

SIMILAR SPECIES: Ringed Plover

SIZE: 14–15 cm (5½–5⅞ in)

HABITAT: Gravel pits, banks of rivers

POPULATION: Scarce

This attractive little member of the plover family – barely bigger than a sparrow – is adept at colonizing new areas created by human beings. Having evolved to nest on bare gravel by rivers, where their eggs and chicks are best camouflaged against the threat from predators, they nowadays breed in working gravel quarries, seemingly oblivious to the noise and activity from the digging machines. Once hatched, the tiny chicks will soon fly all the way to Africa to spend the winter there.

Slightly smaller, slimmer and longer-winged than its commoner relative the Ringed Plover, the Little Ringed can be told apart by its paler upperparts, yellowish (as opposed to orange) legs, lack of orange on the beak and, when seen closely, the bright yellow ring around the eye. In flight, the longer, narrower wings give a rather tern-like appearance, and also enable the bird to be identified: they lack the pale wing bar shown by the Ringed Plover.

Predatory Risks

Little Ringed Plovers return north fairly early in the spring, in late March and early April, and soon settle down to nest. Four eggs are laid in a shallow scrape amongst bare shingle and, if the first brood is successful, a second will usually follow. However, as with other ground-nesting birds, Little Ringed Plovers are at risk from predators, bad weather and, nowadays, from accidents with gravel machines – though most quarry owners do their best to protect these charming little birds.

In Britain, the species has done well since first colonizing around the time of the Second World War. Thanks to the boom in house-building and road construction, there has been no shortage of working quarries where the birds can nest; though in recent years they have also begun nesting in their more traditional habitat of shingle river banks.

BELOW
The Little Ringed Plover is a round wader with a black and white face.

PECTORAL SANDPIPER

SCIENTIFIC NAME: Calidris melanotos

IDENTIFYING FEATURES:
Neat streaked breast-band

SIMILAR SPECIES: Ruff, Curlew Sandpiper

SIZE: 19–23 cm (7½–9 in)

HABITAT: Freshwater marshes

POPULATION: Rare

This attractive, medium-sized wader is one of North America's most familiar shorebird species, although like many other Arctic nesting species its breeding range also extends westwards across the Bering Strait into Russia. A long-distance migrant, Pectoral Sandpipers mainly winter in southern South America. As a result, the species is also the commonest North American species in Europe, with dozens turning up in Britain every year, and on occasions even attempting to breed.

Although superficially similar to many other waders on both sides of the Atlantic (such as Baird's and White-rumped Sandpipers in North America, and Ruff in Europe), when seen well the Pectoral Sandpiper is fairly easy to identify. As its name suggests, the key identification feature is the clear, well-marked streaking on the throat, neck and upper breast, neatly demarcated from the white lower breast and belly. The bird's upright stance, longish neck and slightly down-curved bill are also distinctive; and in flight, as one would expect from such a global traveller, it shows long, narrow wings.

Arctic Breeder

Like so many waders, the Pectoral Sandpiper breeds in the tundra of the Arctic, usually north of the treeline. After breeding, both adults and first-year birds head south, often flying out into the Atlantic Ocean in order to take the most direct route. When caught in autumn gales or the tail-end of hurricanes, a few individuals travel across the Atlantic and end up in Europe: predominately in Britain or on the Azores.

Unlike songbird vagrants, which almost certainly die soon after they arrive, waders tend to be adaptable and fairly long-lived, so as a result there are spring records of Pectoral Sandpipers that may have crossed the ocean one or more autumns earlier. As a result, eventually the species is likely to colonize Europe as a breeding bird.

RUFF

SIZE: 20–30 cm (7⅞–11⅞ in)

HABITAT: Freshwater marshes, often near the coast

POPULATION: Scarce

SCIENTIFIC NAME: Philomachus pugnax

IDENTIFYING FEATURES:
huge ruff when breeding; short bill in winter

SIMILAR SPECIES: none

The Ruff gets its name from the Elizabethan-fashion neckwear.

Name Origins

Strangely, and unlike the kite and crane, the bird was named after the fashion item rather than the other way around, the name first appearing in the seventeenth century. This is despite the fact that the Ruff was a well-known item on the menu of the Tudor court – showing that the bird must have been a much commoner breeder than it is today. Thanks to the draining of its wetland habitats the Ruff has declined across much of Europe in recent years.

The Ruff is well-known for its extraordinary courtship habits, in which males gather together in a 'lek' to show off their prowess in front of watching females. To do so, the males have adopted an incredible plumage feature: the ruff of feathers around the bird's neck that gives the species its English name. The scientific name also reflects this behaviour, which can be translated as 'the fighting bird that loves fighting'!

During the short breeding season, from April to about June, the male Ruff is simply unmistakable, sporting an impossibly ornate ruff around his neck that resembles that worn by Tudor courtiers. This can be a whole range of colours: from almost pure white, through white flecked with black, to chestnut and dark brown and black. The head and bill poke out rather comically, though once the birds start fighting the scene is very serious indeed.

Outside the breeding period, the Ruff is a rather unassuming-looking, medium-sized wader; with the short, slightly decurved bill and longish neck the best identification features. Males and females are very different in size: the males being up to 50 per cent larger, and often looking like two quite different species.

JACK SNIPE

SCIENTIFIC NAME: Lymnocryptes minimus

IDENTIFYING FEATURES:
Small size; habit of bobbing up and down

SIMILAR SPECIES: Common Snipe

SIZE: 17–19 cm (6¾–7½ in)

HABITAT: Freshwater marshes,
damp grassland, swamps and fens

POPULATION: Scarce

This tiny wader – about one third smaller than the Common Snipe – is also one of the most elusive and hard to see of all birds to occur regularly in Britain. Despite being quite widespread during the autumn and winter months, it is rarely seen, often not flying until almost trodden on. Occasionally Jack Snipe venture out into the open at the edge of a reedbed, where their characteristic bobbing movements may draw attention to their presence amongst their commoner relative.

As well as being much smaller than the Common Snipe, Jack Snipe (the word 'jack' means small) is also subtly different in shape and posture. The bill appears shorter in relation to the head (about one and a half times longer rather than twice as long), and the legs shorter, creating a rather hunched appearance.

Remote Breeding Locations

Another useful identification feature are the two pale yellowish lines running along the back, which are broader and more pronounced than in its larger relative. In flight the small size and more rounded wings may be apparent, as is the bird's usual habit of landing not far away from where it is flushed.

Jack Snipe is a breeding bird of the sub-Arctic regions of northern Europe and Asia, although its exact breeding areas and populations are poorly known because of their remote location, and the bird's elusive habits.

Populations of Jack Snipe have been declining steadily and sadly they are now a rare sight.

Although the species has experienced a prolonged decline, recent surveys suggest the population may have stabilized. For such a shy bird, it does have one notable feature: the extraordinary call, which sounds like a cantering horse, which it gives during a brief display flight above its breeding grounds, and can be heard at a considerable distance.

COMMON SNIPE

SIZE: 25–27 cm (9⅞–10⅝ in)

HABITAT: Freshwater marshes and flooded fields

POPULATION: Common

SCIENTIFIC NAME: Gallinago gallinago

IDENTIFYING FEATURES: Short legs; long bill

SIMILAR SPECIES: Jack Snipe, Woodcock

LEFT

Common Snipe have a fast, zig-zag flight pattern that allows them to out-manoeuvre predators.

The Snipe has long been a favourite bird amongst shooters, because its erratic, zig-zagging flight makes it very difficult to hit. The Snipe also appeals to birders for its attractive plumage and distinctive feeding habits: probing that enormously long bill down into the soft mud in order to feel for underground prey such as worms, which it finds by using sensitive hairs at the tip of its bill. It is also one of the few birds to use a non-vocal sound during display: using specially adapted feathers in its tail to produce a distinctive 'drumming'.

Common Snipe often gather in small flocks on areas of open mud, though their subtly camouflaged plumage means that they can easily conceal themselves against the background vegetation. No other common wader has the Snipe's combination of short legs and long, straight bill; and the attractive, subtle tones of the mainly brown and black plumage are also distinctive.

Breeding Habits

During the breeding season, Common Snipe usually seek out damp grassland such as traditionally managed water meadows – which means that in recent years they have suffered a major decline in developed areas of western Europe, where modern farming methods and the draining of many wetlands have left them with nowhere to breed. As a result, breeding Snipe are now mainly found on protected nature reserves. In autumn and winter they will frequent a wide range of well-vegetated wetland habitats, from flooded fields to freshwater marshes, as well as marshy areas near the coast. When flushed from where they are feeding, they will fly away very fast on rapidly beating wings, zig-zagging from side to side to outwit aerial predators such as Merlins.

BLACK-TAILED GODWIT

SCIENTIFIC NAME: Limosa limosa

IDENTIFYING FEATURES:
Black and white wing-bars; long, straight bill

SIMILAR SPECIES: Bar-tailed Godwit

SIZE: 40–44 cm (15¾–17¾ in)

HABITAT: Freshwater and coastal marshes

POPULATION: Common

This large, striking wader is the larger of the two godwits to occur regularly in Europe, and the second largest of the world's four godwit species (being marginally smaller than the Marbled Godwit of North America). It is a sociable bird, especially outside the breeding season, when it gathers in large flocks to feed on areas of coastal marsh. These take part in communal feeding, probing their long bills down into the mud below shallow water, and sometimes feeding with their heads completely underwater.

Like all godwits, Black-tailed is a large, long-legged shore bird with a very long bill and stately bearing. In the breeding season it sports a striking bright orange head, neck and breast (almost pinky-orange in the case of the Icelandic race), shading to brown on the upper back and white below. Once breeding is over, the adults moult into a plain greyish brown non-breeding garb: less scalloped than that of the Bar-tailed. The best way to distinguish the two species at all times of year is not the tail pattern, which is often barely visible, but in flight: the Black-tailed Godwit has a prominent black and white wing pattern, easily visible even at a distance. The two species also have a subtly different overall look: the Black-tailed being a more elegant, longer-legged bird, with a straighter (rather than up-curved) bill.

Name Meaning

Unlike the Bar-tailed, which is a true global traveller, the Black-tailed Godwit is a relatively short-distance migrant, with Icelandic birds wintering in western Europe, while the European race travels to southern Europe and North Africa. The name 'godwit' excites much curiosity as to its origins: experts suggest that it is an onomatopoeic representation of the bird's call. A local East Anglian name, 'yarwhelp', also refers to the sound the bird makes.

WHIMBREL

SIZE: 40–42 cm (15¼–16½ in)

HABITAT: Freshwater
and coastal marshes

POPULATION: Scarce

SCIENTIFIC NAME: Numenius phaeopus

IDENTIFYING FEATURES:
Decurved bill, clear white rump in flight

SIMILAR SPECIES: Curlew

A medium-sized relative of the Curlew, the Whimbrel is a bird of the sub-Arctic regions around much of the Northern Hemisphere, from Alaska, through Canada and Greenland, to Scandinavia and Russia: with a few hundred pairs clinging on in one of their southernmost outposts, in northern Scotland. There, it is sometimes known as the May Bird, as Whimbrels return each year from their African winter quarters in late April and early May, coinciding with the May Day celebrations.

A neat, attractive wader, resembling a miniature Curlew in size and shape, though with a relatively smaller and less decurved bill compared to that of its larger relative. Another key distinguishing feature is the

BELOW

The Whimbrel shares characteristics with the Curlew, although it is much smaller.

presence of two dark stripes along the Whimbrel's crown and, in flight, the more sharply demarcated white rump than the Curlew's.

Diverse Breeding Areas

There could hardly be a greater contrast between the breeding areas of the Whimbrel and its winter quarters. Whimbrels breed in the boreal regions of northern Europe and America, but winter south of the Sahara Desert in Africa, or on the coasts of Central

and South America and the islands of the Indian Ocean. It is thought that first-year birds stay put in their winter quarters throughout the year after they arrive, before returning north to breed when they are almost two years old.

The bill, being smaller and less downward-curved than that of the Curlew, is not usually used to probe into sand or mud. Instead, the Whimbrel tends to pick food off the surface, or from just beneath the sand or mud. When eating crabs, they have been observed breaking off each leg in turn before feeding off the body.

COMMON REDSHANK

SCIENTIFIC NAME: Tringa totanus

IDENTIFYING FEATURES: Orange-red legs

SIMILAR SPECIES: Spotted Redshank, Greenshank

SIZE: 27–29 cm (10⅝–11½ in)

HABITAT: Freshwater and coastal marshes

POPULATION: Common

The Redshank is by far the commonest and most widespread medium-sized European wader, found in a wide range of habitats from coastal marsh to inland water meadows. It is sometimes known as 'the sentinel of the marsh', a name given as a result of the Redshank's habit of sounding a noisy alarm call when any intruder – human or animal – enters its breeding territory. For this reason, many other wader species, including Oystercatcher, Ringed Plover and Dunlin, nest near pairs of Redshanks.

Fascinating Facts

Although it is impossible to know the bird population of the world, experts have estimated that there are between 100,000 and 200,000 million adult birds in the world.

RIGHT

Common Redshanks breed on meadows and other grasslands, although they are mainly water birds.

Easily the most obvious feature of the Redshank – at least at rest – is the orange-red colour of the legs that give the species its name. These are also visible in flight, when another useful field mark, the white rear edge to the wings, is also easy to see. Like its larger relatives, the Spotted Redshank and Greenshank, it also shows a white rump when flying. Otherwise, the Redshank is a relatively nondescript wading bird: with an olive-brown plumage, mottled with darker shades of brown, which appears brighter during the breeding season. The bill is also tinged with orange-red, and is considerably shorter than that of its two cousins.

Breeding Habits

Although Redshanks primarily winter on or near the coast, often in large mixed flocks of other wader species, they usually breed on meadows and other grassland. Like so many species they have suffered from modern farming methods, which have greatly reduced the amount and quality of the food-rich pasture the species needs to raise a family.

When breeding, Redshanks often perch on a gate or fence post in order to survey their territory and watch out for rival birds and predators. As a result, they are usually very easy to see compared to other waders.

GREENSHANK

SCIENTIFIC NAME: Tringa nebularia

IDENTIFYING FEATURES:
Elegant shape; pale plumage; green legs

SIMILAR SPECIES:
Spotted Redshank, Common Redshank

SIZE: 30–33 cm (11⅞–13 in)

HABITAT: Freshwater and coastal marshes

POPULATION: Scarce

This slim, elegant wader is the largest of the five common European and North American 'shanks', with long legs and a long, slightly up-curved bill. In Britain and western Europe it is primarily a passage migrant, being seen regularly on spring and autumn migration between its northern breeding grounds and African winter quarters. However, a few stay put on west coast estuaries during the winter, while a thousand or so pairs breed in the remote Flow Country of northern Scotland.

Seen well, the Greenshank is relatively easy to identify. No other common wader has the same combination of large size, long, slightly upturned bill, and pale plumage – as well as, of course, the green legs that give the species its name. In breeding plumage, the adult also acquires prominent spotting to the sides of the head, neck, breast and flanks; while the leg colour becomes noticeably brighter in hue.

Mating Habits

Greenshanks are generally faithful to a single mate – sometimes for life – and begin courtship soon after arriving back on their boggy breeding areas. The male impresses the female, and strengthens the pair bond, by a complex series of courtship displays. These include flashing his white rump and pale underwings while dancing on the ground; and flying up to 300 m (1,000 ft) in the air and singing to his mate, while plunging down and swooping upwards.

No doubt suitably impressed, the female lays her clutch in a small scrape on the ground, where her cryptically-coloured plumage makes her relatively safe from predators. The young are also well camouflaged, and spend up to a month following their parents for food until they are ready to fledge.

BELOW
The Greenshank has an elaborate courtship display.

GREEN SANDPIPER

SCIENTIFIC NAME: Tringa ochropus

IDENTIFYING FEATURES:
Contrasting dark above, white below; white rump

SIMILAR SPECIES:
Common Sandpiper, Wood Sandpiper

SIZE: 21–24 cm (8¼–9½ in)

HABITAT: Freshwater marshes and ditches

POPULATION: Scarce

A flash of what appears to be black and white may be the first sign of this rather retiring little bird, as it flies away from danger. Once it lands, the dark green upperparts and snow-white underparts are revealed. Yet on its breeding grounds the Green Sandpiper changes its behaviour utterly: the male often perching high on a tree in a forest clearing to broadcast his surprisingly tuneful song.

dark bands across the tail, is an excellent identification feature. The overall effect can be like a large House Martin!

Although not much larger than the Common Sandpiper, Green Sandpipers lack the dumpy, squat appearance of that species, and generally appear quite neat and well proportioned. Seen close, the green upperparts show tiny white spots, while the head, neck and upper breast are covered with dark streaks that form a neat breast-band. White feathering around the eye gives a distinctive 'staring' appearance, while in flight the white rump, contrasting with the very dark upper wings and

Breeding Grounds

Green Sandpipers breed mainly in northern and eastern Europe, and east across northern Asia. They are birds of the boreal zone, generally breeding in forested areas near fresh water where they can obtain plenty of their invertebrate food.

The western populations migrate to Africa, while eastern birds mainly head south-east, wintering in South East Asia (and a few even reaching Australia). Although some birds do not return to their north Russian breeding grounds until June, a few (probably non-breeders or those whose breeding attempts have failed) can be seen heading south in early July – the first sign that the autumn migration is underway!

WOOD SANDPIPER

SCIENTIFIC NAME: Tringa glareola

IDENTIFYING FEATURES:
Slender shape; yellowish-green legs

SIMILAR SPECIES:
Common Sandpiper, Green Sandpiper

SIZE: 19–21 cm (7½–8¼ in)

HABITAT: Freshwater marshes

POPULATION: Scarce

The slimmest member of the three freshwater sandpipers regularly found in Britain and northern Europe is also the scarcest – with small numbers passing through in spring and autumn on their way to their wintering areas south of the Sahara. An unassuming but attractive bird, Wood Sandpipers also breed in very small numbers in the Scottish Highlands, although their nests are very hard to find in this vast wilderness.

A small to medium-sized sandpiper – rather like a miniature Redshank in shape and stature, with a fairly short, straight bill, mottled upperparts and fairly plain pale underparts. In all plumages, the best distinguishing feature is the pale supercilium running above the eye. The legs are yellowish-green in colour, while the bill is dark.

Bird of the Bogs

The Wood Sandpiper is a bird of the northern forests and bogs of Europe and Asia, its main range stretching from Norway in the west to Kamchatka and Sakhalin Island in the east. It is quite varied in its choice of breeding habitat, ranging from open tundra, covered with dwarf willow and birch, to open marshy and boggy clearings in the vast forests of this region.

The male and female time their journey back to the breeding grounds so that they arrive together, helping to strengthen their monogamous pair bond. Once the downy young hatch, however, they are usually looked after by a single parent – generally the male.

Outside the breeding season, it does not, as do other waders, head for coastal areas. Instead, it prefers open wetland habitats. In Africa, it can often be found on the edge of pools, lakes and waterholes in the open grassy savannah. Unlike the generally solitary Green Sandpiper it can be rather sociable, sometimes gathering in flocks to exploit suitable feeding areas.

TOP LEFT
A Wood Sandpiper grasps a tadpole in its beak. They also eat insects, worms, spiders, shellfish and small fish.

COMMON SANDPIPER

SCIENTIFIC NAME: Actitis hypoleucos

IDENTIFYING FEATURES: Dumpy shape; short bill

SIMILAR SPECIES:
Green Sandpiper, Wood Sandpiper

SIZE: 19–21 cm (7½–8¼ in)

HABITAT: Freshwater marshes, streams

POPULATION: Common

Unlike its close relatives, which are predominately northern breeders, the Common Sandpiper has a wide geographical range stretching from northern Scandinavia all the way south to the Mediterranean Sea, and Ireland and Portugal in the west to central Asia and Japan in the east. Most of these birds migrate south to spend the winter in Africa or southern Asia, although some remain in the western, more maritime, parts of their range, where the winters are milder.

The sight of a Common Sandpiper bobbing up and down as it feeds beside a rushing hillside stream is one of the characteristic sights of upland areas in Britain and much of continental Europe. The dumpy shape, short legs and contrasting dark

upperparts and white underparts distinguish it from most other waders, apart from the slightly larger and slimmer Green and Wood Sandpipers. Closer to, the short, yellowish bill, greenish legs and long body are noticeable; while in flight the dark rump separates it from its close relatives, and the whirring wing action from most other waders.

River Bird

Despite its wide geographical range, Common Sandpipers tend to choose similar habitats for breeding: preferring fast-flowing rivers and streams, or clear upland lakes. After breeding the species may be

found in almost any area of fresh water, including tiny pools and ditches – anywhere it can find tiny insects or invertebrate food which it picks up with that short but effective bill.

As might be expected for such a common bird, the name 'sandpiper' was originally given to this particular species of sandpiper – despite the fact that it is rarely found on beaches as such. A more appropriate name is one used commonly in the nineteenth century, but which has since died out: 'summer snipe'.

LEFT

Its contrasting upperparts and underparts help to make the Common Sandpiper stand out among other wading birds.

RED-NECKED PHALAROPE

SIZE: 18–19 cm (7–7½ in)

HABITAT: Freshwater marshes and pools

POPULATION: Rare

SCIENTIFIC NAME: Phalaropus lobatus

IDENTIFYING FEATURES: Small size; needle-like bill; orange-red neck (breeding)

SIMILAR SPECIES: Grey Phalarope

This charming little wader has several features in terms of its behaviour, including the ability to swim – hence the Shetland name 'pirrie duc' meaning little duck! Its breeding behaviour is also very unusual: the female takes the lead in courtship, sports a brighter plumage than her mate, and regularly fights off rival females to defend her tiny territory. Her adoption of traditional male behaviour continues: after laying her eggs, she has nothing more to do with raising the young.

In breeding plumage, the Red-necked Phalarope is a very distinctive little bird: tiny, with a pointed, needle-thin bill and mottled grey and brown plumage, set off by the orange-red patch on the side of the neck. The brighter female also adopts a handsome grey head pattern, while the male's is browner and less bright. Outside the breeding season, both males and females moult into their drabber winter garb: pale grey above and white below, with a narrow black band through the eye. At this time of year it can be confused with the slightly larger and bulkier Grey Phalarope, though the latter is even paler grey and has a distinctly thicker bill.

Winter Season

Red-necked Phalaropes spend the winter very far away from their breeding areas: migrating overland, and then out to the open ocean, where they gather in vast numbers off the coasts of South America, Asia and in the Arabian Sea. Incredibly, although they must overwinter somewhere in the South Atlantic Ocean, we have yet to discover where.

In late spring they return north, to breed in the sub-Arctic. They can be found all around the North Pole, from Alaska and Canada, through Scandinavia and Siberia – with a tiny outpost in the far north of Scotland, on the Shetland Islands.

Fascinating Facts

Phalaropes spin around rapidly on the top of the water; this creates a sort of whirlpool that sucks tiny creatures to the surface, which the birds then eat.

BELOW

No one knows where the Red-necked Phalarope chooses to spend its winters – it remains a mystery.

COMMON KINGFISHER

SCIENTIFIC NAME: Alcedo atthis

IDENTIFYING FEATURES:
Electric blue above, orange below

SIMILAR SPECIES: None

SIZE: 16-17 cm (6¼–6¾ in)

HABITAT: Rivers, streams

POPULATION: Common

This jewel-like creature is surely the most stunningly beautiful of any British – perhaps even European – bird. Tinier than most people imagine (barely bigger than a sparrow), the Kingfisher's dazzling blue and orange plumage, combined with its ability to catch fish by diving into the water from a perch, makes it a favourite amongst birders and the wider public alike. Yet its retiring habits mean it is not always easy to see, despite its bright attire.

Kingfisher's plumage become apparent: the blue shades from dark on the wings to pale on the back and rump. Males and females can be told apart from each other by the colour on the lower part of their bill: dark greyish-black in the male, orange in the female.

Freshwater Bird

Kingfishers are classic birds of freshwater streams and rivers, although in hard winter weather they will move to the coast to find food. Harsh winters used to greatly reduce the population, but the trend towards milder winter weather in north-western Europe has enabled them to thrive.

Simply unmistakeable: electric blue above, and orange below, with a white throat, orange cheeks and a white streak on the side of the neck. Look closer, if you can, and the subtleties of the

As their name suggests, they feed mainly on small fish which they catch by plunge-diving below the surface of the water. Once they return to their perch, they bash the fish to stun or kill it, then turn it round to swallow it head first; unless the male has decided to present his catch as a token to the female, in which he will hold it by the tail and offer the head to her!

SAND MARTIN

SIZE: 12 cm (4¾ in)

HABITAT: Rivers, sand and gravel quarries

POPULATION: Common

SCIENTIFIC NAME: Riparia riparia

IDENTIFYING FEATURES:
Brown above, white below; brown breast-band

SIMILAR SPECIES: House Martin, Swallow

Adapting to Habitats

In recent years, Sand Martins have learned to take advantage of a habitat provided by us: choosing to nest in sand and gravel quarries rather than along riverbanks. The advantages are obvious: sand banks along rivers often flood in winter (and even sometimes in spring and summer) – destroying the nest burrow.

In recent years, enlightened quarry owners have left sandbanks from year to year so the returning birds can make their home there.

After nesting, the young martins will gather along telegraph wires – often in mixed flocks with their relatives. Then, as autumn nears, they head back south – though not as far as Swallows and House Martins. Most British and west European Sand Martins winter in the west African Sahel Zone rather than southern Africa.

The brown and white colouring of the Sand Martin distinguishes them from other martins and swallows.

The smallest member of the hirundines (swallows and martins) found in Europe, the Sand Martin is one of the earliest migrants to return from its African winter quarters, with some individuals arriving as early as February and March, while the bulk have got back by mid April. They soon get down to excavating their nests in a sandbank; or if the colony has not been flooded in the winter, tidying up the old nests.

Sand Martins are generally brown and white in colour, making them relatively easy to tell apart from all other European swallows and martins apart from the larger and bulkier Crag Martin. Close to, the pale brown upperparts, white throat and underparts, and the narrow brown breast-band are obvious. Sand Martins are also shorter tailed, shorter winged and more compact-looking than House Martins and Swallows, a feature apparent even at a distance.

WATER PIPIT

SCIENTIFIC NAME: Anthus spinoletta

IDENTIFYING FEATURES: Pale underparts; whitish supercilium; grey head and pinkish breast (breeding)

SIMILAR SPECIES: Rock Pipit

SIZE: 17 cm (6¾ in)

HABITAT: Alpine meadows (summer), riverbanks and freshwater marshes (winter)

POPULATION: Scarce

Once considered to be the same species as the Rock Pipit, the Water Pipit is in fact a very distinctive bird, in its habits as well as its appearance. Breeding on the flower-rich Alpine meadows of Europe and Asia's mountain ranges, often at elevations of up to three thousand metres, it then spends the winter at lower elevations down to sea level, in a range of wetland habitats including mountain rivers, water meadows and along river banks.

In the breeding season, the Water Pipit sports one of the most delicately beautiful plumages of any European songbird: with its grey head and streaked brown upperparts contrasting with the pale underparts, often suffused with the most delicate shade of pink. Outside the breeding season it adopts a drabber, much less distinctive plumage, and can be confused with Meadow and Rock Pipits. The best features to look out for are the Water Pipit's stronger double wing-bars and the more streaked underparts.

Wintering Birds

In Europe, Water Pipits have the odd distinction of being virtually the only songbird on the continent to move north for the winter; with birds from the Alps regularly wintering in southern England. Others head south-west, to spend the winter in the Iberian Peninsula or north-west Africa; while birds from further east head into the Middle East.

Wintering birds are often very faithful to a particular site: birds in watercress beds in southern Britain have been found to feed in an area of only a few square metres for weeks on end. During the breeding season, like other pipits, they have a distinctive display flight, taking off and landing at the same point.

YELLOW WAGTAIL

SIZE: 15–16 cm (5⅞–6¼ in)

HABITAT: Freshwater meadows and marshes

POPULATION: Scarce

SCIENTIFIC NAME: Motacilla flava

IDENTIFYING FEATURES: Lemon-yellow underparts; greenish back; long tail

SIMILAR SPECIES: Grey Wagtail

This elegant and attractive summer visitor is the only one of the three British wagtails to migrate. Each autumn Yellow Wagtails head south to spend the winter in Africa, where they rub shoulders with big game animals, before returning north in the spring to breed. Yellow Wagtail populations have declined in recent years because of modern farming methods, which have largely destroyed their delicate breeding habitats. With help from conservationists, however, they are beginning to make a comeback.

A long, slender bird with the characteristic long tail of the wagtail family, which appears mainly yellow, especially in flight. A closer look reveals greenish upperparts and lemon-yellow underparts. During the breeding season, Yellow Wagtails are found mainly on damp grazing meadows or freshwater marshes, farmed in the traditional way using livestock to manage the vegetation levels. On migration they can turn up in a range of places, including coastal marshes, reservoirs and gravel pits.

Nesting

Yellow Wagtails begin nesting soon after returning from Africa in late April, but some with second broods may lay eggs as late as August. They build a nest from grass and leaves, lined with hair or wool, in a shallow scrape on the ground. Four to six glossy eggs are laid, pale buff to greyish-white in colour, and are incubated for 11–13 days. The young leave the nest after 10–13 days and fledge a few days later.

Yellow Wagtails feed exclusively on small insects and other tiny invertebrates, which they hunt by foraging; picking them up off the ground or the waters surface with quick, darting runs.

LEFT
The different races of Yellow Wagtail can vary in head pattern – such as this one, in Alaska.

There are many different races of the Yellow Wagtail, some of which may be regarded as full species in their own right.

GREY WAGTAIL

SCIENTIFIC NAME: Motacilla cinerea

IDENTIFYING FEATURES:
Lemon-yellow underparts; grey back; long tail

SIMILAR SPECIES: Yellow Wagtail

SIZE: 17–20 cm (6¾–7⅞ in)

HABITAT: Rivers and streams

POPULATION: Common

The name of this species is surely one of the least appropriate of all English bird names – although it does have grey in its plumage the most striking feature is the lemon-yellow underparts and elongated shape. A resident species, it often lives near fast-flowing water, nesting in holes and cavities of stone bridges, just inches away from the torrent. Like other wagtails, it has the endearing habit of pumping its tail up and down while walking along.

The Grey Wagtail is often confused with its slightly smaller relative, the Yellow Wagtail. Both have yellow in the plumage, but whereas the Yellow Wagtail has entirely yellow underparts and greenish upperparts, the Grey Wagtail has a slate-grey head and back; and in the breeding season the male has a smart black throat bordered with white.

Range of Habitats

Although the species is often associated with rivers and streams, it can be found in a range of other habitats, especially outside the breeding season, when it occasionally appears in gardens and along grassy verges, in the company of its commoner relative the Pied Wagtail. In the breeding season, pairs hold territory along a length of river or stream, and are often seen perched on half-submerged rocks or stones along the edge or the centre of the flow, looking for insects. The nest – a cup made of grass and twigs and lined with hair – is built in a hole or cavity along the bank or in a bridge. The female lays four to six eggs, which are incubated for 11-13 days. The young fledge and leave the nest two weeks later, and the adults often have a second, and sometimes even a third, brood.

PIED WAGTAIL

SIZE: 18 cm (7 in)

HABITAT: Gardens, roadsides

POPULATION: Abundant

SCIENTIFIC NAME: Motacilla alba

IDENTIFYING FEATURES:
Black and white plumage; long tail

SIMILAR SPECIES: None

One of the most distinctive of all European songbirds, with a combination of black, white and grey that gives the species its name. The race found in Britain, Ireland and parts of continental Europe has a darker back than the 'White' Wagtail, whose pale grey upperparts contrast with the darker head and tail. All races of the species have a white face, dark breast and white belly; and of course the long tail, constantly wagged while the bird is walking.

Urban Roosts

Pied Wagtails are well known for their association with human beings, and are one of the most urban of all our birds, able to thrive in built-up areas. They have taken advantage of this in several ways: most notably in their habit of gathering together in large flocks to roost for the night, especially during the winter months.

These roosts are often in well-lit, man-made areas such as high streets, shopping malls, service stations and car parks – anywhere with a few trees, plenty of light to keep the predators away, and the extra heat generated by buildings to keep the birds warm. Yet despite the noisy contact calls they make to each other as they gather just before dusk, many people are still oblivious to the activity going on just above their heads, before the birds settle down to sleep.

LEFT

The Pied Wagtail will often seek out wetland habitat in order to feed.

The Pied Wagtail (known elsewhere in Europe and North America as the White Wagtail) is one of the most familiar of all garden birds; yet it is easily overlooked as it goes about its business, feeding on tiny insects picked up from the cracks between paving stones or the surface of the pavement itself. But when Pied Wagtails take to the wing, and utter their distinctive two-syllable call, they are much more likely to be noticed.

DIPPER

SCIENTIFIC NAME: Cinclus cinclus

IDENTIFYING FEATURES: Cocked tail; white breast

SIMILAR SPECIES: None

SIZE: 18 cm (7 in)

HABITAT: Rivers, streams, especially in upland areas

POPULATION: Scarce

A bird distantly related to the wrens, robins and thrushes in your garden, which lives along fast-flowing rivers and habitually plunges beneath the surface of the water for food, deserves attention. Amongst Europe's songbirds, the Dipper is unique in its aquatic habits and lifestyle – and watching the birds as they bob up and down by the river's edge before plunging into the frothy waters is a sight well worth seeing.

Seen well, it is impossible to mistake the Dipper for any other bird. No other European bird has the combination of dark brown plumage relieved by the bright white breast, or of course the bird's aquatic habits. British Dippers have a brown belly, whereas European birds are darker –

appearing almost black at a distance. Dippers need to live along fast-flowing, well-oxygenated rivers and streams, often (though not exclusively) in upland areas. This is because only fast-flowing water contains enough oxygen to support the large insects and other aquatic invertebrates on which the Dipper feeds.

Hunting Habits

Dippers hunt by diving down beneath the water's surface, then either swimming or walking along the bottom of the river bed, picking off their prey as they go. Even young Dippers are able to use this feeding method as soon as they leave the nest.

They nest along streams and river banks, usually in a cavity or on a ledge just

ABOVE

Dippers hunt by diving to the bottom of a river bed and feasting on the prey found there.

above the water level, making the young very vulnerable to flooding.

Dippers have suffered from population declines and range contractions in recent years, due mainly to the pollution of upland rivers by the airborne chemicals known as 'acid rain'. Fortunately, now that air pollution is being curtailed, numbers are beginning to bounce back.

CETTI'S WARBLER

SIZE: 13.5 cm (5¼ in)

HABITAT: Freshwater marshes

POPULATION: Scarce

SCIENTIFIC NAME: Cettia cetti

IDENTIFYING FEATURES: Chestnut plumage; incredibly loud and distinctive song

SIMILAR SPECIES: Reed Warbler

LEFT

Cetti's Warbler does not migrate in the winter, preferring to stay in its freshwater habitat.

An incredibly loud, explosive burst of notes, ending in a Wren-like flourish, is usually the first indication of the presence of Cetti's Warblers in a wetland habitat. Yet despite their very obvious and distinctive sound, the species is one of the most skulking of all its family, and is rarely seen well. Originally named after an eighteenth-century Italian ornithologist and priest, Cetti's Warbler underwent a notable expansion in range during the twentieth century, moving north from its Mediterranean stronghold to colonize north-west Europe, and eventually southern Britain.

One of the reasons why Cetti's Warbler has such a loud song, yet such skulking habits, is thought to be the advantage it gives to birds defending their territory against rival males. The theory is that by singing loudly from one place, then moving unseen to another location and singing again a few minutes later, the male Cetti's Warbler hoodwinks his rivals into assuming that there are several males occupying the area. It certainly works with human listeners, who get extremely frustrated trying to catch a glimpse of the songster, only to hear the same bird a few metres behind them!

Identification

When seen, Cetti's Warbler is actually quite distinctive. Like the Reed Warbler, it is unstreaked, darker above and pale below; but has far deeper, richer and more rufous upperparts (reminiscent of a Nightingale), and colder, greyish underparts. Uniquely for a European songbird, it has ten (rather than twelve) feathers in its tail.

Unlike most other members of its family, Cetti's Warbler is basically sedentary, staying put in the winter months, making it occasionally vulnerable to hard winters. It also lays very distinctive brick-red eggs, and (unlike other warblers) is polygamous, the male often mating with at least two females.

SEDGE WARBLER

SCIENTIFIC NAME: Acrocephalus schoenobaenus

IDENTIFYING FEATURES:
Streaked plumage

SIMILAR SPECIES: Reed Warbler

SIZE: 13 cm (5 in)

HABITAT: Freshwater marshes
and reedbeds

POPULATION: Common

One of the great long-distance migrants of the Old World, Sedge Warblers travel thousands of miles in just two or three hops from their European breeding grounds to their winter quarters in Africa, well south of the Sahara. To do so they feed frantically in the weeks before they depart, putting on a thick layer of fat beneath their skin to enable them to travel so far with only a few 'pitstops' for feeding along the way.

The first sign that Sedge Warblers have returned to their breeding areas in wetlands across northern Europe and Asia is usually the sight of the male launching himself into the air from a low, scrubby bush and singing his song – a collection of excitable notes and phrases sounding like a jazz musician playing an impromptu tune. A close look at the singer reveals a small, streaked bird – basically brown above and paler buff below, with a pale throat and distinctive buffish yellow eye-stripe – the easiest way to distinguish the Sedge Warbler from its close relative the Reed Warbler.

Arctic Breeder

In contrast to other members of its genus, which are mostly confined to middle latitudes with temperate climates, the Sedge Warbler breeds right up into the high Arctic, reaching well into the Arctic Circle.

Like other Arctic breeders, it takes advantage of the abundance of insects found in the long summer days; but like them, it must raise a family quickly before the nights start to draw in and the food supply disappears.

In their winter quarters, Sedge Warblers are mainly solitary, and can be found across a broad swathe of Africa from Senegal in the west to Ethiopia in the east, and all the way down to Cape Province in South Africa.

MARSH WARBLER

SIZE: 13 cm (5 in)

HABITAT: Scrub and bushes, often near wetland areas

POPULATION: Very rare

SCIENTIFIC NAME: Acrocephalus palustris

IDENTIFYING FEATURES: Unstreaked, grey-brown plumage; extraordinary song

SIMILAR SPECIES: Reed Warbler

Plumage

Seen closely, the Marsh Warbler lacks the rufous tones of the Reed Warbler, being more uniformly grey-brown above, with off-white underparts which sometimes show a yellowish (rather than buff) tinge. However, these differences are extremely subjective and are best left to the real experts!

Marsh Warblers are a breeding bird of cool temperate, middle latitudes, preferring the warmer, drier summers found in Continental Europe and western central Asia rather than the damper, cooler summer climate of Britain – hence it has always been an extremely rare breeder there.

After breeding, Marsh Warblers head south-east, passing through the Middle East and into Africa, where they mainly winter in the south and east of that vast continent. They migrate early (in July or August) and return late, usually arriving back from late May to mid-June, and as a result spend about three times as long in their winter quarters as on their breeding areas.

BELOW
The Marsh Warbler is probably best identified by its unusual and distinctive song.

The quintessential 'little brown job' – a small, grey-brown warbler with no real identification features, save for one – its extraordinary ability to mimic other birds in its song. Marsh Warblers have been found to mimic more than 200 European and African species, with individuals managing to include up to 70 different species in their own repertoire. And despite its name, the Marsh Warbler prefers to nest in areas of scrubby vegetation rather than reedbeds, although it usually lives fairly close to fresh water.

Very similar to its close relative the Reed Warbler, and often the best way to tell the two species apart is by their contrasting songs: compared to the Reed Warbler's repetitive, laboured efforts the Marsh Warbler will always stand out.

REED WARBLER

SCIENTIFIC NAME: *Acrocephalus scirpaceus*

IDENTIFYING FEATURES:
Plain brown, unstreaked plumage

SIMILAR SPECIES: Marsh Warbler, Sedge Warbler

SIZE: 13 cm (5 in)

HABITAT: Reedbeds

POPULATION: Common

One of the best adapted birds to a reedbed existence, the Reed Warbler has an incredible ability to clamber about its habitat of vertical stems in order to find its food – mainly tiny insects, spiders and the odd snail. It also builds its nest in the reeds: suspending a neat cup-shaped structure made from grass, reed stems, leaves and spiders' webs, by weaving it around the stems of the reeds so that it stays in place.

The Reed Warbler is *the* characteristic bird of spring and summer in freshwater reedbeds across Europe and western Asia – its breeding range spanning as far north as Scandinavia and as far south as Morocco, and from Ireland in the west to Iran in the east. Like other members of its genus it is a fairly skulking creature, usually first located by its distinctive song: a series of repeated notes, usually given in twos and threes, with a deep, throaty tone.

ABOVE

The Reed Warbler is a familiar bird of freshwater habitats across Britain and Europe.

Victim of the Cuckoo

When seen (usually on sunny, windless days as it perches on a reed stem), it reveals itself as an unremarkable little bird, brown above (with a slightly warm tinge to the rump), and paler buff below, with a fairly obvious whitish throat, which often stands out when the male is singing.

Reed Warblers are one of the most frequent hosts of the Cuckoo. After the young Cuckoo has hatched, it will use its strength to throw out any remaining Reed Warbler eggs or chicks; after which the unsuspecting host parents will continue to feed it until it fledges. All Reed Warblers are transcontinental migrants, with the entire European and west Asian population migrating south, across the Sahara Desert, to spend the winter in tropical and equatorial Africa.

REED BUNTING

SIZE: 15–16 cm (5⅞–6¼ in)

HABITAT: Reedbeds (summer); farmland, marshes (winter)

POPULATION: Common

SCIENTIFIC NAME: Emberiza schoeniclus

IDENTIFYING FEATURES: Male has black head and white collar; white outer tail feathers

SIMILAR SPECIES: Corn Bunting, House Sparrow

Unlike most other members of its family, which are mainly birds of farmland or the open steppe grasslands of Asia, the Reed Bunting generally prefers wetland habitats, always nesting where the soil is moist. It has one of the broadest breeding ranges of any bunting, being able to breed anywhere from the high Arctic regions of northern Scandinavia to the very southern-most tip of Europe in Andalucía in southern Spain.

In breeding plumage, the male Reed Bunting is a handsome and very distinctive bird: sporting a jet-black head, face and throat, offset by a snow-white collar and white line from the base of the bill to the neck. In winter he loses his finery, though head and throat remain dark. The female, by contrast, is basically a rather nondescript, streaky chestnut brown, with the best diagnostic feature at all times of the year being the white outer tail feathers, easily seen in flight.

Song

For such a handsome bird, the Reed Bunting's song is rather disappointing: a hesitant series of notes, sounding rather like a bored sound engineer doing a microphone test: 'One… two… testing…'

Reed Buntings, like so many seed-eating birds dependent on farmland for food in autumn and winter, have declined heavily in recent years. This is almost entirely due to modern farming methods, which plant crops all year round and leave little or no 'waste' seed for the birds to feed on in the autumn and winter months. As a result, Reed Buntings have followed the example of several other seed-eating birds, and now turn up regularly in gardens, where they can take advantage of food provided by us.

BELOW
The Reed Bunting builds its nest in arable fields, in oilseed rape for example .

BEARDED TIT

SCIENTIFIC NAME: Panurus biarmicus

IDENTIFYING FEATURES: Long tail, grey head, orange-buff plumage, black 'beards' (male)

SIMILAR SPECIES: None

SIZE: 12.5 cm (4⅞ in)

HABITAT: Reedbeds

POPULATION: Scarce

The Bearded Tit is not in fact a true tit at all, but the only representative of an Asiatic family, the parrotbills, to be found in Europe. Oddly, this close relative of the babblers has evolved to live in a most unusual and challenging habitat: the reeds that give the species its alternative name of 'bearded reedling'. A sociable little bird, it can be elusive as it feeds in dense reedbeds, but when seen may give prolonged and outstanding views.

Given good views, it is impossible to mistake the Bearded Tit for any other bird. No other European species has the same combination of delicately marked plumage, long tail and, in the case of the male bird, the black patches either side of the bill that give the species its name. Close views reveal a subtly shaded bird: a greyish-mauve head shading into buffish orange upperparts, wings streaked with black, and an orange tail which, at seven centimetres long, is more than half the total length of the bird itself. Females and juveniles are less strongly marked, and lack the male's grey head and black 'beards' (though 'moustached tit' might be a better name!). Juvenile birds, which stay with their parents in loose family parties long after fledging, are blacker on the wings.

Sedentary Bird

Bearded Tits are generally very sedentary, staying put in the same area of reedbeds. But when harsh winter weather threatens to cut off their food supply they will often travel some distance to try to escape it, turning up in unexpected places. Nevertheless, it is a species very hard hit by cold winters, which might be expected to thrive – and even expand its range northwards – as a result of global climate change.

Coasts

Where the sea meets the land, birders often meet birds. It is a rich convergence, making up such distinctive habitats as estuaries, sand-dunes, beaches, sea-cliff, offshore islands and river inlets, each with their own favoured birds. And this is apart from the sea itself, which contains plenty of food for birds. Coastlines are also excellent places to watch migration, since following the sea allows an uncluttered journey, and the edge of land is there for safety from storms.

Many of our most familiar birds are primarily coastal. These include the many sea birds, such as terns, gulls, cormorants, auks, gannets and shearwaters, plus those that are essentially water birds, such as ducks. Waders use the juxtaposition of land and sea to feed on the inter-tidal multitudes found in mud or sand, mainly worms, molluscs and crustaceans – and indeed, there are few coastal birds that do not eat animals from these groups.

On the whole, coastal birds tend to differ from other birds by being essentially large bodied. There are only a small number of passerines in this biome. Furthermore, most coastal birds are dark above and pale below, remaining cryptic to predators looking down and to food items, such as fish, looking up.

Many of our coastal birds change their spots in the breeding season, and become birds of the tundra. Sea Ducks are typical in this regard, and they swap the worm-mollusc-crustacean diet for the abundant insects on and around freshwater tundra bogs and pools. For some, this is a major dietary change.

Another feature of coastal birds is that, on the whole, they are great travellers. Like the shifting seas themselves, they seem perpetually on the move; some, indeed, such as the Arctic Tern, routinely span the globe.

BEAN GOOSE

SCIENTIFIC NAME: Anser fabalis

IDENTIFYING FEATURES: Large goose with orange legs and orange and black bill; dark head and neck contrast with paler breast

SIMILAR SPECIES: Pink-footed, Greylag and White-fronted Geese

SIZE: 66–84 cm (26–33 in)

HABITAT: Open country, usually near lakes

POPULATION: Rare winter visitor

Identification

On the whole this is a large goose, almost as big as a Greylag, but it shows a thinner neck than that species, and its head is darker, contrasting with a paler belly. In Britain it tends to form smaller flocks than the other wild geese, and it is much less vocal and conversational, making the odd call that is distinctly like a woodwind instrument.

The diet of the Bean Goose is not much different from the other wild geese, despite its name. It feeds on various grasses, cereals and other agricultural crops and, like the rest, it makes predictable daily movements between its feeding and roosting sites.

Although it has a widespread distribution across northern Eurasia, the Bean Goose is a rare bird in Britain. There are only two regular flocks, one in Norfolk, England, and one in south-west Scotland, together numbering 400–500 birds; in addition, odd individuals or small groups can turn up almost anywhere. This species is very much a winter visitor, arriving in November at the earliest and leaving by the first week of March. Indeed, many individuals do not turn up at all until the New Year.

amidst the desolate pools and bogs of the tundra zone. The tundra birds have heavier bills but shorter necks than the more elegant, larger taiga birds. The taiga birds also tend to have more orange on their longer bills.

BELOW
The Bean Goose is a shy bird, but it will feed among other types of goose.

There are actually two forms of Bean Goose. The more common form is known as the Taiga Bean Goose, and makes up the majority of our visitors. It breeds as close as Scandinavia, in the forest zone known as the taiga, and is indeed unusual among geese in nesting among the trees. The other form, the Tundra Bean Goose, breeds much further away in Russia, and places its nest

PINK-FOOTED GOOSE

SCIENTIFIC NAME: Anser brachyrhynchus

SIZE: 60–75 cm (23⅝–29½ in)

HABITAT: Estuaries, farmland, moors

POPULATION: Localized but numerous winter visitor

IDENTIFYING FEATURES: Brownish goose with distinctive frosty look to upper wings

SIMILAR SPECIES:
Bean, White-fronted and Greylag Goose

To see a large flock of wintering **Pink-footed Geese** is one of the great experiences of British birding. When these birds make their commuting movements at dusk and dawn, flying between the inland fields where they feed and the coastal salt marshes where they roost, they do so in magnificent style. Thousands move together, their well-ordered V-shaped skeins lettering the twilight sky, while their 'ang-ang, wink-wink!' calls coalesce into a clanging chorus of voices.

The Pink-footed Goose does not breed in Britain, but is a migrant from Iceland and Greenland. More than half a million of these northern travellers arrive in October and settle in a few favoured parts of the country, including Scotland, northern England and East Anglia, departing in March and April. Despite the large numbers involved, the species is rather rare outside its normal range. During their time here they take advantage of our limited frosts and snow cover to forage over open fields, where they graze on grass and take grain, winter cereals and potatoes. If conditions are favourable, they sometimes manage to feed by a full moon.

Breeding Sites

Up north, where these birds breed, they select various sites for breeding, including large tracts of tundra and, especially in Iceland, gorges and other steep rocky slopes where they nest upon ledges. The latter site can make life difficult for the goslings, since it means that they will have to negotiate some tricky terrain before reaching water, but at least they will be alive to make the journey, having escaped the predation from ground enemies such as Arctic Foxes.

The nest itself is the usual goose creation of a mound of grasses moulded into a cup on the top, and lined with copious down. The goslings, of which there may be between three and six, hatch after nearly a month and are soon on their way. They take another two months to fly, and then follow their parents first to Greenland, to moult, and then down to Britain for the winter.

WHITE-FRONTED GOOSE

SCIENTIFIC NAME: Anser albifrons

IDENTIFYING FEATURES: Light brown with white blaze on forehead and dark markings on belly

SIMILAR SPECIES:
Pink-footed, Greylag and Bean Goose

SIZE: 64–68 cm (25⅛–26⅞ in)

HABITAT: Wet grassland, farmland

POPULATION: Uncommon and localized winter visitor

The White-fronted Goose is a long-distance migrant of high predictability; individuals breed on the same patch of tundra from year to year, and almost invariably use the same wintering areas. They migrate the same routes at more or less the same time each year, stopping for a rest in the same places, and the goslings follow their travelling parents and remain in the family fold until it is time to retrace the traditional routes north in the spring.

Easily identified by their white foreheads and splodges of black on the belly, White-fronted Geese spend the winter in agricultural and grassland areas, usually either close to the coast or to large areas of shallow water. They roost on the latter and feed over the former, and they prefer not to travel more than about 20 km (12 miles) from the two. On their wintering grounds they feed on various grasses, cereals and root crops such as potatoes. They are extremely selective about what they eat; they will, for example, only use particular parts of a field, or eat particular plant species when they are there. Once on the tundra they at first eat subterranean storage organs such as bulbs, before reverting to fresh new growth of grass.

Bonding and Nesting

Before leaving for the tundra in spring, both sexes feed prodigiously, with the female doubling her fat reserves. Another three weeks of hard eating gets the birds in breeding condition, and the female then makes a nest among low bushes. It is usually placed on a hummock or other eminence, both to ensure a good all round view in case of danger, and to ensure that the summer thaw does not flood the nest.

RIGHT
White-fronted Geese pair for life and travel to and fro on migration together.

BARNACLE GOOSE

SCIENTIFIC NAME: Branta leucopsis

SIZE: 58–71 cm (22⅞–28 in)

HABITAT: Estuaries, bogs, farmland

POPULATION: Local and uncommon winter visitor

IDENTIFYING FEATURES:
White or yellowish face; pale grey belly

SIMILAR SPECIES: Brent Goose, Canada Goose

Truly wild Barnacle Geese are found only in a few places in Britain. Flocks of them, always tight-knit, busy and excitable, occur in Scotland, Ireland and along the Solway Firth during the winter. In recent years, however, the very same species has begun to breed in many places elsewhere, even in southern England. These populations arise from birds that have escaped from captivity and established themselves as self-sustaining in the wild. One day, perhaps they will become as familiar as Canada Geese.

That would be an odd outcome for a bird of such good Arctic credentials. Most of the world's Barnacle Geese breed in Greenland, Svalbard and the coast of northern Russia, well above the Arctic Circle. The Greenland birds travel via Iceland to winter in Ireland and the Hebrides; the Svalbard birds winter along the Solway Firth; and the Russian birds winter across the Channel, with small numbers occasionally visiting the east coast. However, the last few decades have seen the Barnacle Goose establish itself on some of the predator-free islands of the Baltic, too, at the same latitude as Britain. So this species is evidently changing in its requirements.

Survival in the Wild

The entry of a Barnacle Goose into the world can be dramatic. The Greenland and Russian populations, in particular, usually nest in colonies on precipitous cliffs, using ledges out of reach of predators such as the Arctic Fox and Polar Bear. Fine though this might be for the safe hatching of eggs, it does present a challenge to the goslings. They have to leap from a ledge if they are to find the safety of water, and this can entail a plunge of 20 m (66 ft) or more from their cliff-top birthplace.

In common with other geese, Barnacles travel in family parties. In the wintertime they feed on grass and clover and, early on, spilt grain. In contrast to other geese, they only make short commuting runs between feeding and roosting areas, 5 km (3 miles) at most.

RIGHT

Barnacle Geese are short-necked, with a white patch on the face.

BRENT GOOSE

SCIENTIFIC NAME: Branta bernicla

IDENTIFYING FEATURES: Dark plumage, with white neck-ring, bright white 'stern'

SIMILAR SPECIES: Barnacle Goose

SIZE: 56–61 cm (22–24 in)

HABITAT: Coasts, estuaries, adjacent farmland

POPULATION: Common winter visitor

This is one goose that is hardly ever found away from the coast, except occasionally on migration. It breeds close to the sea in the high Arctic, and it winters in shallow, often estuarine, waters in the temperate zone. To most bird-watchers, flocks of Brent Geese are a familiar sight grazing on mudflats and salt marshes, or bobbing up and down with the waves of shallow waters at high tide. Their rolling, croaking calls are a constant part of the coastal soundscape.

The Brent Goose has a more specialized winter diet than other geese, traditionally relying on eel-grass (*Zostera*), one of the world's very few flowering plants that grows completely submerged by the sea. When foraging, the geese will graze upon it at low tide, grub it up while paddling, or will up-end to reach it when swimming. The birds do also eat some seaweed, and have recently taken to foraging on coastal fields where they graze grasses and the shoots of winter wheat, but the distribution of eel-grass tends to determine where the birds are found.

Identification and Variation

Brents are very small geese, and they are highly distinctive with their oil-black plumage and white undertails. The previous season's youngsters are easy to pick out from the adults by their lack of white neck collar and four white parallel lines formed by the tips of their wing-coverts; since wintering birds are seen in family parties, it is thus easy to assess how well the previous breeding season went. By midwinter, these differences disappear.

Throughout their range Brent Geese are fairly racially variable. Birds breeding in Canada and Greenland have pale bellies, contrasting very strongly with the black breast, whereas Brent Geese from elsewhere have darker bellies.

SHELDUCK

SIZE: 58–67 cm (22⅞–26⅜ in)

HABITAT: Estuaries, salt marshes, dunes, gravel pits

POPULATION: Common

SCIENTIFIC NAME: Tadorna tadorna

IDENTIFYING FEATURES: Bottle-green head and neck; chestnut breast-band

SIMILAR SPECIES: Goosander, Avocet

With its long neck, ease of gait, comparatively large size and similarity of plumage between male and female – none of which are typical duck features – the Shelduck seems to fit midway between a duck and a goose, and is not closely related to the rest of the ducks. It is, however, usually found in company with them, either feeding over the mud of an estuary or salt marsh, or swimming alongside them at gravel pits and other freshwater sites inland.

This conspicuous species has a number of interesting behavioural quirks. The most frequent nest-site, for example, is an old rabbit hole, although birds will also use other natural holes and occasional artificial ones. Such sites may be eight m (26 ft) off the ground, giving the young birds an interesting start to life when they have to jump out. Once hatched, they are led to a nursery area, where they join the other local broods and learn to feed for themselves.

Aunties

Curiously, though, before the young are fully grown, the adults depart the area and leave their young in the care of a few non-breeding adults, known as 'aunties', who oversee their development to adulthood. The parents, meanwhile, take a short easterly flight to a huge area of mudflats on the north coast of Germany, part of the region known as the Waddensee. Here they gather with other adults from all over Europe and moult, losing their wing feathers almost simultaneously and becoming flightless for a period. Only when the moult is fully complete do they return to their wintering or breeding areas.

The salt marshes in Britain and in Germany provide Shelducks with a diet of inter-tidal invertebrates, including worms, shrimps and – a great favourite – a small snail known as *Hydrobia*.

BELOW
The Shelduck has a distinctive chestnut band around its chest.

SCAUP

SCIENTIFIC NAME: Aythya marila

IDENTIFYING FEATURES: Broad body; large bill; large, evenly-rounded head

SIMILAR SPECIES: Tufted Duck, Pochard

SIZE: 42–51 cm (16½–20 in)

HABITAT: Shallow coasts, sometimes freshwater lakes

POPULATION: Uncommon and localized winter visitor

To most birders the Scaup is very much a sea duck, a bird usually seen in the winter in shallow bays not far offshore. It often feeds in large, tightly knit flocks near abundant food sources, and has a habit of being active on a rising tide, the birds diving down every few moments as they take advantage of the newly active shellfish covered by shallow water. These birds usually do not go very deep, just 1–6 m (3–20 ft) down. Their bursts of feeding activity can be brief; when the tide is too high they simply rest in large rafts, preening or sleeping.

The Scaup leads something of a double life. Despite being almost entirely marine in winter, and feeding on molluscs such as mussels, clams, snails and oysters, the Scaup eschews this habitat in the breeding season to settle instead beside freshwater lakes. Here it will eat large amounts of plant material, especially pondweeds, as well as some insect larvae and only a few molluscs. It is quite a transformation.

Breeding

For breeding the Scaup always selects a site very close to the water, as this heavy duck is very awkward on land – it is also no lightweight in the air, being quite reluctant to fly and taking off with a considerable

run-up. Although usually carefully hidden in a tussock on dry land, sometimes the nest is actually placed on a raft of floating vegetation. The female selects the site and builds the nest, a shallow depression lined with dead plant material and down.

ABOVE
The grey back of the Scaup distinguishes it from the Tufted Duck.

The male leaves the female before the eggs hatch and the pair are unlikely to breed together again.

Where they are numerous, Scaups will often breed close together in informal colonies of a few nests. After the 26 to 28 days of incubation the young, of which there are usually about 10, often gather with the youngsters of neighbouring broods to form a crèche.

EIDER

SCIENTIFIC NAME: Somateria mollissima

IDENTIFYING FEATURES: Large head and massive bill; black crown and nape

SIMILAR SPECIES: Female Mallard or Velvet Scoter

SIZE: 50–71 cm (19¼–28 in)

HABITAT: Sea coast

POPULATION: Common

Although there may be plenty of ducks on the sea, the Eider can usually be picked out quite easily. Not only does the male have the reverse of the usual sea bird plumage, by being dark below and white above, but both sexes have an unusually shaped, Roman-nose type bill. Huge and wedge-shaped, it is used to crush bottom-dwelling animals such as mussels, cockles and starfish. To get at them, Eiders prefer to feed in shallow water, perhaps 2–4 m (6.5–13 ft) deep, although a remarkable 20 m (66 ft) has been recorded.

When diving, Eiders descend with their wings open, and they use their wings, as well as their feet, for propulsion. Although the bird is heavy, and the wings do not look especially strong, Eiders are among the fastest flying birds recorded, with 76 km/h (47 mph) reliably clocked.

A Sociable Bird

These birds are extremely sociable, and quite enormous flocks are often seen in favoured areas and on migration, with thousands of birds sharing bays and rocky coastlines. In the winter the sound from such gatherings is truly memorable, with the males throwing their heads back and uttering their gorgeous, rather suggestive cooing, to a backdrop of unimpressed muttering by the females.

Sociability extends into the breeding season, with many Eiders gathering together into colonies on offshore islets, sometimes among rocks or simply on a flat surface. These colonies have economic importance in some parts of the Eider's range, for the down plucked from the female's breast and used to line the nest is famous for its insulating properties, and is still used in bedding for humans. The male leaves the female during incubation, while the female sits tight. The Eider lays four to six eggs and remains on them for 25–28 days. Once they hatch, the young soon feed themselves under the supervision of their parent, sometimes gathering into crèches with other broods.

ABOVE

The Eider is heavier than the Mallard, but more compact.

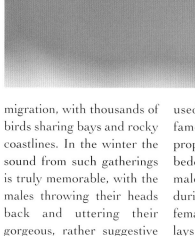

LONG-TAILED DUCK

SCIENTIFIC NAME: Clangula hyemalis

IDENTIFYING FEATURES: Plain dark brown,
no wing-bars; complex but distinctive plumage

SIMILAR SPECIES:
Common Eider, female Common Scoter

SIZE: 36–47 cm (14½–18½ in)

HABITAT: Coasts; occasionally
large inland waters

POPULATION: Uncommon
winter visitor

T his is the epitome of a sea duck. It does not just paddle in the shallows, but takes the plunge into marine waters in every sense, going further out than most other ducks, coping with more choppy waters than most, and diving deeper than any recorded. Its typical dives are down to 3–10 m (10–33 ft), but much greater depths have been claimed. Not surprisingly, it typically spends a long time underwater, searching for its favoured diet of small molluscs, amphipod crustaceans and fish.

At all seasons the Long-tailed Duck is distinctive, and not just because of the male's pin-tailed plumage. It has an unusual shape with a small head and dumpy body. When it flies, the short wings beat furiously, but only seemingly below the horizontal, and the bird tilts from side to side as it goes low over the water, eventually landing with a splash. These are restless birds, moving around a lot, and among flocks there may be much diving and splashing about.

Calls and Breeding

This is an unusually vocal duck. Even in winter flocks it can be noisy, the males making an unmistakable, musical clanging phrase, which may be individually variable; the birds have contortions in their trachea that give rise to the sound. The calls often accompany visual displays, including a lifting of the long tail.

Despite their marine lifestyle in winter, Long-tailed Ducks are abundant breeders on freshwater tundra pools. Pairs form in winter flocks, and male and female migrate north together. Nesting starts rather late, rarely before June, the female selecting a patch of dry ground close to the water's edge, usually on an island. Pairs often nest close together in small groups. The female lays an average of seven eggs and incubates them for 26 days, taking two feeding breaks a day between 09.00 and 10.00 and 16.00 and 18.30. Once hatched, the young must fledge fast, before the water freezes once again on the tundra.

COMMON SCOTER

SIZE: 44–54 cm (17⅓–21¼ in)

HABITAT: Coasts; breeds on northern lakes

POPULATION: Common winter visitor; rare breeder

SCIENTIFIC NAME: Melanitta nigra

IDENTIFYING FEATURES: No obvious wing markings; male all black with yellow on bill; female dark brown

SIMILAR SPECIES: Velvet Scoter, Eider

Most bird-watchers know this bird as a sea-going duck, an intensely sociable species gathering into flocks that pepper the waves. It is much less well known as a secretive tundra bird. Of course, in common with many 'sea ducks' it leads a double life, swapping the salt water in winter for freshwater pools in the far north. The diet changes, too. In winter it feeds mainly on molluscs, especially bivalves such as mussels, plus the odd starfish; in the breeding season, many insect larvae find their way on to the menu.

In winter and on migration, the Common Scoter has a habit of flying low over the sea, quite far out in large, dense flocks. Birds at the front tend to bunch, making a distinctive shape with a 'body' and a 'tail'. The birds are also distinctive on the water, with the males' all-black plumage easily distinguishing them from all other ducks except other Scoters. They often sit quite high in the water with their tails cocked up; as the breeding season approaches the males incorporate something similar into their displays, rushing forward with their heads low and raising the tail past the vertical over the back.

LEFT

Outside the breeding season, Scoters can mainly be found out at sea.

Breeding Biology

Common Scoter breeding biology is not especially well known, but besides the rushing display, males also have a sonar-like whistle that they utter in the early spring. Furthermore, they have a modified outer primary feather which makes a whistling sound to accompany nuptial flights.

The nest site can be in a variety of habitats: beside tundra pools, on a bank or island, or even far from water in low scrub. In contrast to the case of some ducks, the nests are always well dispersed.

The female lays eight or nine eggs in a shallow depression lined with down. The eggs hatch after a month or so, and quickly follow the female down to the water, where they soon feed themselves on abundant midges and other insects.

VELVET SCOTER

SCIENTIFIC NAME: Melanitta fusca

IDENTIFYING FEATURES: Flat crown and large, wedge-shaped bill; white trailing edge to inner wing

SIMILAR SPECIES: Common Scoter, female Eider

SIZE: 51–58 cm (20–22⅞ in)

HABITAT: Coasts

POPULATION: Scarce winter visitor

This is the largest and heaviest of the Scoters, a rather big duck quite close in bulk and shape to the Eider. It enjoys a similar diet to that species in the winter, too, diving down to scoop molluscs such as mussels, cockles and whelks from the bottom of relatively shallow, usually sandy-bottomed coastal waters. It takes a few crustaceans, worms and fish as well, and when diving down differs from the Common Scoter by sinking down with wings open, rather than making a leap with wings held in.

Velvet Scoters, in common with most sea ducks, are sociable creatures, and indeed the scoter species often flock together. When this happens, the Velvet is instantly distinguished as soon as the birds take flight, with its blazing white bar on the secondaries being impossible to miss. The white or pale patches on the head are far more difficult to see. As is typical, marine winter flocks are good places for male and female to meet and pair up. They are not vocal like the Common Scoter, and have a highly distinctive display in which the female leads a number of males on an underwater chase, as if they were all kids in a swimming pool.

Nesting

In the breeding season Velvet Scoters usually abandon the sea air for the boreal zone, where they nest beside freshwater lakes. At this point their diet changes to include large numbers of creatures known as amphipods; in particular the female feasts on these in order to get into condition to lay the eggs. Caddis larvae and crustaceans are also important during the breeding season.

The nest is made on the ground, often on an island in a small lake, but sometimes up to 3 km (1.9 miles) from the nearest water. Several females may breed close together, and they may also share their sites with colonies of gulls or terns. The female lays between seven and nine eggs, which are incubated for on average

ABOVE

Velvet Scoters can be distinguished from Common Scoters by the white bar on their wings.

27 days, but apparently without much dedication. The female routinely leaves the nest for a break, covering the eggs with vegetation.

RED-BREASTED MERGANSER

SIZE: 52–58 cm (20½–22⅞ in)

HABITAT: Harbours, bays and estuaries, usually on or near the coast

POPULATION: Scarce; mainly winter visitor

SCIENTIFIC NAME: Mergus serrator

IDENTIFYING FEATURES:
Long, thin bill; slender body

SIMILAR SPECIES: Goosander

LEFT
The male Red-breasted Merganser has a distinctive punk hairstyle!

Male and Female Characteristics

The female Red-breasted Merganser is much harder to tell apart from the female Goosander: though given good views, the slender red bill (lacking the downward tip of the Goosander's bill) and less obvious border between the brownish head and grey breast are apparent.

Red-breasted Mergansers are predominately coastal birds, although they prefer more sheltered areas than other 'sea ducks', such as estuaries, coastal pools and harbours. They are usually seen in small flocks.

Like other sawbill species, Red-breasted Mergansers feed mainly on fish, which they hunt by ducking their heads underwater, then diving after their target prey. Unlike the Goosander, however, they use their wings as well as their legs and feet to propel themselves when beneath the surface.

This large duck is a member of the 'sawbill' tribe, distinguished, as its scientific name suggests, by the serrated edge to its long, thin bill. The English name, 'merganser', means 'diving goose' – an understandable confusion given the large size of the species. Mergansers are also sometimes confused with cormorants and divers, with whom they share a long, slender body, low-slung posture in the water, and slender bill.

The male Red-breasted Merganser is a rather handsome duck, though his neat plumage is slightly spoilt by the effect of the 'punk hair-do' formed by the wispy feathers on the back of his head, and the slightly comical expression on the bird's face. The male is darker than the male Goosander, with a greenish head, speckled brown breast and pale grey flanks. In flight the inside of the upperwing shows white, contrasting with the darker outer feathers.

GREAT NORTHERN DIVER

SCIENTIFIC NAME: Gavia immer

IDENTIFYING FEATURES: Large size; huge bill

SIMILAR SPECIES:
Black-throated and Red-throated Divers

SIZE: 69–91 cm (27⅛–35⅞ in)

HABITAT: Off coast;
also on reservoirs in winter

POPULATION: Scarce winter visitor

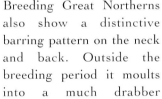

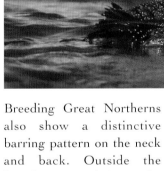

Despite its name, this is not the largest member of the diver family – that honour goes to the White-billed – but is nevertheless an impressive bird. In America divers are known as loons, a name thought to derive from the species' far-carrying and haunting call. Although found in winter in Britain and other parts of northern Europe, the Great Northern Diver is essentially a North American species, its only regular European breeding location being Iceland.

In the breeding season the Great Northern Diver is hard to confuse with any other bird: its large size, jet-black head, and all-black bill being the key distinguishing field marks.

Breeding Great Northerns also show a distinctive barring pattern on the neck and back. Outside the breeding period it moults into a much drabber autumn and winter garb, during which time it can be mistaken for a pale-bellied Cormorant. However, the two birds are very different in shape and posture: the diver being thick-necked and with a dagger-shaped, pale bill usually held at an upright angle.

Coasts and Inland Waters

The Great Northern Diver is generally a coastal bird, although singles and pairs do turn up regularly on inland reservoirs, often staying for the whole of the winter. Even so they can be surprisingly inconspicuous for such a bulky bird, perhaps because they are highly mobile, and spend much of the time diving beneath the water's surface to find food. The species has also bred in Britain on a handful of occasions.

Although graceful on the water, like all divers the Great Northern is clumsy on land, due to the fact that its feet are so far back on its body to achieve propulsion under water.

GOLDENEYE

SIZE: 42–50 cm (16½–19¾ in)

HABITAT: Breeds by freshwater lakes in forests; in winter on lakes, rivers or coast

POPULATION: Scarce breeding bird; common winter visitor

SCIENTIFIC NAME: Bucephala clangula

IDENTIFYING FEATURES: Male has bottle-green head, dark on back; female white line mid-body

SIMILAR SPECIES: Tufted Duck, Scaup, Pochard

The Goldeneye is an unusual-looking duck; not because of its bold plumage pattern, though, but because of its curiously bulbous head. Broad at the back, and with a peaked crown in the middle, the head looks too large for the slender neck, and this feature, as much as anything, makes the Goldeneye easy to identify. On the lakes or coasts where it occurs, it tends to keep itself to itself, not mixing freely with other ducks, finding its own corners.

LEFT

Goldeneyes can be found in areas with some tree cover and fresh water nearby.

The Goldeneye is a bird of forested areas dotted with lakes. The latter, which it uses for foraging, need to be deep and uncluttered. In many places they are relatively unproductive bodies of water lacking fish, and the Goldeneyes will hunt them for aquatic insects, molluscs and crustaceans, often turning over stones underwater to find their hidden prey. The forests, meanwhile, provide the Goldeneye with its rather unusual nest site: large holes in trees. The holes need to be within 2 km (1.2 miles) of water and no more than 5 m (16 ft) above ground; these nest sites usually result from heart-rot, or are made by woodpeckers, and they are always at a premium. Competition is rife, and female Goldeneyes routinely lay their own eggs in the nests of other birds. Mixed broods, sometimes with other tree-nesting ducks such as Goosanders, are routine.

Nesting Season

If all goes well a Goldeneye will lay between eight and 12 eggs of its own, but 28 have been recorded in a single nest. They are incubated for 28 to 32 days, and the young jump out about a day after hatching.

After breeding, many Goldeneyes opt to leave their forested habitat to winter in a quite different one, sheltered coastlines. Here their diet shifts towards such creatures as crabs, shrimps and barnacles, with a few small fish.

FULMAR

SCIENTIFIC NAME: Fulmarus glacialis

IDENTIFYING FEATURES:
Long, parallel-edged wings; thick bill

SIMILAR SPECIES: Gulls, Manx Shearwater

SIZE: 45–50 cm (17¼–19¾ in)

HABITAT: Breeds on sea cliffs; winters at sea

POPULATION: Common

At first sight the Fulmar resembles a gull, being of similar size and having basically grey and white plumage. The flight style soon gives it away, though; instead of the gulls' languid motion, the Fulmar flies on wings held rigidly out, alternating bouts of quick flaps with long, stiff-winged glides. Those long, narrow wings enable the Fulmar to fly for enormous distances, riding the sea currents with supreme efficiency. It is thus very much a sea bird, often seen out in the very depths of the ocean, hundreds of kilometres from land.

Out on the ocean the Fulmar eats a variety of sea animals, including squid (a favourite), fish, crustaceans and marine worms, all of them seized by a quick lunge when the bird is swimming, or occasionally during a brief dive. The Fulmar's bill is strong, with a hooked tip, allowing it to pick off pieces of meat from the floating carcasses of sea mammals, another useful food source on the open ocean. Fulmars will also compete in the scrum of sea birds feeding on offal thrown out from trawlers.

Eggs and Chicks

Fulmars breed on sea cliffs and islands, usually on a ledge but sometimes on an earthy slope. They lay a single egg not in a nest, but more or less directly upon the substrate (whether it be rocky, earthy or other), although a few artistic pairs add a stone for lining. The egg is then incubated for an extraordinarily long time, sometimes up to 53 days; the female starts and then has a week off to recuperate from egg laying.

Not surprisingly, having invested so much effort, the parents are very protective of their hatched chick, never leaving it for the first two weeks. Fulmars are also capable of spitting an extremely foul-smelling concoction of stomach-oil at any intruders, a talent that the young inherit in the nest.

Remarkably, if the young Fulmar survives its nestling phase and reaches fledging at 46 days, it has a long haul to adulthood: some individuals do not breed until they are 12 years old. They may reach an age of 50 or more.

MANX SHEARWATER

SIZE: 31–36 cm (12¼–14⅓ in)

HABITAT: Sea; breeds on islands

POPULATION: Common

SCIENTIFIC NAME: Puffinus puffinus

IDENTIFYING FEATURES:
Black cap; underwings bordered black

SIMILAR SPECIES: Fulmar

It is likely that the name 'shear water' came from this species, named after its habit, shared by many species, of flying so low to the waves that its wing tips seem to touch the surface. Typically, it moves along with alternate quick flaps of the wings and longer glides, tipping from one side to the other so that it appears dark one moment and light the next. Groups of Manx Shearwaters often fly along in lines; they are very sociable birds, gathering in flocks, sometimes very large ones, at all times of the year.

The Manx Shearwater is, like many sea birds, an extraordinary traveller. Breeding on both sides of the North Atlantic, in temperate western Europe and in north-eastern Canada and the USA, these birds begin migrating earnestly south in September and do not stop until they are between 20° and 40° south of the Equator, off the south-east coast of South America. They keep themselves going on a diet of fish and a few squid, and return northwards again to reach their breeding colonies the following March, having travelled almost to the bottom of the world and back.

Colonies

Breeding colonies are on islands, where the birds make burrows in the earth, appropriate old rabbit holes or nest under rocks, the sites usually on flat, open terrain. In common with a number of their relatives, they only attend these burrows at night, in order to avoid predators. Colonies often contain thousands of pairs, and on spring nights the visitor can hear a remarkable cacophony of unearthly crooning, howling and screaming as the birds declare territorial rights.

Manx Shearwaters lay just one egg, which the female lays after a two-week sabbatical at sea, away from the colony. It is incubated for 50 days, with both parents taking shifts of a week or so each. The youngster is fed on regurgitated food until, after 60 days, the parents stop coming and the chick has to pluck up the courage to leave on its own.

RIGHT
Although a sea-going bird, the Manx Shearwater comes ashore to breed.

STORM PETREL

SCIENTIFIC NAME: Hydrobates pelagicus

IDENTIFYING FEATURES: Sooty-black, white rump, white stripe on underwing

SIMILAR SPECIES: Leach's Storm-Petrel, House Martin

SIZE: 14–18 cm (5½–7 in)

HABITAT: Rocky islands; sea

POPULATION: Common but localized summer visitor

It seems extraordinary that such a small bird as a Storm Petrel – not much bigger than a Sparrow – could survive on the turbulent waters of the ocean. But this is the life the Storm Petrel leads, foraging over the water with rapid, bat-like beats of its wings, hugging the waves. It feeds on small fish, plankton, squid and fatty droplets, all these collected from the surface of the water while the bird is airborne.

When a Storm Petrel is feeding, it dips down to the surface and often patters the water with its feet, raising its wings in a V or hovering as it does so. It is thought that this might help to disturb food, or otherwise make it easier to

find. On the oceans, Storm Petrels often feed in large flocks at rich feeding areas. They sometimes follow ships

and, in recent years, it has been shown that they may come close to shore at night to feed on inter-tidal organisms. Although they are seen flying most of the time, these small birds swim well, and are buoyant on the water.

Fascinating Facts

The name 'Petrel' comes from St Peter, who was believed to have walked on water, as these coastal birds seem to do.

RIGHT
The Storm Petrel has a distinctive white rump.

A Wary Breeder

Storm Petrels nest on rocky islands that are predator-free, utilizing small burrows or cracks between rocks and walls, with a diameter of perhaps 5–8 cm (2–3 in). There is a chamber at the end containing a slight depression where the egg is laid, sometimes among some scraps of plant material. The adults, wary of predation, only visit the burrows at night. In early season pairs fly around

the burrow, making a remarkable purring 'song' interspersed with clucks.

Just the single egg is laid, which may equal as much as 25 per cent of a female's weight. The adults take alternate stints at incubation for a total of 40 days and, when the egg hatches, they look after it for a couple of months, bringing in food only at night. The youngster becomes independent as soon as it leaves the nest, and heads for the open sea.

LEACH'S STORM-PETREL

SIZE: 20 cm (7⅞ in)

HABITAT: Breeds on rocky islands; otherwise open ocean

POPULATION: Localized summer visitor

SCIENTIFIC NAME: Oceanodroma leucorhoa

IDENTIFYING FEATURES: Central pale grey panel on upper side; tail slightly forked

SIMILAR SPECIES: Storm Petrel, House Martin

Occurring widely in the Northern Hemisphere, the Leach's Storm-Petrel ought to be a well-known bird. But it is not; it is actually obscure and mysterious. This is partly because it is seldom seen from land, usually feeding at least 50 km (30 miles) out, even when breeding. Another factor is that it only breeds on offshore rocky islands. And furthermore, when it does visit its breeding grounds, it only does so at night. All these things make it a difficult bird to see.

In common with other storm petrels, the Leach's is a tiny,

Swallow-like sea bird that feeds from the surface of the water with a jinking, dipping flight, with frequent hovering. The Leach's long wings make it look rather like a diminutive tern. Its diet mainly consists of crustaceans, including amphipods and copepods, but it will also take a few small fish and squid. This sea bird often follows whales and seals, feeding from their waste products, but it seldom follows ships. It is also less sociable than many other sea birds, usually feeding alone but sometimes in small groups. There is some evidence that it uses its sense of smell to detect some of its food.

LEFT

The Leach's Storm-Petrel is larger than the Storm Petrel, with a lighter colouring.

Nesting and Incubation

The Leach's Storm-Petrel breeds on offshore islands, nesting in burrows or crevices. Males can construct their burrows in the earth by digging with their feet. The burrow is quite long, often more than a metre, and at the end of it is a chamber where the single egg is laid. The parents take turns to incubate the egg for an average of 43 days, each shift lasting about three days. Once the egg hatches, the chick is fed for a couple of months, the adults visiting during the night. But the visits are not frequent; on 35 per cent of nights the adults do not call in at all.

GANNET

SCIENTIFIC NAME: Sula bassana

IDENTIFYING FEATURES: Dagger-shaped bill; orange-yellow on adult head

SIMILAR SPECIES: None

SIZE: 87–100 cm (34¼–39½ in)

HABITAT: Breeds on rocky cliffs or islands; winters at sea

POPULATION: Numerous breeding bird, common offshore

The Gannet is one of the largest sea birds in the world and, with its long, black-tipped white wings, long bill and pointed tail, it is also one of the most distinctive. It flies over the sea with slow, languid wing beats alternated with long glides, and it breaks this relaxed pattern only when it spots some food below. It then gains height to 30 m (100 ft) or more above the surface, checks below and then tumbles into a spectacular nosedive, closing its wings at the last moment and making a splash on impact.

The Gannet finds and catches its food, medium-sized fish. It specializes in shoaling species such as herring and cod, and the sight of one Gannet feeding often brings others in. In order to cope with their extreme feeding method, Gannets have forward-facing eyes to judge their dives, air-sacs under the skin to absorb the shock of plunges, and nostrils opening internally to the bill to prevent water being forced up them.

Cliff-top Colonies

Gannets breed in large colonies on northern sea-cliffs and rocky islands, often tightly packed together. Pairs mate for life and have a series of entertaining displays to keep the bond strong, including a mutual 'fencing' of the bills combined with bowing. The male builds a nest out of seaweed, feathers, grass and earth cemented together by the birds' droppings, making a pile at least 30 cm (12 in) high, but reaching as high as 2 m (6.5 ft) over the years.

Just a single egg is laid each year, and it hatches, if all goes well, after 42–46 days. The young Gannet is fed by both parents on regurgitated fish. The adults may make very long round-trips, of 400 km (250 miles) or more, just to find food for a single visit. After some 80 days the adults cease their endeavour and no longer visit; after a week or so, the youngster gets the message and leaves to begin the long road – five to six years – to breeding maturity.

CORMORANT

SIZE: 80–100 (31½–39⅜ in)

HABITAT: Sea coasts; inland lakes and rivers

POPULATION: Common

SCIENTIFIC NAME: Phalacrocorax carbo

IDENTIFYING FEATURES: Long neck; heavy bill; white on thighs in breeding season

SIMILAR SPECIES: Shag

For a water bird, it is surprising how little time the Cormorant actually spends in the water. If it has a ready supply of food, this large fish-eater may only spend a few minutes each day actually foraging, while the rest of the time it simply sits out on a perch such as a rock, a jetty or the branch of a tree, and watches the world go by. As it does so, it often holds out its wings in characteristic fashion, allowing them to dry.

Indeed, for a water bird, the Cormorant is not very waterproof. The drying of the wings is necessary because the body feathers, apart from an inner layer of down, are specially adapted to absorb, not repel water, so that the Cormorant is not too buoyant. When feeding, it chases fish underwater using its back-set feet to propel it, so it pays to be able to sink easily. The Cormorant's bones are denser than most other birds', reducing buoyancy, and the Cormorant will also swallow stones to help it dive. The Cormorant's eyes are also special; they can adapt to seeing equally well in water and air.

LEFT

Cormorants can be found on large lakes in the winter months, although ostensibly a sea bird.

Food Supply

Most of the fish that the Cormorant catches are bottom-dwellers, especially flatfish, but it depends on what is available, and to this end the Cormorant is quite adaptable. Most live on cliffs and do their fishing in the sea, but small and increasing numbers breed inland, nesting in trees and feeding on the fish of rivers or lakes. This habit may bring them into conflict with anglers.

Pairs of Cormorants form when the male opens its wings and flashes its white thigh patch, a seasonal 'badge' to attract a mate. Once hitched, both sexes contribute to building a large platform of sticks and debris, upon which the three to four eggs are laid. Cormorants usually nest in colonies, and theft of nest material is commonplace. After 30 days the eggs hatch and the young, which are brown with white bellies, then enjoy a long period of being fed, which may last for another three months.

SHAG

SCIENTIFIC NAME: Phalacrocorax aristotelis

IDENTIFYING FEATURES: High crown; thin neck; no white plumage

SIMILAR SPECIES: Cormorant

SIZE: 65–80 cm (25⅗–31½ in)

HABITAT: Sea coast

POPULATION: Common

Many bird-watchers find it difficult to tell the difference between a Cormorant and a Shag, and although former is considerably larger than the latter, it is not always easy to tell the size. The best year-round difference is in the head and neck structure. Cormorants have thick bills that seem to be sunk into the skull, and they have a thick neck; Shags, however, have a thin, snake-like neck and the bill is thin enough, one might imagine, to 'snap off', making a sharp angle to the forehead.

In contrast to Cormorants, Shags are virtually never seen away from the sea, being far more marine than their adaptable counterparts. In many ways they seem more 'at home' when swimming, revelling in more turbulent waters and performing a tremendous leap before diving in (the Cormorant's equivalent leap is less marked). They are known to submerge deeper than Cormorants, too, regularly to 15 m (50 ft) and sometimes down as far as 60 m (200 ft) – an impressive dive by any standards, and while they are down they take advantage of a slightly wider range of foods, including many different species of fish, plus some crustaceans.

Breeding Sites

For breeding, Shags invariably select a site within touching distance of the sea, quite often secluded away in a sea cave and usually more sheltered than a site used by a Cormorant. Shags have crests in the breeding season, another useful distinction from Cormorants when present, and these vary in size in both sexes. Interestingly, birds with larger crests seem to enjoy higher breeding success than the rest.

In common with the Cormorant, Shags build nests out of vegetation such as seaweed and, for example, dead stems of plants. They do breed in colonies, but these are usually rather small and well spaced. The clutch is usually of three eggs, and these are incubated for a month. The young fledge two months after this.

ABOVE

Shags are less prolific than Cormorants, although they breed in larger colonies.

WHITE-TAILED EAGLE

SCIENTIFIC NAME: Haliaeetus albicilla

IDENTIFYING FEATURES: 'Fingered' wings; wedge-shaped tail; pale head

SIMILAR SPECIES: Golden Eagle

SIZE: 70–90 cm (27⅝–35⅜ in)

HABITAT: Sea coasts; large lakes

POPULATION: Rare

Always a magnificent sight in the wild, the White-tailed Eagle is Britain's largest bird of prey. It has huge, long, broad wings, together with a long neck and short tail, giving it a highly distinctive profile as it flies along with slow, deep wing beats interspersed with glides. Even given a distant view, you can see this bird's massive bill, yellow in adults, a tool that can clearly do a great deal of damage to prey large and small.

The White-tailed Eagle is an adaptable predator, taking a wide variety of food items in a wide variety of ways. It is probably best known for its hunting of fish, in which it flies low over the water and snatches fish from the surface, without breaking wing stride. It is an exciting spectacle, but the White-tailed Eagle is equally likely to wade mundanely into shallow water to snatch fish at its feet. It is also famous for its extended harassment of individual birds such as ducks, which may keep trying to escape by diving until becoming fatally exhausted. But it will also fly serenely down to eat a little carrion, with not a flourish nor a drama.

A Rare Sight

These marvellous birds are rare in Britain, breeding in Scotland and occasionally visiting other parts of the country. However, they were formerly much rarer than this. With the White-tailed Eagle having been driven to extinction by 1918, a programme of artificial reintroduction into its previous haunts on the coasts of the Western Isles began in 1975. It has continued exhaustively ever since, and only now has produced a small but self-sustaining population.

BELOW

White-tailed Eagles build huge stick nests on cliff ledges or in trees, and hatch at best a couple of chicks a year. Pairs stay together in their home range for life.

ROUGH-LEGGED BUZZARD

SCIENTIFIC NAME: Buteo lagopus

IDENTIFYING FEATURES: Tail white at base
with black band; black carpal patches

SIMILAR SPECIES:
Buzzard, Honey Buzzard, Hen Harrier

SIZE: 50–60 cm (19¾–23⅝ in)

HABITAT: Open country near coast

POPULATION: Rare winter visitor

'Rough-legged' would seem to be rather a strange name for any bird, but it turns out to be perfectly appropriate. It refers to the feathering on this raptor's belly, which, instead of leaving the tarsus bare, covers the legs right down to the base of the toes. This provides a clue that the Rough-legged Buzzard is very much a bird of cold climates; the feathering keeps the bird warm, like a pair of leggings.

Up in the tundra, the core habitat for this bird, the Rough-legged Buzzard is a common specialist in small mammals, especially voles and lemmings. These it will hunt in several ways, but the most distinctive is a persistent hovering, hanging still in the air over a fixed point, homing in on an individual mammal. The Rough-legged Buzzard hunts in this way more than most of its congeners.

Changing Populations

The fate of Rough-legged Buzzards is strongly influenced by the cyclical abundance of their prey. Voles and lemmings tend to have cycles of boom and bust, with a boom typically happening some three years after a crash. In good years, Rough-legged Buzzards will lay more eggs than usual (five to seven instead of two to three), and they will breed further south than usual, sometimes well into the forest zone to the south of the tundra. In poor years individuals may range widely in search of an area

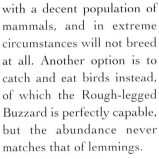

with a decent population of mammals, and in extreme circumstances will not breed at all. Another option is to catch and eat birds instead, of which the Rough-legged Buzzard is perfectly capable, but the abundance never matches that of lemmings.

Rough-legged Buzzards nest on cliffs, as opposed to the trees favoured by many of their relatives. The young are incubated by the female for a month, while the male brings in food. If little is available, some chicks may eat their smaller siblings to make up for the lack.

OYSTERCATCHER

SCIENTIFIC NAME: Haematopus ostralegus

IDENTIFYING FEATURES:
Pied plumage; huge orange bill

SIMILAR SPECIES: None

SIZE: 40–45 cm (15¾–17¾ in)

HABITAT: Coastal marshes and beaches

POPULATION: Common

With its distinctive black and white plumage, plump shape and that amazing orange bill, it is hard to mistake the Oystercatcher for any other bird. Although primarily a coastal species, Oystercatchers are adaptable creatures, and have been known to nest and feed in a wide range of habitats, including grassland, golf courses, gravel pits and even the roofs of industrial estates. But they remain a quintessential bird of the coast, gathering in huge flocks to exploit the food-rich mud revealed at every low tide.

LEFT

The Oystercatcher has a particularly distinctive plumage among waders.

A characteristic trilling, piping call is often the first indication of the presence of Oystercatchers on a coastal marsh or beach; soon followed by the sight of these plump, sociable birds cruising low in flight, or stopping to feed along the exposed mud on the tideline. No other wader has the Oystercatcher's distinctive plumage: black above and on the upper chest; pure white below; with short, stumpy pink legs. But the most obvious feature is the thick, straight, orange bill – likened by some observers to a carrot – which the Oystercatcher uses to probe deep into soft sand or mud in order to reach its favourite food; not oysters, but cockles, mussels and other shellfish.

Shellfish Wars

Their ability to eat cockles has brought them into conflict with shellfish gatherers, although in fact the Oystercatcher is an adaptable feeder, and will often gather in freshly ploughed fields to pick up earthworms.

The courtship display of the Oystercatcher is an elaborate one: birds will dip their bill downwards and approach their mate, piping as they go. Once paired up, the birds nest in a scrape on the ground, making them very vulnerable to mammal predators.

LEFT

Oystercatchers are adaptable feeders.

RINGED PLOVER

SCIENTIFIC NAME: Charadrius hiaticula

IDENTIFYING FEATURES: Orange base to bill; orange legs; wing-bar in flight

SIMILAR SPECIES: Little Ringed Plover

SIZE: 18–20 cm (7–7⅞ in)

HABITAT: Coastal marshes, beaches

POPULATION: Common

The Ringed Plover is an unassuming little wader with a fascinating story to tell regarding its migration. Whereas birds nesting in temperate latitudes, such as the British Isles, move fairly short distances south for the winter, those nesting in the High Arctic regions undertake major migratory journeys, heading thousands of kilometres south to Africa. This strategy, known as 'leapfrog migration', is thought to have evolved as the species expanded its breeding range to the north after the last Ice Age.

The Ringed Plover is a typical bird of shorelines, coastal marshes and beaches throughout coastal Britain and Europe, and is also sometimes found inland, where it may feed and breed in the same locations as its smaller relative the Little Ringed Plover.

Identifying Plovers

With close attention it is fairly straightforward to tell the two species apart: the Ringed Plover is larger and

bulkier, and much less elegant on the wing. Its orange legs, orange base to the bill and pale wing-bar are all key identification features, and also help distinguish it from its other close European relative, the Kentish Plover.

When breeding, Ringed Plovers generally nest on the bare ground or amongst low vegetation, where their blotchy eggs can be well camouflaged. If approached, the adult will often move away from the

ABOVE

It is unusual to see Ringed Plovers in large flocks – they are generally a solitary species.

nest or chicks and begin a 'distraction display'. This involves stretching out its wing as if it is broken, as a trick to lure away predators such as foxes.

Unlike many other waders, Ringed Plovers are rarely seen in large flocks during the autumn and winter, but will often gather in small groups with other species, picking small items off the surface of the mud.

GREY PLOVER

SCIENTIFIC NAME: Pluvialis squatarola

SIZE: 27–30 cm (10⅝–11⅞ in)

HABITAT: Coastal marshes, beaches

POPULATION: Common

IDENTIFYING FEATURES: black belly in summer; short bill, dark underwings in winter

SIMILAR SPECIES: Golden Plover

In its full breeding plumage this is one of the most handsome and striking of all the world's waders; but outside the breeding season it moults into an unprepossessing greyish plumage that renders it virtually anonymous, and lives up to its English name. Yet it is in fact one of the great global voyagers of the bird world, with birds heading south from their Arctic breeding grounds to coastlines all over the Southern Hemisphere.

In breeding plumage, simply unmistakable: no other wader has the combination of jet-black underparts, silver-spangled upperparts, and broad white band extending from its forehead down its sides. Outside the breeding season, it is best told apart from other greyish waders by its short bill, stocky shape and – in flight – the distinctive black feathering along the border between its body and underwings.

Nesting Habits

Although sometimes gathering in flocks, Grey Plovers are often seen feeding on their own: running a few steps, stopping, and then picking small items of food off the surface of the exposed mud. At high tide they will gather with other wading birds to roost.

Grey Plovers return to their breeding grounds on the open tundra in May or June, and settle down quickly to breed in the short Arctic summer. They lay four oval eggs in a shallow scrape in the open, and after the chicks hatch the race begins to feed on as many insects as possible – taking advantage of virtual 24-hour daylight in order to do so. As soon as the young have grown to full size, they head back south, stopping off on coastal marshes in temperate Europe, Asia and North America on their way.

SANDERLING

SCIENTIFIC NAME: Calidris alba

IDENTIFYING FEATURES:
Pale plumage, habit of running along tideline

SIMILAR SPECIES: Dunlin

SIZE: 20–21 cm (7⅞–8¼ in)

HABITAT: Beaches, coastal mudflats

POPULATION: Common

Open Tundra

On its breeding grounds, the Sanderling is a bird of the open tundra. Like other Arctic-nesting waders they arrive in early summer, to coincide with the outburst of tiny insects; though they will also take plant food if insects are not available because of poor weather.

After breeding, Sanderlings head south, in long hops of several thousand miles at a time. To do so, they need to put on huge reserves of fat to give them energy: increasing their body weight from about 60-70 grams to as much as 100 grams – a rise of more than two thirds! Only by doing so will they be able to make the journey without dying from exhaustion.

This delightful little wader is known the world over for its characteristic habit of running along the tideline like a tiny clockwork toy, the waves lapping at its feet as it seeks out tiny morsels of food to eat. Yet it is also one of the great global voyagers: nesting in the high regions of the Arctic, before travelling south along the world's coastlines, and spending the winter in the Southern Hemisphere, in South America, Africa and Australasia.

their Arctic breeding areas are likely to see them in their full glory, however: with scalloped black, grey and chestnut on the back, chestnut-coloured cheeks and a distinctive dark breast-band above a white belly.

Sanderlings are mainly seen in their non-breeding plumage: in which they have an almost frosted appearance, being silver-grey above and mainly white below, with black legs and a short, black bill. In early autumn, they may also be seen while in moult, with traces of their chestnut breeding plumage visible. Only those who travel to

AVOCET

SIZE: 42–45 cm (16½–17¼ in)

HABITAT: Coastal lagoons; estuaries

POPULATION: Scarce

SCIENTIFIC NAME: Recurvirostra avosetta

IDENTIFYING FEATURES: Black and white plumage; uptilted bill; bluish legs

SIMILAR SPECIES: None

No other bird looks quite like an Avocet, with its peculiar-shaped, sharply uptilted bill and its extremely long, bluish-grey legs. It clearly does something unusual, and this is indeed the case: it wades through shallow water, sweeping its bill from side to side, hoping to touch some edible item in suspension, which it then swallows. The angle of the upward tilt allows the bird to lean down with the bill horizontal to the water, thus covering as wide an area as possible.

Another advantage of having a curved, as opposed to a straight, bill is that it can be opened to a consistent gap all the way down, rather than being broader at the tip; this helps the Avocet's filtering system, keeping outsize objects out. In order to feed efficiently, the Avocet wades in water up to 15 cm (5⅞ in) deep. However, it is also capable of feeding in very soft mud, so the bill is not quite as fragile as it looks. The main prey of Avocets consists of crustaceans such as shrimps, insects and worms. These it obtains in saline or brackish, very sheltered waters.

Saved from Extinction

Avocets are rare breeding birds in Britain, but they are doing better now than at the beginning of the twentieth century, when they were nearly extinct. They nested after a long gap in Suffolk in the 1940s, and soon caught the imagination of conservationists, being adopted as the symbol of the fast-growing Royal Society for the Protection of Birds.

These elegant birds make a nest on bare ground, making a scrape that may hold a shallow cup of marsh vegetation. They breed in colonies, and are collectively aggressive to every predator that intrudes anywhere near. They lay three or four eggs, which are incubated for up to 25 days. Already noisy, the intensity of the Avocet's 'kluut, kluut' calling increases vastly with the hatching of the chicks.

KENTISH PLOVER

SCIENTIFIC NAME: Charadrius alexandrinus

IDENTIFYING FEATURES:
Incomplete black collar; pale plumage

SIMILAR SPECIES: Ringed Plover,
Little Ringed Plover

SIZE: 15–17 cm (5⅞–6¼ in)

HABITAT: Sandy beaches; mud

POPULATION: Rare passage migrant

Much as they are attractive to humans, sandy beaches are not, on the whole, great places for birds, especially for breeding. One bird does, however, make this habitat its heartland, and that is the Kentish Plover. It likes sand or mud free from obstructions, where it can run along freely on its noticeably long legs. Here, as in many other such habitats near coasts or inland lakes, there are plenty of crustaceans, molluscs and insects on which to feed.

In common with other Plovers, the Kentish feeds in a very distinctive way, alternating periods of standing still and watching with fast-paced runs, either to relocate and watch again or to catch up with some prey spotted during the reconnaissance. With its sandy-brown plumage and bold, black markings on the head and neck, the bird is both camouflaged against its background by its colour, and concealed in the way that the bold marks draw the eye of the predator and break up the bird's shape. Such efficient camouflage is highly necessary in the open habitats where this bird lives.

A Good Neighbour

In the breeding season Kentish Plovers often nest close to others of their kind, as little as 2 m (6.5 ft) at times. In such situations it does not pay to be territorial, so they avoid too much bickering and tend to feed in neutral areas away from the nest site. The nest itself is basically a scrape in the sand, one of several that the male constructs for the female to choose. On to it the female lays two to four eggs, which are sometimes covered by the birds with sand to protect them from the sun.

Sometimes, during the 24- to 27-day incubation period, one of the parents seems to get fed up with its duties and simply leaves the area – occasionally even to re-pair elsewhere.

RIGHT
The Kentish Plover is camouflaged by its sand-coloured feathers with black markings.

KNOT

SIZE: 23–26 cm (9–10¼ in)

HABITAT: Muddy estuaries; beaches

POPULATION: Fairly common winter visitor; passage migrant

SCIENTIFIC NAME: Calidris canutus

IDENTIFYING FEATURES:
White supercilium; grey tail; white rump

SIMILAR SPECIES: Dunlin, Redshank, Grey Plover

The Knot is certainly no ordinary wader, it is not just another dot among the host of actively feeding dots on a muddy estuary in winter. It might look dumpy, dull and grey, but it has a tendency towards the spectacular and extreme. It does, for example, nest further north into the extreme Arctic than most other relatives; it also has a truly dramatic breeding plumage of glorious sunset-red. And it can also gather into enormous flocks in grand style.

In the winter, this wader shares the inter-tidal habitat with many others, although

it also adopts sandy beaches in some areas, overlapping with the Sanderling. On the mud it feeds predominately on hard-shelled molluscs, for which it has a specialized highly muscular stomach to crush them. It commonly takes these just below the surface of the mud, pushing its bill forward to make a furrow, using its sense of touch to locate them. It is the touch-feeding technique that allows the Knot to be intensely sociable, the birds feeding almost shoulder to shoulder without interfering with each other.

Aerial Displays

All inter-tidal feeders are governed by the tides, and when the water rises Knots seek a place to roost. When this happens they commonly perform spectacular pre- roosting aerial manoeuvres, thousands of birds flying this way and that, the whole flock joining as a single globular unit, resembling a giant amoeba at a distance.

The birds breed well above the Arctic Circle, usually on the open tundra, where the lichens and other short plants may match the birds' impressive colours. The female lays three to four eggs and these may hatch in a mere 20–21 days (several days fewer than average for a bird of this size), reflecting the short summer season. Often, once the eggs hatch, the female leaves the area, while the male tends the brood alone.

BELOW
Knots breed in the high Arctic of Greenland and Canada.

LITTLE STINT

SCIENTIFIC NAME: Calidris minuta

IDENTIFYING FEATURES:
Short, straight bill; rapid, feverish movements

SIMILAR SPECIES: Temminck's Stint

SIZE: 12–14 cm (4¾–5½ in)

HABITAT: Coastal pools, some inland waters

POPULATION: Uncommon passage migrant

Looking at a picture of a Little Stint, at first sight it would appear to be just like any other small wader. But in fact it is surprisingly distinctive. It is not only Britain's smallest wader, smaller indeed than a Sparrow, but it also has a signature shape and character. Its bill is very short, and the bird uses it to make somewhat feverish picking movements from the mud, faster than those of other waders. It is also notably tame and preoccupied, often the last wader to flush when disturbed.

This is very much an autumn speciality. It does not breed in Britain, but passes through on the way between its breeding centres in the Norwegian and Russian Arctic and its wintering headquarters in West Africa, being most common in August and September. In spring, however, it is seldom ever seen, so it seems that it takes a different route in the spring, missing Britain out and perhaps passing over Continental Europe. Such a system, taking different routes to and from the same places in different seasons, is known as a 'loop migration'.

Feeding Habits

In common with most waders, the Little Stint feeds on small invertebrates, including worms, insects and the least bulky crustaceans and molluscs. It also eats some plant material, mainly seeds.

Up in the high Arctic, it occupies coastal tundra, making a cup nest of leaves and grass on the ground and usually in the open. Its breeding system is intriguing, with many individual birds being bigamous. Frequently, a female will lay two clutches of four eggs, the first being incubated by one male and the second by the female herself, the product of a different father. After incubation, which lasts a mere 20–21 days, the two parts of the 'family' sometimes meet up again.

TEMMINCK'S STINT

SIZE: 13–15 cm (5–5⅞ in)

HABITAT: Freshwater pools and marshes

POPULATION: Rare passage migrant

SCIENTIFIC NAME: Calidris temminckii

IDENTIFYING FEATURES: Grey-brown above, white below; yellow-green legs

SIMILAR SPECIES: Little Stint, Dunlin, Common Sandpiper

Although it breeds in minute numbers in Scotland, the Temminck's Stint is far less well known in Britain and Europe than its commoner migrant relative the Little Stint. It is a far scarcer bird, with only 100 or so being seen passing through each year, as opposed to almost 800 Little Stints. The Temminck's is also more of a skulking bird. While the Little Stint feeds well out in the open in energetic style, the Temminck's Stint occupies more sheltered habitats, often far from the coast, and feeds with more deliberation and more furtively.

There is also an interesting difference in the way these birds respond to danger. The Little Stint is tame, and does not usually flush far when disturbed. The Temminck's, on the other hand, almost overreacts, flying high and far – sometimes out of sight.

Breeding Habitats

Although, like many waders, the Temminck's Stint is at heart an Arctic breeding bird, it actually occupies much less severe habitats than many, extending down into the boreal zone. Here, rather than open tundra, it seeks out rich riverbanks, stream-sides and the edges of fjords – habitats rather similar to those it prefers during migration.

On the breeding grounds the male performs a splendid song-flight, circling over its territory with a hovering action, with the wings held up in a V and the tail spread. It is accompanied by an almost insect-like trilling. In common with Little Stints, Temminck's also have a breeding system geared to rapid reproduction. A given female may mate with one, two or more males. If there is only one, the sexes share incubation; if two, the female allows her first mate to incubate the first clutch and she will incubate the second; if more than two, she will always incubate the last. Each clutch contains four eggs, which hatch after 21–22 days.

LEFT
Temminck's Stints are much less sociable than Little Stints, forming small parties at best.

TURNSTONE

SCIENTIFIC NAME: Arenaria interpres

IDENTIFYING FEATURES: White belly; thick bill; tortoiseshell pattern on back when breeding

SIMILAR SPECIES: Purple Sandpiper

SIZE: 22–24 cm (8⅝–9½ in)

HABITAT: Rocky coastlines

POPULATION: Common winter visitor

With its short bill and legs, dumpy shape and characteristic tortoiseshell plumage pattern, the Turnstone is one of the easiest to identify of all waders. It is also equally easy to appreciate how it operates, and how it gets its name. The feeding method is based on using its bill to turn over objects, including stones but also seaweed, shells and all manner of tideline debris to see what edible items might be hidden underneath. It is capable of shifting objects weighing up to about 100 g (3.5 oz) and, if something is too large and bulky, it will sometimes gather a small team to heave it away together.

These birds have a distinctly catholic diet, wider than that of any other wader. Apart from the expected molluscs (mussels, periwinkles), crustaceans (crabs, barnacles) and worms, it also eats fish, sea urchins and a variety of edible scraps thrown out by people. It will

scavenge on dead animals (even a human corpse has been recorded) and take eggs from the nests of sea birds. It has also been seen feasting on a bar of soap. Meanwhile, on the tundra where it nests, its main sustenance actually comes from insects.

Flock Hierarchy

Turnstones are sociable creatures, living in small groups, but they are not necessarily friendly. Flocks have strict hierarchies, and the dominant birds in each group tend to hog the best feeding opportunities. The

hierarchy is maintained easily, because each bird has an individually recognizable face pattern. If a bird attempts to feed outside its allotted station, it might be attacked or even killed.

In the breeding season Turnstones are found in the tundra zone of the High Arctic, where they prefer sites near water, usually close to the coast. The nest may be in the open or concealed, and contains the usual wader complement of four eggs. As so often happens among this family of birds when they nest this far north, the young tend only to be overseen in their later stages by one parent, in this case the male.

RIGHT
Turnstones can be identified in flight by the white wing-bar and white tail.

CURLEW SANDPIPER

SIZE: 18–19 cm (7–7½ in)

HABITAT: Freshwater and coastal marshes

POPULATION: Scarce

SCIENTIFIC NAME: Calidris ferruginea

IDENTIFYING FEATURES: Long, decurved bill

SIMILAR SPECIES: Dunlin

across it. Young birds are very neat, with delicate buff on the breast and a lack of streaking which tells them apart from the Dunlin. Adults are generally greyer and a bit more tatty-looking.

Best Times to See

Most Curlew Sandpipers are seen in autumn: with the parents arriving from early August, soon followed by their fresher-looking, buff-coloured juveniles in September and October. In spring, they may be seen coming into their breeding plumage: a gaudy chestnut-orange colour, traces of which may also be seen on adult birds in early autumn. Once they pass through western Europe, Curlew Sandpipers cross the Mediterranean Sea and the Sahara, and then spread out across the whole of sub-Saharan Africa; before heading north the following spring. Why they take such an indirect route is hard to say; but fans of this attractive little wader are pleased that they do.

This unassuming little wading bird gets its name from the distinctive, down-curved bill – reminiscent of a miniature Curlew. But its real claim to fame is that it breeds further to the east than any other regular migrant through western Europe. Despite nesting no closer than eastern Siberia, a quarter of the globe east of the British Isles, large numbers pass through every autumn on their migratory journey to spend the winter in sub-Saharan Africa.

Curlew Sandpipers resemble a larger, more elegant version of the Dunlin: though observers should beware races of the Dunlin with longer bills, which may be seen alongside their shorter-billed cousins and cause confusion. The cast-iron way to tell the two species apart is in flight: the Curlew Sandpiper has a bright white rump rather than one with a dark bar

PURPLE SANDPIPER

SCIENTIFIC NAME: Calidris maritima

IDENTIFYING FEATURES:
Dark plumage; hunched shape

SIMILAR SPECIES: Knot

SIZE: 20–22 cm (7⅞–8⅝ in)

HABITAT: Rocky shores, breakwaters

POPULATION: Scarce

This rather drab, unassuming wader is known to most birders as a coastal bird, often found hunched together with Turnstones on a rocky shore, pier or breakwater. But in spring it undergoes a Cinderella-like transformation into an attractive purplish-tinged plumage, before heading north to its breeding grounds on the Arctic tundra. Here, it displays to its mate before breeding, then returning south to rocky shores for the autumn and winter.

No other European wader looks so dark – either in breeding or winter plumage – which usually makes the Purple Sandpiper fairly easy to identify. Close to, the paler, orangey base to the bill and stocky appearance are also apparent. In breeding plumage the breast and belly become more streaky, with a pale stripe above the eye giving the bird a more 'capped' appearance; while the purplish tinge to the upperparts (especially in bright sunlight) can be quite striking. More often, though, wintering Purple Sandpipers are identified simply by their location: sitting hunched up on the edge of the shore as waves break nearby. Wintering Purple Sandpipers are remarkably loyal, with the same individuals coming back year after year to the same locations – usually in the company of a larger flock of another Arctic wader, the Turnstone.

Foraging Habits

Unlike Turnstones, though, Purple Sandpipers hardly ever venture on to open sandy beaches to feed, preferring to root about on the rocks and find tiny invertebrates and molluscs amongst the seaweed. At high tide they simply retreat to just above the tideline and go to sleep.

Purple Sandpipers have a justified reputation for tameness, perhaps because they rarely encounter human beings – few will venture very close to the rocky outcrops where they prefer to feed.

DUNLIN

SCIENTIFIC NAME: Calidris alpina

IDENTIFYING FEATURES:
Down-curved bill; black belly in summer

SIMILAR SPECIES: Knot, Sanderling

SIZE: 16–20 cm (6¼–7⅞ in)

HABITAT: Coasts, marshes

POPULATION: Abundant

The Dunlin is the ubiquitous small wader across much of the coastal areas of the Northern Hemisphere, being equally common and widespread on both sides of the Atlantic Ocean, and also found in Asia. Nesting in a wide range of locations and habitats, Dunlins do not travel so far outside the breeding season as many other waders, with virtually all wintering in the Northern Hemisphre, and only a handful ever making it beyond the Equator.

In breeding plumage, the Dunlin is a striking and distinctive little bird, with a chestnut-brown back contrasting with a black belly. The bill is also an obvious feature: decurved, and varying considerably in length, depending which particular race the individual bird belongs to. Outside the breeding season, after moulting into its winter plumage, the Dunlin's name – meaning 'brown-coloured bird' – is more appropriate. Having lost the rich chestnut and black, wintering Dunlins are a grey-brown colour, with paler underparts. At this time of year they can be confused with a variety of other small to medium-sized waders including the larger Knot and much paler Sanderling.

An Adaptable Bird

Much of the Dunlin's success comes down to its adaptability: it is equally at home on beaches, coastal and freshwater marshes and even riverbanks – and on migration may be seen almost anywhere with a patch of wet mud where the birds can stop to refuel.

When breeding, Dunlins seek out a wide range of grassy areas, from coastal meadows to upland moors, where its distinctive trilling call is a characteristic part of the scene. As ground-nesters they are especially vulnerable to mammal predators, and as a result many pairs must make several breeding attempts before they are successful.

BAR-TAILED GODWIT

SCIENTIFIC NAME: Limosa lapponica

IDENTIFYING FEATURES:
Scalloped plumage; slightly upturned bill

SIMILAR SPECIES: Black-tailed Godwit

SIZE: 37–39 cm (14⅝–15⅜ in)

HABITAT: Coastal marshes, beaches

POPULATION: Common

Bar-tailed Godwits have always had a deserved reputation as one of the great global travellers of the bird world, being known to cross the Pacific Ocean from north to south on their migratory journeys, but until recently no-one was sure just how far an individual bird could fly. Now, thanks to satellite tracking, we know that one bird flew all the way from Alaska to New Zealand – a journey of more than 11,000 km (6,800 miles) – nonstop!

To do so, the bird flew at an altitude of up to 4,500 m (15,000 ft), and lost as much as half its body weight. It compensates for this enormous expenditure of energy by fattening up for several weeks before embarking on its journey south, depositing a thick layer of yellow fat beneath the surface of its skin.

Breeding and Eating

To look at a Bar-tailed Godwit in non-breeding plumage – a medium to large wader with streaky brown plumage and a prominent, slightly upturned bill – you would hardly think that it could be capable of such a feat. In breeding garb it is a more striking bird: with bright orange underparts, and brownish upperparts; together with the black and white barred tail that gives the species its name.

Bar-tailed Godwit breeds far to the north of its Black-tailed relative: mainly on coastal tundra, including peat bogs, accompanied by other species of wader. After breeding, it is a much more coastal species than its larger relative, often seen in flocks on beaches or amongst areas of salt marsh.

Like other larger waders such as Curlews, Bar-tailed Godwits use their long bills to probe into soft sand or mud, sometimes immersing their heads completely, and usually walking along while feeding. Their main prey are molluscs, crustaceans and marine worms.

CURLEW

SIZE: 50–60 cm (19¾–23⅝ in)

HABITAT: Coastal marshes and beaches; moorland when breeding

POPULATION: Common

SCIENTIFIC NAME: Numenius arquata

IDENTIFYING FEATURES: Large size; very long, decurved bill

SIMILAR SPECIES: Whimbrel

The Curlew is the largest European wader, and one of the best-known, being found in a wide range of habitats from coastal marshes and beaches to high moorland, where its far-carrying call is a characteristic spring and summer sound. The call – rather than the curved bill – is also the origin of the species' name, although the species has a large and varied vocal repertoire, including a haunting, bubbling call often delivered in flight.

Seen well, the Curlew cannot be confused with any other wader, being appreciably larger than both the godwits and Whimbrel, and with a much longer,

strongly decurved bill – up to one quarter of its entire body length. The plumage is generally buffish brown in tone, with delicate and intricate markings visible at close range, streaked underparts and a plain, pale

area under the tail. The legs are very long and greenish in colour.

Nesting

In the southern parts of its European breeding range, the Curlew is generally a bird of upland areas, nesting at between 500 and 700 m (1,650 and 2,300 ft) above sea level on moorland, peat bogs and heaths. Like most nesting waders it dislikes heavily vegetated or forested landscapes, preferring to nest where it can easily see for a wide range around it, so it can take evasive action should a predator approach the nest.

After breeding, Curlews usually head to the coast. Like other maritime waders, it follows a tidal regime: feeding when low tide exposes extensive areas of open mud, where it can probe that huge bill deep down in search of invertebrate prey. As the waters rise, it makes a twice-daily journey to an area of higher ground where it is able to rest amongst waders for safety and security until the tide retreats again.

SPOTTED REDSHANK

SCIENTIFIC NAME: Tringa erythropus

IDENTIFYING FEATURES:
Very long bill; pale plumage (winter)

SIMILAR SPECIES: Common Redshank, Greenshank

SIZE: 29–31 cm (11½–12¼ in)

HABITAT: Coastal marshes

POPULATION: Scarce

Feeding Habits

Most striking of all, however, are the Spotted Redshank's feeding habits. Birds will wade into far deeper water than most waders, often completely covering their legs until they are virtually swimming; then probe their long bill down through the water into the mud and move it back and forth in a 'sewing-machine' action.

Also known as the Dusky Redshank, this elegant and attractive wader sports two very distinct plumages. In the breeding season, high in the northern latitudes of Europe and Asia, it is a dark, almost black bird, delicately marked with silvery-white spots on the back, flanks and wings. Yet outside the breeding season, as it heads south through Europe and Asia to its wintering grounds in West Africa and South East Asia, it adopts a very pale grey plumage – in almost complete contrast to its breeding garb.

Birds in full breeding plumage are very rarely seen on migration, but it is quite common to come across those in moult, in which the dark feathering is either being replaced by paler plumage (autumn) or vice versa (spring). At a distance, Spotted Redshanks are more likely to be identified amongst their commoner cousins by their larger size, more elegant shape, and longer bill. Close to, the deeper crimson red of the bill and deep red (rather than orange, as in the Common Redshank) of the legs are also evident.

This technique may be carried out by individual birds, but is also used in communal feeding by flocks, which behave almost like ducks as they herd the tiny fish they are hunting into an area of water, then vacuum them up as quickly as possible.

GREY PHALAROPE

SIZE: 20–22 cm (7⅞–8⅝ in)

HABITAT: Ocean

POPULATION: Rare storm-blown passage migrant

SCIENTIFIC NAME: Phalaropus fulicaria

IDENTIFYING FEATURES: Chestnut-red when breeding; pale grey with black spot by eye

SIMILAR SPECIES: Red-necked Phalarope

This is a difficult bird to see, seemingly programmed to keep out of the way of people, including birders. It breeds in the brief Arctic summer rather locally on the tundra, and then heads with indecorous speed out to sea, where it passes the time in mid-ocean, often ending up well down into the Southern Hemisphere. Only a visit to the Arctic, or a brief encounter of a storm-driven bird, will put it on the average birder's list.

It is a fascinating bird nonetheless. In contrast to all the other waders, except other phalaropes, it typically feeds by swimming, floating on both turbulent ocean waters and gentle tundra pools with the buoyancy of a cork, spinning round to disturb edible organisms at its feet. On the ocean it eats plankton and small fish, opening its surprisingly broad bill just enough to allow surface tension to scoop them up. To feed effectively it requires relatively rich parts of the ocean's surface, so it is drawn to the edge of patches of floating seaweed or other detritus, to places where currents meet and bring up nutrients from the seabed, and to the activity of marine mammals such as whales, whose daily movements it may follow.

Life on the Tundra

On the tundra the Grey Phalarope has a quite different diet, consisting mainly of insects, especially flies, which it can catch from the air with dexterous snaps of the bill. Naturally, it comes here for the seasonal bloom of food, which makes the feeding ridiculously easy. In common with the other phalaropes, the Grey practises the same role reversal breeding system, in which the brightly coloured female initiates display and otherwise 'wears the trousers', while the relatively dowdy, deferential male usually takes on all incubation and breeding duties alone. Sometimes, with one clutch safely installed in a shallow, grass-lined scrape, a given female will seek a second mate, and lay another batch of four eggs.

BELOW
The female Grey Phalarope performs the display to attract a mate, unlike many other bird species.

POMARINE SKUA

SCIENTIFIC NAME: Stercorarius pomarinus

IDENTIFYING FEATURES: Dark with pale bases to primaries above and below

SIMILAR SPECIES: Arctic Skua, Great Skua, Long-tailed Skua

SIZE: 46–51 cm (18–20 in)

HABITAT: Sea

POPULATION: Rare passage migrant

This gull-sized Skua is generally a rare and difficult bird to see, breeding up in the Arctic tundra in summer, and then transferring out to sea for the rest of the year. Nevertheless, it is a regular sight during spring and autumn off most coasts of the British Isles, though it is nowhere guaranteed. It can normally be picked out from the more abundant Arctic Skuas by being larger, much heavier and with slower, more ponderous wing beats. A good rule of thumb is that, if it is an Arctic Skua that reminds you of a Great Skua, it is a Pomarine!

Out to sea the Pomarine Skua mixes its skills, being a food-robber one moment, a conventional forager the next and a predator the next. It often simply eats such birds as phalaropes, while larger birds, such as terns and Kittiwakes, are

ambushed and chased until they disgorge whatever it is they have caught. Yet the Pomarine Skua can also dip to the surface to pick up fish or other sea creatures.

Tundra Scavenger

On its breeding grounds on the tundra, however, quite a different foodstuff dominates the menu. As its colleague the Long-tailed Skua drools over lemmings and voles, so does the Pomarine. In contrast to that species, it often catches these small mammals on the ground, and will also sometimes dig them out of their burrows. When

lemmings are in short supply, as they regularly are, it will turn its attention to the eggs and chicks of fellow sea birds.

As a breeding bird it is noted for its extreme paranoid protection of its

territory against other birds, especially other skuas; it will chase them off the premises and far away. It is rather more tolerant of people. It lays two eggs, laid in a nest placed on coastal, lowland tundra.

ARCTIC SKUA

SCIENTIFIC NAME: Stercorarius parasiticus

IDENTIFYING FEATURES:
Slender shape, pointed tail

SIMILAR SPECIES:
Pomarine and Long-tailed Skuas

SIZE: 41–46 cm (16½–18 in)

HABITAT: Islands, coasts

POPULATION: Scarce

Also known as the Parasitic Jaeger, due to its extraordinary habit of hunting down other sea birds such as auks and Kittiwakes, then chasing them in mid-air until they have either dropped their catch or regurgitated it. This habit, known as kleptoparasitism, makes them feared amongst other sea birds; whilst their habit of targeting human intruders in their nesting territories, and hitting them with their powerful feet, has earned them the healthy respect of locals and birders alike.

Like some other species of skua, Arctic Skuas come in two very distinct forms known as 'morphs' – a light morph, in which the breast and belly are a pale creamy-white, and the cheeks are yellowish; and a dark morph, in which the entire underparts are chocolate-brown in colour. Although incredibly distinctive, these are not separate races, and will freely interbreed with each other, with mixed pairs commonly seen throughout their range.

Medium Skua

The Arctic Skua is the medium-sized of the three smaller skuas to occur in Britain and Europe: slightly larger and bulkier than the elegant Long-tailed, but slimmer than the bulky Pomarine – though individual birds, especially juveniles, can cause confusion.

As their name suggests, Arctic Skuas are found all around the Arctic, though in fact they breed further south than their two close relatives, and are often found in loose mixed colonies with the largest member of their family, the Great Skua.

They are monogamous, forming lifelong partnerships – hence their aggressive behaviour towards any rival males entering the territory.

After breeding, they head on a leisurely journey south, with most spending the winter far away from their nesting areas, off the coasts of Patagonia and South West Africa.

BELOW

An Arctic Skua in its light morph phase. Compare to the dark morphs on the far left.

GREAT SKUA

SCIENTIFIC NAME: Stercorarius skua

IDENTIFYING FEATURES: Large, bulky, all-dark plumage

SIMILAR SPECIES: Pomarine Skua

SIZE: 53–58 cm (21–22⅛ in)

HABITAT: Islands, coasts

POPULATION: Scarce

The largest member of the skua family in Europe, the Great Skua probably evolved in the Antarctic, where several of its close relatives still live. It also has the smallest breeding range of any of the Northern Hemisphere skuas, nesting in a small area of north-west Europe, from Iceland in the west to north-west Arctic Russia in the east, and south to Scotland. Indeed the Scottish colonies, mainly on the Shetland Islands, account for about two thirds of all the world's Great Skuas.

The largest and bulkiest of the skuas, with a dumpier, barrel-chested and more gull-like shape, compared with the slim, falcon-like appearance of its smaller relatives. Great Skuas are generally brown in colour: paler beneath, and darker on the head, back and wings. In flight the white patches towards the tip of the wing are obvious, and a good identification feature even at a considerable distance.

Kleptoparasite

Like other skuas, they are kleptoparasites, chasing and harassing other sea birds until they drop or regurgitate their fishy catch. However, Great Skuas are also fearsome predators, especially when fish stocks are low, and will chase and kill smaller birds, especially Kittiwakes. At times when the Kittiwake population is already suffering from a shortage of sand-eels, this can be a double blow to their survival.

Like their relatives, Great Skuas are highly territorial, readily chasing away any intruder – human or animal – that ventures too close to their nest, and threatens their precious eggs or chicks. Their aggressive habits – and reputation for taking lambs – have not always made them popular, but they are a vital part of Britain's ornithological heritage.

Great Skuas are still often known today by their Shetland name of 'Bonxie' (derived from a Norse word meaning 'dumpy bird').

LONG-TAILED SKUA

SCIENTIFIC NAME: Stercorarius longicaudus

SIZE: 48–53 cm (19–21 in)

HABITAT: Sea

POPULATION: Rare passage migrant

IDENTIFYING FEATURES: Long tail-streamers; black cap with yellow-buff nape

SIMILAR SPECIES: Arctic Skua

This supremely elegant sea bird is the smallest of the skuas. A breeding bird of the Arctic tundra, it quickly disappears out to sea by the end of summer and is then a scarce passage migrant off northern coasts during the autumn and following spring. In between, intriguingly, its winter quarters are virtually unknown, making it one of the very few species to keep such a secret. It undoubtedly wanders the oceans, and probably goes south below the Equator, but the precise area is yet to be discovered.

Long-tailed Skuas in adult plumage are easy to identify, especially since their dark phase is exceptionally rare or non-existent. The long tail plumes are unmistakable, but it is also their general elegance and demeanour that marks them out. They are only about the size of a small gull, and they fly with the lightness and grace of a tern.

Predatory Nature

On the breeding grounds Long-tailed Skuas feed

ABOVE
Long-tailed Skuas perform spectacular aerial displays before settling down to build their nests.

mainly on small mammals, which they hunt in a style more redolent of a Kestrel than a sea bird, by hovering some 20–50 m (65–165 ft) above ground and then plunging down. Once on the ground they show their predatory side, devouring the small furry creatures and picking out only their entrails. Although the diet can be 99 per cent lemmings in a good year, these Skuas can also eat

birds' eggs, insects and even berries. Being small, the Long-tailed Skua cannot make a career out of food-piracy like its near relatives.

These birds may perform some spectacular swooping aerial displays in the spring, but soon get down to business, building no great nest – just a few bits of plant debris on a depression – on the ground in the tundra. They lay two eggs and when these hatch, after 23–25 days, the adults protect the young with the same zeal shown by other skuas, swooping down and striking intruders with bill or feet.

LITTLE GULL

SCIENTIFIC NAME: Larus minutus

IDENTIFYING FEATURES: Pale grey plumage; black hood; dark underwings. Winter plumage: white head, with darker cap and eye-spot

SIMILAR SPECIES: Black-headed Gull, Kittiwake

SIZE: 25–27 cm (9⅞–10⅝ in)

HABITAT: Mainly coastal

POPULATION: Scarce passage migrant and winter visitor

It is hard to believe that a gull might be dainty, but that certainly is a fair description of the Little Gull. With its diminutive size and buoyant, graceful flight on rather short, rounded wings, it is a far cry from some of the hulking brutes of its family.

It is also a good deal less fearsome and predatory than other members of its family. It mainly eats insects and small fish, so, although it is not quite true to say it wouldn't hurt a fly, the Little Gull does not eat eggs, carrion, chicks or small mammals, and thus poses less of a threat to its coastal neighbours. Its main method of feeding is to snatch food from the surface of the water in flight, a technique that works both on the freshwater lakes where it breeds, and on the sea where it spends the winter. It is not a common bird in Britain, being essentially a passage migrant and scarce winter visitor.

ABOVE
The Little Gull is easiest to see on the coast, but also visits inland waters.

MEDITERRANEAN GULL

SCIENTIFIC NAME: Larus melanocephalus

IDENTIFYING FEATURES: Clear white wing-tips (except black line on outermost primary)

SIMILAR SPECIES: Black-headed Gull, Common Gull

SIZE: 36–38 cm (14½–15 in)

HABITAT: Mainly coastal

POPULATION: Scarce

The Mediterranean Gull is what a Black-headed Gull should look like. It is an exceptionally smart Gull, much beloved by birders, with a pitch black head, deep-red bill and legs and almost entirely white wings in the breeding season. It is usually found in Britain in company with Black-headed Gulls, making them look dowdy.

Despite its exotic name, this is more a bird of eastern Europe than the Mediterranean. It was once rare in Britain, but has become steadily more common since first breeding here in 1968.

This species feeds on the expected range of foods for gulls in the winter, but in spring it has a notable bias towards insects and other invertebrates. It has been recorded following the plough.

The nest is a shallow depression on bare ground, lined with a few bits and pieces of feathers or grass. In display, the adults sometimes shut their eyes to show off their white eye crescents to best effect.

BLACK-HEADED GULL

SCIENTIFIC NAME: Larus ridibundus

SIZE: 34–37 cm (13½–14⅝ in)

HABITAT: Breeds in salt marshes; inland within reach of freshwater

POPULATION: Common breeding bird; abundant in winter

IDENTIFYING FEATURES: Red legs and bill; white isosceles triangle at front of outer wing

SIMILAR SPECIES: Common Gull, Mediterranean Gull, Kittiwake

'Sea gull' is never a very accurate term, and no species shoots down the concept quite like the Black-headed Gull. In the winter this elegant species, with its slender wings with sharp points, its red legs and its smudge behind the eye, is found all over inland Britain, in huge flocks on reservoirs, in wheeling groups at rubbish tips, following the plough and competing with ducks for slices of thrown-out bread.

Bizarrely, the Black-headed Gull does not have a black head at any stage of its life; in the breeding season it merely has a very smart chocolate-brown hood, with a neat white eye-ring. The colour is at least dark, and the hood plays an important part in communication, as well as probably absorbing the sun's light to prevent glare to the eye. When being aggressive, Black-headed Gulls usually bow their heads towards a rival, whether on land or water.

these gulls also eat all kinds of scraps, grain, berries and insects, and will fly around swarming ants on hot summer days.

ABOVE

The Black-headed Gull is one of Britain and Europe's most common birds.

Omnivorous Eater

In common with most gulls, the Black-headed Gull is impressively omnivorous. Its main food in winter is invertebrates found in the soil, especially worms, while its main diet on the breeding grounds, where these are coastal, is marine invertebrates. However,

The species breeds in colonies, which are often large, and invariably extremely noisy; the calls are harsher and less trumpeting in tone than those of larger species. Pairs hold a small territory on a patch of shingle, marsh, dune or moorland and defend it from rivals and predators. The female lays two to three eggs in a neat pile of vegetation, and incubates them for 23–26 days. When the youngsters hatch, they need to be careful to avoid trespassing on to their neighbours' territory, for they could elicit a violent response.

COMMON GULL

SCIENTIFIC NAME: Larus canus

IDENTIFYING FEATURES: Black on wing-tip with large white blob; grey on back

SIMILAR SPECIES: Herring Gull, Kittiwake

SIZE: 40–42 cm (15¾–16½ in)

HABITAT: Marshes, lakes when breeding; inland freshwater in winter

POPULATION: Common

One look at the Common Gull and you might easily guess that it was not as predatory as most of its fellow gulls. It has a much thinner bill than a Herring Gull, for example, and, for what it is worth, its face carries a much gentler expression. The facts bear out this impression. The Common Gull does not normally feed on young birds or small mammals, instead confining itself to smaller creatures such as worms, insects and other invertebrates.

It is, however, still a successful and resourceful bird. It does, for example, occur both on the coast and inland, breeding and wintering on both. It also utilizes all kinds of food sources from rubbish dumps (although less habitually than many gulls) to berries, and from fish to carrion. Intriguingly, it is also remarkably adaptable in where it places its nest. Some nests are on the ground in conventional gull fashion, in dunes, rocks and beaches, whereas others are in more unusual sites, including on mats of floating vegetation, gravel roofs of buildings and

trees, especially tree stumps. In such eclectic places the Common Gull builds differently; on the ground the nest is little more than a lined scrape, while tree and marsh nests are quite substantial heaps of vegetation.

Solitary Tendencies

Common Gulls are sometimes colonial, but they have more of a tendency than some gulls to nest alone. They lay the usual gull tally of three eggs which are incubated for

23–28 days. Chicks on the ground may leave the nest early, while those in elevated sites stay put.

The Common Gull is noted for its voice, even among such a clamorous group of birds. Its calls are often higher pitched than the rest, and, with imagination, the American name of Mew Gull seems vaguely appropriate. But really, it would be a cat in distress, such is the ear-splitting nature of some of its squeals.

ABOVE

The Common Gull is resourceful.

LESSER BLACK-BACKED GULL

SCIENTIFIC NAME: Larus fuscus

SIZE: 52–67 cm (20½–26⅛ in)

HABITAT: Breeds on coastal dunes and islands

POPULATION: Common

IDENTIFYING FEATURES: White spots on wing-tips; dark back; long wings

SIMILAR SPECIES: Great Black-backed Gull, Herring Gull, Yellow-legged Gull

Among the region's club of very similar-looking gulls, it is very easy for this species to get lost in the crowd. Often mistaken for the brutish Great Black-backed Gull, this is a far more elegant and graceful species, with different breeding habitats and a much stronger mastery of the air. The Lesser Black-back is closely related to the Herring Gull but, once again, it is subtly different: more liable to be seen out to sea, far more migratory and, once again, a far more efficient flying machine.

Much has changed in the life of the Lesser Black-backed Gull in the last 30 or 40 years. British birds, and some of their Continental counterparts, used to be migrants, travelling to the Mediterranean region, or even further, for the winter. Now, with conditions suiting them further north (perhaps more food available, perhaps climatic amelioration), they tend to stay put and winter 'at home'. Young birds might still make the journey, but the adults tend not to. In the meantime, the Scandinavian versions of the Lesser Black-backed Gull also flood Britain in the winter. These gulls have much darker backs than their British breeding counterparts, making them look like Great Black-backed Gulls – no wonder people get confused.

Gull Colonies

The Lesser Black-backed Gull breeds in typically gull-infested sites in summer, such as sand dunes and shingle banks; it also frequently nests inland, on moorland. It usually forms colonies and these can be very large, and they are often mixed colonies with Herring Gulls. The two keep apart because of, among other things, their subtly different displays; when proclaiming territory, for example, Lesser Black-backs lift their heads higher than Herring Gulls. The Lessers also breed in areas with more vegetation cover, and their nests are more densely packed in.

In common with other gulls, the Lesser Black-back lays an average of three eggs, which hatch after 24–27 days. After another month the young fly, and it will then be at least three years before they begin to breed themselves.

YELLOW-LEGGED GULL

SCIENTIFIC NAME: Larus michahellis

IDENTIFYING FEATURES: Large patch of orange
on yellow bill; small white spots on wing-tips

SIMILAR SPECIES:
Herring Gull, Lesser Black-backed Gull

SIZE: 55–57 cm (21¼–22⅛ in)

HABITAT: Coasts

POPULATION: Scarce but regular
visitor; very rare breeder

A few years ago this species did not exist – at least not in the minds of birders. It was only recently that, in view of its having slightly different plumage, yellow legs, a different call and a tendency not to interbreed in mixed colonies, the Yellow-legged Gull has been considered as a separate species from the Herring Gull in its own right. To those who find gull identification difficult, it is another headache.

But this is a splendid bird, with a tendency to look immaculate, and with practice, distinguishing it is a pleasure. The yellow legs always look bright yellow, very different from the dull flesh colour of Herring Gulls. The mantle is slightly darker grey, there is a larger orange spot on the yellow bill, and the head usually remains brilliant white in winter, as opposed to being strongly freckled. The legs and wings are longer, and the bird is altogether a more slimline product.

Yellow-legged vs. Herring Gull

As yet, very few differences in behaviour between the two species have been worked out. The Yellow-legged Gull does seem to be more restricted to coastal areas, and there are some very subtle differences in display. But, like the Herring Gull, the Yellow-legged Gull is an omnivore, taking such items as fish, shellfish, plant material, small land vertebrates, carrion and a wide range of insalubrious items from dumps. It will rob food with the best of them, and is probably no more gentle or overbearing than the more common bird.

For breeding, Yellow-legged Gulls tend to form exclusive colonies, or at least their own neighbourhoods within colonies. These are usually on sea cliffs, offshore islands or salt marshes. In common with other gulls they build up a mound of vegetation for the nest and lay three eggs. There are occasional mixed pairs with Herring Gulls, but their progeny die well before fledging.

ABOVE
The Yellow-legged Gull has only quite recently been considered a separate species from the Herring Gull.

HERRING GULL

SCIENTIFIC NAME: Larus argentatus

IDENTIFYING FEATURES: Pale eye and low crown; white blobs on wing-tips

SIMILAR SPECIES: Yellow-legged Gull, Lesser Black-backed Gull, Common Gull, Glaucous Gull

SIZE: 55–67 cm (21¼–26⅜ in)

HABITAT: Coasts; inland waters and dumps

POPULATION: Abundant

The irrepressible Herring Gull is an abundant, successful and somewhat boorish bird – the sort that it is very difficult to overlook. It is most overbearing on the coast, where its many wailing calls make up an important part of the seaside atmosphere. Although primarily a breeding bird of cliffs, dunes or beaches, it thinks nothing of living out its nesting season, with its noisy triumphs and disasters, on the flat roofs of coastal towns, commuting no great distance to rubbish dumps, dockyards and the nearest beach.

Herring Gulls are usually very sociable, and most of the population breeds in colonies. Pair formation actually usually occurs away from the breeding centres, at gathering spots known as 'clubs', while the colonies themselves are usually subdivided into neighbourhoods where egg-laying and hatching is closely synchronized. Gull society is full of complicated gestures, including head-nodding, facing away or standing erect, all combining into a universally understood sign language that oils the wheels of social cohesion. Between

males and females the most important gestures are actually very practical; for much of the period before and during egg-laying, the male brings in offerings of food for the female, to save her the trouble of feeding herself. Many times a day, the provider male arrives on the territory and throws up chivalrously, often goaded by open-mouthed begging postures from the female.

Herring Gull Society

There are several interesting quirks that happen in Herring Gull society.

Sometimes females form pairs with other females and, aided by sperm from 'donor' males, may actually raise chicks. And the chicks themselves, of which there are usually three to a brood, will sometimes abandon their parents and attempt to be adopted by their neighbours, whom they

deem to be better suppliers of food. Usually, however, the young gulls remain with their parents for the 35–40 days they take to gain full flight.

BELOW

Herring Gulls are not only found on the coasts – they have become a problem in some cities, too.

GLAUCOUS GULL

SCIENTIFIC NAME: Larus hyperboreus

IDENTIFYING FEATURES: Entirely white wing-tips; small pale eyes; bright pink legs

SIMILAR SPECIES: Herring Gull

SIZE: 62–68 cm (24⅜–26⅞ in)

HABITAT: Coasts

POPULATION: Scarce winter visitor

You might almost guess that this was a bird of the Arctic, with its mainly very pale grey and white plumage. And so it is – indeed, it is the only large gull to reach into the High Arctic zone. It does, however, wander south in winter to be a rather scarce visitor to more temperate coasts, where it mixes in with flocks of other gulls. It is second only in size to the Great Black-backed Gull, and follows in some of that species' highly aggressive tendencies.

As are most gulls, the Glaucous Gull is a highly adaptable omnivore, taking all kinds of animal food, thrown out rubbish, carrion and even some plant material. Its core diet revolves around fish and shellfish, together with the eggs and chicks of young birds. In the latter case, it can and frequently does take a heavy toll around the northern sea bird colonies. Pairs of Glaucous Gulls may divide parts of a large colony of auks, for example, among them, each patrolling a 'private' allocation of ledges.

Pirate of the Skies

The Glaucous Gull is a notable food-pirate, routinely stealing food from other birds instead of going to the trouble of finding its own. It seems to be particularly merciless towards flocks of Eiders, hounding any individuals that bring shellfish to the surface until the rightful owners reluctantly give up their catch. However, out of season, these fearsome birds prove perfectly adept at obtaining their own food, often ranging far out to sea and sometimes following marine mammals, picking off scraps that they bring to the surface.

For breeding, Glaucous Gulls select rocky areas, both cliffs and level ground, sometimes placing their platform of seaweed, grass and moss straight on to snow or ice. Not surprisingly they are not very popular with other birds and tend to form single-species colonies, usually of no great size. The female lays the usual three eggs, which hatch after 27–28 days. Unusually, once they are out, the youngsters leave the nest area altogether and move to special temporary rearing territories.

GREAT BLACK-BACKED GULL

SIZE: 64–78 cm (25⅛–30¾ in)

HABITAT: Mainly coastal; some inland dumps or lakes

POPULATION: Common

SCIENTIFIC NAME: Larus marinus

IDENTIFYING FEATURES: Pitch-black back with large white spots on tips; broad, blunt wings

SIMILAR SPECIES: Lesser Black-backed Gull

The world's largest gull, the Great Black-backed Gull does not hesitate to throw its weight about. It commonly steals food from other bird species, including other gulls; it is at the top of every gull hierarchy; and it is also one of the most predatory species, having no hesitation in eating young sea birds and sometimes adults, too. It has a thick, powerful neck and body, a truly fearsome bill with sharp cutting edges, and a mean-looking small eye amidst a frowning expression.

This is one of the more marine gulls, generally uncommon away from the coast. It will be found on inland rubbish dumps and some large wetlands, but it has not expanded to the land like many other species. Nevertheless, it is just as omnivorous and opportunistic as the other species. It is a frequent visitor to fishing boats when the catch is made, it will regularly resort to eating carrion, and on the beach it will often drop shellfish down on to a hard surface while flying, in order to break them open. It even has the dexterity, on occasion, to catch birds in flight.

Great Black-backed Gulls will eat almost anything, and are one of the most predatory coastal species.

flat rooftops are far less frequently used. It can be colonial, but has a tendency to breed alone that is rather more pronounced than for other gulls. Appropriately, perhaps, it often selects the topmost part of a cliff, or some other eminence, as if to lord it over the other birds nearby. Breeding birds are quite vocal, giving a marvellously gruff and bad-tempered range of calls.

Great Black-backs build a typical gull mound of grass, seaweed and other plant

Colonies and Calls

For breeding, Great Black-backed Gulls are usually found on sea cliffs and rocky islands. Flatter sites such as marshes, beaches and even material for the nest, and lay the regulation two to three eggs. Both adults incubate, and look after their chicks with a tenderness quite out of keeping with the general character of this bird.

KITTIWAKE

SCIENTIFIC NAME: Rissa tridactyla

IDENTIFYING FEATURES: Black legs; inky-black wing-tips without white blobs

SIMILAR SPECIES: Common Gull, Black-headed Gull

SIZE: 38–40 cm (15–15¼ in)

HABITAT: Sea and cliffs

POPULATION: Common

The Kittiwake is the acceptable face of the gull family. It lives a blameless life of eating fish and crustaceans and spends no time harassing other gulls or victimizing young sea birds in that overweening way that other species have. It has a mild, gentle expression to go with its demeanour. And it never shows up in the insalubrious surroundings of the rubbish dump. Indeed, it is really a proper sea bird, keeping a healthy lifestyle in the marine air.

The odd name comes from the Kittiwake's call. Birds at the breeding colony are exceptionally boisterous (it is a true gull, after all), uttering the bird's name incessantly in a sort of pleading, complaining, and often ear-splitting manner.

The sound often rebounds off the precipitous cliffs where this species breeds, the noise mixing with the waves and creating an atmosphere of wildness and urgency.

Cliff-top Homes

The nests are remarkable. They are platforms made from mud collected from nearby freshwater pools, seaweed and grass, and they are distinctly better built structures than those of other gulls. They need to be, too. Most are placed on the tallest and most precipitous of sea-cliffs, often lodged on to small rock projections, and they can look highly precarious with the frightening drop below them. However, they are very safe from predators. There are usually two eggs instead of the usual three for a gull, and the youngsters, when they are hatched, stay still on the platform instead of wandering around and risking an early death.

Once the young have left the nest, Kittiwakes leave the coast and venture out to sea, often hundreds of miles offshore. Here they find food

by dipping down to the surface in flight, or even making short plunges to a metre or so down. They often accompany whales and other sea mammals on their travels around the oceans of the Northern Hemisphere.

BELOW
The Kittiwake gets its name from its distinctive cry.

LITTLE TERN

SCIENTIFIC NAME: Sterna albifrons

IDENTIFYING FEATURES:
White forehead; black stripe through eye

SIMILAR SPECIES: Common, Arctic
and Roseate Terns

SIZE: 22–24 cm (8⅝–9½ in)

HABITAT: Coastal beaches

POPULATION: Scarce summer visitor

This diminutive species really lives up to its name – not much bigger than a Starling, albeit with much longer wings. It has a more fluttery, butterfly-like flight than other terns, typically feeding in hovering flight close in to shore. It feeds on small fish 3–6 cm (1⅛–2⅜ in) long, and on crustaceans such as shrimps.

The Little Tern mainly breeds on beaches, both of the shingle and sandy types. Both make it very vulnerable to disturbance, and its numbers have declined markedly in the last few decades. The nest is no more than a scrape in the ground, on to which the one to three well-camouflaged eggs are laid. The young hatch after 18–22 days and are fed assiduously by the parents. A Little Tern feeding young has been known to make 109 dives in

the course of an hour, and visit its young more than 30 times a day.

After breeding, Little Terns migrate to winter off the coast of West Africa.

ROSEATE TERN

SCIENTIFIC NAME: Sterna dougallii

IDENTIFYING FEATURES: Rosy flush to underparts in breeding season; mainly black bill; long tail streamers

SIMILAR SPECIES:
Common Tern, Arctic Tern, Sandwich Tern

SIZE: 33–38 cm (13–15 in)

HABITAT: Marine islands and jetties

POPULATION: Rare summer visitor

This beautiful tern is now one of our rarest sea birds. After a long decline the population in Britain is down to only about 60 pairs (from 3,500 pairs in the 1960s). Nobody

RIGHT

The population of Roseate Terns has declined dramatically over the past 50 years.

is quite sure why a crash has occurred, but disturbance at its colonies, together with persecution on its wintering grounds in West Africa, where the birds are eaten, may be to blame.

It is not an easy bird to distinguish from its two very similar relatives, the Arctic and Common Terns, but it always looks much whiter, and has much shallower, quicker wing-beats. It does not usually hover much before diving, instead simply angling down and crashing in without breaking stride, making it quite a dynamic hunter. Its main food is fish and, in contrast to its closest relatives, it is strictly coastal, virtually never venturing inland.

The breeding site is marine islands, either rocky or sandy, within reach of shallow, calm water. It has a tendency to nest among vegetation, sometimes quite tall.

BLACK TERN

SCIENTIFIC NAME: Chlidonias niger

IDENTIFYING FEATURES: Insignificant notch in tail; sooty black in spring; black shoulder patch outside breeding

SIMILAR SPECIES: Other terns

SIZE: 22–24 cm (8⅝–9½ in)

HABITAT: Coasts and inland freshwater

POPULATION: Fairly common passage migrant

The Black Tern belongs to a small group of terns known as the Marsh Terns, to be contrasted to the rest, broadly known as Sea Terns. The Marsh Terns are named for their habit of nesting in freshwater marshes, often on floating vegetation, but there are other differences, too. Marsh Terns do not normally plunge into the water to catch food, merely tiptoeing down in buoyant flight to snatch items from or above the surface. And in the summer they usually eat insects, rather than fish.

In fact, as far as the Black Tern is concerned, the line between the groups is slightly blurred by this species' remarkable ecological defection in the winter. While its relatives in the Old World stay on freshwater, the Black Tern becomes a sea bird and eats fish, taken in typical Marsh Tern fashion. After breeding, it migrates down the coast to winter in the tropics.

Easy Nester

In common with many other terns, Black Terns are fussy about where they nest and are prone, especially in early season, to abandon sites that are not right. They will sometimes spend a couple of weeks in the general area, visiting the actual site for just a short time each day to get a feel, before finally settling down. Early seasons are characterized by a 'high-flying' display, in which up to 20 birds fly up almost out of sight, making a great deal of noise.

The nest, which is essentially a mound of waterweed, is usually on floating vegetation in 50 cm (19¾ in) of water, although sometimes it is actually among plants on muddy ground. Typically there are two to four eggs in the clutch, and these are incubated for 21–22 days. When the young hatch they soon hide in the vegetation, and they fly when about three weeks old.

SANDWICH TERN

SCIENTIFIC NAME: Thalasseus sandvicensis

IDENTIFYING FEATURES: Clean white plumage; short tail; shaggy black crest in summer

SIMILAR SPECIES:
Roseate Tern, Common Tern, Arctic Tern

SIZE: 36–41 cm (14⅛–16⅛ in)

HABITAT: Coasts; breeds on beaches and islands

POPULATION: Common summer visitor

Always looking whiter and a bit chunkier than the similar Common or Arctic Terns, the Sandwich is a distinctive species with a shaggy crest in summer and a very long, black bill with a yellow tip, the latter looking as though dipped in mustard. This species has a habit of flying along with its head distinctly angled down before making its impressive plunge-dives to catch surface-dwelling fish. Usually going in from a height of 10 m (33 ft) or more, its dives are higher than those of most other similar species.

This is a strictly coastal bird, rarely venturing inland. It breeds in very low-lying habitats such as shingle islands and beaches, usually in very densely packed colonies – five to seven nests per metre is average. It is strangely reluctant to nest entirely on its own, almost always breeding in company with other species, notably Black-headed Gulls in Britain and Royal Terns in North America. Late-arriving Sandwich Terns sometimes actually displace nesting Black-headed Gulls from the centre of the colony, which is hardly an expression of gratitude. Ever nervous, Sandwich Terns are notorious for their tendency to desert sites early in the season when disturbed, but once egg-laying begins, this stops.

Colony Defence

Sandwich Terns are excellent defenders of their colonies (although doubtless their near neighbours are also helpful), flying up as one and harassing intruders mercilessly. They also, in common with other terns, make mass panic-flights above the colony for no obvious reason at all, as if the danger was no more than a rumour; such false alarms are known as 'dreads'.

There is little nest except for a scrape in the ground. In it the female lays one or two eggs which are incubated by both adults. Young Sandwich Terns, once they hatch, may stay on the nest site, or they may form crèches with neighbouring young. Either way, when the adults visit, they can still easily recognize their own young by call.

RIGHT
Although they breed on beaches, Sandwich Terns can largely be seen out at sea.

COMMON TERN

SCIENTIFIC NAME: Sterna hirundo

IDENTIFYING FEATURES: Black-tipped red bill; clean black cap; white face and underparts

SIMILAR SPECIES: Arctic Tern, Roseate Tern, Sandwich Tern

SIZE: 31–35 cm (12¼–13¾ in)

HABITAT: Breeds on islands and beaches; at sea in winter

POPULATION: Common

Very much the typical tern, the Common Tern has the usual greyish plumage, smart black cap and long, dagger-shaped bill shared by most of the family. It has a long, strongly forked tail and supremely angular wings, with the sharp tips that distinguish them so well from gulls. It flies with very full wing-beats, the wings slightly angled back. Typically, it flies to and fro over shallow water, either fresh or salty, intermittently hovering and plunge-diving down.

Fish are supremely important in the Common Tern's life. They constitute the main diet, and it is only when these are in short supply that this tern will take serious quantities of invertebrates, such as crustaceans. Fish also play an important role in courtship. For much of the immediate period before egg-laying, the male brings fish to the female every day to help her get into peak condition; this provision is of great importance to the pair bond. If the provider slips below the expected six-per-hour provisioning rate, the partnership could split up. The condition of the eggs could also be compromised: the more efficiently the female is fed, the larger the eggs she will lay and the healthier the young will be.

Nesting

Common Terns will nest as an isolated pair, but far more often they gather into colonies, which are usually quite substantial, with 200 or more nests. The usual site is on an island or beach and, although this is primarily a coastal species, it frequently nests inland as well, on freshwater lakes and marshes. In typical tern style, the nest would not win any construction prizes, being just a scrape in the ground lined with a few bits of debris. The clutch varies between one and three eggs.

After breeding, Common Terns retreat south to winter in tropical seas. They do not migrate in any rush, and can still be seen into October, or even later.

ABOVE

The Common Tern is, as its name suggests, the most common tern found in Europe.

ARCTIC TERN

SCIENTIFIC NAME: Sterna paradisaea

IDENTIFYING FEATURES: Longer tail-streamers, narrower wings and shorter legs than Common Tern

SIMILAR SPECIES:
Common Tern, Roseate Tern, Sandwich Tern

SIZE: 33–35 cm (13–13¼ in)

HABITAT: Coasts, islands, rivers

POPULATION: Common summer visitor

Terns are identified on the finest points, and to those who have the experience and confidence, the best way to tell an Arctic Tern is in its manner of flight. Compared to its closely related species, the Arctic has a more bouncy, flickering flight, with a snappier, faster upstroke, and the narrow wings look slightly forward set, rather than centred. When hunting over the sea, this bird has a distinct tendency to hover, descend and then hover again before finally plunging in.

There must be something special in those wings, because the Arctic Tern is famous for having what is perhaps the longest regular migration of any bird in the world – although some shearwaters push it close. Often breeding well into the High Arctic, it travels to the Antarctic, no less, for the winter, swapping one side of the world for the other. It will migrate along coast and sea, but there is evidence to suggest that some birds might take an overland route at great altitude. Once arriving in the Antarctic, some individuals actually fly around that continent and might travel as much as 50,000 km (31,000 miles) in a year altogether. In doing so, they see more daylight in a year than any other living organism.

Nesting and Parenting

On the breeding grounds there are no such wonders; it follows the basic pattern of most of its family. It settles in the tundra, on coasts or even rough pastureland, as long as the vegetation is not too high – it has very short legs.

Breeding in colonies, each pair builds a shallow scrape for the one to three eggs, which the parents incubate for three weeks. Up in the north, the diet tends not always to consist of fish, since there is such an abundance of flying insects that the terns take advantage of these.

Once breeding, the Arctic becomes a coastal bird again. The chicks fly at three or four weeks of age, the beginning of a record-breaking career aloft. One Arctic Tern was known to have lived 29 years – and seen the world many times over.

ABOVE
The Arctic Tern has the longest migratory flight of any bird in the world.

GUILLEMOT

SCIENTIFIC NAME: Uria aalge

IDENTIFYING FEATURES: Dark above and white below; dagger-like bill; black legs

SIMILAR SPECIES: Razorbill, Puffin, Little Auk

SIZE: 38–41 cm (15–16¼ in)

HABITAT: Inshore coasts, cliffs and islands; at sea in winter

POPULATION: Common

At first sight the Guillemot looks like a Northern Hemisphere version of a penguin, with its upright stance, small wings and sharply contrasting plumage, dark above and white below. In the water the resemblance remains, as it powers itself below the surface by a rowing action of the wings and with its back-positioned feet. It is only when it takes off on slightly over-fast wing beats, and makes its safely into the air that you realize that it is actually quite a different bird.

In common with the other auks, chasing food underwater is the main method of finding sustenance. In the Guillemot's case this is mainly fish, and it has been known to go down 30 m (100 ft) below the surface and fly out more than 50 km (31 miles) from the colony to get a good supply.

Independent Young

The breeding of Guillemots is in many ways remarkable. They tend to nest on tall cliffs, often occupying very narrow ledges at terrifying heights (up to 300 m/1,000 ft) above the sea. It may be safe, but it is also desperately cramped, because Guillemots have the most densely packed colonies of birds in the world – 20 nests may be crammed into a square metre. They lay a single egg, which is incubated for up to 38 days, although usually less. The egg is intricately marked with squiggles and splodges, and it seems that each is different; their unique eggs help Guillemots find their nest-sites in the crowded colony.

Both sexes incubate and feed the chick until, when only 15–25 days old and only half grown at best, it leaves the nest. Astonishingly, there is only one way to do this – to jump. The young are light, with partly grown wings and, so long as they do not hit rocks or get snatched by predators, they land on the sea safely. Once there, they find their male parent and the two swim out to sea until, after a month, the youngster becomes independent.

RAZORBILL

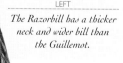

SIZE: 37–39 cm (14⅝–15⅜ in)

HABITAT: Inshore coasts, cliffs and islands; at sea in winter

POPULATION: Common

SCIENTIFIC NAME: Alca torda

IDENTIFYING FEATURES: Broad, thin bill with subterminal white bands; white streak starts above bill and goes to eye; clean white 'armpits' in flight

SIMILAR SPECIES: Guillemot, Puffin, Little Auk

At first sight this auk looks similar to a Guillemot, and indeed its lifestyle, nesting on cliffs but living mainly at sea, is not very different. However, to look at, the Razorbill has a longer tail than the Guillemot, which can be obvious on the water, and its bill is much thicker in profile. As the name suggests, if viewed from above or below, the bill is narrow and file-like, and there is also a smart white stripe near its tip.

In common with the Guillemot, the Razorbill feeds under the water, chasing fish. However, it has a more catholic diet than the Guillemot, frequently incorporating significant numbers of crustaceans, too.

It seems unable to dive as deep as a Guillemot, rarely venturing more than 7 m (23 ft) down. Another significant difference between the two species is that, when a Razorbill brings food to its young in the nest, it does not take in just one held lengthwise in the bill, as a Guillemot does, but can carry up to 20, fitted crosswise in the same way as a Puffin.

Razorbills frequently share the same cliffs as Guillemots in the breeding season, but they occupy distinctly different sites, with a little more luxury and a lot more space. Their ledges tend to be wide, often with an overhang, and they will sometimes choose flat sites among rocks and boulders. Just a single egg is laid and incubated by both parents for 36 days.

Leaving the nest carries the same dramas that afflict the young Guillemot. At 18 days old the chick departs the breeding ledge, well before it is fully grown, and does so by a straight jump down to the sea, feeble, undeveloped wings fluttering. In contrast to the Guillemot chicks, however, which leave in the evening during the light, Razorbill chicks wait until 9 p.m. at least, when night has fallen in late summer. This literal leap in the dark is probably good to avoid predators, but the chick's heart must be in its mouth as it casts off into the blackness.

LEFT
The Razorbill has a thicker neck and wider bill than the Guillemot.

BLACK GUILLEMOT

SCIENTIFIC NAME: Cepphus grylle

IDENTIFYING FEATURES: Red legs and gape; thin bill; large white wing-patch

SIMILAR SPECIES: None

SIZE: 30–32 cm (11⅞–12⅝ in)

HABITAT: Rocky coasts

POPULATION: Fairly common locally

Plumage-wise, the Black Guillemot is very much a bird of contrasts. Dressed in smart sooty-black in summer, with a brilliant white patch on the wing-coverts and equally brilliant red legs, it swaps this tuxedo smartness for a winter plumage of mainly white, with black bars on the wings and upperparts. It could easily be a different species from one season to the next – and it is at least always highly distinctive.

This auk differs quite markedly from the rest in its ecology – it is very much a bird of inshore waters throughout the year, although in the Arctic it feeds around the pack ice. It is far less a fish-eater than other large auks, taking a wide variety of other foods such as

BELOW

In the early mornings, Black Guillemots can be seen performing their displays.

crabs, shrimps, molluscs, marine worms and even plant material. To obtain these it eschews the chase-searching method of the rest in favour of a methodical search of the seabed in shallow water. It only goes down to about 8 m (26 ft) at best, and will often come up a long way from where it began its dive.

Breeding Biology

Such a strategy of searching carefully in shallow inshore waters allows Black Guillemots the chance to lay two eggs instead of the usual one – they do not have so far

to travel. These are placed in a crevice in a rock, or perhaps under a boulder or even a piece of driftwood. The youngsters hatch after 23–29 days, and if they are fortunate the adults will visit up to 15 times a day, more

often than Guillemot parents. Thankfully for the chicks, they do not have the traumatic departure from the nest-site suffered by Guillemots or Razorbills; their nest sites are usually close to the water, and they do not leave until at least a month old. They still cannot fly, though.

Thus, the Black Guillemot differs markedly from other auks in its breeding biology. Intriguingly, it also makes a remarkably different sound; instead of the grunts and wails of Guillemots, for example, it utters high-pitched, electronic-sounding peeps.

LITTLE AUK

SIZE: 17–19 cm (6¾–7½ in)

HABITAT: Coasts

POPULATION: Uncommon winter visitor

SCIENTIFIC NAME: Alle alle

IDENTIFYING FEATURES: Black above, white below; tiny but quite thick bill; looks almost tail-less

SIMILAR SPECIES: Guillemot, Razorbill, Puffin, Starling (in flight)

Feeding

During the breeding season, Little Auks feed their young a similar diet. In order to carry it, they have special pouches in the throat, which mix the plankton with mucus to produce a sort of paste. A single helping can hold as many as 600 different minute items, so the young grow fast.

Up in their breeding grounds, which are centred further north than those of any other auk in the world, these small birds nest in small crevices or among rocks on slopes. They are sociable, forming colonies that can be enormous, up to about a million pairs. There is a single egg, incubated for 28–31 days, and, in contrast to the situation among Guillemots or Razorbills, the youngster leaves only when fully grown, after 23 or more days.

BELOW

Breeding as they do well above the Arctic Circle, even above 80°N, Little Auks have some interesting predators, including hardy human beings and Polar Bears.

As auks go, this is not the quite the smallest, but it is still only the size of a Starling. It is a tiny, energetic sea bird that can be seen in wild, inhospitable places, such as far out into the ocean, and around the pack ice in the gut-wrenchingly cold waters of the Arctic. Nevertheless, it is not immune to the hazards of the sea; severe storms and long periods of northerly winds do sometimes force it further south than it is used to, to temperate coasts, and even inland.

The Little Auk feeds mainly on plankton, particularly guzzling the larval stages of crustaceans, but it will eat fish and small molluscs, too. The plankton occurs in enormous concentrations in northern waters, especially where convection currents around floating ice bring it near the surface. Thus Little Auks usually do not need to dive especially deep, going down 20 m (65 ft) at most.

PUFFIN

SCIENTIFIC NAME: Fratercula arctica

IDENTIFYING FEATURES: Broad, colourful bill; white cheek; red legs; triangular eye-patch

SIMILAR SPECIES: None

SIZE: 26–29 cm (10¼–11½ in)

HABITAT: Sea cliffs and islands; oceans

POPULATION: Numerous but local summer visitor

This engaging and colourful sea bird is not easy to see. Although it breeds in large colonies in certain sites, it is only present for a few months of the year (March to July) and then quickly, almost instantaneously, disappears out to sea, often well out of sight of land – it has been known to cross the Atlantic. But wherever it occurs, it makes a very popular attraction. The upright posture and comical gait have a certain human resonance, and the huge, brilliantly patterned bill make it look like a dumpy, sea-living parrot.

The main breeding habitats for Puffins are tall cliffs and offshore islands, where they nest in a rock crevice or, more frequently, a burrow. The latter is usually dug out by the birds themselves, using their feet, and it is up to 2 m (6.5 ft) long. Not surprisingly, Puffins usually require the turf on top of cliffs rather than living on the cliffs themselves.

Fish Tricks

As in many auks, there is only one egg, laid in the burrow amidst a sparse lining of grass and root fragments, feathers and other dry material. Both sexes incubate for 39–43 days, with shifts of about 32 hours each, and the chick hatches with a covering of down.

Puffins are celebrated for their neat trick of bringing in a lot of fish at the same time, all held crossways in the bill. They do this firstly by having backward-pointing edges to the bill, that hold the fish by friction, and by hooking their

tongue around them. It is by no means unusual to see a Puffin bringing in 10 fish so arranged, although a remarkable 62 has been reliably recorded.

The youngster leaves the nest when about two months old and more or less fully grown. It does so under cover of darkness, alone and unknown to its parents.

ROCK DOVE

SIZE: 34 cm (13⅓ in)

HABITAT: Coastal cliffs

POPULATION: Common

SCIENTIFIC NAME: Columba livia

IDENTIFYING FEATURES: Dark blue-grey head; iridescence on the neck and wings; grey-pink bill

SIMILAR SPECIES: Feral Pigeon, Woodpigeon

The Rock Dove is related to the Feral Pigeon and the Woodpigeon of the woodland or urban realms, and the grandfather of domestic pigeons all over the world. They share similar features with those of their family. They are chunky in build, with a short, rounded tail. They often have dark bands across the wing and a blue-grey band across the tail. Plumage can be diverse, though, ranging from a true slate grey to a more reddish colouring. Some can even be entirely black.

Rock Doves nest in rocky seaside cliffs, but usually only if these are close to farmland or other open country. They feed mainly on seeds in open country, but those that venture into urban areas will eat almost anything they can find. Rock Doves will breed at any time of year and the pair bond is made for life. The male will build the nest – usually quite crudely made from sticks and debris – and both male and female will incubate the eggs (usually two), which hatch around 19 days after being laid.

RIGHT

The Rock Dove is closely related to both the Feral Pigeon and the Woodpigeon.

SHORELARK

SIZE: 14–17 cm (5½–6¾ in)

HABITAT: Beaches, fields and dunes near sea

POPULATION: Rare winter visitor

SCIENTIFIC NAME: Eremophila alpestris

IDENTIFYING FEATURES: Strong yellow and black head pattern; male has short 'horns'

SIMILAR SPECIES: Skylark

At heart this lark is an inhabitant of the tundra, being perfectly at home in cold, barren terrain with short vegetation. It also occurs in mountains and, in some parts of its wide world range, in many other open country habitats. Everywhere, it forages on the ground, walking or running, searching out plant material in winter, insects in summer.

The Shorelark would be an average small brown bird were it not for its unusual, distinctive head pattern of black and (usually) pale yellow. Only the male has the two unusual 'horns' (wispy tufts) on top of the rear crown. The nest is made on the ground, usually

in a depression which can be natural or excavated by the female. Quite often the builder places clods of earth or pebbles around the nest, and places it carefully out of the wind. In common with other larks, male Shorelarks rise into the air to sing. Sometimes they go as high as 250 m (820 ft).

ABOVE

A female Shorelark at her nest full of begging chicks.

ROCK PIPIT

SCIENTIFIC NAME: Anthus petrosus

IDENTIFYING FEATURES: Streaky plumage;
dark legs; buff outer tail feathers; dark bill

SIMILAR SPECIES:
Water Pipit, Meadow Pipit, Tree Pipit

SIZE: 16.5–17 cm (6½–6¾ in)

HABITAT: Rocky coasts

POPULATION: Common

The Rock Pipit is similar to the other British pipits in appearance and sound, but the bird itself is special. Very few other small passerines share its unusual maritime habitat, even for short periods. It is this bird alone that will be alongside auks and Kittiwakes at their breeding cliffs, and it is this one alone that is likely to be at the feet of waders such as Turnstones as they feed along the seaweed-covered rocks by the seashore. As such, and for its tendency to be seen inland only occasionally, it is very unusual.

It is not much to look at, though – a small, streaky bird with rather long legs and a habit of running or walking rather than hopping. It is best distinguished from the very similar Meadow Pipit by its dark legs, rather broad streaks down the breast and its overall dark plumage. The call is fuller than that of the Meadow Pipit, like that same species but with a cold, and the Rock Pipit uses it sparingly, in contrast to the Meadow Pipit's attacks of panic.

Flight

In some ways its lifestyle is similar to other pipits. For example, the male performs a song-flight along party lines, flying up slowly as it delivers its trilling song, then returning to earth like

a paper aeroplane, wings still, tail spread and with a twisting flight-path. The Rock Pipit also feeds in the typical manner for the family, wandering over the ground in an apparently aimless manner, intermittently picking at

ABOVE
The Rock Pipit is large, with a long bill and dark legs.

things. However, as might be expected a few unusual items enter the menu, including molluscs, worms, crabs and small fish.

The Rock Pipit nest is placed inside a hole in a cliff or sometimes under dense vegetation and, besides the usual ingredients of grass and leaves, there is usually some seaweed in the structure. The female lays between four and six eggs.

SNOW BUNTING

SCIENTIFIC NAME: Plectrophenax nivalis

SIZE: 16–17 cm (6¼–6¾ in)

HABITAT: Breeds on mountain tops; mountains and coasts in winter

POPULATION: Common

IDENTIFYING FEATURES: White-headed, black on wings and back when breeding, otherwise warm buff; yellow bill

SIMILAR SPECIES: Lapland Bunting

No other small bird in the world breeds as far north as the Snow Bunting. It is most common on the Arctic tundra and can reach right to the permanent ice. In the winter, it seeks no respite from the cold, and tends to be found in barren, windswept places, including beaches, mountains and wide open pastures.

It is well adapted to such a life. Despite its white and brown plumage, which helps to conceal it, the Snow Bunting is quite robust for a bird of its type, and it has unusually thick plumage. It often walks with the belly feathers covering its legs. When breeding, the male has a white head with white underparts; its black wings have large white patches. The female – as is often the case – is pale brown on the back with a brown cap. Outside breeding season the male can be identified by its white plumage, with a pied pattern on its back and wings. The female outside breeding time has a grey head and dark streaks on her back.

Feeding and Breeding

The Snow Bunting feeds mainly on seeds gathered on the ground, although it takes insects in summer and feeds these to its young. It forages in flocks, with birds at the back often over-flying the leaders, the whole flock rolling forward like snowflakes.

The nest is a large open cup placed in a crevice, lined with feathers and usually on rocky outcrops. Although they can be spotted in the summer in mountainous regions, it is easier to see a Snow Bunting in winter, when they spend more time on sea shores or salt marshes.

RIGHT

The Snow Bunting's habitat is mountainous in summer but coastal in winter.

TWITE

SCIENTIFIC NAME: Carduelis flavirostris

IDENTIFYING FEATURES: Unstreaked throat of rich buff; yellow bill; buff wing-bar and white wing-panel

SIMILAR SPECIES:
Linnet, Lesser Redpoll, Meadow Pipit

SIZE: 14 cm (5½ in)

HABITAT: Coasts, farmland, moorland, mountains

POPULATION: Fairly common but localized

A bird of damp and chilly climates, the Twite is a bird of upland farmland and moorland in the breeding season. It tends not to be found in the vicinity of trees or bushes, and it builds its nest on or very close to the ground. It is in many ways a tough version of the Linnet, eschewing the warmth and sun favoured by that bird.

In the winter this tendency towards bleak spots is even more marked. While breeding birds in Scotland often stay put, Twites from Scandinavia visit eastern Britain and occur on windswept beaches and dunes, where they feed in close-knit flocks on tiny seeds, including those of salt marsh plants.

Pairs form in the winter flocks, and it appears these relationships can be quite enduring, perhaps persisting beyond a single season. The male performs a pleasing song-flight in spring, describing a circle and alternating flaps with glides. If all goes well, the birds can raise two broods in a season.

LAPLAND BUNTING

SCIENTIFIC NAME: Calcarius lapponicus

IDENTIFYING FEATURES: Male has strong black on breast and crown, chestnut on nape

SIMILAR SPECIES:
Reed Bunting, Snow Bunting, Skylark

SIZE: 15–16 cm (5⅞–6¼ in)

HABITAT: Beaches, stubble fields

POPULATION: Uncommon winter visitor

The Lapland Bunting is, like the Snow Bunting, an inhabitant of the northern tundra. Where the Snow Bunting likes desolate, rocky areas, however, this species prefers the mossy and scrubby, more verdant parts of the ecosystem. Nevertheless, it shares similar desolate habitats outside the breeding season.

Male Lapland Buntings may arrive several weeks before the females in spring, and soon settle in territories defended by the birds' sweet, musical song. In their finery, the birds also have a brief song-flight, rising up to 10 m (33 ft) or so before descending in a spiralling glide. The nest is placed in a shallow depression in the moss or other vegetation, and the clutch is four to six eggs. Lapland Buntings can lure predators away from the nest by pretending to be injured.

In the winter, these birds feed mainly on seeds gathered on the ground. The birds forage on the ground, often with Snow Buntings and Shorelarks and they can be highly flighty and restless.

Mountains & Uplands

Upland habitats – mountains and moors – are the last truly great wilderness areas remaining in Britain and Europe, and contain some of our most spectacular and sought-after birds. But these are tough places to live, and only a handful of superbly adapted species can do so, especially during the winter months. Of these, the toughest of all is without question the Ptarmigan, a member of the grouse family that is the only species to stay put all year round on the snow-covered slopes of the Highlands. They may be joined by the mighty Golden Eagle, which patrols these vast uplands in search of dead or dying creatures such as Red Deer, or perhaps a mountain hare that it can chase and kill.

In spring and summer, it is a different story – long hours of daylight and warmer temperatures lead to a brief abundance of food. This attracts one of our most unusual summer migrants – the Dotterel, a member of the plover family that flies here all the way from Africa to take advantage of the seasonal glut of insects.

Lower down, on the moors of northern Britain and across Europe, a few other specialist species have also found a way to make their home. Many are birds of prey: the Hen Harrier, Merlin and Peregrine; or the day-flying Short-eared Owl. Others are songbirds such as the Ring Ouzel and Northern Wheatear, both members of the thrush family, whose songs can be heard on fine spring days. Neither species could survive the winter here: both migrate south to Africa each autumn before returning to our uplands the following spring.

The main resident species on our moors is the famous Red Grouse, whose habitat has been artificially maintained by burning to preserve the species for hunting; to the benefit of the grouse and several other moorland birds.

RED GROUSE

SCIENTIFIC NAME: Lagopus lagopus

IDENTIFYING FEATURES:
Russet plumage, red above eye

SIMILAR SPECIES: Black Grouse (female)

SIZE: 37–42 cm (14⅝–16½ in)

HABITAT: Moorlands

POPULATION: Scarce

The Red Grouse was once thought to be the only endemic British species of bird, but is now considered to be a race of the widespread Willow Grouse. However, unlike the Willow Grouse, the British race does not moult into an all-white winter plumage. The Red Grouse has a unique status as the most prized of all game birds, much sought-after when the shooting season begins every year on the 'Glorious Twelfth' of August.

Grouse moors – mostly in the north of England and Scotland – are specially managed for Red Grouse, so any fast-flying game bird seen here is usually of this species. It can be identified by its chestnut-brown plumage, and the crimson red patch above the eye.

The only likely confusion is with female Black Grouse, a greyer, darker and slightly larger bird that lacks the red markings on the head.

RIGHT
The Red Grouse is the classic bird of heather moorland.

Life on the Moorland

The habitat requirements for the Red Grouse are highly complex, requiring careful management by a team of gamekeepers. They need a succession of heather plants at different stages of growth, so they can feed and breed in the same small area of moor. This is usually achieved by careful burning of the moor at different times, so there are always succulent new plants for the birds.

Red Grouse nest in a shallow scrape amongst the heather, incubating their clutch for three to four weeks. Once the chicks have hatched, they are remarkably precocious: capable of flying at just 12 days old, despite their tiny size.

Because grouse shooting is so expensive, it has been in decline for the past century or so; with the grouse population falling from a peak of several million birds to fewer than 250,000 pairs today. Whether or not it can continue to survive the social and economic changes of the twenty-first century is debatable.

PTARMIGAN

SIZE: 34–36 cm (13⅓–14⅓ in)

HABITAT: Mountain tops

POPULATION: Scarce

SCIENTIFIC NAME: Lagopus mutus

IDENTIFYING FEATURES: All-white plumage (winter); white wings (summer)

SIMILAR SPECIES: None

The Ptarmigan is the quintessential bird of the high Arctic-alpine plateaux of Europe and it is the only British bird whose plumage turns white in winter. It also has a unique means of keeping warm, with dense feathering covering its whole body, legs and face, so that it keeps heat loss to a minimum. When really harsh conditions occur, the Ptarmigan burrows deep into the snow until the storm has abated, using the insulating properties of the snow to keep itself warm.

The name 'Ptarmigan' – which has long puzzled birders and the general public alike – derives from a Gaelic word *tarmachan*, meaning 'croaker', a reference to the bird's extraordinary croaking call. The silent 'p' (derived from ancient Greek) was added by a seventeenth-century scholar who wanted to give the name a classical feel.

Plumage and Feeding Habits

The Ptarmigan is also unique in having several distinctive plumages throughout the year, rather than just one or two as do other birds. These range from the snow-white winter garb, through spring browns, and autumn greys – always with pure white wings revealed when the bird takes to the air. These plumage changes enable the Ptarmigan to conceal itself from predators – notably Golden Eagles – as the snow advances and recedes during the four seasons.

The Ptarmigan feeds on berries, shoots and catkins of specialized upland plants, on which most birds and animals would struggle to survive. Yet recently the Ptarmigan too has been under threat from global warming: as climate change leads to more unpredictable snowfalls – and sometimes none at all – the bird may find itself unable to find the food plants it needs to survive.

BELOW

The Ptarmigan is smaller and more slender than its close relatives.

BLACK GROUSE

SCIENTIFIC NAME: Tetrao tetrix

IDENTIFYING FEATURES:
Purplish-black plumage (male)

SIMILAR SPECIES: Capercaillie, Red Grouse

SIZE: 40–55 cm (15¾–21¼ in)

HABITAT: Wooded moorland and heath

POPULATION: Scarce

The Black Grouse has suffered a major population decline and contraction in range in recent years, and is now absent from many parts of Britain and Europe, and becoming scarce in its other strongholds of the northern uplands. Careful management of its habitat is now reversing this downward trend, however, and prospects look better for the first time in decades.

The lekking behaviour of the Black Grouse – in which females stand watching on the sidelines as males fight each other for the privilege of mating – is one of the most extraordinary spectacles found in the bird world. Males face up to each other like prize fighters, fanning their tails, puffing up their feathers and strutting their stuff. The winner is the male who manages, over time, to fend off all his rivals – after which he gets the ultimate prize, to mate with the females.

Once copulation is over, the male Black Grouse – or Blackcock, as he is often known – has nothing more to do with the female (Greyhen) leaving her to raise the young. This is typical of birds that use the lekking system of courtship. The system works simply because there is enough food widely available for the grouse chicks, so there is no need for the male to defend a territory to safeguard a food supply for his family.

Male and Female Colouring

The male Black Grouse is an extraordinarily striking and beautiful bird: with his purplish-black plumage contrasting with snow-white belly, lyre-shaped tail and red patch above the eye. The female is smaller and much less spectacular: basically greyish-brown, in order to camouflage herself at the nest or when she is with the chicks.

HEN HARRIER

SCIENTIFIC NAME: Circus cyaneus

IDENTIFYING FEATURES: Grey plumage,
black wing-tips (male); brown plumage with
white rump (female)

SIMILAR SPECIES: Marsh and Montagu's Harriers

SIZE: 44–52 cm (17½–20½ in)

HABITAT: Open moorland;
lowland wetlands (winter)

POPULATION: Scarce

Male and Female Features

The male Hen Harrier is a beautiful creature: floating through the air on long, slim wings; the pale grey of its body and wings, and pale underparts, offset by the inky black wingtips. The female – as in other birds of prey – is appreciably larger and bulkier than her mate. Her plumage is mainly brown, with a contrasting white rump revealed in flight.

The difference between the two sexes, and their similarity with the male and female plumages of another species, Montagu's Harrier, led to the two species being mixed up until the early nineteenth century, when George Montagu managed to separate them and sort out the confusion. The Hen Harrier is the larger of the two, and the only one to be found in Europe during the winter, when Montagu's Harriers instead migrate south to Africa.

Hen Harriers, like many other moorland species, nest on the ground, and lay a large clutch of eggs – sometimes as many as eight. The young stay in the nest for several weeks after hatching, with the male bringing back food for them and his mate. The male chicks usually leave the nest slightly earlier than the females.

Some Hen Harriers will indulge in polygamy and will seek out more than one female.

This elegant bird is one of the most persecuted of all Britain's raptors, because of its habit of making its nest on upland grouse moors, and taking the adults and chicks of that species to feed its own young. As a result, it remains one of the rarest and most threatened birds of prey. Outside the breeding season, Hen Harriers often move to the coast or freshwater marshes, where they hunt for prey on slender, uptilted wings.

GOLDEN EAGLE

SCIENTIFIC NAME: Aquila chrysaetos

IDENTIFYING FEATURES:
Huge size, long wings, golden feathers on neck

SIMILAR SPECIES: Buzzard

SIZE: 75–88 cm (29½–34¾ in)

HABITAT: Mountains and moorland

POPULATION: Scarce

This magnificent raptor is truly the king of all it surveys, making its territory amongst some of the harshest regions of the northern uplands, and surviving on a combination of hunting skills and the ability to find and scavenge carrion, especially during the long winter months. Few birds are so well suited to such a harsh environment, and the Golden Eagle is thriving, despite occasional persecution from farmers and gamekeepers.

Many people visit Scotland and come home happy that they have seen a Golden Eagle, whereas in fact they have seen what the locals disparagingly call a 'tourist eagle' – the much smaller and more common Buzzard. When the real thing does come into view, it is quite unmistakeable: a huge bird floating on long, straight-edged wings, with massive 'fingers' of the primary feathers at each wing-tip. Seen closer, the shaggy feathering around the neck may also be visible; as is the golden tinge to the upper wings. Juveniles are even easier to identify: their white rump and white patches on the upper wings are very distinctive.

Nesting Habits

Golden Eagles often nest lower than you might think: the theory being that it is easier to carry heavy prey – such as hares – down rather than up the mountainside to reach the nest. They lay two eggs in a huge nest made from sticks; but in what is known as 'Cain and Abel syndrome', the larger, elder chick usually causes the death of its younger sibling by taking the lion's share of

Fascinating Facts

The world's largest bird of prey is the Andean Condor, which has a wingspan of around 3 m (10 ft).

LEFT

The Golden Eagle is the most magnificent of the upland-dwelling birds.

the food. As a result, only in one out of every five nests does the second chick survive. The young eagles remain in the nest for about nine or 10 weeks before they fledge and then go off to fend for themselves.

MERLIN

SIZE: 25–30 cm (9⅞–11⅞ in)

HABITAT: Moorlands

POPULATION: Scarce

SCIENTIFIC NAME: Falco columbarius

IDENTIFYING FEATURES:
Small size; blue-grey plumage (male)

SIMILAR SPECIES: Peregrine, Hobby

The smallest of all British and European falcons, yet what it lacks in size it makes up for in its ability to hunt and kill birds almost as big as itself, which it hunts by chasing low over the ground and using the element of surprise to strike its prey unawares. With its acrobatic flight, it manages to chase – and sometimes catch – a variety of small songbirds including Meadow Pipits and even Skylarks, which it seizes in mid-air before dispatching with its powerful talons.

The Merlin may be confused with one of the largest falcons, the mighty Peregrine, as both birds share similar plumage features, including dark upperparts, streaked underparts and dark on the head. They are also quite structurally similar: with a compact shape and triangular wings. Apart from the obvious size difference, however, the Merlin's wings are noticeably shorter, giving it a stocky shape.

RIGHT
Merlins prey on small birds that frequent the mountain regions.

Colouring and Comparisons

The male Merlin is greyish-blue above, with darker wing-tips and orangey underparts, with only a light streaking compared with the heavy barring on the breast and belly of the Peregrine. The female Merlin is browner, with pale barring on the tail. Merlins may also be confused with the Hobby, a summer visitor, but the latter is far more slender and elegant, with long, slim wings.

In medieval times, when falconry was a popular sport, the Merlin was generally flown by ladies – as its small size meant that it was considered a suitable bird for their delicate arms. Since those days Merlins have, like so many other birds of prey, been ruthlessly persecuted by gamekeepers, even though they present little or no threat to game bird populations as they mainly feed on songbirds.

PEREGRINE

SCIENTIFIC NAME: Falco peregrinus

IDENTIFYING FEATURES: Large size, blue-grey plumage, black 'moustache'

SIMILAR SPECIES: Merlin, Hobby

SIZE: 36–48 cm (14⅛–19 in)

HABITAT: Mountains and moorlands; coastal cliffs; urban areas

POPULATION: Scarce (but increasing)

The Peregrine was almost wiped out on both sides of the Atlantic during the middle part of the twentieth century, as a result of the widespread use of pesticides such as DDT. This was because the Peregrine was at the summit of the food chain, which resulted in this lethal poison accumulating in their bodies, leading to a thinning of their eggshells and a consequent population crash. Fortunately the problem was discovered just in time, and today Peregrines are not only thriving, they are even moving into major cities to breed.

The largest British falcon, second only to the Gyr Falcon as the biggest of its family in the world, the Peregrine is a true record-breaker. Of all the creatures on earth, this is the fastest of all: capable of reaching speeds of at least 300 km/h (186 mph) in its stooping flight. Its unwary prey does not stand a chance, and probably never realizes what hit it.

Master of the Mountains

Adult Peregrines can be told apart from other falcons by their large size, triangular pointed wings, and barred underparts. Their upperparts are greyish-blue, while juvenile birds are browner.

The dark cap and 'moustache', contrasting with the white collar and throat, are also distinctive; but it is the bird's indefinable quality of appearing to be master of all it surveys that really marks the Peregrine out.

Having once been confined to sea cliffs and upland moors, the Peregrine has recently taken up home in many large cities, where it has found a home from home: high buildings on which it can breed and survey its territory, and plenty of food in the shape of the Feral Pigeon flocks that live there.

LEFT
The peregrine is the fastest bird in the world and an impressive sight as it soars through the air.

DOTTEREL

SIZE: 20–22 cm (7⅞–8⅝ in)

HABITAT: Mountain tops

POPULATION: Rare

SCIENTIFIC NAME: Charadrius morinellus

IDENTIFYING FEATURES:
Orange belly, striped head pattern

SIMILAR SPECIES: Golden Plover

LEFT
*Unlike most birds, the male
Dotterel incubates the eggs and looks
after the chicks by himself.*

buffish-orange belly with a neat white line across the breast, and the pale supercilium above the eyes.

Relict Species

The Dotterel is what is known as a 'relict species', whose range has declined since the last ice age, so that today it is found mainly in the far north of Scandinavia and northern Russia. However, isolated populations continue to breed in high mountain areas of Europe, including the Carpathians of Romania, the Apennines of central Italy, and of course the high tops of the Scottish Cairngorms. A few pairs have also taken to nesting at sea level, on the reclaimed polders of the Netherlands.

The breeding season in the Dotterel's summer homes is short, and it is a race against time for the tiny chicks to put on enough fat reserves – by feeding frantically on insects such as crane flies – before the autumn begins to set in. Then, adults and youngsters will fly south to Africa and the Middle East, not crossing the Sahara Desert as do many other migrants.

This rare and attractive member of the plover family is unusual in that the female bird takes the lead in courtship and breeding behaviour, and is also the brighter plumaged of the pair. Having courted and mated with her spouse, and laid her clutch of eggs, she will then leave everything else up to the male, while she seeks another mate elsewhere. Female Dotterels have been known to lay a clutch in Scotland, and then fly off to Norway to repeat the process there.

The name 'dotterel' means 'foolish bird', and it is certainly true that the species is often very approachable, especially when incubating the eggs. At a distance, the Dotterel is best told apart from other members of its family such as the Golden Plover by the

GOLDEN PLOVER

SCIENTIFIC NAME: Pluvialis apricaria

IDENTIFYING FEATURES: Black underparts
(summer); golden-brown upperparts

SIMILAR SPECIES: Grey Plover

SIZE: 26–29 cm (10¼–11½ in)

HABITAT: Upland areas, moorlands
(summer), farmland (winter)

POPULATION: Common

Golden Plovers are a migratory species, travelling from their northern homes in the winter months.

With its haunting call, the Golden Plover is one of the classic birds of upland areas of Britain and northern Europe, where it adopts its splendid breeding garb of black underparts and spangled golden upperparts. In winter, Golden Plovers are generally found in large flocks, often with Lapwings, feeding either on coastal marshes or ploughed fields. In flight, they glow as they twist and turn in synchrony with each other in mid-air.

In breeding plumage, the Golden Plover is impossible to mistake for any other bird: its black face, breast and belly contrasting with the paler, golden-brown upperparts. Outside the breeding season the species adopts a less striking plumage, and may sometimes be confused with other medium-sized waders such as its close relative the Grey Plover. At all times of year the plump body, long and pointed wings, and the short, stubby bill are distinctive.

In flight, Golden Plovers are fast and direct, and as a result they have traditionally been considered as a game bird because they are a challenge to shoot.

Breeding Habits

Golden Plovers breed mainly on moorland, nesting in tussocky vegetation on the ground, where they lay their clutch of four well-camouflaged eggs. After hatching, the young stay around the nest for about four weeks, and later join their parents in large flocks to spend the winter. The population is massively outnumbered in winter by immigrants from the north and east, with flocks of several thousand birds not uncommon. Unlike many other waders, they often gather at inland sites, usually in the company of even larger flocks of Lapwings. Both species have recently taken to roosting on factory roofs, whose extra warmth and safety from ground predators makes them an ideal place to spend the night.

SHORT-EARED OWL

SCIENTIFIC NAME: Asio flammeus

SIZE: 37–39 cm (14⅝–15⅜ in)

HABITAT: Moorland

POPULATION: Scarce

IDENTIFYING FEATURES:
Long, slender wings; lack of ear-tufts

SIMILAR SPECIES: Long-eared Owl

This large, long-winged owl is very different from other British and European owls in two important ways. First, it has forsaken the traditional woodland habitat of other members of its family for wide open moorland, where it nests on the ground. Second, probably as a result of this habitat change, it hunts mainly by day, and not – as most other owls do – by night. As a result it is generally easier to see than nocturnal species.

The 'ears' of Short-eared and Long-eared Owls are in fact ear-tufts – the real ears are lower down on the face, and hidden from view. As its name suggests, those of the Short-eared Owl are hardly visible, except in a very close view.

Short-eared Owls are generally seen hunting low over heather moorland, where their long wings make it easy to confuse them with another characteristic moorland species, the Hen Harrier. The round face of the owl also looks like that of its relative – suggesting convergent evolution. Both species feed on voles, which the owl hunts using a combination of hearing and its acute sight.

Courtship and Breeding

Male Short-eared Owls perform an extraordinary courtship display, flying high up into the sky and then plummeting down towards the ground, clapping their wings beneath them as they go.

Once the eggs have been laid, the male will bring back voles to the female at the nest. She must sit unobserved, to avoid ground predators; so will often close her bright yellow eyes to avoid being seen.

Populations of Short-eared Owls go up and down depending on the rises and falls in vole populations, but in general the species has

ABOVE
The tufts that many people mistake for the short ears of this owl are actually just feathers.

declined in recent years, especially in winter, with many formerly regular sites now unoccupied.

NORTHERN WHEATEAR

SCIENTIFIC NAME: Oenanthe oenanthe

IDENTIFYING FEATURES:
Black mask (male), grey back, ochre underparts

SIMILAR SPECIES: Whinchat

SIZE: 14.5–15.5 cm (5⅝–6 in)

HABITAT: Moorlands

POPULATION: Common

This attractive member of the thrush family is a summer visitor to Britain, with the first birds returning in March, and usually seen on coastal areas before returning to their breeding grounds on the moors. One race, the 'Greenland' Wheatear, is one of the greatest long-haul songbird migrants in the world, travelling over 13,000 km (8,000 miles) between its breeding grounds in the North American Arctic and its winter quarters in southern Africa.

In breeding plumage, the male Northern Wheatear is a very smart and distinctive bird, with a grey crown and back, dark wings, yellow-ochre underparts and a dark mask across its eyes. The female is duller, brownish above and paler below, with a buffish wash on the breast. Outside the breeding season the male loses his distinctive markings and looks more like the female.

When they take to the wing, both the male and female reveal the bright white rump from which the bird gets its name – 'wheatear' is nothing to do with crops, but a corruption of an Anglo-Saxon word meaning 'white arse'!

A Hardy Species

Like other members of its group, the Northern Wheatear evolved in the stony deserts of North Africa and the Middle East, where the vast majority of the world's couple of dozen species of wheatear still live. Only this species has managed to extend its range into the cool temperate latitudes of northern Europe and find a home north of the Arctic Circle in North America and Scandinavia.

Once they return from their winter quarters in southern Africa, Wheatears build a nest in a crevice among rocks, or even in an old rabbit burrow. They will also often nest in man-made objects such as pipes and dry stone walls.

RING OUZEL

SIZE: 23–24 cm (9–9½ in)

HABITAT: Moorland

POPULATION: Scarce

SCIENTIFIC NAME: Turdus torquatus

IDENTIFYING FEATURES: Black plumage, yellow bill, white crescent on breast

SIMILAR SPECIES: Blackbird

Although the same size and shape as a Blackbird, and with a similar black body and yellow bill, the male Ring Ouzel also sports a distinctive white crescent across its breast, and often variable amounts of white or pale grey on the wings,

---
LEFT

The Ring Ouzel looks similar to the Blackbird, but can be distinguished by its white throat.

---

giving it a less monotone plumage. The underparts may also be marked with white chevrons, while the bill is generally less brightly coloured and can have a black tip. The female is browner, with similar but less distinct markings to the male.

Breeding Locations

The Ring Ouzel is an early spring migrant – many are seen on south-coast watchpoints in March and early April, and most are back on their breeding grounds by late April or early May.

Despite its remote breeding locations, on bleak moors and hillsides of northern and western Britain, the Ring Ouzel is a shy bird, and may be suffering from the increased recreational use of its habitat by climbers and walkers. Whatever the reason, the species has declined significantly in recent years in these areas, and the same is true across much of its European range. Only in Norway can really large numbers still be found.

Also known as the 'mountain Blackbird', this scarce and declining member of the thrush family can be found in upland areas of Britain and parts of Europe, western Asia and North Africa. Like other upland specialists, its range is very fragmented, these relict populations almost certainly hanging on since the retreat of the glaciers at the end of the last Ice Age. Northern populations in Britain, Scandinavia and the Alps are migratory, heading south in autumn to Spain and North Africa, while southern ones stay put for the winter.

CHOUGH

SCIENTIFIC NAME: Pyrrhocorax pyrrhocorax

IDENTIFYING FEATURES: Glossy black plumage, decurved red bill, red feet

SIMILAR SPECIES: Jackdaw, Carrion Crow, Rook

SIZE: 39–40 cm (15⅛–15¼ in)

HABITAT: Upland areas, coastal clifftops with short grass

POPULATION: Scarce

This comical bird is, like so many other members of the crow family, named after its call. The original version – pronounced 'chow' – has for some reason mutated into 'chuff', so the connection between name and sound no longer exists. A bird of upland areas across much of its range (which extends from Portugal in the west to central Asia in the east, and south to Ethiopia), in Britain the Chough is mainly found on coastal clifftops, where grass cropped by sheep is ideal for finding its favourite insect food.

Seen well, the Chough is unmistakeable: a medium-sized crow, a little larger than the Jackdaw, with a large, red, decurved bill and bright red legs and feet. On closer view the plumage – which appears black at a distance – reveals subtle shades of purple and dark brown. In flight, they have broad, ragged wings with pronounced 'fingers' at the tips. Young Choughs have a shorter, yellowish bill, which in some parts of their European range causes confusion with their close relative the Alpine Chough.

Feeding and Population

Choughs are sociable and gregarious birds, almost always seen in loose flocks, and often uttering their distinctive call. They feed mainly on short, cropped grass (eaten by sheep or rabbits), in which they probe deeply to find leatherjackets (the larvae of the crane fly). Having vanished from their symbolic home of Cornwall many years ago, a recent attempt was made to reintroduce them there; which was circumvented by the arrival of genuine wild birds, which probably flew there from Brittany rather than Wales. Hopefully this is a sign of an upturn in the fortunes of this delightful and fascinating bird.

LEFT
The Chough is equally an upland and coastal bird and can be seen, with luck, in either habitat.

RAVEN

SIZE: 64 cm (25⅛ in)

HABITAT: Craggy mountainsides, moorlands

POPULATION: Scarce (but increasing)

SCIENTIFIC NAME: Corvus corax

IDENTIFYING FEATURES: Large size, huge bill, wedge-shaped tail in flight

SIMILAR SPECIES: Carrion Crow, Rook

The Raven is one of the most adaptable birds in the world: able to live almost anywhere, and eat almost anything.

Survival Instincts

Ravens can be found from the High Arctic (some spend their entire lives in the Arctic Circle) to the deserts of North Africa and the Middle East, and in North America from Alaska south to Central America. Ravens have even been seen at altitudes of over 6,000 m (19,700 ft) on Mount Everest, scavenging for food at a mountaineers' camp.

In Britain and Europe they are generally a bird of upland areas, nesting on high crags (many known as 'Raven's Crag' – hence many place names such as Ravenscraig) and also in trees. But their adaptability extends to their nest sites as well – and in recent years they have moved into towns and cities, nesting on large buildings such as cathedrals.

The world's largest member of the Order *Passeriformes* (which accounts for well over half of the world's 10,000 or so bird species), the Raven is a bird rich with symbolism and myth. Ravens are an ancient symbol of evil, yet are also famed for their cleverness. They are one of the few birds to have been observed 'at play', when Ravens were seen to be sliding down a snowy slope, apparently purely for pleasure.

Like all large, black crows, the Raven is best identified on shape and structure rather than plumage differences. Compared to the Carrion Crow, it is larger (almost half as big again with a wingspan of up to 1.5 m/5 ft), bulkier and with a heavier bill. Ravens also have shaggy feathering around their thick neck. In flight, the wedge-shaped tail and huge, broad wings are also obvious.

SNOWY OWL

SCIENTIFIC NAME: Nyctea scandiaca

IDENTIFYING FEATURES: White plumage (male),
white with black spots (female)

SIMILAR SPECIES: None

SIZE: 53–66 cm (21–26 in)

HABITAT: Tundra

POPULATION: Very rare winter visitor
(formerly bred)

This magnificent white owl has become famous in recent years thanks to the massive popularity of the *Harry Potter* books and films, in which Harry's companion is a Snowy Owl. In real life, it is a bird of the High Arctic, found all across the Northern Hemisphere from Scandinavia, across Siberia, to Alaska and Canada. The male is significantly smaller than his mate, and lacks her black markings, making him genuinely 'snowy'.

Seen well, this bird is simply unmistakeable. It is a huge owl (second in bulk only to the Eagle Owl in the Northern Hemisphere), with an all-white plumage and staring yellow eyes. The smaller male is pure white in plumage, while the larger female is marked with flecks of black – more marked on the upperparts, and with a pure white face.

Habitat and Wandering

Snowy Owls nest on the ground, where they lay their clutch of eggs – numbers varying from three to nine depending on the availability of food that year. The chicks are fed for six or seven weeks until they fledge and are able to begin to fend for themselves, after which they begin their nomadic wanderings.

Despite being a bird of the tundra, Snowy Owls occasionally wander south in North America and Europe, to the delight of birders. This tends to happen in bad years for lemmings or voles, their staple diet, when the birds would starve if they stayed where they were. On one memorable occasion, Snowy Owls stayed on to breed in the Shetland Islands, well south of their normal range. A pair bred from 1967 to 1975, and individual birds lingered on for another decade, but sadly the species failed to permanently colonize Britain. Today it remains a rare and much sought-after winter visitor to the shores of Britain and Europe.

Useful Addresses

Bird Observatories Council (BOC)
Department of BioSyB
National Museum Wales
Cardiff
CF10 3NP
Tel: 029 2057 3233
www.birdobscouncil.org.uk

British Ornithologists Union
PO Box 417
Peterborough
PE7 3FX
www.bou.org.uk

British Trust for Ornithology
The Nunnery
Thetford
Norfolk
IP24 2PU
Tel: 01842 750050
www.bto.org

The Countryside Agency
Natural England
Northminster House
Peterborough
PE1 1UA
Tel: 0845 600 3078
www.naturalengland.org.uk

Forestry Commission
231 Corstorphine Road
Edinburgh
EH12 7AT
Tel: 0131 334 0303
www.forestry.gov.uk

The National Trust
PO Box 39
Warrington
WA5 7WD
Tel: 0870 458 4000
www.nationaltrust.org.uk/main/

**Royal Society for the
Protection of Birds (RSPB)**
The Lodge
Potton Road, Sandy
Bedfordshire SG19 2DL
Tel: 01767 680551
www.rspb.org.uk

Scottish Ornithologists Club
Waterston House, Aberlady
East Lothian EH32 0PY
Tel: 01875 871330
www.the-soc.org.uk

Wildfowl and Wetlands Trust
Slimbridge
Gloucestershire GL2 7BT
Tel: 01453 891900
www.wwt.org.uk

Worldwide Fund for Nature
Panda House
Weyside Park, Godalming
Surrey GU7 1XR
Tel: 01483 426444
www.wwf.org.uk

Further Reading

Beddard, Roy, *The Garden Bird Year: A Seasonal Guide to Enjoying the Birds in Your Garden*, New Holland (London, UK), 2007

Beletsky, Les, *Collins Birds of the World: Every Bird Family Illustrated and Explained*, HarperCollins (London, UK), 2007

Birdlife International, *Bird: The Definitive Visual Guide*, Dorling Kindersley (London, UK), 2007

Brown, Roy; Ferguson, John; and Lees, David, *Tracks and Signs of the Birds of Britain and Europe*, Christopher Helm (A&C Black) (London, UK), 1999

Burton, Robert, *Garden Bird Behaviour*, New Holland (London, UK), 2005

Cocker, Mark and Mabey, Richard, *Birds Britannica*, Chatto and Windus (London, UK), 2005

Cook, Katrina and Elphick, Jonathan, *Birds*, Quercus (Colchester, UK), 2007

Couzens, Dominic and Partington, Peter, *Secret Lives of British Birds*, Christopher Helm (A&C Black) (London, UK), 2006

Couzens, Dominic, *Bird Migration*, New Holland (London, UK), 2005

Couzens, Dominic, *Identifying Birds by Behaviour*, HarperCollins (London, UK), 2005

Couzens, Dominic, *The Complete Back Garden Birdwatcher*, New Holland (London, UK), 2005

Couzens, Dominic, *The Secret Life of Garden Birds*, Christopher Helm (A&C Black) (London, UK), 2004

Elphick, Jonathan (Ed.), *Atlas of Bird Migration*, Natural History Museum (London, UK), 2007

Eppinger, Michael, *Field Guide to Birds of Britain and Europe*, New Holland (London, UK), 2006

Farrow, Dave, *A Field Guide to the Bird Songs and Calls of Britain and Northern Europe*, Carlton Books (London, UK), 2008

Greenoak, Francesca, *British Birds: Their Names, Folklore and Literature*, Christopher Helm (A&C Black) (London, UK), 1997

Harrap, Simon and Nurney, David, *RSBP Pocket Guide to British Birds*, A&C Black (London, UK), 2007

Holden, Peter and Cleeves, Tim, *RSPB Handbook of British Birds*, Christopher Helm (A&C Black), 2006

Hume, Rob and Hayman, Peter, *Bird: The Ultimate Illustrated Guide to the Birds of Britain and Europe*, Mitchell Beazley (London, UK), 2007

Hume, Rob, *RSPB Birds of Britain and Europe*, Dorling Kindersley (London, UK), 2006

Kettle, Ron and Ranft, Richard (Ed.s), *British Birdsounds*, British Library Publishing (London, UK), 2006

Lambert, Mike and Pearson, Alan, *British Birds Identification Guide*, Flame Tree Publishing (London, UK), 2007

Moss, Stephen, *Everything You Always Wanted to Know About Birds … But Were Afraid to Ask*, Christopher Helm (A&C Black), 2005

Moss, Stephen, *How to Birdwatch*, New Holland (London, UK), 2006

Moss, Stephen, *The Garden Bird Handbook: How to Attract, Identify and Watch the Birds in Your Garden*, New Holland (London, UK), 2006

Sample, Geoff, *Bird Songs and Calls of Britain and Northern Europe*, HarperCollins (London, UK), 1996

Sterry, Paul, *Complete British Birds: Photoguide*, HarperCollins (London, UK), 2004

Svensson, Lars and Grant, Peter J., *Collins Bird Guide: The Most Complete Guide to the Birds of Britain and Europe*, HarperCollins (London, UK), 2001

Ward, Mark, *Bird Identification and Fieldcraft*, New Holland (London, UK), 2005

Glossary

altricial
Unable to move around without assistance after hatching.

Archaeopteryx
The earliest known fossil bird, the first example of which was discovered in 1861. This find proved that reptiles with feathers lived around 150 million years ago, forging a link between reptiles and birds.

Aves
The bird class of vertebrates. Aves have feathers and most are able to fly. They are warm-blooded and lay eggs.

avifauna
The birds of a particular region or time.

carrion
Dead and decaying flesh. Birds of prey will feast on carrion, although they prefer to catch their prey live.

cere
A fleshy covering over part of the upper mandible.

cline
When a bird population shows a variation in certain characteristics such as weight or colour across its geographic range.

cloaca
The opening for digestive, reproductive and excretory systems in a bird.

clutch
The number of eggs a bird lays at any one time.

coniferous woodland
Woodland made up mainly of needle-leaved trees with cones. These trees retain their covering all year round.

convergent evolution
The process of evolution through which birds that are unrelated come to share similar characteristics and features.

deciduous woodland
Woodland made up of trees that lose their leaves in the autumn and throughout the winter.

divergent evolution
The process of evolution whereby birds that once shared similar characteristics have adapted over time and developed different ones in order to survive in changing habitats.

DNA
Deoxyribonucleic acid. The material contained inside the nucleus of human and animal cells that contains all the genetic information.

Dromaeosaur
Literally, 'running reptile', a group that includes dinosaurs such as velociraptors.

ecosystem
A self-contained habitat defined by the organisms living there and their relationships with one another and non-living factors such as climate and soil.

endemic
Found only in one place – birds that cannot be found in any other country. Most countries have a number of endemic species, but the Scottish Crossbill is the only bird endemic to the British Isles.

extinction
The process by which an animal or plant dies out completely. Some birds have been hunted to extinction by human predators; others have become extinct by natural selection or destruction of habitats. Conservation efforts are being made to prevent some endangered species from becoming extinct.

fledge
The growth of the first set of feathers of a baby bird.

At this point the birds are known as fledglings.

fossil
The remains of an organism from a period in history, such as a skeleton or imprint of some flora, embedded in the crust of the earth.

game bird
Any bird that is hunted for sport. In Britain, grouse and pheasants are the most popular and widespread game birds.

gape
The expanse of a bird's open bill.

Hirundines
Members of the swallow family.

hybridization
The cross-breeding of certain species with others to create a new species with certain characteristics.

lekking
An elaborate display ritual performed by male birds during the breeding season in order to attract a mate and drive off other potential suitors. Leks often take place in specific areas. The females watch the display before entering the lek to mate with the dominant male.

mandible
The jaws of a bird. Mandibles comprise two parts – upper and lower.

mobbing
A technique carried out by a group of birds, usually of the same species, to protect territory or young by driving out alien predators, by which the birds encircle and attack the alien.

monophyletic species
Pertaining to a group of animals or birds that are descended from one stock or source.

nestling
A young bird that has not yet fledged (grown its first set of feathers).

nominate form
The main form that a species takes. The same species may differentiate from the nominate form across a geographic region through divergent evolution.

non-monophyletic species
Pertaining to a group of animals or birds that are not descended from a single stock or source.

palaeontologist
A scientist who studies prehistoric forms of life through fossils and other evidence.

pelagic
Pertaining to birds that live on the open sea rather than in coastal areas or other regions of inland water.

planform
The shape of a wing (usually relating to its shape as seen from above).

plumage
The type and colouring of feathers on a bird; this can often change between seasons and differ between males and females of the same species.

precocial
Used to describe young birds that develop early and are able to perform functions such as moving about and even flying soon after hatching.

predation
The act of one bird preying and feeding upon another.

primaries
The large, main feathers situated on the distal joint of a bird's wing.

quadruped
Any creature that walks on four legs.

race
Also called subspecies. Made up of a population that has been dispersed geographically and has evolved its own distinguishable set of characteristics such as plumage or migratory habits; such populations can still breed with one another.

raptor
A bird of prey.

remiges
A type of feather that includes both primaries and secondaries; remiges are the feathers that are used in flight.

resident
A bird that lives and breeds in a country and does not make seasonal migrations.

roding
The process of cutting rushes or reeds to create a nest, used by water birds.

scrape
A shallow nest in the ground, usually simply scraped out of the mud or earth; used by ground-nesting birds such as plovers.

secondaries
The feathers that grow along the trailing edge of a bird's wings.

substrate
A surface on which an organism grows.

taxonomy
The science of classifying animals and birds according to a system that is defined by natural relationships and common characteristics.

Theropod
Any of the carnivorous dinosaurs, literally meaning 'beast-footed'.

tubenoses
A group of sea birds with large tubular nostrils situated on the upper bill, allowing them to dive for fish.

vagrant
A migrant bird that has strayed from its typical migratory path and can therefore be seen in areas in which it is not normally resident.

Picture Credits

Illustrations by **Ann Biggs**.

Ardea: Brian Bevan: 190 (tl, cl)

Corbis: 80 (tl), 84 (b); Jonathan Blair: 89 (cl); Bob Krist: 71 (c); Gunter Marx Photography: 78 (t); Joe McDonald: 64 (tl), 69 (tl); Mark Peterson: 68 (b); Pinnacle Pictures: 69 (tr); Joel W. Rogers: 89 (br); Kevin Schafer: 84 (t); Erich Schlegel/Dallas Morning News: 5 (bl), 89 (tr); David Woods: 68 (tl)

FLPA: Terry Andrewartha: 102 (br), 133 (tr), 156 (tl, bl); Jan Van Arkel: 143 (c); Ron Austing: 341 (b); Andrew Bailey: 108 (br), 245 (tr), 99 (tr); Bill Baston: 5 (tl), 41 (t), 52 (tr), 55 (tr), 92 (tl), 103 (tr, bl), 130 (b), 148 (b), 169 (tr), 220 (tl, cl), 224 (cl), 326 (r), 336 (b), 337 (b); Leo Batten: 83 (t); Neil Bowman: 60 (br), 71 (t), 111 (c), 114 (cr), 180 (c), 183 (c), 191 (c), 216 (c), 247 (c), 254 (c), 256 (c), 290 (c), 294 (bl), 322 (tl), 326 (l), 334 (tl), 337 (tr); Frans Van Boxtel: 140 (tl, bl), 144 (cl, br), 185 (c), 187 (b); Jim Brandenburg: 32 (c), 195 (c), 271 (c), 340 (c); Hans Dieter Brandl: 140 (br), 198 (tl, br), 246 (b) 254 (tl, br); Oliver Brandt: 26 (bl); Matthias Breiter: 60 (t), 328 (tl); Ben Van Den Brink: 75 (tr), 138 (cl), 174 (b), 181 (cr, b), 226 (cr), 235 (b), 256 (tl, bl); Richard Brooks: 23 (b), 32 (br), 36 (t), 59 (tl), 97 (bl), 160 (tl, bl), 161 (c), 164 (tl), 170 (c), 173 (tr), 177 (tr), 189 (tr), 192 (c), 192 (b), 193 (tr), 222 (tl, bl), 225 (bcr, bl), 232 (c), 233 (c), 237 (c), 242 (tl, cr), 242 (cl), 247 (tr), 250 (tl), 252 (c), 252 (tl, bl), 263 (tr), 263 (c), 287 (tr), 287 (c), 307 (cr), 318 (c), 335 (c), 336 (tl), 339 (tr); S Charlie Brown: 46 (tr), 110 (bl), 114 (b), 142 (c), 171 (tr), 317 (c); Rino Burgio: 55 (br), 176 (c); David Burton: 70 (br); Peter Cairns: 329 (c); Michael Callan: 29 (b), 37 (b), 61 (br), 95 (tr), 165 (c), 177 (b), 188 (tl, br), 227 (br), 236 (tl, cr), 272 (tl, br), 292 (tl, cr), 301 (tr), 319 (tr, br), 328 (c), 331 (b), 334 (c), 338 (bl); Robert Canis: 52 (b), 65 (tl), 71 (b), 85 (t), 110 (tl, br), 132 (tl), 158 (bl), 158 (tl, br), 166 (tl, br), 193 (c), 236 (cl), 240 (br), 274 (c), 286 (br), 345 (r); Cisca Castelijns: 182 (c), 303 (tr); Nigel Cattlin: 31 (b), 62, 80 (cl); Robin Chittenden: 70 (bl), 122 (tl), 122 (br), 258 (l), 274 (tl), 293 (bl), 298 (bl), 320 (bl), 322 (cr), 325 (b); Hugh Clark: 66 (tr), 105 (c), 172 (tl, cr), 342 (t); Justus de Cuveland: 28 (cr), 47 (tr), 168 (br), 308 (b);Frits Van Daalen: 93 (tl); 137 (br), 146 (tl), 151 (b), 167 (br), 172 (cl), 175 (b), 238 (cr), 265 (tr), 269 (c), 312 (cr); Dembinsky Photo Ass.: 190 (cr); Do Van Dijck: 91 (c), 113 (c), 139 (c), 146 (b), 176 (tl, bl), 207 (tr), 224 (tl, cr), 237 (b), 239 (bl), 243 (c), 297 (cr); R. Dirscherl: 205 (tr, br); Dick Dobbenberg: 53 (cr), 153 (bl); Dickie Duckett: 28 (b), 41 (b), 82 (bl), 93 (tr), 116 (cl), 188 (bl), 196 (bl), 217 (b), 277 (c), 314 (tl, b); Michael Durham 60 (bl), 79 (b), 174 (cl), 332 (tl); Danny Ellinger: 9 (b), 44 (b), 205 (c), 206 (bl), 217 (tr), 237 (tr), 282 (c), 304 (cl), 313 (c), 313 (b); Peter Entwistle: 135 (tr), 140 (c), 147 (b); Yossi Eshbol: 39 (b), 49 (tl), 91 (l), 106 (c), 278 (bl); Otto Faulhaber: 138 (tl, cr); Harry Fiolet: 170 (tl, br); Tim Fitzharris: 79 (tl), 92 (cr), 129 (tr), 203 (br), 220 (cr); Andrew Forsyth: 307 (tr, cl); Foto Natura Stock: 55 (bl), 100 (l), 109 (tr, cr), 175 (tr), 234 (tl), 304 (cr), 326 (c), 330 (tl), 109 (br), 141 (br); Philip Friskorn: 115 (c), 255 (tr), 259 (b); Tom and Pam Gardner: 218 (c); Bob Gibbons: 85 (c); Dwin Giesbers: 207 (c); Patricio Robles Gil/Sierra Madre: 302 (c); Michael Gore 290 (bl), 298 (tl, br); Manfred Grebler: 198 (c); David T. Grewcock: 78 (bl); Tony Hamblin: 48 (b), 50 (bl), 57 (br), 64 (cr), 64 (cl), 74 (cr), 80 (b), 86 (l), 100 (c), 104 (bl), 105 (br), 107 (bl), 112 (bl), 116 (tl, b), 127 (c), 127 (bl), 144 (tl), 145 (cr, br), 151 (c), 166 (bl), 179 (c), 180 (tl, b), 202 (br), 221 (cr), 230 (bl), 241 (c), 241 (b), 243 (tr), 246 (tl), 248 (cl), 261 (tr), 266 (tl), 283 (b), 294 (tl, br), 327 (c); Hannu Hautala: 5 (cr), 99 (cl), 132 (cl, br), 211 (c), 281 (c), 324 (tl); John Hawkins: 14 (tl), 34 (cl), 35 (tl), 36 (br), 50 (br), 51 (l), 53 (cl), 54 (tr), 73 (tr), 83 (b), 92 (cl), 94 (br), 97 (br), 103 (br), 107 (c), 108 (c), 111 (br), 117 (b), 119 (cl), 120 (l), 131 (tr), 135 (b), 136 (br), 136 (c), 137 (tr), 148 (tl), 152 (tl, br), 155 (tr), 157 (c), 159 (c), 160 (br), 171 (c), 171 (b), 173 (b), 185 (b), 187 (tr), 194 (r), 208 (c), 228 (c), 252 (br), 253 (c), 275 (tr, br), 275 (c), 276 (c), 338 (tl, br); Fred Hazelhoff: 102 (cl), 125 (c), 129 (b), 225 (tcr), 249 (tr), 306 (tl, cr), 342 (b); Henk Heerink: 59 (tr), 222 (c); Paul Hobson: 9 (t), 29 (tl), 40 (br), 56 (bl), 58 (tl), 59 (br), 82 (br) 87 (bl), 100 (r), 111 (tr), 117 (cr), 118 (br), 124 (tl, bl), 125 (b), 133 (br), 142 (tl, br), 145 (tr), 153 (tr, cl), 159 (tr), 159 (b), 186 (cl), 192 (tl), 210 (b), 245 (cr), 270 (c), 293 (tr, br), 317 (tr), 327 (b), 331 (c), 334 (b), 338 (c), 339 (b), 339 (c), 340 (bl), 340 (tl, br); Gerard De Hoog: 241 (tr), 292 (cl), 299 (tr, br); Jaap Hoogenboom: 151 (tr), 240 (cl); Adri Hoogendijk: 187 (cr); Michio Hoshino: 8, 341 (c); David Hosking: 14 (b), 17 (tl), 18 (cl), 31 (tl), 34 (cr), 35 (r), 39 (tr), 43 (b), 54 (tl), 58 (tr), 65 (tr), 69 (br), 76 (bl), 88 (tl), 103 (c), 116 (cr), 119 (cr), 122 (c), 126 (br), 138 (b), 141 (c), 150 (b), 152 (bl), 167 (bl), 168 (bl), 169 (c), 176 (br), 189 (b), 193 (b), 197 (tr, bl), 204 (tl, bl), 210 (tl), 213 (cr), 215 (tr), 233 (tr), 238 (tl, b), 250 (c), 250 (b), 255 (b), 256 (br), 259 (tl), 261 (c), 269 (b), 279 (tr), 284 (tl), 287 (b), 289 (tr), 291 (b), 298 (c), 310 (tl, bl), 311 (br), 323 (b), 336 (c); Roger Hosking 33 (cr), 36 (bl); Frits Houtkamp: 106 (tl, bl); Wayne Hutchinson: 82 (tr), 327 (tr); Mitsuaki Iwago: 316 (b); Horst Jegen: 43 (tl), 98 (t), 127 (tl, br), 181 (tr); Mike Jones: 34 (tl), 38 (tr); Rolf De Kam: 21 (b); Wim Klomp: 85 (b), 11 (r), 48 (tl), 52 (tl), 131 (c), 156 (c), 221 (tr), 235 (tr), 297 (cl); Marko König: 88 (tr); Jos Korenromp: 184 (tl, bl); Michael Krabs: 198 (bl), 223 (b), 262 (br), 308 (c); Heinz Kühbauch: 307 (br); Erwin Van Laar: 105 (tr, bl); Gerard Lacz: 222 (br); Mike Lane: 5 (tr), 13 (t), 25 (tr), 40 (tl), 41 (tr), 44 (tr), 45 (b), 49 (tr), 57 (bl), 61 (tl), 70 (t), 73 (b), 75 (br), 91 (r), 95 (b), 123 (b), 101 (bl), 119 (b), 139 (tr), 139 (b), 149 (c), 150 (tl), 181 (cl), 209 (cr), 211 (bl), 212 (tl, br), 220 (b), 234 (b), 246 (c), 248 (tl, cr), 258 (c), 260 (tl, bl), 268 (b), 277 (tr, br), 282 (tl, br), 286 (c), 296 (b), 300 (br), 301 (b), 301 (c), 305 (b), 323 (c), 329 (tr, br); Bob De Lange: 144 (cr); Frans Lanting: 3, 12 (cl), 14 (tr), 22 (t), 24 (b), 38 (tl), 44 (tl), 67 (br), 74 (tl), 96 (bl), 196 (c), 200 (tl, bl), 321 (cr), 321 (tr); Simon Litten: 18 (cr), 80 (cr); Ad Van Lokven: 134 (c); Marcel Maierhofer: 1, 26 (tl); S & D & K Maslowski: 23 (tr), 46 (l), 63 (r), 64 (b), 81 (b), 93 (b), 206 (tl, br), 219 (c), 236 (b), 271 (tr), 295 (tr), 302 (b), 316 (tl, c), 345 (cl); Phil McLean: 22 (br), 101 (br), 120 (r), 124 (br), 128 (tl), 132 (cr), 150 (c), 155 (b), 306 (b); Wil Meinderts: 35 (b), 200 (c), 230 (tl, c), 257 (tr), 272 (bl), 278 (br), 308 (tl); Eric Menkveld: 324 (b); Hans Menop: 76 (br), 182 (tl); Claus Meyer: 16 (l); Derek Middleton: 11 (c), 31 (tr), 42 (cl), 48 (cl), 51 (r), 61 (tr), 90, 112 (c), 120 (c), 128 (cl), 142 (bl), 143 (b), 154 (c), 165 (tr, br), 168 (tl, c), 178 (bl), 182 (bl), 189 (c), 300 (tl, bl), 325 (tr, cl), 335 (b), 341 (tr); Hiroya Minakuchi: 26 (br); Oene Moedt: 164 (c), 203 (c), 265 (c), 296 (tl); Mark Moffett: 49 (br); Yva Momatiuk & John Eastcott: 15 (bl), 32 (tl), 33 (t), 277 (bl); Tom Mueller: 67 (cl); Rinie Van Muers: 281 (b), 320 (tl, cl); Piet Munsterman: 45 (tl), 162 (cr), 186 (b); Elliott Neep: 77 (tr); Mark Newman: 56 (cr), 199 (tr, bl), 199 (c), 218 (tl), 218 (b), 347; Ulrich Niehoff: 81 (tr); Leendert Noordzij: 106 (br); Flip De Nooyer: 26 (tr), 98 (bl), 115 (br), 135 (c), 141 (tr, bl), 143 (tr), 178 (tl, br), 210 (c), 214 (br), 228 (tl), 231 (c), 235 (c), 243 (b), 251 (b), 283 (c), 295 (b), 313 (tr), 314 (cr), 318 (bl), 335 (tr); Pete Oxford: 15 (br); Panda Photo: 123 (cr); Philip Perry: 274 (b); Fritz Polking: 5 (cl), 25 (tl), 96 (br), 225 (tr), 227 (bl), 231 (bl), 280 (tl, bl), 280 (c), 280 (bl), 285 (tr, br), 310 (br); Michael Quinton: 11 (l), 32 (bl), 34 (b), 37 (tr), 124 (cl), 271 (b); Robert Reijen: 153 (cr); Guy Robbrecht: 226 (tl, b); Derek A Robinson: 126 (cl); Walter Rohdich: 157 (tr); Michael Rose: 136 (tl, bl), 202 (c), 345 (b); Tui De Roy: 65 (b), 68 (tr), 72 (cr), 309 (tr); L Lee Rue: 264 (c); Thomas Ruffer: 82 (tl); Steven Ruiter: 209 (tl, cl), (c), 331 (tr); Cyril Ruoso: 321 (bl); Chris Schenk: 87 (br), 95 (tl), 167 (tr), 208 (br), 215 (b), 232 (b), 238 (cl), 267 (tr, bl), 273 (tr), 284 (c), 292 (b), 296 (c), 297 (tr), 302 (tl), 309 (b), 312 (cl, br), 325 (cr), 328 (b); Hans Schouten: 28 (tl), 30 (br), 87 (tr), 130 (tl), 184 (c), 216 (tl, br), 242 (b), 262 (tl, c), 262 (bl), 288 (tl, bl), 289 (c), 305 (tr), 310 (cl), 312 (tl); Ingo Schulz: 12 (b), 305 (c); Malcolm Schuyl: 15 (t), 24 (tl), 25 (b), 48 (cr), 56 (tl), 63 (c), 75 (bl), 77 (b), 94 (bl), 158 (c), 161 (tr), 186 (tl), 194 (l), 195 (tr), 197 (c), 199 (br), 201 (c), 215 (c), 219 (b), 229 (b), 230 (br), 244 (c), 249 (c), 270 (br), 273 (c), 279 (c); Silvestris Fotoservice: 57 (tr), 161 (b), 163 (tr, b), 194 (c), 212 (cl), 245 (cl), 251 (c), 333 (c); Mark Sisson: 17 (tr), 20 (tr), 74 (b), 117 (tr), 162 (tl), 244 (bl), 266 (c), 286 (tl, bl), 318 (tl, br); Jan Sleurink: 203 (tr, bl), 212 (cr), 293 (c); Wim Smeets: 169 (b), 323 (tr), 247 (b); Jan Smit: 104 (tl, br), 283 (tr); Don Smith: 128 (b); Gary K Smith: 40 (bl), 43 (tr), 58 (b), 107 (tr, br), 191 (br), 200 (br), 201 (tr), 239 (tr, br), 259 (c), 263 (b), 285 (c), 289 (b), 291 (c), 295 (c), 320 (br), 324 (c), 345 (cr); Lars Soerink: 206 (c); Jurgen & Christine Sohns: 17 (br), 45 (tr), 50 (t), 54 (b), 72 (b), 81 (tl), 101 (tl, tr), 188 (c), 223 (c), 224 (b), 229 (tr), 272 (c); Sunset: 30 (t), 47 (bl), 97 (t), 157 (b); Krystyna Szulecka: 47 (br), 79 (tr), 96 (t), 201 (b), 213 (tr, cl), 279 (b), 306 (cl), 311 (c); Mike J Thomas: 28 (cl); Roger Tidman: 5 (br), 21 (tr), 33 (br), 39 (tl), 42 (b), 46 (b), 77 (cl), 78 (br), 87 (tl), 88 (b), 99 (br), 104 (cl), 109 (bl), 115 (tr, bl), 118 (c), 126 (tl), 134 (tl, br), 155 (c), 160 (c), 163 (c), 166 (c), 172 (b), 174 (tl), 204 (cr), 205 (bl), 207 (b), 213 (br), 226 (cl), 229 (c), 232 (tl), 234 (c), 253 (tr), 258 (r), 260 (c), 260 (br), 261 (b), 264 (br), 266 (b), 275 (bl), 281 (tr), 288 (br), 290 (tl, br), 291 (tr), 299 (c), 300 (c), 309 (c), 315 (b), 322 (cl, br), 337 (c), 343, 345 (l), 348; G.F.J. Tik: 175 (c); Brian Turner: 98 (br), 170 (bl); Duncan Usher: 183 (br), 195 (b); Jan Vermeer: 118 (tl, bl); Tom Vezo: 21 (tl), 37 (tl), 63 (l), 66 (tl, b), 233 (b), 248 (b), 294 (c), 315 (c), 317 (b); Albert Visage: 130 (c), 214 (c); Michaela Walch: 121 (tr, bl); Maurice Walker: 113 (br), 145 (cl), 147 (tr), 147 (c); David Warren: 123 (tr); John Watkins: 10, 23 (tl), 94 (t), 112 (tl, br), 149 (tr, br), 149 (bl), 196 (tl, br), 204 (cl), 211 (tr, br), 253 (b), 267 (c), 267 (br), 269 (tr); Michael Weber: 223 (tr); Wim Weenink: 113 (tr, bl), 184 (br), 185 (tr), 227 (tr, cr), 254 (bl); Andre Wieringa: 18 (tl); Roger Wilmshurst: 27 (bl), 29 (tr), 42 (tl, cr), 53 (t), 72 (tl), 76 (t), 102 (tl, bl), 108 (tl, bl), 110 (c), 129 (c), 131 (b), 133 (c), 146 (c), 148 (c), 152 (c), 154 (l), 156 (br), 173 (c), 177 (c), 179 (tr), 191 (tr), 202 (tl, bl), 209 (b), 228 (b), 239 (c), 249 (b), 257 (bl), 257 (cr), 265 (b), 268 (c), 268 (tl), 303 (bcr, bl), 304 (tl, bl), 311 (tr, bl), 314 (cl); Peter Wilson: 72 (cl); Winfried Wisniewski: 219 (tr), 231 (tr, br), 264 (tl, bl), 278 (tl, c), 299 (bl), 319 (bl), 208 (tl, bl); Martin B Withers: 19 (c), 134 (bl), 137 (c), 154 (r), 183 (tr), 216 (bl), 240 (tl), 251 (tr), 284 (b), 332 (c); Martin Woike: 255 (c), 282 (bl), 330 (b); Konrad Wothe: 4, 86 (r), 114 (tl, cl), 121 (br), 121 (c), 125 (tr), 197 (br), 244 (tl, br), 270 (tl, bl), 273 (b), 332 (b); John Van Der Wouw: 178 (c); Steve Young: 214 (tl, bl), 276 (tl), 303 (tcr), 315 (tr); Bernd Zoller: 20 (tl), 73 (tl), 92 (b), 162 (cl), 217 (c), 333 (tr, b); Gerhard Zwerger-Schoner: 221 (b);

NHPA: George Bernard: 16 (tr), 67 (tr); Jordi Bas Casas: 17 (bl); Andrea Ferrari: 12 (cr); Daniel Heuclin: 13 (b); Stephen Krasemann: 12 (tl)

Index of Scientific Names

General Index